Archa Verbi

Yearbook for the Study of Medieval Theology

1 (2004)

Archa Verbi

Yearbook for the Study of
Medieval Theology

1 (2004)

Aschendorff Verlag Münster

Archa Verbi
Annuarium Societatis Internationalis pro Studiis
Theologiae Medii Aevi promovendis

Annuaire de la Société Internationale pour l'Étude de la Théologie Médiévale
Annuario della Società Internazionale per lo Studio della Teologia Medievale
Anuario de la Sociedad Internacional para los Estudios de la Teología Medieval
Jahrbuch der Internationalen Gesellschaft für Theologische Mediävistik
Yearbook of the International Society for the Study of Medieval Theology

Abbildungsnachweis:
Bildarchiv Foto Marburg, Neg. 166.092, Laon, Kathedrale, Archivolten.

Satz: Christiane Storeck (Hugo von Sankt Viktor-Institut mit TUSTEP)

Gesamtherstellung: Druckhaus Aschendorff, Münster, 2005
Gedruckt auf säurefreiem, alterungsbeständigem Papier ∞
ISSN 1612-3964
ISBN 3-402-00840-8

Liminaire

La Société Internationale pour l'Étude de la Théologie médiévale, ainsi que la maison éditoriale Aschendorff, se réjouissent de présenter au public le premier volume de leur annuaire *Archa Verbi*. Le sous-titre, « Yearbook for the Study of Medieval Theology », indique bien l'objet et le cadre que les éditeurs se sont fixés pour cette publication.

Notre Société Internationale – Internationale Gesellschaft für Theologische Mediävistik (I.G.T.M.) –, s'est constituée en association en 2002 à Francfort sur le Main après avoir travaillé pendant quelques années en tant que groupe de recherche libre. Elle a pour objet de promouvoir toute approche scientifique de l'histoire du christianisme au moyen âge, couvrant une période allant, à peu près, de la mort de Grégoire le Grand († 604) jusqu'à l'époque de la Réforme (fin XVIe siècle). D'après ses statuts, la Société veille également à offrir des possibilités de formation en ce domaine à des jeunes chercheurs. Dans cette visée, l'I.G.T.M. a décidé de publier, en priorité, un périodique destiné à recevoir des articles et des éditions de textes de toute nature correspondant à la période établie et au but de la Société. Sous la métaphore bien connue des lecteurs de l'Écriture Sainte, *Archa Verbi* en évoque la mission: rendre compte, par ses travaux, de la Parole révélée.

Le fait religieux et son histoire ne cessent d'attirer l'attention des historiens. La période médiévale se prête particulièrement aux recherches scientifiques car il s'agit d'un temps-clé qui ouvre la voie à la lente émergence du monde moderne. Quand, à la fin du XVIe siècle, les premiers témoignages de la nouvelle conscience d'une ère nouvelle ont été recueillis, les générations précédantes tombèrent, définitivement, en déconsidération. Par la suite, l'opposition au dit moyen âge s'est articulée et s'est élaborée de différentes manières. Les tendances restauratrices du XIXe et du XXe siècles, au sein desquelles cet âge a été embelli par des idéalismes divers, ne pouvaient guère, pour leur part, retarder l'avènement des catastrophes humaines du siècle dernier. La renaissance d'un certain intérêt pour le moyen âge pendant les trente dernières années, semble se nourrir d'une source toute autre que le romanticisme.

En ce qui concerne l'histoire de l'Église, de nombreuses études, sous tous les aspects institutionnels, continuent d'être menées selon les différentes disciplines des sciences historiques. En fait, ceci n'a rien de surprenant puisque l'Église et la société médiévale se sont retrouvées dans un face à face des plus étroites possibles. Bien évidemment, la relation entre les institutions ecclésiastiques proprement dites et celles du pouvoir séculier était en évolution permanente durant tout ce temps-là. Tous ceux qui, aujourd'hui, désirent étudier l'histoire de l'Église au moyen âge, sont exposés au fait que le christianisme avait imprégné la société de l'époque à toutes les échelles. De ce point de vue, à la recherche scientifique portant sur la (pré-)histoire médiévale de l'Europe participent les historiens, membres des Facultés de Théologie, aussi bien que ceux qui sont membres d'un département de Sciences Humaines dans une université d'État.

Il y va de même pour l'ensemble des pratiques religieuses et leur histoire. L'évolution des diverses liturgies en cours au moyen âge demande non seulement à ce que les historiens du culte retracent leurs origines et dénomment les influences qu'elles ont subies. Mais aussi les historiens de l'art, par exemple, sont appelés à expliquer le cadre de la liturgie, à savoir les ornements, la musique, les bâtiments, etc. afin de mieux saisir la portée humaine et chrétienne de l'agir liturgique. Par ailleurs, l'instruction chrétienne a éte intimement liée à l'essor scolaire et universitaire des sociétés médiévales. L'annonce de la Parole présuppose la capacité à lire et à écrire. L'historiographie de la catéchèse ne s'applique pas seulement à une activité spécifique aux chrétiens; elle va aussi mettre en avant le rôle décisif de l'enseignement chrétien pour le progrès des sciences et le développement de l'économie médiévales. La spiritualité chrétienne, enfin, dans la mesure où elle relève d'un caractère pratique, amène les historiens à s'interroger sur le regard que les chrétiens du moyen âge ont porté sur le monde. En quel sens un regard particulier serait-il perceptible? La perception de soi-même reflète inévitablement l'image que l'individu se construit de l'autre. Là encore, la recherche sur les mouvements spirituels et les formes de vie spirituelle, par exemple, au lieu de se restreindre, elle s'étend à l'histoire médiévale des concepts d'altérité et d'identité, sur lesquelles se fondent les relations avec autrui.

Dans le domaine de l'histoire des doctrines, enfin, les études médiévales en théologie se retrouvent dans un carrefour où un certain nombre de lignes d'influence doivent être prises en compte. De prime abord, la lente formation d'une pensée théologique à proprement parler, se nourrit de tout ce que l'on a l'habitude d'appeler philosophie, aussi bien l'héritage intellectuel classique avec sa relecture chrétienne ancienne que les nouveaux auteurs de la renaissance du XIIe siècle, peu importe s'ils écrivaient en latin ou dans une langue à traduire. Grâce à l'évolution des pratiques scientifiques depuis une génération, l'histoire des doctrines médiévales n'accordera plus une place privilégiée aux divers systèmes de pensée théologique encore récents, qui réclamaient chacun sa provenance médiévale.

En livrant le premier volume d'*Archa Verbi* à ses lecteurs, notre Société se propose d'ouvrir un espace au débat scientifique à deux objectifs: Nous invitons, tout d'abord, à mener des recherches et à en publier les résultats, qui découvrent les réalités les plus diverses et les conditions les plus circonstanciées du témoignage de la foi au cours du moyen âge. Nous avons ensuite l'intention de contribuer à déceler les continuités et les fissures, voire les ruptures, dans l'univers du sentiment religieux de l'époque. L'I.G.T.M. s'engage ainsi – en reconnaissance, certes, d'une option prise – sur un chemin à parcourir.

Rainer Berndt sj
PRAESES SOCIETATIS

TABULA

RECENSIONES

ABKÜRZUNGEN UND SIGLEN

Die in den Bibliographien verwendeten Siglen sind entnommen dem TRE-*Abkürzungsverzeichnis*, 2., überarbeitete und erweiterte Auflage, zusammengestellt von SIEGFRIED M. SCHWERTNER, Berlin/New York 1994.

Archa Verbi 1 (2004) 11–24

Book V of Bede's *Historia ecclesiastica gentis Anglorum* Perspectives on Salvation History and Eschatology

by RALPH WALTERSPACHER

Book V is the last of the five parts into which Bede divided his *Historia ecclesiastica gentis Anglorum* (*HE*). One would expect the themes touched upon in the preceding four books to be brought to a close here, and the historical narrative brought up to date. Concerning the latter, a number of commentators have already remarked that this is not the case. Bede seemed to have "... precious little material ... and so created a narrative of sorts with miracles, pilgrimages to Rome, episcopal successions (all evidence of catholicity), the Frisian mission and an obituary of Wilfrid."[1] Such an assertion is understandable from the historian's point of view, who seeks to mine *HE* for factual information, of which book V produces comparatively little. At the same time, however, this statement is an indication of a lack of understanding of the metaphysical level. In book V we can discern a carefully constructed opposition between ecclesiastical history understood as part of the unfolding history of salvation and chapters intended to make the reader consider his individual judgement. The aim of this article is to show how Bede achieved a synthesis of these themes in the last book of his *HE*.

WIDENING THE PERSPECTIVE

Book V begins with a chapter on Cuthbert's successor Oethelwald, which Bede uses to establish a link with the last chapters of book IV. Just as book IV closed with the posthumous miracles worked by Northumbria's greatest saint, so book V continues the theme of the miraculous. From the second chapter onwards, however, Bede's account helps to set the scene for a wider perspective than the mainly insular one of the previous book.

Patristic exegesis, in the tradition of which Bede stood, regarded the present, the sixth age, as that of the church.[2] Its earliest history was recorded mainly in the apostolic letters and Luke's Acts of the Apostles. In the latter, Bede saw parallels with the events that had taken place in the recent history of Northumbria. At the opening of book V, Bishop John appears performing healing miracles which are strongly reminiscent of those performed by the apostles Peter and Paul.[3] As they do in Acts, the miracles here form an intrin-

1 DUNCAN 1981, p. 42.

2 Cf. MARKUS 1970, pp. 1–21 with special reference to AUGUSTINUS *De civitate Dei*, XX.9, pp. 715–719.

3 BEDA VENERABILIS *HE*, V, 2–6, pp. 434–447; cf. Apg 3,1–10; 9,32–35 and 36–43; 14,8–18; 20,7–12.

sic part of the wider context of book V, rather than being part of a particular hagiographic narrative, as a comparison with *HE*'s account of St. Cuthbert can show.[4] Bede deals with Cuthbert in the context of his life, but he does not do so with John, as it is mainly his miracles that interest Bede. His episcopal career, which, given that he was bishop of Hexham and York, could hardly have been particularly obscure to Bede, was only of the most marginal interest.

In order to understand the significance of these miracles for Bede, both in Acts and in book V, his comments on Peter raising Tabitha from the dead are very instructive. Bede interpreted the grace Tabitha received in terms of the penitent's need for repentance and the intercessory value of good deeds. Crucially, however, Bede could interpret this passage allegorically so that, besides the literal meaning, this miracle showed that both apostolic teaching and the example of the saints had come to Tabitha's aid.[5] In book V, John of Beverley appears as both such a saintly example and teacher, who came to help those who were in need in his day, in exactly the same way as the apostles had done. As book V unfolds, he does not remain the only such *exemplum*.

A key theme of *HE*, that of the English conversion, had already been brought to a close before the last book even began, so Wallace-Hadrill has pointed out with reference to the lack of a heading in book V specifying "the ecclesiastical history of the English people", which is present in all preceding chapters.[6] One should be careful not to stress the peculiar omission of the book heading too much here, but it seems fair to say that Bede was quite aware that he was venturing into terrain that was outside the confines of the previous four books. Indeed, the last conversions of Anglo-Saxon kingdoms occur in book IV. Bede's readers, however, encounter a further instance of conversion from paganism in book V. With Wihtberht and Willibrord, English missionaries reach Frisia.[7] Thence Willibrord's companion Suithberht proceeds to the Boructuari but remains as unsuccessful as Wihtberht had been with his initial efforts among the Frisians. Finally two English missionaries called Hewald become martyrs among the Saxons.[8]

It has been a matter of considerable debate among historians whether originally the choice of the German mission-field was motivated by the fact that a related *gens* lived there, or whether it was simply the nearest opportunity for missionary work.[9] Based upon an examination of the peoples mentioned in a list provided by Bede in the context of Ecgberht's thoughts about becoming a missionary, Fritze has argued that it expresses a universal view of mission

4 Beda Venerabilis *HE*, IV, 27–31, pp. 410–427.

5 Cf. Beda Venerabilis *Expositio Actuum Apostolorum*, IX, 36–41, p. 47f.; *Commentary on Acts*, pp. 91–93.

6 Wallace-Hadrill 1991, p. 174.

7 Beda Venerabilis *HE*, V, 9–11, pp. 452–463.

8 Beda Venerabilis *HE*, V, 10, pp. 456–461. Bishop Wilfrid's mission in Frisia, which was prior to the Wihtberht's is referred to briefly in Beda Venerabilis *HE*, V, 19. More on this below.

9 For the first view, see for example: Ewig 1966, p. 12. For the second: Fritze 1969, pp. 121–123 and Schäferdiek 1994, pp. 176–180. Cf. von Padberg 1995, pp. 63–65.

which transcends ethnic links.[10] Wherever this list may have originated,[11] it seems fair to interpret further this *opus apostolicum*, as Bede calls it, in the context of the chapter on Ecgberht in which it appears.

Bede portrays Ecgberht, who lived the life of a penitential exile in Ireland, as making a crucial equation: if his resolution to become a missionary proved impossible, then the alternative would be a pilgrimage to Rome and its shrines of saints.[12] It does not appear that a distinction is made between these ways of pursuing salvation.[13] Indeed, as Levison has pointed out, pilgrimage was as much about saving one's own soul as it was about saving the soul of others. So it could become a foundation of medieval missionary work.[14] As Bede said about Ecgberht, it was *pluribus prodesse* that mattered.[15] This notion not only transcended ethnic links, it also included a wide variety of Christian ways of living. In fact, in the case of Ecgberht it even included getting involved in politics in order to prevent war.[16]

For the present purposes this means that we need to apply a wide definition of missionary work, or better works assisting conversion, to the interpretation of book V.[17] The last book of *HE* is about conversion in a much broader way than in the modern missionary sense.

The second theme about which Bede made comments in every book of *HE*, and which can serve to illustrate the point just made, concerns catholic theology and religious observances. The key event here can be located in book III with its account of the Council of Whitby and the official triumph of Catholicism over divergent Irish practices.[18] On the other hand, Bede did not neglect the positive role and achievements of Irish and more specifically Ionan Christianity. The Irish, unlike the British Christians, had, in his view, played a crucial part in the conversion of the English, particularly in Northumbria. The key figure he used to illustrate the reconciliation of both traditions is Cuthbert, who towers high in the final chapters of Book IV.[19] "In Bede's eyes Cuthbert was the epitome of the old Celtic holiness and the Celtic virtues, now

10 "Quarum in Germania plurimas nouerat esse nationes, a quibus Angli uel Saxones, qui nunc Brittaniam incolunt, genus et originem duxisse noscuntur; unde hactenus a uicina gente Brettonum corrupte Garmani nuncupantur. Sunt autem Fresones, Rugini, Danai, Hunni, Antiqui Saxones, Boructuari." (Beda Venerabilis *HE*, V, 9, p. 452f). Cf. Fritze 1969, pp. 78–80.

11 Cf. von Padberg 1995, p. 64 n. 14 for a summary of the debate.

12 "… uel, si hoc fieri non posset, Romam uenire ad uidenda atque adoranda beatorum apostolorum ac martyrum Christi limina cogitauit." (Beda Venerabilis *HE*, V, 9, p. 454f).

13 Cf. Rollason 2001, p. 15.

14 Cf. Levison 1946, p. 44.

15 Cf. Schäferdiek 1994, p. 175.

16 "… sed quoniam anno praecedente noluerat audire reuerentissimum patrem Ecgberctum, ne Scottiam nil se laedentem inpugnaret, datum est illi ex poena peccati illius, ne nunc eos, qui ipsum ab interitu reuocare cubiebant, audiret." (Beda Venerabilis *HE*, IV, 26, p. 408f).

17 Against the narrow definition of Wood 2001, p. 18.

18 Beda Venerabilis *HE*, III, 25, pp. 282–295. Cf. Mayr-Harting 1991, pp. 103–113.

19 Cf. Charles-Edwards 1983, pp. 42–52.

poured into the Roman mould and brought, with Lindisfarne, into the new order of the English Church."[20] Thus, another main theme of *HE* seems to have reached its climax before the last book has even begun.

Yet, here too the perspective widens in book V. Bearing in mind Thacker's assessment of Bede's portrayal of Cuthbert as an ideal teacher, we can better understand Abbot Adomnan's and Ecgberht's role.[21] The former, instructed in Northumbria in Catholic doctrine and practice, brought the Irish who lived on the mainland to the catholic Easter.[22] The latter, a Northumbria-born religious exile in Ireland, brought about the change of Iona's celebration of Easter; a *conuersio*, as Bede saw it.[23] It was this role as teacher which put both of them directly in the succession of the apostles, "to whose *ordo* they belonged and whose role they fulfilled in the contemporary church."[24] Book V thus shows how Northumbrian models of catholic practice and teaching were applied in true apostolic tradition for the benefit and *conuersio* of the wider church, in this instance the Irish church to which Northumbrian Christianity owed so much.[25]

The more than individual or national significance of the missionary Willibrord and Ecgberht the catholic teacher is underlined by the fact that both of them were mentioned in Bede's Greater Chronicle. Placing them in the context of the six world ages by mentioning their main achievements under an *annus mundi* date, they received a place in the universal history of salvation.[26] In the sixth age, the Christian era, the unfolding of history was about the spread of faith among all nations which would then be followed by the conversion of Israel.[27] Bede here followed a well established line of thought and

20 Markus 1975, p. 7.

21 Thacker 1983, pp. 136–42.

22 Beda Venerabilis *HE*, V, 15, pp. 480–483. Cf. Picard 1984 for an assessment of how much of this may have been Bede's fiction.

23 Beda Venerabilis *HE*, III, 4, p. 218f. and V, 22, p. 530f.: "… eodem die et ipse migrauit ad Dominum, ac gaudium summae festiuitatis, quod cum fratribus, quos ad unitatis gratiam *conuerterat*, inchoauit, cum Domino et apostolis ceterisque caeli ciuibus conpleuit, immo id ipsum celebrare sine fine non desinit." My italics. The same term is used in Beda Venerabilis *De temporum ratione*, c. 66 (Chronica maiora), s.a. 4670, p. 532f.: "Ecberectus, uir sanctus de gente Anglorum et sacerdotium monachica uita, etiam pro caelesti patria peregrinus exornans, plurimas Scotticae gentis prouincias ad canonicam paschalis temporis obseruantiam, a qua diutius aberrauerant, pia praedicatione *conuertit*, anno ab incarnatione domini DCCXVI." My italics. Bede *The Reckoning of Time*, p. 235.

24 Thacker 1983, p. 130 with references to Beda Venerabilis *De tabernaculo*, pp. 26–30. Bede *On the Tabernacle*, pp. 27–31. And Beda Venerabilis *De templo*, pp. 200–203. Bede *On the Temple*, pp. 75–80.

25 Beda Venerabilis *HE*, V, 22, pp. 528–533. See also the instruction of the Picts, whose king Nechtan turned to Jarrow in the question of the correct celebration of Easter, Beda Venerabilis *HE*, V, 21, pp. 506–529.

26 Beda Venerabilis *De temporum ratione*, c. 66 (Chronica maiora), s. a. 4649, p. 529 (Willibrord's mission) and s. a. 4670, p. 532f. (Egbert's pilgrim life in exile in Ireland and reformation of Iona). Bede *The Reckoning of Time*, pp. 233 and 235.

27 Beda Venerabilis *Homeliarum evangelii*, I, 10, p. 70f. Bede *Homilies on the Gospels*, I, 99f. Cf. also Beda Venerabilis *In Tobiam*, VII.2, p. 11. Bede *On Tobit*, p. 44.

understood the broad dynamics of the history of salvation in the tradition of Pope Gregory, as Fritze has shown.[28]

Yet Bede differs from Gregory in one important aspect. Although the pope professed that he did not know the time of the end, "... his sense of nearness is unequalled since the fading of the early Christians' eschatological expectations."[29] Book V of *HE* provides little evidence to substantiate a heightened sense of the impending end such as Gregory had.[30] The conversion of the remotest ends of the earth – as Britain was seen by Gregory and still in Bede's days[31] – may have been achieved yet this was not the end. Bede's comments on the continuing necessity of preaching the faith in his exegetical works and his scepticism about the depth of Christianisation in Britain in his letter to Bishop Ecgberht are a case in point.[32] Similarly, in book V of *HE*, Bede makes it clear that the church had not yet reached all the Gentiles and its missionary expansion was still very much in progress, thus his account of the martyrdom of the two Hewalds.[33] In Frisia, Willibrord and his Frankish protectors had experienced major setbacks, particularly upon the death of Pippin in 714.[34] Furthermore, the conversion of the Jews had not yet occurred, and Bede was quite aware of this.[35]

The end of the conversion process both of Britain and the rest of the world was not imminent. Promising signs (as expressed in Bede's lyrical view of contemporary Northumbria in the penultimate chapter of book V) coexisted with worrying signs, such as the two comets portending disaster mentioned earlier in the same chapter.[36] As Bede commented twice there: the outcome of everything remained unclear – just as was the date of the end of the present age.[37] Resisting the temptation to speculate about portents of the end, Bede seems to have understood the nature of the sixth age as highly ambivalent.[38] Signs of the redemption (the spread of the church) and of growing resistance to Christ could coexist.

28 Fritze 1969, pp. 108–119, esp. pp. 111–114.

29 Markus 1997, p. 51. See also von Padberg 1995, p. 43f.

30 Cf. McCready 1994, p. 95 arguing against Bonner 1966, p. 5.

31 Cf. Henderson 1980, p. 9–13.

32 For brief survey of the former, cf. Fritze 1969, p. 117f. For the latter: Beda Venerabilis *Epistola ad Ecgberhtum*, passim. Cf. Blair 1990, pp. 305–307.

33 Beda Venerabilis *HE*, V, 10, pp. 456–461.

34 Cf. Schäferdiek 1994, p. 185.

35 Beda Venerabilis *De temporum ratione*, c. 69, p. 538f. Bede *The Reckoning of Time*, pp. 241–243. Cf. Beda Venerabilis *In regum*, p. 297. Bede *Thirty questions*, p. 93.

36 Beda Venerabilis *HE*, V, 23, p. 532–536.

37 Beda Venerabilis *HE*, V, 23, p. 534f.: "[Ceoluulf] ... cuius regni et principia et processus tot ac tantis redundauere rerum aduersantium motibus, ut, quid de his scribi debeat quemue habitura sint finem singula, necdum sciri ualeat." On the present peaceful times, p. 536f.: "Quae res quem sit habitura finem, posterior aetas uidebit." More theologically: Beda Venerabilis *De temporum ratione*, c. 67, p. 537f. Bede *The Reckoning of Time*, p. 240f. Cf. McCready 1994, p. 94f.

38 Cf. Davidse 1982, p. 666f.

Focussing on the Individual

Bede may have been fairly quiet about the imminence of the end of the sixth age, yet he was not so reticent when it came to the individual's own end and judgement. In book V he is very much concerned with this second aspect of eschatology, which was also an important feature of Luke's Gospel and the Acts of the Apostles. As Markus has rightly pointed out, in *HE* Bede intended to act as a teacher of morals, and therefore was aiming at the individual, and his/her response to the eschatological themes that had come up.[39] This means we now have to look at the response that Bede wanted to create in his readers. The believer, who through the beginning of eschatological action in Christ lives in an eschatologically characterised age, is expected to modify his behaviour in response to this.[40] A *conuersio* is intended. Here lies the fundamental continuity between history and the present. In addition to establishing the connection of the present age with that of the early church, Bede therefore also shows his readers in book V the considerations and reactions of people confronted with imminent judgement and retribution in the afterlife.[41]

The occurrence of visions concerning the afterlife seems to go against the flow of the widening of Bede's perspective, which we have witnessed so far. Yet visionary experiences are not an uncommon theme in *HE*. They occur in every book, featuring perhaps most prominently as the cause of Edwin's conversion.[42] In book IV, we encounter the biggest cluster of visions, mostly in connection with events in Essex, at the monastery of Barking. A nun had a vision of a holy man who appeared with a message as a portent for her imminent death.[43] Another nun, Torhtgyth, had a vision acting as a portent of the death of the holy abbess of the convent and saw a vision of the same abbess acting as a portent of her own death.[44] This series of visions in a monastic context is followed by a similar vision seen by the retired king Sebbi of Essex which also indicated the time of his death.[45] In every one of these cases, we are dealing with Christians who had chosen the religious life (even if they had only done so at the very end of their lives) and who had nothing to fear from the transition of this life to the next. Torhtgyth, in particular, being struck with illness, comes across as very eager to follow her abbess to the afterlife. The visions here have the character of a promise.

Book V is the only other book of *HE* which features a similar cluster of visions. Again, their concern is to serve the edification and salvation of posterity, which is the reason which Bede gives for including them in his history.[46]

39 Markus 1975, p. 6.

40 Daley e.a 1986, p. 82.

41 Beda Venerabilis *HE*, V, 12–14, pp. 462–481.

42 Cf. Chapter headings to book II (s. c. 12), Beda Venerabilis *HE*, p. 122f.: "Vt Eduini per uisionem quondam sibi exuli ostensam sit ad credendum prouocatus."

43 Beda Venerabilis *HE*, IV, 8, pp. 342–345.

44 Beda Venerabilis *HE*, IV, 9, pp. 344–349.

45 Beda Venerabilis *HE*, IV, 11, pp. 350–353.

46 Beda Venerabilis *HE*, IV, 7, p. 343f.: "In hoc etenim monasterio plura uirtutum sunt signa patrata, quae et ad memoriam aedificationemque sequentium ab his, qui nouere,

Dryhthelm's long vision of the pleasures and tortures of the afterlife differs from the other visions, in so far as we are here dealing with a 'guided tour' through the visionary space in which heaven, hell and different intermediate transitory stages appear in close proximity.[47] Returned to life, this experience moved him to the extent that he radically changed his lifestyle, leaving his wife and children, distributing all his property to them and the poor, entering a monastery and pursuing the most rigorous ascetic practices of the day. It is clearly the fear of judgement and eternal punishment that speaks out of his answers to enquirers about this radical change of life and asceticism.[48] It was the neglect of a similar kind of repenting response to the exhortations of his king that led to the vision of a Mercian thegn, which showed him his own judgement for the many evil deeds he had committed and for which, due to his lack of repentance, he would now have to suffer for ever.[49] Finally, a monk who neglected his religious duties, had a vision of hell where he saw a place prepared for him.[50] In this case, there was no question of repenting at the last minute, the judgement having already been passed and there was no time left to change his life. As Dryhthelm made it his duty to tell everyone about his experience so that they might repent, so, according to Gregorian tradition,[51] Bede interpreted the other two visions as having occurred not for the benefit of the lost souls who experienced them, but as a spur for others, that they might repent in time and a sudden death not condemn them unrepented for ever.[52] Here, in contrast to book IV, the visions have taken on the character of a warning, but note that this is a warning to the individual in the light of his own judgement, not in the light of the impending consummation of the age.

Bede wanted these visions to elicit a response in his readers and therefore provided some *exempla* for them. The sort of response he had in mind had already come up in the context of King Sebbi's vision of his peaceful death.[53] After having reigned as a pious king for thirty years, he, upon falling ill, decided to finally pursue the religious life, left his kingdom and went to London, where he became a monk. In book V such a radical abandonment of royal office occurs no less than four times. First of all, we hear of Cædwalla, the last Anglo-Saxon king to convert (after God's help and Bishop Wilfrid's

descripta habentur a multis; e quibus et nos aliqua historiae nostrae ecclesiasticae inserere curauimus." Also Beda Venerabilis *HE*, V, 12, p. 462f.: "Namque ad excitationem uiuentium de morte animae quidam aliquandiu mortuus ad uitam resurrexit corporis, et multa memoratu digna, quae uiderat, narrauit."

47 Cf. Dinzelbacher 1981, pp. 90–145, esp. p. 111. Cf. also Carozzi 1994, pp. 226–253. Note, however, the exception of Fursa's vision in Beda Venerabilis *HE*, III, 19 (pp. 256–265), which strikes a similar chord. Bede included this vision at an earlier part in *HE*, where it fitted in well not only with his narrative (conversion of East Anglia) but also with the general chronology.

48 Cf. Dinzelbacher 1981, p. 202f.

49 Beda Venerabilis *HE*, V, 13, pp. 474–477.

50 Beda Venerabilis *HE*, V, 14, pp. 476–481.

51 Beda Venerabilis *HE*, V, 13, p. 476f. Cf. Gregorius *Dialogi*, IV, 40, pp. 138–147.

52 Cf. Dinzelbacher 1991, pp. 62–69.

53 Beda Venerabilis *HE*, IV, 11, pp. 350–353.

advice had ensured his accession to the kingship of Wessex and his conquest of Sussex and the Isle of Wight).[54] He was wounded in battle, which may explain his desire for a dramatic change of life, as well as the fact that he seems to have committed major genocide on Wight. Illness or a physical affliction often acted as a prelude to visions of death or judgement and the afterlife, as in most of the instances discussed above, and as the final impulse for Sebbi. Being washed in the waters of baptism meant complete forgiveness of sins, which is why Bede made the immediate link between baptism and Cædwalla's desire to die in Rome. A complete change of his way of life (and his ontological status) was implied by this baptism in Rome. It was definite and no turning back was possible, so he had come to Rome to remain there until his death.

Among those kings who were to follow Cædwalla's example, were Coenred of Mercia and Offa (probably king of the East Saxons).[55] A link between Coenred's and Cædwalla's retirement was further made in *HE* V, 24 where they are both listed as retiring to Rome. Coenred's and Offa's decision was also about a complete change of way of life and status, for they, like Sebbi before them, became monks. The charismatic character associated with both Cædwalla and Coenred was Wilfrid.[56] Inspired by him, according to Bede, Alhfrith and Oswiu had already contemplated pilgrimages to Rome.[57] Yet his influence alone cannot act as the whole explanation for this phenomenon. The Irish understanding of *peregrinatio*, which was also entertained by Bede, meant a long-lasting exile, abandoning the security of one's home and with this the safety and benefits of one's kindred.[58] It is this Irish tradition which becomes perceptible in Bede's positive evaluation of royal retirement in book V.

At the same time, however, Bede makes a very obvious point about the retiring kings and the destination of their journey, i.e. Rome and the veneration of the apostles in *HE* V, 19. He seems to have deliberately lengthened the already long chapter containing Wilfrid's biography, in order to make clearer the association between him, Rome and the retiring kings, although never explicitly. Wallace-Hadrill calls *HE* V, 19 "a chapter of *Romipetentes*", pointing out that Bede emphasizes "... the Roman aspect of Wilfrid's life, not his wanderings among English kings and the reasons for them."[59] This Roman aspect shows how much the Anglo-Saxons had already made Irish traditions their own and expressed them in a genuinely English way. For them, *peregrinatio* could be a way of life, as in Ireland, but it could also be combined with a particular devotion to the apostles and the Holy See, which, as Bede informed his readers, had played such a significant role in the conversion of the English.

54 Beda Venerabilis *HE*, IV, 15–16, pp. 364–367.

55 Cf. Yorke 1985, p. 17f.

56 Cf. Stancliffe 1983, p. 170f. with further references.

57 Beda Venerabilis *HE*, IV, 5, p. 334f. for Oswiu and for Alhfrith Beda Venerabilis *Historia abbatum*, c. 2, p. 365f. Bede *History of the Abbots*, p. 188.

58 Cf. Charles-Edwards 1976, pp. 44–46.

59 Wallace-Hadrill 1991, p. 191.

Wallace-Hadrill has noted that by the time of Alcuin's writings on kingship in a Carolingian context, the religious aspect of the royal office had become so exalted that royal retirement would have directly contravened what was expected of a Christian king.[60] Stancliffe however points out that Bede himself, while collecting examples of monk-kings, did much to promote a view of kingship entailing particular responsibilities.[61] Care for the faith of the inhabitants of his kingdom was the most prominent of these – and something with which Bede was concerned throughout *HE*. In the light of the apparent ambivalence in Bede's views, Stancliffe suggests that his approval of royal retirement in these monk-kings should rather be interpreted in the context of "... the cautionary tales in *HE* V, 13–14, urging the very Irish concern of penance."[62] However, as we have seen above, these "cautionary tales" were concerned with the individual reader's response to his impending judgement which had been revealed to him for the benefit of others, immediately before the end of his life. Bede's concern with individual judgement then seems to have been so significant that he would rather put up with an ambiguous portrayal of kingship than miss an opportunity to bring home to his readers a lesson on individual salvation.

Finally, we need to consider briefly the biographical chapter on Bishop Wilfrid. Although Bede wanted to make an association between the *Romipetentes* Coenred, Offa and Wilfrid, who all turned to Rome for judgement (or the avoidance of an unfavourable eternal judgement) in their own cases, the perspective begins to broaden again in *HE* V, 19, returning to the now familiar apostolic themes. For example, Wilfrid's missionary work, having been rather neglected at the chronological points where it would have fitted into the main narrative of *HE*, is now given due consideration.

Wilfrid's life was not so different from St. Paul's, who also came into frequent conflict with the authorities and, in a similar way embarked on important missionary journeys, spreading the faith even when he was in chains. Stephen of Ripon wants to make this link with apostolic times. In his Life of Wilfrid, he makes obvious comparisons between Wilfrid and St. Paul, the *doctor gentium*.[63] Yet Bede in *HE* V, 19 does not associate any miracles with the missionary Wilfrid nor is the apostolic aspect very pronounced.[64] Foley suggests that we seek the cause for this in Bede's and Stephen's different episcopal ideal and views of sanctity.[65]

This is not the place to enter into a debate about Bede's views on Wilfrid. In the present context, it is more relevant that Bede ended his account of Wilfrid, unlike Stephen, with Wilfrid's vision. It was concerned with the time the

60 Wallace-Hadrill 1971, pp. 101–105.

61 Stancliffe 1983, p. 175.

62 Stancliffe 1983, p. 176.

63 Stephen *Vita Wilfridi*, cc. 5. 26, pp. 10–13. 52f.

64 Note, however, that Bede had touched upon the miraculous associated with Wilfrid in the context of the main narrative of *HE*, when dealing with the conversion of Sussex and the plague-miracle of Selsey. Cf. Isenberg 1978, pp. 28f. and 58–73.

65 Trent Foley 1992, pp. 40–42. 72–76. 110–118.

bishop had left to live, so Bede could include him in his theme on individual judgement. Levison has highlighted that Wilfrid's vision did not fit the pattern of the visions in book V, which were concerned with judgement and retribution.[66] It should rather be seen in the context of the revelation of his time of death to Archbishop Theodore (*HE* V, 8) and the visions in book IV. It can thus be understood as a clear indication that, in Bede's view, Wilfrid had nothing to worry about. His vision promised further life and the restitution of his possessions. It did not urge him at all to change his way of life. Just like the retiring kings with whom he is associated, Wilfrid shines as an *exemplum* in the light of his promised benign individual judgement in *HE* V, 19.

The 'narrative of sorts' presented in book V of *HE* and even Bede's portrait of individual figures in Northumbrian history can be further unravelled when the reader bears the two aspects of salvation history and individual judgement in mind. From the outset of book V Bede established a link with apostolic times, chiefly through the *exempla* of Bishop John of Beverley, Willibrord and Ecgbhert. His outlook on the subject of mission was universal, rather than national, and it needs to be understood in a wider sense of assisting conversion, encompassing works of asceticism such as Ecgberht's voluntary exile as well as helping to spread catholic orthodoxy as Adomnan, Ecgberht and the monks of Jarrow had done. This thread is then picked up by a cluster of visions which help to illustrate that the subject of conversion was as important when it concerned the individual as when it did other nations. Bede's concern for individual salvation led him to incur inconsistencies in his portrait of royal and episcopal ideals rather than compromising his message to individual readers. Finally, despite the heightened sense of judgement expressed in the visions concerning the afterlife, Bede avoided speculation about the time of the end of the sixth age and its eschatological prefiguring, which was so apparent in the writings of some of his predecessors such as Gregory the Great. This, as well as the lack of 'history' in book V (except for a few chapters which complete episcopal successions)[67] seems due to the fact that Bede wanted his moral lesson to remain unobscured by worldly worries.

66 Levison 1948, pp. 229–235.

67 Beda Venerabilis *HE*, V, 8, pp. 450–453; V, 18, pp. 486–489; V, 20, pp. 504–507 and V, 23, pp. 532–535.

Bibliography

Sources

BEDA VENERABILIS

De tabernaculo

BEDA VENERABILIS: *De tabernaculo et vasis eius ac vestibus sacerdotum libri III*, ed. DAVID HURST (CChr.SL 119A), Turnhout 1969, 1–139.

On the Tabernacle

BEDE: *On the Tabernacle*, transl. ARTHUR G. HOLDER (TTH 18), Liverpool 1994.

De templo

BEDA VENERABILIS: *De templo libri II*, ed. DAVID HURST (CChr.SL 119A), Turnhout 1969, 143–234.

On the Temple

BEDE: *On the Temple*, transl. SEÁN CONNOLLY (TTH 21), Liverpool 1995.

De temporum ratione

BEDA VENERABILIS: *De temporum ratione liber Chronica Maiora includens*, ed. CHARLES W. JONES et TH. MOMMSEN (CChr.SL 123B), Turnhout 1977, 241–544.

The Reckoning of Time

BEDE: *The Reckoning of Time*, transl. FAITH WALLIS (TTH 29), Liverpool 1999.

Epistola ad Ecgberhtum

BEDA VENERABILIS: *Epistola ad Ecgberhtum Episcopum*, in *Venerabilis Baedae opera historica*, ed. CHARLES PLUMMER, I, Oxford 1896, 405–423.

Letter to Egbert

BEDE: *Letter to Egbert*, in *The Ecclesiastical History of the English People*, transl. JUDITH MCCLURE, ROGER COLLINS, Oxford 1994, 341–357.

Expositio Actuum Apostolorum

BEDA VENERABILIS: *Expositio Actuum Apostolorum*, ed. MAX L. W. LAISTNER (CChr.SL 121), Turnhout 1983, 1–99.

Commentary on Acts

THE VENERABLE BEDE: *Commentary on the Acts of the Apostles*, transl. LAWRENCE T. MARTIN (CistSS 117), Kalamazoo MI 1989.

Historia abbatum

BEDA VENERABILIS: *Historia abbatum*, in *Venerabilis Baedae opera historica*, ed. CHARLES PLUMMER, I, Oxford 1896, 364–387.

History of the Abbots

BEDE: *Lives of the Abbots of Wearmouth and Jarrow*, in *The Age of Bede*, transl. DAVID H. FARMER, Harmondsworth 1998, 185–220.

HE

BEDA VENERABILIS: *Historia ecclesiastica gentis Anglorum*, ed. et transl. GÜNTER SPITZBART, Darmstadt [2]1997.

Homeliarum Evangelii

BEDA VENERABILIS: *Homeliarum Evangelii Libri II*, ed. DAVID HURST (CChr.SL 122), Turnhout 1955, 1–378.

Homilies on the Gospels
BEDE THE VENERABLE: *Homilies on the Gospels*, transl. LAWRENCE T. MARTIN and DAVID HURST, I-II (CistSS 110 and 111), Kalamazoo MI 1991.
In regum
BEDA VENERABILIS: *In regum librum* XXX *quaestiones*, ed. DAVID HURST (CChr.SL 119), Turnhout 1962, 289–322.
Thirty questions
BEDE: *Thirty Questions on the Book of Kings*, transl. W. TRENT FOLEY in BEDE: *A Biblical Miscellany*, transl. W. TRENT FOLEY and ARTHUR G. HOLDER (TTH 28), Liverpool 1999, 89–138.
In Tobiam
BEDA VENERABILIS: *In Tobiam*, ed. DAVID HURST (CChr.SL 119B), Turnhout 1983, 1–19.
On Tobit
BEDE: *On Tobit and on the Canticle of Habakkuk*, transl. SEÁN CONNOLLY, Dublin/Portland OR 1997, 39–63.

Other Medieval Sources

AUGUSTINUS *De civitate Dei*
AUGUSTINUS HIPPONENSIS: *De civitate Dei*, ed. BERNHARD DOMBART et ALFONS KALB (CChr.SL 47–48), Turnhout 1955.
GREGORIUS *Dialogi*
GRÉGOIRE LE GRAND: *Dialogues*, ed. et transl. ADALBERT DE VOGÜÉ (SC 251. 260. 265), Paris 1978. 1979. 1980.
STEPHANUS *Vita Wilfridi*
The Life of Bishop Wilfrid by Eddius Stephanus, ed. et transl. BERTRAM COLGRAVE, Cambridge 1927.

Secondary Literature

BONNER 1996
GERALD BONNER: *Saint Bede in the Tradition of Western Apocalyptic Commentary* (Jarrow Lecture 9), Jarrow 1966.
CAROZZI 1994
CLAUDE CAROZZI: *Le voyage de l'âme dans l'au-delà d'après la littérature latine (Ve-XIIIe siècle)* (Collection de l'École française de Rome 189), Roma 1994.
CHARLES-EDWARDS 1976
THOMAS CHARLES-EDWARDS: "The Social Background to Irish Peregrinatio", in *Celtica 11* (1976) 43–59.
CHARLES-EDWARDS 1983
THOMAS CHARLES-EDWARDS: "Bede, the Irish and the Britons", in *Celtica 15* (1983) 42–52.

DALEY e.a. 1986
BRIAN DALEY, JOSEF SCHREINER, HORACIO E. LONA: *Eschatologie in der Schrift und der Patristik* (Handbuch der Dogmengeschichte IV.7), Freiburg/Basel/Wien 1986.

DAVIDSE 1982
JAN DAVIDSE: "The Sense of History in the Works of the Venerable Bede", in *Studi Medievali 21* (1982) 647–695.

DINZELBACHER 1981
PETER DINZELBACHER: *Vision und Visionsliteratur im Mittelalter* (Monographien zur Geschichte des Mittelalters 23), Stuttgart 1981.

DINZELBACHER 1991
PETER DINZELBACHER: *Revelationes* (Typologie des sources du moyen âge occidental 57), Turnhout 1991.

DUNCAN 1981
ARCHIBALD A. M. DUNCAN: "Bede, Iona and the Picts", in *The Writing of History in the Middle Ages.* Essays Presented to R. W. Southern, ed. by RALPH H. C. DAVIS and JOHN-MICHAEL WALLACE-HADRILL, Oxford 1981, 1–42.

EWIG 1966
EUGEN EWIG: "Die Abwendung des Papsttums vom Imperium und seine Hinwendung zu den Franken", in *Handbuch der Kirchengeschichte,* hg. von HUBERT JEDIN, III.1, Freiburg/Basel/Wien 1966, 3–30.

FRITZE 1969
WOLFGANG H. FRITZE: "Universalis gentium confessio. Formeln, Träger und Wege universalmissionarischen Denkens im 7. Jahrhundert", in *Frühmittelalterliche Studien 3* (1969) 78–130.

HANNING 1966
ROBERT W. HANNING: *The Vision of History in Early Britain,* Columbia 1966.

HENDERSON 1980
GEORGE HENDERSON: *Bede and the Visual Arts* (Jarrow Lecture 23), Jarrow 1980.

HUNTER BLAIR 1990
PETER HUNTER BLAIR: *The World of Bede,* Cambridge (new ed.) 1990.

ISENBERG 1978
GABRIELE ISENBERG: *Die Würdigung Wilfrieds von York in der Historia Ecclesiastica gentis Anglorum Bedas und in der Vita Wilfridi des Eddius. Ein Vergleich der verschiedenen literarischen Intentionen und der unterschiedlichen historischen Voraussetzungen,* Diss. masch., Universität Münster 1978.

LEVISON 1946
WILHELM LEVISON: *England and the Continent in the Eighth Century* (The Ford Lectures 1943), London 1946, repr. 1998.

LEVISON 1948
WILHELM LEVISON: "Die Politik in den Jenseitsvisionen des frühen Mittelalters", in *Aus rheinischer und fränkischer Frühzeit. Ausgewählte Aufsätze,* hg. von WILHELM LEVISON, Düsseldorf 1948, 229–246.

MARKUS 1970
ROBERT A. MARKUS: *Saeculum: History and Society in the Theology of St. Augustine*, Cambridge 1970.
MARKUS 1975
ROBERT A. MARKUS: *Bede and the Tradition of Ecclesiastical Historiogaphy* (Jarrow Lecture 18), Jarrow 1975.
MARKUS 1997
ROBERT A. MARKUS: *Gregory the Great and His World*, Cambridge 1997.
MCCREADY 1994
WILLIAM D. MCCREADY: *Miracles and the Venerable Bede* (Studies and Texts 118), Toronto 1994.
VON PADBERG 1995
LUTZ E. VON PADBERG: *Mission und Christianisierung. Formen und Folgen bei Angelsachsen und Franken im 7. und 8. Jahrhundert*, Stuttgart 1995.
PICARD 1984
JEAN-MICHEL PICARD: "Bede, Adomnan and the Writing of History", in *Peritia 3* (1984) 50–70.
ROLLASON 2001
DAVID W. ROLLASON: *Bede and Germany* (Jarrow Lecture 44), Jarrow 2001.
SCHÄFERDIEK 1994
KNUT SCHÄFERDIEK: "Fragen der frühen angelsächsischen Festlandsmission", in *Frühmittelalterliche Studien 28* (1994) 172–195.
STANCLIFFE 1983
CLARE STANCLIFFE: "Kings Who Opted Out", in WORMALD e.a. 1983, 59–94.
THACKER 1983
ALAN THACKER: "Bede's Ideal of Reform", in WORMALD e.a. 1983, 130–153.
TRENT FOLEY 1992
WILLIAM TRENT FOLEY: *Images of Sanctity in Eddius Stephanus' Life of Bishop Wilfrid*, Lewiston/Queenston/Lampeter 1992.
WALLACE-HADRILL 1971
JOHN-MICHAEL WALLACE-HADRILL: *Early Germanic Kingship in England and the Continent*, Oxford 1971.
WALLACE-HADRILL 1991
JOHN-MICHAEL WALLACE-HADRILL: *Bede's Ecclesiastical History of the English People. A Historical Commentary*, Oxford [2]1991.
WOOD 2001
IAN WOOD: *The Missionary Life. Saints and the Evangelisation of Europe, 400–1050*, Harlow 2001.
WORMALD e.a. 1983
Ideal and Reality in Frankish and Anglo-Saxon Society. Studies presented to J. M. Wallace-Hadrill, ed. by PATRICK WORMALD, DONALD BULLOUGH, ROGER COLLINS, Oxford 1983.
YORKE 1985
BARBARA YORKE: "The Kingdom of the East Saxons", in *Anglo-Saxon England 14* (1985) 1–36.

Archa Verbi 1 (2004) 25–41

The origins of the Trinitarian attributes *potentia, sapientia, benignitas*[1]

by Matthias Perkams

One major theme in 12th-century theological literature is the discussion about the extent to which the Trinity can be understood by human reason. A crucial point is the explanation of the Trinity with the help of an image taken from the perfection of God's activity as creator of the world. This had a vast influence on the medieval discussion of Trinitarian theology: the three persons of the Trinity are compared to God's omnipotence, wisdom and benignity or goodness respectively (*potentia, sapientia, benignitas* or *bonitas* in the most usual terminology).[2] This triad of concepts can be traced back to Middle Platonic philosophical discussions and was first used in a Christian context by Irenaeus of Lyon, who quotes it as δύναμις, σοφία, ἀγαθότης.[3] It is, however, a difficult question, by what route the formula found its way to the medieval discussions about the Trinity: the three concepts cannot be derived directly from Irenaeus, because in the Latin translation of his work they are rendered as *virtus, sapientia, bonitas.* They are not found either, as one triad, in Augustine's Trinitarian theology, which was the main source for the medieval discussion on this topic. It is hard to explain, then, why the triad appears, in the form *potentia, sapientia, benignitas,* around 1120 in the works of two leading theologians of this time: in Peter Abelard's *Theologia 'Summi Boni'* and in Hugh of Saint Victor's *De tribus diebus.*[4] Because neither of these contemporaries cites the other, it is not clear who was the first to introduce *potentia, sapientia, benignitas* in the Trinitarian context in which it became so important in the later tradition.

In a major study on Hugh of Saint Victor's *De tribus diebus* and its sources, Dominique Poirel could throw some light on the history of the formula. He shows that Hugh of Saint Victor could have had knowledge of the triad through Ambrose's *Expositio in Hexaemeron* and from the *De fide, spe et caritate* by the 9th-century abbot Paschasius Radbertus,[5] a work which was apparently not widely read in the 12th century.[6]

1 This paper is the fruit of discussions after a speech at the 11th International Conference for Medieval Philosophy at Porto in August 2002. I thank Constant Mews for reading previous versions of it and preventing me from many errors in content and, last but not least, in my English. For further corrections of my English I thank Morwenna Ludlow.

2 On the variable terminology of Hugh cf. Poirel 2002, pp. 327–343; Abelard is generally more consistent, but he can also use *caritas* instead of *bonitas* or *benignitas* regarding the Holy Spirit, e.g. Abaelardus *Tsum,* 1, 17, p. 92, 160f.

3 Irenaeus *Adversus haereses,* 4, 38, 3; Whittaker 1987, pp. 282–287.

4 Abaelardus *Tsum,* 1, 1–5, p. 86–88; Hugo *trib. dieb.,* 1, pp. 4–6; with explicit regard to the Trinity: ibid. 25, p. 64, 1131f.; 27, pp. 69f.

5 Poirel 2002, pp. 163–165.

Paschasius was obviously the first medieval Theologian to use *potentia, sapientia, voluntas* as a triad of nouns, not of adjectives. Poirel concludes from this that Hugh, contrary to the most current opinion on this issue, did not have to rely on Abelard to re-introduce this formula into Trinitarian theology. Therefore he holds that "c'est très probablement Hugues qui fut la source d'Abélard et non l'inverse."[7] By this he gets a new *terminus ante quem* for the *De tribus diebus* at around 1120, when Abelard's *Theologia 'Summi Boni'* was published.

While it is surely true that Hugh might have known the triad from the sources mentioned by Poirel, it does not necessarily follow from this that he, and not Abelard, was the first to apply the formula to the Trinity. Indeed, there are some arguments in favor of establishing Abelard in this regard. In the first part of my paper, I shall explain, how he could have coined the formula, relying on earlier discussions in Paris and Laon, but without presupposing Hugh's treatise. Indeed, it is indicated by some points of contact between the *De tribus diebus* and the *Theologia 'Summi Boni'*, which I shall discuss in the second part, that more probably Hugh was relying on Abelard than the other way around. In a third part, I shall discuss Poirel's arguments for claiming that Hugh was the first to apply the formula to the Trinity.

1. Abelard and the contemporary discussions

At the time of Abelard and Hugh, the discussion about the Trinity was already going on for some decades in the schools of Paris, Laon and other cities. Within the texts which inform us about the ideas developed here, there are some passages that show elements of the application of *potentia, sapientia, benignitas* to the Trinity. These texts are products of the schools where Abelard was educated.[8] We can safely assume that he knew the discussions and arguments which we find within them, even if we cannot say for sure that he knew exactly these texts or that they are, in their present form, anterior to the *Theologia 'Summi Boni'*. But, as I want to demonstrate more clearly, his own Trinitarian teaching, based on the use of the triadic formula in a Trinitarian context, can easily be understood as a reaction to the opinions attested here.

The first text which is relevant here is attributed to William of Champeaux in the *Liber pancrisis*, an anthology of theological teachings from the early twelfth century, which brings together opinions of the Church Fathers and of some contemporary masters. William, who had been Abelard's teacher for some years, is reported as describing *sapientia* as the Son (a traditional Pauline concept) and *caritas* as the Holy Spirit (a traditional Augustinian concept), whereas he mentions *potentia* in connection with the divine substance, but without linking it explicitly with the Father:

6 Poirel 2002, pp. 351–356.

7 Poirel 2002, p. 376.

8 Both are cited by Poirel, but not linked with Abelard; cf. already the critical apparatus to Abaelardus *Tsum*, 1, 1.

One has to hold firmly that the simple substance of the godness is totally free from all forms or parts. Because of its dignity and its potency it is necessary to believe much about it which cannot be grasped by human reason. ... Also the catholic church judges that one shall not hear those who say that some creatures have existed all the time along with the Creator, like the sun which by its nature is prior to its light, but in no time is without its light ... so they say that also the Creator does not exist in any time without some effects of himself. ... For he created ... everything from nothing ... by his wisdom and loved it by his charity. This wisdom is called the Son of the Father, and the charity of both of them the Holy Spirit.[9]

By contrast with Abelard and Hugh, *potentia* is not used here as an attribute of the father,[10] but as an attribute of the divine substance. It is, however, only a little step to the complete Trinitarian formula, if someone is looking for a suitable attribute for the father.[11] William stresses that the divine substance and the Trinity cannot be understood by human reason because it transcends its categories; consequently, they are objects of the real faith which believes what is not visible. In spite of that, William thinks that a rational explanation of the Trinity is possible with the help of analogies (*similitudines*),[12] the same method, which Abelard uses extensively in the different versions of his *Theologia.*[13] So we have good reasons to assume that he knew this teaching by William.

The same holds true for the second text I want to hint at which has especially close links to Abelard's theology. This text, the *Sententiae divinae paginae* (from now on *SDP*), is a collection of Sentences the exact date of wich is difficult to determine. The editor F. P. Bliemetzrieder suspects it to be a work by Anselm of Laon,[14] but it is more probably a product of his school or a

9 "Illud tamen firmiter est tenendum, illam simplicem divinitatis substantiam omnium tam formarum quam partium omnino esse expertum. De qua propter dignitatem ipsius et potentiam multa credi oportet que capi ratione non possunt humana. ... Nec enim catholica ecclesia illos iudicat audiendos, qui aliquas ex creaturis dicunt semper cum creatore fuisse ac sicut sol, qui natura prior est suo lumine, nunquam tamen est sine suo lumine ... sic et ipsum creatorem, potentia et dignitate priorem, nunquam tamen sine aliquo suo dicunt exstitisse effectu. ... Ipse enim ... omnia de nihilo ... sua sapientia creavit et sua caritate dilexit. Que quidem sapientia Filius Patris, caritas vero Spiritus utriusque sanctus nominatur." (GUILLELMUS CAMPELLENSIS *Sententiae*, nr. 236, pp. 191, 58–192, 85).

10 POIREL 2002, pp. 363–366.

11 Cf. also the text cited by POIREL 2002, p. 367, whose date is, however, difficult to establish.

12 "Est enim unus Deus et trinus, unus quidem in substantia, trinus in personis; quod qualiter explicare possim non video, quoniam in nulla rerum natura simile quod possit inveniri. Dici tamen et credi oportet Deum unum tres habere personas quarum una Pater dicitur, propterea quod ex se credatur aliam generare personam que Filius nominatur. De qua generatione per similitudinem id dicamus quod possumus; et quod similitudo describere non poterit fides sola defendat." (GUILLELMUS CAMPELLENSIS *Sententiae*, p. 192, 85–92).

13 Cf. ABAELARDUS *Tsum*, *Capitula librorum* 3; 2, 65; 3, 52, p. 85, 14f.; p. 135, 572f.; p. 179, 623f., and elsewhere.

14 BLIEMETZRIEDER 1919, p. 31*f.

collection of notes taken from his lectures.[15] The structure of the text shows remarkable parallels to William's *Sententiae*:[16] it contains discussion of the Trinity immediately after an opening chapter which deals at some length with the divine essence and its incomprehensibility by human reason, yet then goes on to give rational arguments about identity and difference. This structural parallel is interesting because it is not found in the other Sentence collections of the School of Laon with the one exception of the *Sententiae Atrebatenses* which cite extensively the *SDP*, but without mentioning the Trinitarian attributes:[17] the so called *Sententiae Anselmi* discuss the divine substance and the Trinity very briefly while they are otherwise much longer than the *SDP*;[18] the *De conditione angelica et humana* does not contain a Trinitarian discussion at all;[19] the *Sententiae Berolinenses* open with a long chapter on the Trinity, but without a preceding part on the divine essence and without mentioning the Trinitarian attributes.[20] If we find at all a discussion of the Trinitarian attributes in one of these collections, we find it in the section concerning the creation of man, and the argument is quite Augustinian without touching upon the new developments discussed in the present article.[21] So both the structure of William's Sentences and the *SDP* and the mentioning of the Trinitarian attributes in both texts hint at a certain relationship between them. On the other hand, as regards the content, the doctrine of the *SDP* is quite different from William's teaching. This is clearly shown by the following extract, which directly concerns our question:

> The cognition of this Trinity seems to be materially within the human reason. Because, when the human reason regards that all these changeable things have taken and have got a beginning from something, it regards in this moment the person of the Father from whom everything is. But when it recognizes that everything has been made in wisdom, it attends then the person of the Son, that is the wisdom of the Father. And when it recognizes that everything has been made in goodness, there is the Holy Spirit, that is the goodness of God the Father.[22]

15 On the possibility of notes taken from systematic lectures at this period cf. Lefèvre 1959, p. 254f.

16 Constant Mews also sees a close relationship of both texts in the sixth chapter of his forthcoming book on Peter Abelard; I thank him for sending me a draft of this chapter.

17 *Sententiae Atrebatenses*, 1, pp. 206f.

18 *Sententiae Anselmi*, 1, pp. 47f.

19 *Liber de conditione*, p. 256.

20 *Sententiae Berolinenses*, pp. 39, 1–40, 40.

21 E.g. *Sententiae Berolinenses*, p. 47, 1–8; *Sententiae Atrebatenses*, 5, pp. 213, 19–214, 32.

22 "Cognitio etiam istius trinitatis materialiter videtur insita humane rationi. Cum enim humana ratio attendit omnia hec mutabilia cepisse et habuisse exordium ab aliquo, ibidem attendit patris personam, a quo omnia. Cum autem omnia in sapientia facta esse dinoscit, ibi personam filii, quod est sapientia patris. Cum vero omnia in bonitate facta dinoscit, ibi spiritus sanctus, quod est bonitas Dei patris" (*Sententiae Divinae Paginae*, 3, pp. 7–8).

The author of these *Sentences* is obviously less critical as regards an understanding of the Trinity by human reason than William of Champeaux. One could read both texts as directly opposed to each other in this respect, but perhaps it is better to see both of them as representative of one tradition within which they present a more or less rational standpoint. Anyway, the *SDP* speaks more openly about the use of reason in Trinitarian debate than Abelard who, like William, does not claim that the Trinity can be grasped directly by human reason, but recurs to *similitudines* for its explanation. But in spite of that, there are certain affinities between the argument of the *SDP* and the beginning of Abelard's *Theologia 'Summi Boni'*: in both texts the Trinity is explained by a triad of concepts which are assumed to be necessary to a perfect creator.

The *SDP* argues from basic assumptions about creation to the nature of the Creator: creation is created, so there has to be a Creator; it is created wisely, so this Creator has to be wise; it is created well, so he has to be good. These conclusions are supposed to give human reason an understanding of the divine Trinity. The creator who, as the divine substance, has in William's Sentences the attribute of *potentia,* is identified in the *SDP* as the first person of the Trinity.

It is easy to see that the argument of the *SDP* was open to criticisms from theologians which were more critical about the use of reason in Trinitarian theology. On the other hand, the idea of explaining the doctrine of the Trinity rationally could have seemed more attractive to those theologians with an interest in logic greater than the rather restrictive approach of William of Champeaux. Peter Abelard was such a theologian: he was taught by William of Champeaux with whom he had deep disagreements.[23] He also studied with Roscelin of Compiègne whose Trinitarian theology we do not know very precisely, but who was interested in this topic and who put forward a theory obviously very different from William's.[24] And Abelard studied with Anselm of Laon whose school could have been the place where the *SDP* has been produced.[25] So it is quite probable that Abelard knew also the terminology and the opinions attested by this collection of sentences. If he intended to explain the doctrine of the Trinity from the point of view of a logician, as he in fact did, his endeavour can be rendered as a correction of the simplifications which he found in positions like the *SDP,* by changing the run of the argument according to his own methods. This can be seen from the beginning of the *Theologia 'Summi Boni'*:

> The incarnate wisdom of God, Christ the Lord, in describing the perfection of the Highest Good, which is God, carefully distinguished it with three names when he called the one and single, totally undivided and simple divine substance Father, Son, and Holy Spirit, for three reasons. ... To call God three persons, that is Father and Son and Holy Spirit, amounts to saying that the divine substance is potent, wise, benign, or

23 Abaelardus *Historia calamitatum,* pp. 64, 31–67, 154.

24 Cf. Anselmus *Epistola* 136, p. 279, 3–8; Niggli 1991, p. 271, note on 177, 10.

25 Abaelardus *Historia calamitatum,* pp. 68,164–69,221.

again that it is potency[26] itself, wisdom itself, benignity itself. But in those three, potency, wisdom, benignity, consists all the perfection of the good.[27]

Rather schematically, one can summarize Abelard's argument as follows: he starts from the signification of the word *summum bonum* (this notion is mentioned in the *SDP* shortly before the passage quoted[28]). From this signification he draws conclusions regarding the implications of this notion: a *summum bonum* which is about to create something has to be mighty, so it has to have *potentia*; it has to be wise, so it must have *sapientia*; and it has to be good, so it has to have *benignitas* or *bonitas*. Abelard explains the Trinity by the same triad of concepts relevant to creation, as was already used in the *SDP*; but his account is far more sophisticated: he does not have to recur to human reason for the invention of these concepts, but he can ascribe them to an authority, the words of Christ. So he can present the doctrine of the Trinity in a way which is both rationally or scientifically sound (according to the standards of the time, of course) and not based on an obvious rationalism, but presented as a clarification of the tradition.

While Abelard took over the tendency of the *SDP* to explain the Trinity by a rational analysis of the creator, he could borrow from William the term *potentia* to designate God the Father who lacks an own attribute in the *SDP*. It was not difficult for him to introduce this term into the discussion of the Trinity. In fact, the use of *potentia* in this context is the most original point in Abelard's and Hugh's Trinitarian explanation both because of the newness and because of the special signification of this word in Abelard's work.[29] Abelard could have been moved to do so also by Boethius, who writes in his *Consolatio philosophiae* that man lives in a world where often the virtues are trodden underfoot, and states that this is hard to bear in the reign of an omnipotent, omniscient and benevolent God.[30] In this text which the logician Abelard probably

26 The translation of the Latin *potentia* in Abelard's Trinitarian doctrine is difficult, because Abelard unifies in this term the idea of God's power and the Aristotelian notion of δύναμις, which could be rendered as "possibility". The term potency tries to give a compromise, which allows to discern both senses of the Abelardian term; with the same aim I will use in my forthcoming German translation of the *Theologia 'Scholarium'* the word "Mächtigkeit".

27 "Summi boni perfectionem quod deus est, ipsa dei sapientia incarnata Christus dominus describendo tribus nominibus diligenter distinxit, cum unicam et singularem, individuam penitus ac simplicem substantiam divinam patrem et filium et spiritum sanctum tribus de causis appellaverit. ... Tale est ergo deum esse tres personas, hoc est patrem et filium et spiritum sanctum, ac si dicamus divinam substantiam esse potentem, sapientem benignam, immo etiam esse ipsam potentiam, ipsam sapientiam, ipsam benignitatem. In his autem tribus, potentia scilicet, sapientia, benignitate, tota boni perfectio consistit" (Abaelardus *Tsum*, 1, 1–3, pp. 86, 4–8. 87, 21–26).

28 *Sententiae divinae paginae*, 2, p. 6.

29 I discussed Abelard's concept of potency in Perkams 2003, pp. 101–107.

30 "Quae fieri in regno scientis omnia, potentis omnia, sed bona tantummodo volentis Dei nemo satis potest nec ammirari nec conqueri" (Boethius *consolatio*, 4, 1, 5, p. 65, 15–17).

knew quite early in his career[31] we find all the three elements which Abelard adduces, and it should be pointed out that they appear in a discussion of the unlimited goodness of God. It is of course possible that Abelard knew also the writings of Ambrose and Paschasius Radbertus quoted by Poirel, which, however, show closer parallels with Hugh's treatment of the question.[32] However that may be, the evidence adduced up to now shows clearly enough that it was no less possible for Abelard than for any of his contemporaries to introduce *potentia, sapientia, benignitas* into the Trinitarian discussion. As to whether he or Hugh was earlier in doing so, we can only look out for traces of possible mutual influences in the earliest texts in which they used the formula, i.e. in Hugh's *De tribus diebus* and in Abelard's *Theologia 'Summi Boni'*.

2. The *De tribus diebus* and the *Theologia 'Summi Boni'*

Ralf Stammberger has shown that there are many parallels in Hugh's and Abelard's theological writings, though the approaches of both authors in the above works are quite different from each other. "Where Hugh presents an exegesis of nature Abelard analyses the texts of Jews and Gentiles."[33] Now, I want to draw the attention to some points of contact between them which could hint at an acquaintance of Hugh with the *Theologia 'Summi Boni'* already at the time of writing the *De tribus diebus*.

The most obvious parallel between the *Theologia 'Summi Boni'* and the *De tribus diebus* is the triad *potentia, sapientia, benignitas* itself. This parallel is remarkable, because only one of the three notions is an uncontroversial part of the tradition, as to say *sapientia*, which can be found already in Augustine as part of triads describing the Trinity. *Potentia* is more difficult, but it could be found in Paschasius or Ambrose and was used already by William of Champeaux in Trinitarian theology. *Benignitas* is another remarkable term: while *bonitas, caritas* or *voluntas* are frequent attributes of the Holy Spirit in the theological tradition, *benignitas* is, as far as I know, never used as an attribute of the Holy Spirit before Abelard and Hugh.[34] While its equivalents do not disappear totally, *benignitas* is clearly the preferred attribute of the Holy Spirit in Abelard and in the *De tribus diebus*. This fact requires an explanation: which considerations could have led Abelard or Hugh to use *benignitas* rather than *bonitas*?

In the case of Abelard, this is not difficult to see: he needs a term to describe his concept of charity, which is, according to him, a good will directed

31 According to the *Index scriptorum* of CChr.CM 13 Abelard cited the *Consolatio* three times in Abaelardus *Tsum* and still more often in the subsequent versions of the *Theologia*.

32 Poirel 2002, pp. 348–356.

33 Stammberger 2002, pp. 69–76 (quotation: pp. 72f.).

34 Poirel 2002, p. 348 hints at Sap. 1, 6 ("Benignus est enim spiritus sapientiae") and Gal. 5, 22 ("Fructus spiritus est caritas, gaudium, pax, patientia, benignitas ...") as scriptural testimonies for *benignitas*, but he does not cite authorities using this notion in a Trinitarian context. On Augustine he writes (p. 358) "*amor, voluntas* ou *benignitas* sont pareillement appropriées au Fils et au Saint-Esprit", but without citing a passage where *benignitas* is used.

towards the other creatures without any interest of his own.[35] *Bonitas* is problematic in this respect, because it could be understood as describing the everlasting and immutable goodness of God, but *benignitas* serves Abelard's purpose very well. It also has a corresponding adjective, *benignus*, by the help of which Abelard can describe the character of the Holy Spirit.[36] On the other hand, this term does not have a special function in Hugh, who does not explain in the *De tribus diebus*, what *benignitas* means, and uses the adjective *benignus* only in few cases. It seems that benignity is a term coined by Abelard to serve his special purposes.

There are some parallels between Hugh and Abelard, as regards the function of the triadic formula: according to both authors, its cognition has a moral effect. For example, Hugh writes at the end of the second part of his treatise:

> Consequently, he shows to you in his work how much he is able to do concerning your redemption. ... Nobody can resist him, because he is omnipotent; nobody can deceive him, because he is the wisest; nobody can corrupt him, because he is the best.[37]

These formulations are very close to what Abelard says at the beginning of the *Theologia 'Summi Boni'*:

> (Christ called) the Father according to the unique potency of his majesty which is omnipotence, because nothing can resist him; but he called the same divine substance the Son according to the acumen of his own wisdom by which he can judge without being mistaken and understand everything, so that nothing can be hidden to him by which he would be deceived; also he called him Holy Spirit according to the grace of his benignity by which God prepares evil to nobody, but is ready to redeem all.[38]

It is obvious that at least the omnipotence and the wisdom of God have the same significance in both authors and are described by almost identical formulations. The statements on *benignitas* are similar, too, though Hugh does not adhere to Abelard's pneumatology and, consequently, does not ascribe a special sense to the word *benignitas*. We can follow up these parallels further. A few lines later Hugh writes:

> When the recognized omnipotence of God excites our heart to admiration, this is the day of the Father; but when the wisdom of God illuminates our heart, because we have got cognition of the truth, this is the day of the Son; but when the hope that the

35 Cf. Abaelardus *Tsum*, 3, 88f., pp. 195, 1195–196, 1202. 196, 1212–1219.

36 Abaelardus *Tsum*, 1, 1–4, p. 13, 86–88.

37 "Monstrat ergo tibi in suo opere, quantum possit in tua redemptione. ... Nemo resistere ei potest, quia omnipotens est; nemo fallere eum potest, quia sapientissimus est; nemo eum corrumpere potest, quia optimus est" (Hugo *trib. dieb.*, 24, p. 60, 1063–1067).

38 "Patrem quidem secundum illam unicam maiestatis sue potentiam, que est omnipotentia, qua scilicet efficere potest quicquid vult, cum nichil ei resistere queat; filium autem eandem divinam substantiam dixit secundum proprie sapientie discretionem, qua videlicet cuncta veraciter diiudicare ac discernere potest, ut nichil eam latere possit quo decipiatur; spiritum sanctum etiam vocavit ipsam secundum benignitatis sue gratiam, qua scilicet nulli malum machinatur deus, sed paratus est cunctos salvare" (Abaelardus *Tsum*, 1, 1, pp. 86,11–87,18; this passage is situated between the two quoted above, n. 49).

> benignity of God inflames our heart to love, this is the day of the Holy Spirit. ... In the day of potency we die from fear; in the day of wisdom we get buried by the contemplation of the truth; in the day of benignity we arise through the love and the desire of the eternal goods.[39]

The same connections between potency and fear and between benignity and love we find also at the beginning of the *Theologia 'Summi Boni'*:

> There are two things which make us completely subject to God, these are fear and love. Potency and wisdom instil especially fear, because we recognize that God is able to punish faults and that nothing is hidden to him. But his benignity is related to love, such that we love most intensely whom we see to be the most benign.[40]

There are some obvious parallels between both works also in these passages, while some differences remain: Abelard wants to distinguish sharply between fear and love which are the two modes of human piety; he understands love as a decision of someone's own will while fear is an obedience which is not chosen freely.[41] Hugh, on the other hand, compares the human behaviour towards God to three different days, each of which has certain properties related to the invisible attributes of God. By doing so, Hugh creates the triad of *timor, veritas* and *amor,* carrying on the triadic way of thought which is predominant in the *De tribus diebus.* In the same manner, he relates the triad of *potentia, sapientia, benignitas* to the resurrection of Christ which is of no interest to Abelard in this context.

These parallels show that Abelard and Hugh took part in the same theological debate (which is in any case very plausible, because both lived at the same time in the same city, Paris) and that they without doubt influenced each other. In some way, both of their treatises have the same goal, that is to make God's nature and its Trinity comprehensible with the help of the attributes *potentia, sapientia, benignitas* which are themselves concepts of human reason. Though Hugh does not relate this triad to the Trinity at the beginning of his work, he does so at the end, leading the reader towards the same point which Abelard makes at the very beginning of his own treatise.

But what does all this mean for our main question: did Abelard borrow the triadic formula from Hugh or the other way around? Or did both of them rely on the same oral or written sources? What makes answering these questions so difficult is, that both of them were so outstanding theologians: each reworked

39 "Quando ergo omnipotentia Dei considerata in admirationem cor nostrum excitat, dies Patris est; quando vero sapientia Dei inspecta agnitione veritatis cor nostrum illuminat, dies Filii est; quando autem benignitas Dei attenta ad amorem cor nostrum inflammat, dies Spiritus sancti est. ... In die potentiae per timorem morimur; in die sapientiae per contemplationem veritatis a strepitu huius mundi sepelimur; in die benignitatis per amorem et desiderium aeternorum bonorum resurgimus" (Hugo *trib. dieb.*, p. 69, 1237–1245; cf. also ibid., pp. 63,1126–64,1131).

40 "Duo quippe sunt que nos omnino Deo subiectos efficiunt, timor videlicet atque amor. Potentia quidem et sapientia maxime timorem incutiunt, cum eum et posse punire errata et nichil latere cognoscimus. Benignitas autem eius ad amorem pertinet, ut quam benignissimum habemus, potissimum diligamus" (Abaelardus *Tsum*, 1, 4, p. 88, 41–46).

41 Cf. Perkams 2001a.

the material which he had at his disposal according to his own ideas. Neither of them quotes the other, and it is very improbable that either would have done so, had he used the other's work.[42] So, it is equally conceivable that Abelard borrowed some concepts from Hugh and adapted them to his own interests and that Hugh read the introduction to the *Theologia 'Summi Boni'* before writing a treatise in which some of its ideas are reproduced in a different theological framework.

Having said so much, I still think that there are some reasons to suppose that Hugh drew on Abelard: 1) Abelard's *Theologia 'Summi Boni'* is closely related to the theological project of his teacher William of Champeaux. There are no such parallels between Hugh and William, but only between Hugh and Abelard. The easiest way to explain this is that Hugh used Abelard's work as a starting point for his own reflections. 2) A second argument is the significance of the triad in Abelard: *potentia* and *benignitas* are key concepts which he needs to develop his explanation of the Trinity with the help of ethical presuppositions. Without the ambivalent *potentia* he cannot link Trinitarian theology to the exegesis of Aristotle, as I have shown elsewhere.[43] *Benignitas* is crucial to him for ascribing to God his concept of Charity. There is no similar relevance of these terms in Hugh's theological framework. 3) Around 1120 Abelard was already a famous master whose ideas were without doubt widely read and discussed. In this perspective it would be more natural that the young Hugh read the *Theologia 'Summi Boni'* and picked up a few ideas from it than that Abelard used key concepts of the first major work of the young Hugh to shape his Theology.

3. Poirel's arguments in favor of Hugh as being earlier

So, we have good reasons to think that Abelard was the first one to apply the complete triad of *potentia, sapientia, benignitas* to Trinitarian theology. However, Poirel puts forward some arguments in the opposite direction, which deserve to be discussed shortly.

The first point is the dating of the *De tribus diebus* itself. Poirel, criticizing Damien van den Eynde,[44] makes a new attempt to date the *De tribus diebus.*[45] The only sure date he supplies for this treatise is a hint which the author gives in his *Libellus de formatione arche*, an appendix to the larger *De archa Noe*, which must have been completed in 1126/27. Because one has to reckon with a span of time between this work and the *De tribus diebus*, according to Poirel the *terminus ante quem* of the latter is 1125/26.[46] This date is some years after the *terminus ante quem* which one can establish for the *Theologia 'Summi Boni'*: one can date this work with certainty to the time around 1120 or still earlier, as it must have been completed by March 1121, when it was condemned at the

42 Cf. Poirel 2002, p. 169.
43 Cf. Perkams 2003.
44 van den Eynde 1960.
45 Poirel 2002, pp. 131–150.
46 Poirel 2002, pp. 150f.

Council of Soissons. If we allow some time for the discussions which led to this assembly, keeping in mind also that Abelard had time to enlarge his treatise at least once, probably before Soissons, it seems likely that he composed the first version, which already contains the Trinitarian terminology, not later than 1119.[47] On the other hand, we do not have a precise *terminus post quem* for the *De tribus diebus*, so that it could theoretically have been completed before Abelard's work. This is what Poirel tries to prove: his assumption that the formula *potentia, sapientia, benignitas* is presupposed in Abelard's treatise is his crucial argument for dating the *De tribus diebus* to the time before the *Theologia 'Summi Boni'* was composed. If this is true and if Hugh arrived at Paris, as far as we know, between 1115–1118[48] the time in which the *De tribus diebus* could have been composed must be the span between 1115/18–1120.[49] However, the dating of the treatise is completely dependent on the priority of Hugh in coining the Trinitarian formula. Which arguments does Poirel give for this assumption?

His first point is the development in the use of *potentia, sapientia, benignitas* in Hugh's treatise: the triad is applied to the Trinity not from the very beginning of the work, but only towards the end.[50] Hugh's aim is to understand the Creator by attributes which can be deduced from creation, while a Trinitarian perspective is not the main goal of the *De tribus diebus.*[51] Abelard, on the other hand, starts with the three concepts as Trinitarian attributes.[52] According to Poirel, we can conclude from this that he knew the development of Hugh's thought within the *De tribus diebus.*[53] However, we have seen that Abelard probably knew the Trinitarian connotations of the three concepts already from William of Champeaux and, consequently, did not have to rely on Hugh for their invention.[54]

Furthermore, Poirel hints at the fact that the triad *potentia, sapientia, benignitas* is used also by Bernard of Clairvaux who is in this regard dependent on the *De tribus diebus.*[55] He concludes from this "on voit mal saint Bernard attaquer Abélard pour hérésie et lui emprunter dans le même temps un de ses thèmes les plus litigieux. Une telle attitude nuancée ne s'explique que si la triade avait aux yeux de l'abbé de Clairvaux une origine plus respectable et plus 'autorisée' qu'Abélard".[56] However, Poirel himself cites no passage of

47 We also know that Roscelin of Compiègne wrote a letter to bishop Gilbert of Paris against Abaelardus *Tsum*, to which an answer by Abelard still exists. Both letters have to be dated between the publication of Abaelardus *Tsum* and the Council of Soissons. Mews 1987, pp. 54f. An enlargement to Abaelardus *Tsum* by Abelard himself is witnessed by ms. B (Berlin, Staatsbibl. Preuß. Kulturbesitz, theol. lat. oct. 95). Cf. Mews 1987, pp. 67f.

48 Poirel 2002, p. 152, following Taylor 1957, p. 67.

49 Poirel 2002, pp. 150–152.

50 Hugo *trib. dieb.*, p. 64, 1131f.

51 Poirel 2002, pp. 249–258. 318–327.

52 Abaelardus *Tsum*, 1, 1–5, pp. 86, 4–88, 62.

53 Poirel 2002, pp. 376–378.

54 Cf. above p. 24–27.

55 Poirel 2002, pp. 177–181.

56 Poirel 2002, p. 373.

Bernard in which the three notions are used as Trinitarian attributes, which is the only novelty introduced around 1120. His argument, then, is not conclusive: on the one hand, there is no reason to suspect that Bernard refuted every teaching of Abelard only because it was the invention of the Parisian master; this holds especially true for Bernard's works which were written before the synod of Sens in 1141, as is Bernard's 6th sermon on the Canticum from 1135/36 where he uses the triad for the first time.[57] Secondly, the triad *potentia, sapientia, benignitas* itself was not controversial between Abelard and his adversaries. Crucial is the role of these notions as divine attributes and especially the relationship between the omnipotence of the Father and the lesser omnipotence Abelard seems to ascribe to the Son. So, there was nothing that should have prevented Bernard from using this triad without touching the Trinitarian question at all. Furthermore, we cannot be sure that Bernard should have known that Abelard's use of the triad was borrowed from the *De tribus diebus.* There is no reason to assume that he was specially informed or peculiarly interested in the origin of this formula.

The last argument proposed by Poirel draws on the content of Abelard's work: "On comprend mal pourquoi le maître breton aurait, de son propre chef, inventé la triade *potentia, sapientia, benignitas* ainsi que son emploi trinitaire."[58] Abelard would be concerned with the texts of the theological tradition and would not intend to present innovations. This argument is crucial, for two reasons: on the one hand, Abelard is quite able and eager to invent and develop new arguments if they suit his purposes; his use of sources is heavily determined by his own preoccupations.[59] On the other hand, as I have shown,[60] the triad *potentia, sapientia, benignitas* fits very well into Abelard's way of doing theology. It allows him to explain the Trinity as *summum bonum* with the help of certain words as they are commonly understood, and it gives an ideal basis for a theology, which has close links to ethical questions. Though Abelard develops his ethical ideas for the most part after the *Theologia 'Summi Boni'*, it is quite probable that he was interested in these questions already before 1120.[61] So, he had good reasons and was able to coin the triadic formula, if he had its single elements at his disposal, as has been shown above.

57 BERNARDUS *Sermones in Cant.*, 6, 3, in *Opera*, I, p. 27. For the date cf. KÖPF 1994, p. 32. For the date of the synod of Sens which until recently has been situated in 1140, cf. now MEWS 2002.

58 POIREL 2002, p. 379.

59 I studied this point regarding Abelard's use of Cicero in PERKAMS 2001b.

60 Cf. above p. 27–29.

61 A large portion of it is already present in Abelard's *Theologia christiana*, composed not long after 1121; PERKAMS 2001a, 31–54. In this article, I cite only ABAELARDUS *Tsum*, while paying no attention to the development of Abelard's thought in the later versions of his *Theologia.*

4. Conclusion

In sum, it is still plausible to ascribe to Abelard the introduction of *potentia, sapientia, benignitas* into Trinitarian theology. What we know about the chronology of the respective works speaks more in favour of this hypothesis: there is no proof that the *De tribus diebus* is earlier than the *Theologia 'Summi Boni'*. The *terminus ante quem* of Hugh's treatise remains 1125/26. Perhaps he wrote it as to give a really theological treatment of the rational comprehensibility of God's nature, a popular theme in those days the treatment of which through Abelard, however, could have seemed to Hugh too dialectical.[62]

A second point is more important: a composition of the triad by Abelard is quite possible. Firstly, it can easily be understood as a resolution of problems which emerged in the schools where he learned. This way of looking for new solutions to old problems by his own experience as a logician fits very well with Abelard's overall way of thinking, while it is hard to conceive that he borrowed his ideas from Hugh's treatise which was so alien to his own interests. A second point is that the triad *potentia, sapientia, benignitas* suits Abelard's theological project especially well, because he relies heavily on the ambivalence of *potentia* and by *benignitas* he can clarify his own theory of God's Charity.

In spite of these reasons one should reflect, given the difficulty of the question, on another idea on the development of the origin of this triad, namely that it was produced in oral discussions, based on Patristic teaching at the school of William of Champeaux in Paris.[63] This idea seems to be attractive because it can help to explain the surprising fact that Abelard and Hugh begin to use *potentia, sapientia, benignitas* as key concepts in their theological works at nearly exactly the same time. But even this assumption is not without problems: it is hard to see how the triad could have been already the subject of discussions which started much earlier than around 1117/18, the year in which Abelard probably began to work on the *Theologia 'Summi Boni'*, because there is no evidence for this in the many sentences which we still have from these discussions. The testimonies of the *Sententiae* of William of Champeaux and of the *SDP* show that the triad reflects earlier theological discussions, but they show also that these discussions did not yet use this formula as attributes of the Trinitarian persons. Therefore, if one accepts the thesis that the triad is a product of oral discussions, those discussions must have been nearly contemporary with our first written records of the triad, and very probably the two first important users of this formula, Abelard and Hugh, were themselves involved in them. Given this fact and the arguments adduced above, I do not see how we could ascribe the Trinitarian formula to anyone else than Peter Abelard, and I think that it is, also after Poirel, still correct to call it the "Abelardian triad".

62 Cf. Hugh's reserve against the *dialectica* Hugo *sap. an.*, 845f., a passage which could according to Stammberger 2002, p. 78, concern Abelard.

63 This is the position of Ralf Stammberger and Constant Mews; cf. Stammberger 2002, p. 72 with n. 40.

Appendix: The triad and the interpretation of the *Timaeus*

There is one loose end in the picture which I have presented. John Whittaker has pointed out, that the triad is used in 12th century-commentaries on Plato's *Timaeus* to explain Tim. 30A 2–6, a passage, in which already Proclus found the potency, wisdom, and goodness of the creator. One might conclude from this that the 12th-century theologians knew the triad from some interpretation of the *Timaeus*. As far as Abelard is concerned, it is not very probable that he took the triad from an ancient interpretation of this dialogue: he quotes the relevant passage of Plato's work for the first time in the *Theologia christiana*, which has been written some years after the *Theologia 'Summi boni'*. Even then, he is not convinced that Plato's text can be reconciled with Christian doctrine; he is irritated by the phrase that God created everything as good "as the nature of the things, which come into existence, permits" (*prout eorum quae nascuntur natura fert*), because this seems to impose a limit on God's omnipotence.[64] These words, however, are not in Plato, but they are Calcidius' rendering of the Greek κατὰ δύναμιν.[65] This is important for our question, because it was just this expression, which allowed Proclus, with "a little force",[66] to find the potency of the creator in that passage.[67] Abelard, then, did not have at his disposal a text by Plato, in which the complete triad could be found. This problem must have concerned all 12th century-readers of the *Timaeus*. It is not surprising, that William of Conches in his *Glosae in Platonem*, which has been written probably after 1140,[68] does not find the triad in *Timaeus* 30a, but mentions only *essentia, sapientia, bonitas* to explain Aristotle's efficient, formal and final causes;[69] in fact, he knows also the term *potentia*, but he connects it only with *sapientia*, not with *bonitas*.[70] As far as Abelard is concerned, the fact that he links the triad *potentia, sapientia, bonitas* with Plato's text in his *Commentary on the Letter to the Romans*,[71] seems to be a secondary connection of his Trinitarian theology and his teaching on God's omnipotence. It seems, then, that the emergence of our triad in 12th-century-Platonism does not depend on a direct transmission of ancient sources; at least, I am not able to clarify at the moment, "by what route this interpretation of Timaeus 30 A-B … found its way to the Platonists of the twelfth century",[72] though further research on the history of Platonism might change this picture.

64 Abaelardus *Theologia christiana*, 5, 34–36, pp. 361,488–363,511.

65 Plato *Timaeus*, 30A 3; Plato *Timaeus latinus*, 22, 23.

66 Whittaker 1987, p. 283.

67 Proclus *In Timaeum*, 1, pp. 374,30–375,5; 381, 1–5; Whittaker 1987, 282f.

68 Jeauneau 1965, 14f

69 Guillelmus de Conchis *Glosae*, 98; quoted by Whittaker 1987, p. 287.

70 Guillelmus de Conchis *Glosae*, 112. 118.

71 Abaelardus *Ad Romanos*, 1, p. 69, 767–776.

72 Whittaker 1987, p. 287.

Bibliography

Sources

ABAELARDUS *Historia calamitatum*
Abélard. Historia calamitatum. Texte critique, ed. JEAN MONFRIN, Paris ³1978.

ABAELARDUS *Ad Romanos*
Petri Abaelardi commentaria in epistolam Pauli ad Romanos, ed. ELIGIUS M. BUYTAERT (CChr.CM 11), Turnhout 1969, editio 41–340.

ABAELARDUS *Theologia christiana*
Petri Abaelardi Theologia christiana, ed. ELIGIUS M. BUYTAERT (CChr.CM 12), Turnhout 1969, editio 71–372.

ABAELARDUS *Tsum*
Petri Abaelardi Theologia 'Summi Boni', ed. ELIGIUS M. BUYTAERT/CONSTANT J. MEWS (CChr.CM 13), Turnhout 1987, editio 83–201.

ANSELMUS *Epistola* 136
ANSELMUS ARCHIEPISCOPUS CANTUARIENSIS: *Epistola* 136, in *Sancti Anselmi Opera*, ed. FRANCISCUS SALESIUS SCHMITT OSB, III, Stuttgart ²1986, 279–281.

BERNARDUS *Sermones in Cant.*
BERNARDUS CLARAVALLENSIS: *Sermones in Canticum Canticorum*, in *Sancti Bernardi Opera*, VI, Roma 1957.

BOETHIUS *Consolatio*
BOETHIUS: *Consolatio philosophiae*, ed. LUDWIG BIELER (CChr.SL 94), Turnhout 1957.

GUILLELMUS CAMPELLENSIS *Sententiae*
GUILLELMUS CAMPELLENSIS: *Sententiae*, ed. ODON LOTTIN: *Psychologie et morale aux* XIIe et XIIIe *siècles*, V, Gembloux 1959, 191 58–192 85.

GUILLELMUS DE CONCHIS *Glosae*
GUILLAUME DE CONCHES: *Glosae super Platonem.* Texte critique avec introduction, notes et tables par ÉDOUARD JEAUNEAU, Paris 1965.

HUGO *Sap. an.*
HUGO DE SANCTO VICTORE: *De sapientia animae Christi* (PL 176) 857–876.

HUGO *Trib. dieb.*
HUGO DE SANCTO VICTORE: *De tribus diebus*, ed. Dominique Poirel (CChr.CM 177), Turnhout 2002.

IRENAEUS *Adversus Haereses*
IRENÉE DE LYON: *Contre les hérésies*, édition critique sous la direction d'ADELIN ROUSSEAU, IV, 2, Paris 1965.

Liber de conditione
Liber de conditione angelica et humana, ed. LEFÈVRE 1959, cditio 256–275.

PLATO *Timaeus latinus*
Timaeus a Calcidio translatus commentarioque instructus (Plato Latinus 4), ed. J. H. WASZINK, London/Leiden 1962, 7–52.

PROCLUS *In Timaeum*
PROCLUS DIADOCHUS: *In Platonis Timaeum commentaria*, ed. ERNESTUS DIEHL, I, Leipzig 1903.

Sententiae Anselmi

Sententiae Anselmi, ed. FRANZ PAUL BLIEMETZRIEDER, *Anselms von Laon systematische Sentenzen* (BGPhMA 18, 2–3), Münster 1919, 47–106.

Sententiae Atrebatenses

Sententiae Atrebatenses, ed. ODON LOTTIN: "Les *Sententiae Atrebatenses*", in *RThAM 10* (1938) 205–224. 344–357.

Sententiae Berolinenses

Sententiae Berolinenses, ed. FRIEDRICH STEGMÜLLER, "*Sententiae Berolinenses.* Eine neugefundene Sentenzensammlung aus der Schule des Anselm von Laon", in *RThAM 11* (1939) 33–61.

SDP

Sententiae Divinae Paginae, ed. BLIEMETZRIEDER (s. *Sententiae Anselmi*), 3–46.

Literature

BLIEMETZRIEDER 1919

FRANZ PAUL BLIEMETZRIEDER: "Einleitung", *Sententiae Anselmi*, 1*–37*.

JEAUNEAU 1965

ÉDOUARD JEAUNEAU: "Introduction", in GUILLELMUS DE CONCHIS *Glosae*, 9–48.

KÖPF 1994

ULRICH KÖPF: "Einleitung", in BERNHARD VON CLAIRVAUX: *Sämtliche Werke*. Lateinisch-Deutsch, v, Innsbruck 1994, 27–50.

LEFÈVRE 1959

YVES LEFÈVRE: "Le *De conditione angelica et humana* et les *Sententiae Anselmi*", in *AHDL 34* (1959) 249–275.

MEWS 1987

CONSTANT J. MEWS: "Introduction", in ABAELARDUS *Tsum*, 39–81.

MEWS 2002

CONSTANT J. MEWS: "The Council of Sens (1141). Abelard, Bernard, and the Fear of social Upheaval", in *Speculum* 77 (2002) 342–382.

NIGGLI 1991

PETER ABAELARD: *Theologia Summi Boni*. Lateinisch-Deutsch, übersetzt von URSULA NIGGLI, Hamburg ²1991.

PERKAMS 2001a

MATTHIAS PERKAMS: *Liebe als Zentralbegriff der Ethik bei Peter Abaelard* (BGPhThMA. NF 58), Münster 2001.

PERKAMS 2001b

MATTHIAS PERKAMS: "Der Rhetor als Philosoph – Cicero als Zeuge philosophischen Gottesglaubens in den Schriften Peter Abaelards", in *Convenit Selecta 7* (2001) 3–14.

PERKAMS 2003

MATTHIAS PERKAMS: "Divine Omnipotence and Moral Theory in Abelard's Theology", in *Mediaeval Studies 65* (2003) 99–116.

POIREL 2002

DOMINIQUE POIREL: *Livre de la nature et débat trinitaire au* XIIe *siècle. Le* De tribus diebus *de Hugues de Saint Victor* (Bibliotheca Victorina 14), Turnhout 2002.

STAMMBERGER 2002
RALF M. W. STAMMBERGER: "*De longe veritas videtur diversa iudicia parit.* Hugh of Saint Victor and Peter Abelard", in *Revista Portuguesa de Filosofia 58* (2002) 65–92.

TAYLOR 1957
JEROME TAYLOR: *The Origin and Early Life of Hugh of Saint Victor.* An Evaluation of the Tradition (Texts and Studies in the History of Medieval Education 5), Notre Dame 1957.

VAN DEN EYNDE 1960
DAMIEN VAN DEN EYNDE: *Essai sur la succession et la datation des écrits de Hugues de Saint Victor* (SPAA 13), Roma 1960.

WHITTAKER 1987
JOHN WHITTAKER: "Proclus and the Middle Platonists", in *Proclus. Lécteur et interprète des anciens,* ed. by JEAN PÉPIN/HENRY DOMINIQUE SAFFREY, Paris 1987, 277–291.

Archa Verbi 1 (2004) 42–66

Die Bibel als Lehrbuch: Zum »Plan« der Theologie nach mittelalterlichen Kanon-Auslegungen

von Thomas Prügl

Das wichtigste Erbe der mittelalterlichen Scholastik für das moderne Verständnis von Theologie ist zweifelsohne die Herausarbeitung eines Statutes von Theologie als Wissenschaft in Anlehnung an das aristotelische Wissenschaftsmodell, das, vermittelt durch Boethius und die vermehrte Kenntnis aristotelischen Schrifttums im 13. Jahrhundert, zu der standardisierten Einleitungsfrage *Utrum theologia sit scientia?* führte. Diese wurde vorrangig in den Prologen und einleitenden Quästionen der Sentenzenkommentare, aber auch in eigenen *quaestiones disputatae*, und nicht zuletzt in den Kommentaren zu den Werken des Boethius scharfsinnig und äußerst fruchtvoll geführt.[1] Das Modell von Wissenschaft innerhalb dieser Epistemologie ist die axiomatische Prinzipienwissenschaft, die mit Hilfe logischer Denkwerkzeuge von ersten, sichersten Prinzipien Schlußfolgerungen zieht, um zu neuen Denkinhalten und weiteren Gewißheitszusammenhängen zu gelangen. Dabei spielte auch die Qualifizierung der Metaphysik bei Aristoteles als *philosophia prima* und als Weisheit, die sich den höchsten denkbaren Gegenständen zuwendet und dabei an die Grenzen der menschlichen Einsichtsfähigkeit gelangt, eine wichtige Rolle. Theologie ist gleichermaßen Wissenschaft und Weisheit. Der Weise, insofern er sich ganz der Betrachtung der höchsten Wissensbereiche hingibt, partizipiert am göttlichen Intellekt selbst und ordnet wie ein erfahrener Architekt das »niedrigere« Wissen auf die höheren Wahrheiten hin.[2]

In seiner Realisation wurde dieser Idealbegriff von *scientia* jedoch zu keinem Zeitpunkt dem tatsächlichen Aufgabengebiet von Theologie und ihrer faktischen Umsetzung im scholastischen Schulbetrieb gerecht. Sieht man auf die Praxis des theologischen Unterrichts im Mittelalter und sucht gleichsam nach einem Lehrplan, so stößt man als erste und wichtigste Aufgabe des *Magister divinitatis* auf die Schriftauslegung, anhand derer die Glaubenslehren in Übereinstimmung mit der patristischen Auslegungstradition aufgefunden und veranschaulicht wurden. Im Laufe des 12. Jahrhunderts trat zu diesem traditionellen Verständnis vermehrt das Bedürfnis hinzu, die theologischen Inhalte nach systematischen Kritierien zu ordnen, um die literarisch-historischen Erscheinungsformen von Theologie, wie sie in der Heiligen Schrift begegneten und in kirchlicher Lehre festgeschrieben wurden, durch eine einsichtigere Ordnung besser zu präsentieren und in ihrem Zusammenhang zu verstehen. Es braucht an dieser Stelle nicht näher auf die frühen Versuche theo-

1 Trottmann 1999; Köpf 1974; Chenu 1969.

2 Vgl. Thomas *Summa contra gentiles*, I, 1, vol. 2, 2f.

logischer Systematisierung eingegangen zu werden, die einen wirkungsgeschichtlichen Höhepunkt in den vier Sentenzenbüchern des Petrus Lombardus und in der theologischen Summe des Thomas von Aquin fanden.[3] Nach deren Einteilung befaßte sich Theologie grob gesprochen mit dem dreifaltigen Gott, dem Schöpfer und seiner Schöpfung, dem inkarnierten Logos, der sich den Glaubenden gnadenhaft mitteilt und ihr Leben geistlich durchwirkt, bis hin zu den Sakramenten und der Eschatologie. Die Distinktionen der Lombardischen Sentenzen legten die Inhalte fest, nach denen sich der theologische Stoff wie auch der theologische Unterricht zu richten hatten, und in aller Regel auch die weiterführende Begründung und die kritische Reflexion.

Da diese neuen Formen theologischer Reflexion sich offenkundig von der Heiligen Schrift selbst wie auch von der traditionellen Schriftexegese abhoben, setzte sich der Eindruck durch, daß im Mittelalter ›systematische‹ Theologie in der Sentenzenkommentierung und der damit zusammenhängenden Summenliteratur betrieben wurde, während die Bibelexegese sich weithin auf die geistliche Textauslegung im Stil der patristischen Tradition beschränkte. Dabei wird jedoch übersehen, daß als das eigentliche und erste Textbuch der Theologie im Mittelalter nicht die Sentenzen des Lombarden galten, sondern die Heilige Schrift, die es auszulegen galt, aus der die Glaubenswahrheiten aufzuspüren und zu bekräftigen waren.[4] Die Frage nach dem Wesen von Theologie und ihren verschiedenen Aufgaben wurde daher von vielen, ja den allermeisten mittelalterlichen Theologen mit Blick auf die primär zu kommentierenden Texte angegangen. Die Heilige Schrift war das Grunddokument der Theologie, die Sentenzen des Lombarden lediglich ein Lehrbuch, das im Stile wissenschaftlicher Argumentation (*modus argumentativus*) dem *intellectus fidei* nachspürte, der einerseits apologetischer Notwendigkeit entsprang, Kirche und Glauben gegen Irrtümer und Häresien zu schützen, andererseits einem natürlichen intellektuellen Verlangen entsprach, Gründe für das Geglaubte zu finden. Das primär auszulegende Textbuch jedoch war die Schrift. Als solches wurde sie aber auch gleichzeitig als die auslegende Wissenschaft verstanden. *Theologia id est sacra scriptura.* Lehrer und Schüler vollzogen die Wissenschaft durch aneignendes Lernen und vermittelndes Unterweisen mittels der gemeinsamen Anstrengung um das Verständnis des Textes. Der Text konstituierte das Wissen und die Wissenschaft. Daher nahm der mittelalterliche Theologe ganz selbstverständlich an, daß die Heilige Schrift trotz ihres scheinbar zufälligen, kompilatorischen Charakters auf einer inneren Ordnung und Systematik beruhte, die es ermöglichte, ihren Sinn und ihren Zusammenhang zu verstehen. Die Theologie schuf sich also ihre Systematik nicht erst innerhalb der Sentenzenwerke und Summen des 12. und frühen 13. Jahrhunderts, vielmehr wurde diese Systematik als der Heiligen Schrift inhärent zugrunde liegend, und damit dem Exegeten zur Auffindung aufgetragen vorausgesetzt.

3 Heinzmann 1995; Heinzmann 1974; Cloes 1958; vgl. zu dieser Frage auch die seit M.-D. Chenu intensiv geführte Diskussion über den »Plan der Summe« des hl. Thomas von Aquin; dazu zuletzt Johnstone 2002.

4 Hier gilt es, traditionellerweise auf die klassische Studie Denifle 1894 hinzuweisen.

Daher gab es in der mittelalterlichen Scholastik neben der wirkungsgeschichtlich so erfolgreichen und dominierenden Systematik der Sentenzen auch eine ganz anders geartete, nicht minder reiche Reflexion über die ›Ordnung‹ der Heiligen Schrift und damit der Theologie selbst. Solche Überlegungen wurden sogar im Zentrum der mittelalterlichen Selbstbesinnung auf das Wesen von Theologie geführt. Der Anlaß und die Form dafür waren die feierlichen Antrittsvorlesungen, die der angehende Theologieprofessor im Rahmen seiner Promotion bei zwei herausragenden Zeremonien vorzutragen hatte. Diese Vorträge, genannt *Principia*, waren ein fester Bestandteil im Promotionsverfahren der mittelalterlichen Universität. Man erwartete dabei von den angehenden Theologieprofessoren einen programmatischen Entwurf ihres Verständnisses von Schrift, Schriftauslegung und Theologie. Anläßlich der Überreichung der *licentia docendi* hatte der Kandidat eine *Recommendatio sacrae scripturae* zu halten, worin er, in der Tradition der *Accessus ad auctores*, verschiedene Merkmale der Heiligen Schrift herausstellte, etwa ihren Autor, ihre Methode oder ihren literarischen Stil.[5] Der zweite Vortrag, der tags darauf im Rahmen der sogenannten *Resumptio* stattfand, hatte sich dagegen der inhaltlichen Struktur des biblischen Kanons zu widmen und wurde in der Regel als *Divisio seu partitio canonis* bezeichnet. Auffälligstes Kennzeichen dieses zweiten Vortrages war, über die Struktur des Schriftkanons zu einer Einteilung von Theologie als solcher zu gelangen.[6] Ich will im folgenden einige solcher *divisiones canonis* näher untersuchen und die Kriterien beleuchten, anhand derer scholastische Theologen die Prinzipien der biblischen Offenbarung und die innere Bewegung der Heiligen Schrift einzufangen versuchten. Daß angesichts der zahlreichen Promotionen manche Einteilungen eher von dem Bestreben nach rhetorischen Effekten denn von einem ernsthaften Bemühen um Sinn und Struktur der Offenbarung zeugen, darf angesichts der topischen Situation des Redeanlasses nicht allzusehr verwundern. Gleichwohl eröffnet sich ein erstaunlicher Reichtum von originellen Annäherungen an den biblischen Kanon, dessen Sinnstruktur ja nicht kanonisch festgelegt war, sondern eben zu teils kühnen, teils scharfsinnigen Reflexionen herausforderte. Eine nähere Untersuchung der exegetischen Praxis der hier untersuchten Autoren (was zweifelsohne den Rahmen dieser Untersuchung sprengen würde) hätte zu verifizieren, inwieweit solche generellen Überlegungen zu Beginn eines theologischen Magisteriums auch die nachfolgende exegetische Praxis eines Theologen beeinflußten.

5 Über die Zeremonien der *Inceptio* (*Vesperies, Aulica, Resumptio, Principium* etc.) unterrichtet Weijers 1987, S. 407–424. Zu Einfluß und Praxis des *Accessus* in der hochscholastischen Theologie vgl. Minnis 1984; Kelly 1992.

6 Spatz 1992; Spatz 1994a; Spatz 1994; Sulavik 2004.

1. Peter Abaelards Prolog zum Römerbrief

Obgleich die *Principia* erst ab dem frühen 13. Jahrhundert an der Pariser Universität als etablierter Brauch faßbarer werden, gab es wichtige Vorläufer von Kanonerklärungen, die man durchaus als Vorbilder des späteren Genus ansehen darf. Mit zu den wichtigsten Quellen zählte die Vorrede des Hieronymus zum Buch der Könige, die der Kirchenvater selbst *Prologus galeatus* nannte und als Vorwort für seine gesammelten Übersetzungen der alttestamentlichen Bücher betrachtete. Hieronymus nahm darin eine prinzipielle Einteilung des Alten Testamentes vor, die sich am jüdischen Kanon orientierte. Er begnügte sich freilich nur mit einer groben Einteilung des AT in die fünf Bücher Mose, die Propheten (acht Bücher) und die Hagiographen (neun Bücher); eine theologische Deutung dieser Zusammenstellung unternahm er dabei nicht.[7]

Eine solche versuchte aber der Prolog des Römerbriefkommentars des Peter Abaelard (entstanden zwischen 1133 und 1137): Abaelard wählte für seine Einleitung vier Aspekte aus, die deutlich die Tradition der *Accessus ad auctores* widerspiegelten. Neben der Frage nach dem Autor und dem Hauptgegenstand des Buches (*materia*), erörterte er den Stil, oder besser gesagt die stilistische Argumentation des Römerbriefes (*modus tractandi*) sowie dessen Absicht (*intentio*).[8] Auffälligerweise nimmt die Frage nach der *intentio* den wichtigsten Platz innerhalb dieses Prologs ein. Abaelard war zunächst aber nicht an der ›Absicht‹ des unmittelbar zu kommentierenden Buches, des Römerbriefes, interessiert, sondern er fragte vorweg nach der *intentio* der Heiligen Schrift als ganzer. Erst wenn dieser größere Rahmen bekannt ist, gewinnt das einzelne Buch seinen besonderen Sinn und Stellenwert und kann innerhalb dieses Rahmens erklärt und eigentlich erst verstanden werden. Die Heilige Schrift verfolgt Abaelard zufolge eine doppelte Absicht: Sie will lehren und ermahnen (*docere et monere*). Diese zweifache Ausrichtung begegnet innerhalb des gesamten Schriftkanons, im Alten Testament gleichermaßen wie im Neuen. Während die ›Lehre‹ im alten Bund in den fünf Büchern des Mose festgelegt ist, obliegt den Propheten und historischen Bücher die komplementäre Aufgabe der Ermahnung, das Volk zur Treue gegenüber dem Gesetz anzuhalten.[9] Parallel dazu gelten die Evangelien als das ›Lehrbuch‹ des Neuen Testaments, während die übrige Briefliteratur keine im eigentlichen Sinne neuen Lehren enthält, sondern zur Einhaltung und Aneignung der Grundwahrheiten des Evangeliums, nämlich Glaube, Hoffnung und Liebe, anspornen soll.[10] Abaelard spielte damit nicht nur auf seine radikal auf der *caritas*

7 Hieronymus *Prologus Galeatus*.

8 Abaelardus *Ad Romanos*, S. 46. Wir benutzten den teils verbesserten Text in Abaelard *Römerbriefkommentar* I, S. 62–77.

9 Abaelard nennt darüber hinaus auch eine dritte Kategorie der *exempla*, denen jedoch im Grunde dieselbe exhortative Funktion zukommt: »Exempla quoque ex historiis necessarium erat adiungi, in quibus tam remuneratio oboedientium quam poena transgressorum ante oculos ponerentur.« Abaelardus *Ad Romanos*, S. 41; Abaelard *Römerbriefkommentar* I, S. 62.

10 »Similiter et Novi tripertita est disciplina Testamenti, ubi quidem Evangelium pro lege est, quod verae iustitiae ac perfectae formam docet, deinde epistolae cum Apocalypsi

basierende antinomistische Ethik an, die er im weiteren Verlauf des Kommentars näher ausführte,[11] sondern er schuf damit auch eine klare Hierarchie innerhalb des Kanons, dessen Mitte und Zielpunkt die Evangelien sind. Diese stellen die »perfecta forma verae iustitiae« dar, da in ihnen Glaube, Hoffnung, Liebe und die Sakramente grundgelegt sind. Während die Evangelien die für die Religion notwendigen Dokumente enthalten, gleichsam den unaufgebbaren Kernbestand darstellen, hat die neutestamentliche Briefliteratur dagegen – trotz einiger wichtiger doktrinärer Bestimmungen – nur eine komplementär-ornamentale Funktion. Sie steht im Dienst der Evangelien und begründet durch ihren Verpflichtungscharakter in gewisser Weise den rechtlichen Aspekt der Religion. Da sie die ›Kernoffenbarung‹ gleichsam ergänzend ausschmücken, dienen die Briefe der Zier und der Stärkung der Kirche und stehen daher näher bei den Kirchenvätern als bei den Evangelien.[12]

Nachdem Abaelard den großen Rahmen der Theologie, wie sie ihm in der Einteilung der Heiligen Schrift entgegentrat, abgesteckt hatte, wandte er sich der *intentio particularis* des Römerbriefes zu. Paulus wollte mit seinem Schreiben die Römer zu wahrer Demut führen, indem er sie an Gnade und Verdienst erinnerte. Entsprechend wurde die *materia* des Römerbriefes, sein Zentralthema, bestimmt als »göttliche Gnade und menschliches Werk«. Der *modus tractandi* schließlich bestand darin, die Wichtigkeit der Werke zu minimalisieren und gleichzeitig die Gnade Gottes zu »übertreiben«.[13] Dieser letzte Gedanke zeigt, daß Abaelard unter *modus tractandi* nicht die Methode oder den literarischen Stil im engeren Sinn verstand, sondern eher eine Spezifizierung der ihm so wichtigen *intentio*. Mit seinem Verständnis von *intentio* schuf er die Brücke zwischen dem biblischen Text und seiner theologischen Bedeutung. Das Aufspüren der Schriftintention ermöglichte dem Exegeten, seine eigene Theologie als ein Fortdenken und Auslegen des Offenbarungsinhaltes

loco prophetarum ponuntur, quae ad oboediendum Evangelio cohortantur. Actus vero apostolorum et pleraque narrationes evangelicae sacras historias continent.« Abaelardus *Ad Romanos*, S. 41; Abaelard *Römerbriefkommentar* I, S. 64. – »... evangeliorum intentio sit ea, quae sunt saluti necessaria, nos docere, hanc intentionem epistolae tenent, ut ad oboediendum evangelicae doctrinae nos moveant vel nonnulla etiam ad amplificandum vel tutius muniendam salutem tradant.« Abaelardus *Ad Romanos*, S. 43; Abaelard *Römerbriefkommentar* I, S. 68.

11 Vgl. dazu Perkams 2001, zum Römerbrief ebd. S. 99–137.

12 »Sufficere autem saluti fortasse poterant ea, quae Evangelium de fide et spe et caritate seu sacramentis tradiderat, etiam si apostolica non adderentur instituta neque aliquae sanctorum patrum disciplinae vel dispensationes, ut sunt canones vel decreta, regulae monachorum et plurima sanctorum scripta sacris admonitionibus plena. Neque enim aliqua his praetermissis imputanda esset transgressio, si nulla de eis fieret praeceptio. Voluit tamen Dominus et ab apostolis et sanctis patribus quaedam superaddi praecepta vel dispensationes, quibus adornetur vel amplificetur ecclesia ...« Abaelardus *Ad Romanos*, S. 42f; Abaelard *Römerbriefkommentar* I, S. 66–68.

13 »Modus vero tractandi in attenuatione est nostrorum operum, sicut dictum est, et exaggeratione gratiae, ut iam nemo de operibus gloriari praesumat.« Abaelardus *Ad Romanos*, S. 43; Abaelard *Römerbriefkommentar* I, S. 70.

auf der Grundlage der konkreten schriftlichen Offenbarungsgestalt zu entfalten. Man könnte sagen, daß Theologie gerade im Auffinden und Herausstellen der *intentio sacrae scripturae* bestand.[14]

Abaelards Entscheidung, nicht nur den Inhalt und Hauptgegenstand des einzelnen Buches zu bestimmen, sondern zunächst nach der Absicht der gesamten Schrift zu fragen, um durch die Vergewisserung über den Plan des Kanons das einzelne Buch als Teil eines größeren Lehr- und Offenbarungszusammenhanges zu verstehen, fand zahlreiche Nachahmer. Vorgebildet durch die in der *Accessus*-Tradition vorgesehene Frage nach dem Platz des zu kommentierenden Buches im größeren Gesamt der Philosophie,[15] wurde die Kanonerklärung eine obligatorische Fingerübung im Kontext der Feierlichkeiten der theologischen Magisterpromotion.

2. Johannes von Rupella (de La Rochelle) OFM

Ein frühes Beispiel eines theologischen *Principiums* ist uns von dem Franziskaner Johannes von Rupella, der 1236 zum Magister promoviert wurde, erhalten.[16] Im ersten Vortrag umriß Johannes, einem allgemeinen Brauch folgend, das Amt des Theologieprofessors, der nicht nur seine Wissenschaft – sie wird als *intellectus sacrae scripturae* beschrieben – beherrschen mußte, sondern auch einen dieser Wissenschaft entsprechenden Lebenswandel zu pflegen und schließlich die sowohl didaktisch als auch theologisch verstandene Lehre (*doctrina*) zu vermitteln hatte. Der erste Aspekt, *scientia*, zielte auf die Kenntnis der Heiligen Schrift, deren Einteilung später, im zweiten Teil dieses *generalis introitus*, erläutert wurde. Entsprechend der Tradition der frühen Franziskanerschule spezifizierte Johannes *sacra scriptura* als eine praktische, d.h. eine auf das Handeln hin ausgerichtete Wissenschaft. Der theologische Unterricht, die *doctrina*, wurde als Prophetie interpretiert, weil diese das Ziel des menschlichen Lebens unter dem eschatologischen Aspekt zukünftigen Heils oder Unheils verkündet. Beim Schriftkanon selbst ging Johannes von einer losen Gegenüberstellung der beiden Testamente aus. Das AT erfuhr dabei eine sich von Hieronymus dezidiert abhebende und im Mittelalter einzigartige Dreiteilung in Gesetz, Propheten und Psalmen.[17] Das Gesetz wird dabei nicht nur durch den Pentateuch repräsentiert, sondern auch die Geschichtsbücher und die Weisheitsliteratur wurden von Johannes dazu gerechnet. Johannes war sich der Problematik seines recht weit gefaßten Begriffes von Gesetz bewußt, weshalb er den Pentateuch als die *lex specialiter accepta* von den Geschichtsbüchern unterschied, die lediglich als Gesetz *communiter accepta* gelten. Sie wurden

14 Zur Bedeutung der *intentio* in Abaelards Exegese: Mews 2003, S. 51f.

15 Der letzte Punkt des klassischen Accessus innerhalb des von R.W. Hunt bestimmten »Type C« der frühmittelalterlichen *Accessus ad auctores* fragte nach der Teildisziplin des vorzustellenden Lehrbuches: *cui parti philosophiae supponitur.* Minnis 1984, S. 23–28; Hunt 1948, S. 94f.

16 Rupella *Introitus*; Spatz 1992, S. 97–101. Zur Person siehe Hödl 1991.

17 Allerdings kopierte einige Jahre später der Dominikaner Petrus de Scala dieselbe Einteilung. Sulavik, 2002, S. 115.

nochmals in eine *doctrina praeceptorum, exemplorum* und *admonitionum* unterteilt, um dem besonderen Charakter auch der Weisheitsliteratur Rechnung zu tragen.[18] Damit umfaßte die *lex* insgesamt 20 biblische Bücher, während den Psalmen als Einzelbuch eine singuläre Rolle zuerkannt wurde. Diese Dreiteilung verwies für Johannes auf die drei grundlegenden Akte des religiösen Lebens, die aus den drei Schriftgruppen ihre ideelle Grundlage beziehen: Das Gesetz als der *liber mandatorum* sporne zum Handeln an, die Propheten, die Johannes als *liber revelationum* bezeichnete, zielen auf den Glaubensakt, während die Psalmen, der *liber orationum*, zum erflehenden Beten einladen (*ad impetrandum*). Weshalb räumte Johannes dem Buch der Psalmen eine solch ungewöhnliche Auszeichnung ein, daß es als einzelnes Buch geradezu als ein Wesensbestandteil der Schrift herausragte? Die Antwort lag in der christologischen Interpretation des gesamten Kanons. Christus ist das innere Band der Schrift; er wird daher bereits im AT »eingeführt« (*introducitur*) und ist in allen drei Teilen präsent: im Gesetz als Macht (*potestas*), in den Propheten als Wahrheit (*veritas*) und in den Psalmen als Güte (*bonitas*). Die herausgehobene Stellung der Psalmen als *liber orationum* spiegelte ferner die Bedeutung der affektiven Seelenkräfte wider, denen gerade die franziskanische Theologie als das Zielobjekt allen theologischen Unterfangens große Aufmerksamkeit schenkte. Durch das Gebet sporne Christus den Affekt an, was dem Beter im Gegenzug die Gnade der Frömmigkeit erwirke. Theologie wurde in dieser Tradition als wesentlich affektiv, die Seele des Menschen zur Gottesliebe bewegend, verstanden. Daher kam den Psalmen eine solch zentrale Stellung zu innerhalb der *sacra scriptura* zu.[19]

Die Propheten nehmen als Offenbarungsliteratur (*liber revelationum*) das NT vorweg. Die vier großen Propheten finden ihre Entsprechung in den vier Evangelien, die über Christus als das Haupt des mystischen Leibes berichten, während die zwölf kleinen Propheten auf die zwölf Apostel und damit auf die »apostolische« Literatur, d.h. auf den Rest des NT, der von den Gliedern des mystischen Leibes handelt, verweisen. Johannes legte Wert darauf, daß die Propheten »intentional« mit den Evangelien übereinkommen: beiden gehe es um die Offenbarung des menschgewordenen Gottessohnes.[20] Johannes führte die Parallelen zwischen beiden soweit, daß jedem Evangelist ein bestimmter Prophet entsprach: Joh und Jes betonen das Geheimnis der Inkarnation, also die Gottheit Jesu; Mk und Jer stellen insbesondere die Lehre und Predigt Jesu heraus und damit dessen Weisheit; Lk kommt mit Ezechiel darin überein, das Priestertum Jesu und damit seine Güte und Heiligkeit kundzutun, während Mt und Dan auf die Königsherrschaft Jesu und seine Macht abzielen.

Christus ist die Mitte und das Band der gesamten Schrift, was insbesondere in den Evangelien zutage tritt. Der zweite Teil des NT, die *doctrina apostolica*, handelt dagegen vom Leib Christi, der Kirche: als *ecclesia nascens* in Apg, als

18 Rupella *Introitus*, S. 352–356.

19 Rupella *Introitus*, S. 350f.

20 »Unde eadem est intentio quatuor prophetarum et quatuor evangelistarum, et duodecim prophetarum in prophetis, apostolorum in epistolis. Intendunt ergo quatuor prophetae ostendere quoniam Deus et homo unus est Christus.« Rupella *Introitus*, S. 358.

ecclesia proficiens in den Briefen, als *ecclesia finalis* in Offb. Die Zweiteilung des NT verdankt sich also einer christologisch-ekklesiologischen Überlegung, die Johannes bereits in der Prophetenliteratur des AT vorgebildet sah. Diese Einteilung zeigte nur geringes Interesse an den speziellen Inhalten und Eigentümlichkeiten der einzelnen biblischen Bücher selbst, was aber auch nicht Sinn und Zweck der *Principia* war, die eben den größeren Zusammenhang unter den biblischen Büchern herauszustellen versuchten. Dabei favorisierte Johannes von Rupella eine Theologie, in der Christus das dominierende Thema bildete. Er ist nicht nur die Mitte der Schrift, sondern in gewisser Weise auch ihr gesamter Inhalt, wenn auch innerhalb der einzelnen Bücher in recht differenzierter Weise. Wie aber jede Wissenschaft und Lehre ihre Struktur braucht, so findet die Theologie diese im mystischen Leib Christi, den es vom Theologen gleichermaßen zu beschreiben und zu konstruieren gilt.[21]

3. Albert der Grosse OP

Albert der Große erhielt seinen Pariser Magistertitel 1245, im Todesjahr des Johannes von Rupella. Wir kennen von ihm nur ein *Principium*, das sich jedoch ausschließlich mit der Deutung des Kanons befaßt.[22] Der verbindende Gedanke innerhalb der Heiligen Schrift war für Albert nicht Christus, sondern das Gesetz (*lex*). Das Gesetz trug in dieser Konzeption nicht den negativen Aspekt des zu überwindenden Antipoden zur Gnade, sondern wurde in erster Linie als Offenbarungsgut verstanden, das ein bereits ergangenes Erbe sowie eine eschatologische Verheißung miteinschloß. Das Gesetz besteht demnach nicht nur aus Vorschriften, auch die Weise, wie man das Gesetz besitzt und die Haltung, wie man es sich zu eigen macht, gehören zum Gesetz. Wichtiger aber noch ist der Gedanke, daß das Gesetz eine Konsequenz für den, der es befolgt, bereithält und sich so als ein lebendiges Prinzip göttlicher Selbstmitteilung erweist. Aus dieser Zukunftsorientierung des Gesetzesbegriffs

21 Damit findet sich Rupella freilich in einer langen patristischen Tradition wieder, die für das Mittelalter Hugo von St. Viktor prägnant zusammenfaßte: »Materia divinae scripturae est Verbum incarnatum cum omnibus sacramentis suis.« Hugo *De scripturis*, 17, Sp. 24. Vgl. auch Hugo *Didascalicon*, V, 4, S. 324, worin Hugo die sieben Auslegungsregeln des Ticonius referiert, die Augustinus *De doctrina christiana*, III, 31, S. 104, und nach ihm Isidorus *Sententiae*, I, 19, S. 65f., dem Mittelalter überlieferten. Die erste Regel des Ticonius zementierte die Vorstellung von Christus als dem Inhalt und dem *corpus mysticum* als Auslegungsmaxime der gesamten Schrift.

22 Albert Fries legte die ›editio princeps‹ dieses Principiums bereits 1952 vor. Fries 1952. Seit einigen Jahren ist es nun auch in der Editio Coloniensis, der kritischen Gesamtausgabe der Werke Alberts zugänglich. Albertus Magnus *Principium*; vgl. auch die Prolegomena zu der Edition, ebd. p. xlii-xliii, sowie Fries 1951 und Fries 1950. Das *Principium* ist in zwei Handschriften bekannt: Vat. lat. 4245, f. 22va–24ra, und Troyes, Bm 1245, f. 220rb–222vb. Bei diesem Text handelt es sich jedoch lediglich um die *Partitio canonis*, also das zweite *Principium*. Der Frage, ob Albert daneben auch eine erste Rede für die *Aulica* vorgetragen hat, kann an dieser Stelle nicht nachgegangen werden. Vgl. Spatz 1992, S. 101–103.

bezieht Alberts Kanonauslegung ihren ganzen Reichtum.[23] Innerhalb dieser Zielrichtung öffnet sich das Gesetz nicht nur für die Geschicke des Volkes Israel, sondern auch für das Christusereignis, denn Christus gilt als Ziel und Erfüllung des Gesetzes.

Der theologisch reiche Begriff des Gesetzes erhielt somit eine Vielzahl von Aspekten, die durch die Vielfalt der biblischen Bücher eingefangen wurden. Als Bundesgabe an das Volk Gottes umfaßte es zunächst die Vorschriften (*praecepta*); darüber hinaus deutete es auch deren Zweck und unmittelbares Ziel an. Die Befolgung des Gesetzes wurde nämlich von Gott mit der Landgabe belohnt und zielte daher auf Erbe und auf Verheißung. Aus diesem teleologischen Gesetzesmodell gewann Albert eine Dreiteilung des Kanons in »Vorschriften«, »Erbe« und »Verheißungen«. Die *praecepta* fand Albert im Pentateuch, in der Weisheitsliteratur, in den Propheten und in den Psalmen festgelegt. Die *hereditas promissa* bezog sich auf die Landnahme Israels als Lohn für seine Gesetzestreue und ist in den historischen Büchern dokumentiert. Der dritte Teil, die im Gesetz enthaltenen Verheißungen, finden sich in den Büchern des NT, wo Christus als das Ziel und die Erfüllung des Gesetzes hervortritt. Alle drei Teile wurden von Albert nochmals untergliedert, um zu einer feineren inhaltlichen Unterscheidung der einzelnen biblischen Bücher zu kommen. Dabei zeigte sich neben einer großen Vertrautheit Alberts mit dem Schrifttext (was ja im Grunde auf jeden mittelalterlichen Theologen zutraf) ein waches Interesse für die biblische Geschichte und geschichtliche Details. Im Vergleich zur prominenten Stellung des Gesetzes verzichtete Albert allerdings auf eine stärkere theologische Akzentuierung der Propheten und Psalmen, die eher einfallslos unter das *opus praecepti*, also unter die Gesetzesvorschriften im eigentlichen Sinn gerechnet wurden. Während der Pentateuch als das *opus praecepti in actu* vorgestellt wurde, faßte Albert die Sapientialbücher und Propheten recht allgemein als *opus praecepti in comparatione ad virtutum determinationem*, bzw. *in comparatione ad praemia et poenas* zusammen.[24] Gleichwohl hob Albert die Zukunftsorientierung auch der Propheten und Psalmen hervor, weil durch das Gebet die Sehnsucht nach dem Künftigen entfacht und durch die Prophezeiungen die Wahrheit der Verheißungen kundgetan wird.[25] Interessanter dagegen liest sich die Einteilung des (zeitlichen) Erbes Israels, das in den Historialbüchern erzählt wird. Nach Ansicht

23 »Unde sicut praecepta sunt partes legis, ita modus possidendi hereditatem indicat statum legis in observantibus eam ... Est igitur status observationis legis cognitus in modo possidendi hereditatem, totam vel partem, cum molestia inimicorum vel sine molestia.« Albertus Magnus *Principium*, S. 242, lin. 12–25. – Fries beobachtete richtig, daß Albert in seinem *Principium* »das NT nicht so sehr als Gegenstück zum AT (sieht), sondern mehr als dessen Erfüllung und Vollendung und gliedert so das Schriftganze in drei Hauptgruppen: Gesetz als Gebot, Gesetz als Zustand, Gesetz als Erfüllung.« Fries 1951, S. 348.

24 Albertus Magnus *Principium*, S. 243, lin. 54–59.

25 »Ad futura vero ordinatur prophetia et praenuntians et desiderans, et ideo, ut exprimatur desiderium, oportet ut quaedam sint per modum orationis; et ut exprimatur veritas promissionis, oportet ut quaedam sint per modum praenuntiationis.« Albertus Magnus *Principium*, S. 246, lin. 14–18.

Alberts gibt die Geschichte des Volkes Israel Auskunft über Erfolg und Mißerfolg in dem umfassenden Bemühen, das Gesetz als Treue gegenüber Gott zu leben. Die Geschichte Israels läßt somit Rückschlüsse auf den »Status« zu, den das Volk oder Einzelne in ihrer gelebten Beziehung zum Gesetz erwerben. Diese Beziehung entwickelt sich entweder als vorbildhafte Befolgung (*firmiter in lege stando:* Jos; 1 Kön–3 Kön 10), als Mißachtung und Verfehlung des Gesetzes (*in lege claudicando:* 3 Kön 11–4 Kön), als erneute Hinwendung zum Gesetz nach abgeleisteter Reue (*ad legem resurgendo:* 1–2 Makk, Neh, Esra), und schließlich in unerschütterlicher Treue daran festhaltend (*status firmiter adhaerentium:* Tob, Jdt, Ijob, Est). An dieser Stelle gab Albert auch Rechenschaft darüber, warum er in seiner Einteilung des AT von der klassisch jüdischen, von Hieronymus überlieferten Dreiteilung des alttestamentlichen Kanons abwich: Die Juden folgten bei ihrer Einteilung des Kanons nicht der *materia*, sondern der Autorität des Buchautors. Daher würden Jos, Ri, Kön im jüdischen Kanon unter die Propheten gerechnet, weil diese Bücher von Propheten verfaßt worden seien.[26] Umgekehrt läßt sich daraus schließen, daß Albert nach einer sachlichen, dem Inhalt der Bücher gerecht werdenden Ordnung suchte und deshalb die formalen oder stilistischen Eigenarten der einzelnen Bücher außer acht ließ. »Libri idem habent pro materia, sed differunt in modis praedictis«, sagte er beispielsweise über die vier Evangelien.[27]

Die *promissiones*, die den dritten Aspekt des Gesetzes umfassen, seien in der Inkarnation des Gottessohnes, die die Erlösung des Menschengeschlecht herbeiführte, eingelöst worden. Folglich seien die *sacramenta*, die dem Menschengeschlecht mittels der Erlösung erwiesen wurden, die *materia* des NT. Mit den *sacramenta* meinte nun Albert zunächst die Hauptgeheimnisse der Heilsökonomie, allen voran die Inkarnation, in einem weiteren Schritt aber auch die liturgischen Heilsriten. Dabei griff er auf die Einteilung des mystischen Leibes und des dreifachen Status der Kirche von Johannes von Rupella zurück, denn diese *sacramenta* vollzögen sich entweder am Haupt des mystischen Leibes allein (Evangelien), oder an den mit ihm verbundenen Gliedern, nämlich der Kirche.[28] Die Evangelien berichteten demzufolge über ein und denselben

26 »Iudaei, quorum divisionem irritat Hieronymus, materiam in dividendo non sequuntur, sed potius auctoritatem, quam habet liber a scribente; et ideo Iosue, Iudicum, Regum et huiusmodi inter prophet ponunt, quia a prophetis historiae illae scriptae sunt.« Albertus Magnus *Principium*, S. 250, lin. 60–251, lin. 3. Die Vorworte des Hieronymus zur Vulgata wurden von Albert übrigens generell sorgfältig berücksichtigt und dienten ihm neben der *Glossa Ordinaria* als Hauptquelle seiner Kanoneinteilung. Die Quellen in Alberts *Principium* stellte zusammen Fries 1950, S. 202–204.

27 Albertus Magnus *Principium*, S. 251, lin. 57f.

28 »Sacramenta igitur exhibita in redemptione generis humani sunt materia novi testamenti; haec autem sunt aut in capite tantum, aut in membris per coniunctionem ad caput, quia membrum per se sumptum nec membrum est nec aliquod percipit sacramentum. Si in capite tantum tunc est doctrina quattuor evangeliorum. Si autem in membris, hoc tripliciter est secundum triplicem coniunctionem membrorum ad caput, scilicet nascentis, proficientis per augmentum, et consummati in transitu ad gloriam.« Albertus Magnus *Principium*, S. 251, lin. 8–18.

Gegenstand, nämlich Christus; sie seien daher identisch hinsichtlich der *materia* und differierten nur hinsichtlich des Modus. Bei der Einteilung der neutestamentlichen Briefliteratur skizzierte Albert eine breit angelegte Ekklesiologie, denn letztlich ginge es bei den apostolischen Briefen um nichts anders als um das *regimen ecclesiae* (Paulusbriefe) und um einen rechten Lebenswandel *in fide et moribus* (katholische Briefe).[29] Unter »Leitung« (*regimen*) verstand Albert allerdings nicht nur die äußere Verwaltung der Kirche durch Klerus und Hierarchie, sondern jegliche aktive Hinordnung des mystischen Leibes auf sein Haupt Christus. Dadurch kam dem Glauben, der insbesondere in Röm, Eph, Phil, Kol und 1–2 Thess erörtert werde, wenn auch jeweils unter verschiedener Hinsicht, eine wichtige ekklesiologische Dimension zu.[30] Zum zweiten brachte Albert aber neben dem Glauben als kirchenkonstituierendes Moment auch die Sakramente zur Sprache, die er, nach *ritus, minister* und *efficacia* unterschieden, vor allem in 1–2 Kor und Gal thematisiert sah. In den Pastoralbriefen schließlich werde das *regnum ecclesiae* unter dem Gesichtspunkt der Amtsträger beleuchtet. Bevor Albert sich abschließend den katholischen Briefen zuwandte, stellte er wiederum eine Diskrepanz zwischen seiner inhaltlichen Einteilung und der Anordnung der Briefe im Kanon fest.[31] Er vermeinte eine Lösung darin zu sehen, daß der Kanon die Briefe *secundum ordinem membrorum ad caput* aufliste, und daher Hebr den Schlußpunkt bildet, während er selbst die Einteilung des *regimen ecclesiae* nach Glaube, Sakramente und Stand der Gläubigen (Laien, Klerus) bevorzugte.

Dieser letzte Teil des *Principium* mit seiner interessanten ekklesiologischen Interpretation verliert allerdings den zuvor ausgefalteten Begriff des Gesetzes aus den Augen. Insbesondere der Begriff des Glaubens wird in keiner Weise mit dem Gesetz in Beziehung gesetzt, weder als bestimmende Haltung noch als konkurrierende Macht. Dadurch begab sich Albert in gewisser Hinsicht eines schlüssigen, zumindest aber eines symmetrischen Endes seines *Principium.* Obwohl er zuvor mit der *lex* einen umfassenden Gesichtspunkt gefunden hatte, unter dem jeder Teil der schriftlichen Offenbarung einen Platz erhielt und umgekehrt zum Verständnis der Offenbarung als Verdeutlichung

29 »Sacramenta vero, quae sunt ex parte membrorum capiti coniunctorum, secundum quod accipiuntur ut nascentia vel consummata, non subdividuntur, sed illa quae sumuntur penes incrementum, subdividi oportet. Penes illa enim accepta est doctrina universaliter omnium epistularum; haec autem instructio dupliciter consideratur, scilicet secundum regulas universalis regiminis ecclesiae aut secundum specialem modum conversandi in moribus et fide.« Albertus Magnus *Principium,* S. 252, lin. 17–25.

30 »Regimen ordinans ecclesiam ad caput in duobus est, scilicet in fide operante per dilectionem, et ritu sive efficacia sacramentorum. Si in fide operante per dilectionem, hoc contingit dupliciter, aut ex parte vocationis ad fidem aut ex parte status in fide percepta. Et primo quidem modo accipitur doctrina epistulae ad Romanos ...« Albertus Magnus *Principium,* S. 252, lin. 42–49.

31 »Sed secundum hanc divisionem dubium incidit de ordine, quia non eodem ordine ponuntur quo exeunt per divisionem. Ad quod dicendum, quod ordinantur epistulae secundum ordinem membrorum ad caput ...« Albertus Magnus *Principium,* S. 253, lin. 72–254, lin. 1.

und Kundgabe des Gesetzes beitrug, erfuhr dieses Leitmotiv nicht die Zuspitzung, die es über seine Bedeutung als lediglich formales Strukturmoment hinaus auch zur theologischen Leitidee erhoben hätte.[32]

4. Bonaventura da Bagnoregio OFM

Von Bonaventura ist bislang kein separates *Principium* bekannt, allerdings gibt es einen Text von ihm, der alle Fragen, die üblicherweise in den *Principia* angeschnitten wurden, enthält: das Vorwort zu Bonaventuras *Breviloquium*. Es ist dies einer der dichtesten bibelhermeneutischen Texte des gesamten Mittelalters. Bonaventura legte darin auch eine Einteilung des Kanons vor, aber seine Absicht im Prolog zum *Breviloquium* reichte sehr viel weiter.[33]

In sieben Kapiteln entwarf er eine theologische Hermeneutik unter dem Aspekt der Bibelauslegung. Theologie als Weisheit und als Weg zu Gott beginnt beim Glauben, denn die Heilige Schrift ist nicht das Ergebnis menschlichen Forschens, sondern göttlicher Offenbarung. Die Wissensform ist daher nicht der schlußfolgernde Beweis, sondern das gläubige Entgegennehmen. Alles Schriftverständnis »fließt« (*fluit*) aus dem Glauben, der selbst durch den »Ein-fluß« (*influxus*) Gottes hervorgebracht wird. Der Glaube verleiht eine anfanghafte Vertrautheit (*notitia*) mit der Heiligen Schrift, was als Voraussetzung, gleichsam als theologisches Grundwissen, das Schriftstudium erst ermöglicht. Im Glauben erschließt sich der Reichtum der Schrift, in ihr wird – »quasi in quadam summa« – das gesamte Universum verständlich. Freilich ist diese »Summe« nicht als eine Universalenzyklopädie zu verstehen, ihr Universum ist nicht das Weltwissen, sondern das Heilswissen. Sie bringt all jene Kenntnis hervor, die den Menschen zum Heil, zum Ziel führt.[34] Der hermeneutische Rahmen der Exegese Bonaventuras erstreckt sich somit zwischen Glauben und der Fülle aller Erkenntnis und Liebe in der ewigen Glückseligkeit. Schriftauslegung ist der Weg zwischen diesen beiden Polen, wofür der Theologe eine Wegbeschreibung, ein *Itinerarium* bereitstellt.

32 Näheren Aufschluß über die Beziehung des Glaubens zum Gesetz könnte ein Kommentar Alberts zu den Paulusbriefen geben, den er aller Wahrscheinlichkeit jedoch niemals verfaßt hat. Zwar versichern einige Chroniken, Albert habe »super totam bibliam per modum postillae« geschrieben, doch gibt es gerade für die Paulusbriefe keine Indizien dafür. Vosté 1932/1933, I, S. 4f. – Mit den hermeneutischen Fragen der Schriftauslegung Alberts, vor allem seiner Theorie des mehrfachen Schriftsinnes befaßt sich Olszewski 2001.

33 Bonaventura *Breviloquium*, S. 201–208 (Prolog); vgl. auch Bonaventura *Breviloquium* (dt.). Zur Exegese Bonaventuras siehe Riedlinger 1984; Riedlinger 1987; Monti 1979; Falque 2000, S. 31–52; Klauck 1974; Mercker 1971.

34 »Mediante igitur hac fide, datur nobis notitia sacrae Scripturae, secundum influentiam Trinitatis beatae. ... Sed potius, cum secundum lumen supernaturale procedat ad dandam homini viatori notitiam rerum sufficientem, secundum quod expedit ad salutem, partim per plana verba, partim per mystica describit totius universi continentiam quasi in quadam summa ... Et sic describit totum universum, quantum expedit de ipso habere notitiam ad salutem.« Bonaventura *Breviloquium*, 201b–202a.

Auf dem Hintergrund dieser ›Weg-Hermeneutik‹ stellte die Betrachtung des Schriftkanons nur einen Aspekt des Schriftverständnisses dar. Bonaventura nannte ihn in Anspielung an Eph 3,18, das er als Thema seines Prologs (und vielleicht auch seines *Principiums*) gewählt hatte, die »Breite« (*latitudo*) der Heiligen Schrift, dem sich Betrachtungen über die »Länge«, die »Höhe« und die »Tiefe« der Schrift anschlossen, in denen die Heilige Schrift unter den Aspekten der Heilsgeschichte, der Hierarchienlehre und der geistlichen Schriftsinne nebst einigen weiteren Auslegungsmaximen betrachtet wurde. Entsprechend der Wegmetaphorik verglich Bonaventura die Entstehung der Heiligen Schrift und des Kanons mit einem Fluß, der in seinem Verlauf durch hinzustoßende Nebenflüsse anschwillt, bis er mit der Lehre der Apostel, also mit den letzten Büchern der Bibel, seinen Höchststand, seine Fülle erreicht.[35] Trotz dieses linearen Aufrisses, der einen Zuwachs an Erkenntnis innerhalb der Offenbarung ausdrückt, entsprechen sich AT und NT in den vier literarischen Hauptgruppen. Die Gesetzesbücher, historischen Bücher, Weisheitsbücher und Propheten des AT spiegeln sich im NT in den Evangelien, der Apostelgeschichte, der Briefliteratur und der Johannesoffenbarung. Jedes Buch, jeder Einzeltext steht im Dienst des Weg-Prozesses, indem es den Glaubenden »vom Bösen wegruft und zum Guten hinbewegt«.[36] Hauptziel der Schrift wie der Auslegung ist es, den Menschen zum Guten geneigt zu machen, damit er zum Heil gelange. Diesen Zweck unterstützen die Gesetzesbücher *per praecepta maiestatis*, die historischen Bücher *per exempla bonitatis*, die Weisheitsbücher *per documenta veritatis* und die Prophetenbücher auf alle diese drei Weisen zusammen.[37] Schließlich wies Bonaventura recht interessant auf die ekklesiale Verwurzelung der Heiligen Schrift hin, ein Zusammenhang, den andere Theologen im 13. Jahrhundert nur selten für erwähnenswert erachteten. Die Apostel haben, nachdem die Schrift materiell abgeschlossen und der Kanon komplett war, diese der Kirche übergeben, damit die *notitia Christi* auch nach deren Tod verbreitet würde. Damit ist Schrift gleichsam als apostolisches Erbe in die Hände der Kirche gelegt.[38]

35 »Est igitur Scriptura sacra similis latissimo fluvio, qui ex concursu multarum aquarum aggregatur magis ac magis, secundum quod longius decurrit.« Bonaventura *Breviloquium*, S. 203b.

36 »Quoniam igitur Scriptura sacra est notitia movens ad bonum et revocans a malo; et hoc est per timorem et amorem: ideo dividitur in duo testamenta, quorum brevis differentia est timor et amor.« Bonaventura *Breviloquium*, S. 203a. Die Unterscheidung der beiden Testamente als *timor et amor*, ein Allgemeinplatz im Mittelalter, stammt von Augustinus *Contra Adimantum*, 17 (S. 166f.): »Nam haec est brevissima et apertissima differentia duorum testamentorum, timor et amor: illud ad veterem, hoc ad novum pertinet, utrumque tamen unius Dei misericordissima dispensatione prolatum atque coniunctum.«

37 »Nam libri legales movent per praecepta maiestatis omnipotentissimae, historiales per exempla bonitatis innocentissimae, sapientiales per documenta veritatis providentissimae, prophetales movent ex omnium praedictorum aggregatione, sicut manifeste in eis apparet. Unde ipsi sunt quasi rememorativi totius legalis sapientiae et doctrinae.« Bonaventura *Breviloquium*, S. 203a-b.

38 »... et tandem doctrina evangelica revelata est, per os carnis Christi prolata, per Evangelistas conscripta, per sanctos Apostolos divulgata; additis etiam documentis, qua Spi-

Bonaventura hat sich, wie auch alle anderen hier untersuchten Theologen, ausführlich zur Systematik des Lombarden geäußert und wichtige Präzisionen im Wissenschaftsverständnis von Theologie beigetragen. Seine »Einführung in die Heilige Schrift« zeigt jedoch, wie er sich als Theologe und Kommentator treu geblieben ist. Auch die vier Bücher des Lombarden werden mit dem Bild der Paradiesflüsse als Veranschaulichung des göttlichen *influxus* gedeutet, der sich auf verschiedene Weise, heilsgeschichtlich, noetisch, geistlich, prophetisch und nicht zuletzt mittels der Heiligen Schrift den Menschen mitteilt.[39] Theologie bedeutete für ihn die Bewegung der göttlichen Selbstmitteilung zur Seele und den Aufstieg der Seele zu Gott verstehend nachzuvollziehen. Für diesen Prozeß liegt in der Heiligen Schrift ebenso wie in der gesamten geschaffenen Wirklichkeit ein unsichtbarer Plan zugrunde, der diese Bewegung transparent macht und nachschreitet. Von daher wollte Bonaventura den einzelnen Büchern auch keine eigene *materia*, d.h. keine spezifischen Inhalte zuschreiben, die das jeweilige Buch im Kanon unverwechselbar machen oder als Leitmotive der Auslegung dienen könnten, denn alle spiegeln sie dieselbe Grundwahrheit des Weges zu Gott wieder.

5. Matthäus von Acquasparta OFM

Der Aufriß von Theologie und Heiliger Schrift, der uns in der frühen Franziskanerschule, bei Alexander von Hales, Johannes von Rupella und Bonaventura entgegentrat, fand sich eine Generation später bei Matthäus von Acquasparta wieder, wenn auch nun in stark formalisierter und schematischer Gestalt.[40] Matthäus wählte für sein *Principium* eine Einteilung nach den vier aristotelischen *causae*, wobei die *causa efficiens* den Autor der Schrift, Gott, beleuchtet, die *causa finalis* das eschatologische Ziel der Theologie, die *causa materialis* die Gestalt von Theologie als »Weisheit« und die *causa formalis* den Inhalt und die Einteilung des theologischen Stoffes. Unter diesem letzten Aspekt legte Matthäus seine *divisio canonis* dar, in der viele Gedanken seiner Lehrer wieder begegnen. Der Kanon als ganzer zeichnet sich durch *brevitas, ordo* und *concordia* aus. AT und NT unterscheiden sich nach dem Gegensatzpaar von *timor* und *amor*, wobei das NT den Inhalt des AT mit *nova praecepta,*

ritus sanctus, super eos veniens docuit nos per eos: ut sic omnem veritatem, per Spiritum sanctum iuxta divinum promissum edocti, omnis veritatis salutaris doctrinam Ecclesiae Christi darent et sacram Scripturam consummando veritatis notitiam dilatarent.« Bonaventura *Breviloquium*, S. 203b.

39 Vgl. den umfangreichen Prolog samt Quästionen in Bonaventura *In I Sent.*, S. 1–25. Als Thema des Eröffnungssermo wählte Bonaventura Hiob 27,11 (»Profunda fluviorum scrutatus est, et abscondita produxit in lucem«). Der gesamte Prolog des Sentenzenkommentars kreist um die Fluß-Metapher: »Propter quod notandum, quod iuxta quadruplicem proprietatem fluvii materialis quadruplex est fluvius spiritualis, de quo secundum quadruplicem differentiam sunt quattuor libri Sententiarum.« Bonaventura *In I Sent.*, S. 1a.

40 Matthaeus ab Aquasparta *De excellentia sacrae Scripturae*. Vgl. Spatz 1992, S. 123–127. Zum Autor: Leppin 1997; Huning 1993.

nova sacramenta und *nova promissa* übertrifft. Auf sicherem Terrain bewegt sich Acquasparta auch bei der Einteilung des AT in die vier Gruppen Gesetz (*libri legales*), Geschichtsbücher, Weisheitsbücher und Propheten. Diesen entsprächen im NT die Evangelien (*praecepta Domini*), die Apostelgeschichte (*exempla apostolica*), die paulinischen und katholischen Briefe (*documenta canonica*) und die Johannesoffenbarung (*oracula prophetica*). Sowohl die Geschichtsbücher als auch der Pentateuch geben vor allem historische Auskunft über die Geschicke des Volkes Israel. Dem Aspekt der Prophetie kam besondere Bedeutung zu. Da Matthäus die Psalmen unter die prophetischen Bücher rechnete, schlug er eine dreifache Einteilung vor: *per medium orationis* (Pss), *per medium praedicationis* (Jes, Jer, Ez, Dan), *per medium testificationis* (Zwölfprophetenbuch). Matthäus wiederholte auch die Typologie, die die vier großen Propheten mit den vier Evangelien verbindet. Man urteilt wohl nicht zu hart, wenn man das *Principium* des Matthäus von Acquasparta nicht als originellen Gesamtentwurf einstuft. Seine Gedanken finden sich fast ausnahmslos bereits in früheren Einleitungen und Antrittsvorlesungen und wirken bisweilen als *en bloc* übernommen. Sein Vortrag mag deshalb als Beispiel dafür dienen, wie sich manche Theologen der Aufgabe der *recommendatio* und der *divisio sacrae Scripturae* vergleichsweise konventionell entledigten.

6. Thomas von Aquin OP

Während Bonaventura mit seiner Hermeneutik des Weges ein Aufstiegsmodell verfolgte, das den Theologen wie den Gläubigen vom Glauben zur mystischen Liebe führen will, könnte man die Hermeneutik des Thomas von Aquin als ein Abstiegsmodell umschreiben, in dem sich die göttliche Weisheit den Gläubigen intellektuell vermittelt. Das Medium dieser Mitteilung sah Thomas in der Theologie, verstanden als *sacra doctrina*. Die Heilige Schrift, *sacra scriptura*, teilt die Struktur von *sacra doctrina*, die im letzten eine aktive Teilnahme und gnadenhafte Teilhabe am göttlichen Verstand selbst ist. Theologie unterrichtet über Gott, indem sie Gottes Pläne einsehbar macht gemäß einem *ordo doctrinae*, der wie ein guter »Lehrplan« die Schüler zum Verstehen und zur Einsicht führt. *Doctrina* ist aber nun für Thomas kein starres System katechetisch abfragbaren Wissens, sondern über den Lehrinhalt hinaus ein Vermittlungs- und Verständnisprozeß, der sich in einem Kommunikationsgeschehen vollzieht.[41]

Der Aquinate legte dies umrißartig in seinem ersten *Principium* dar, worin er Theologie als Interaktion von Lehrinhalt, Lehrer, Hörer und Lehrvermittlung skizzierte. Mehr als die zuvor erwähnten Autoren insistierte Thomas auf dem Amt des Lehrers, obwohl die Frage nach dem *auctor* oder der *causa efficiens* der Heiligen Schrift durchaus eine geläufige innerhalb der *Principia*-Literatur war. Thomas jedoch gab hier, zu Beginn seiner Laufbahn als akademischer Lehrer,

41 Die Literatur zum Verständnis von *sacra doctrina* bei Thomas von Aquin ist Legion. Vgl. stellvertretend Torrell 1996; Johnson 1999; Shanley 1997; Donohoo 1999; Ofilada Mina 2000.

eine sehr selbstbewußte, optimistische Sicht seines Berufsstandes.[42] Die Lehrer wurden mit Bergen verglichen, über die es in Ps 104,13 heißt »Er tränkt die Berge aus seinen Kammern«, oder nach der Vulgata: »Er benetzt die Berge von oben her«. Dies Bild macht deutlich, daß die Lehrer die göttliche Weisheit als erste empfangen und diese an die Hörer weitervermitteln. Berge ragen heraus, sie stehen dem Himmel näher als der Erde, sie lassen das Tosen der Welt hinter sich und schöpfen aus der Stille der Höhe. Den Berg trifft das Licht der Sonne zuerst und macht ihn leuchtend.[43] Wen meinte Thomas? Er schien von den *sacri doctores*, von den Verfassern der Heiligen Schrift zu sprechen, die ihre Inspiration wie eine Erleuchtung von oben erhalten. Aber im weiteren Verlauf schwenkte er unmerklich zu den Lehrern in der Kirche (*doctores ecclesiae*) über, und spätestens als er auf die akademischen Pflichten – Predigt, Vorlesung und Disputation – zu sprechen kam, war klar, daß seiner Ansicht nach dem Amt des Theologieprofessors strukturell dieselbe Bedeutung und Würde zukomme wie den inspirierten biblischen Schriftstellern. Beide nehmen in der Vermittlung von *sacra doctrina* den Platz des Lehrers ein, der die göttliche Weisheit an die Hörer vermittelt. Thomas hatte aber auch klare Erwartungen an die Studenten. Sie sind die fruchtbare Erde, die von den Bergen das Wasser erhält. Daher haben sie demütig zu sein, aber auch einen Sinn für das Richtige zu entwickeln. Sie unterwerfen sich der Zucht des geduldigen Zuhörens. Ihren »rechten Sinn« (*rectitudo sensus*) sollen sie anwenden, um das Gehörte richtig einzuschätzen, damit sie einst selbst »Frucht bringen«, d.h. produktiv werden und sich zu Verkündigern entwickeln.

Vor diesem Hintergrund von *sacra doctrina* führte Thomas in seinem zweiten *Principium* eine Einteilung des Schriftkanons durch.[44] Die Anordnung der Bücher wurde dort vom Ziel und Zweck des Schriftstudiums her illustriert. Diesen Zweck (*utilitas*) erläuterte Thomas als »Leben«, zu dem die Heilige Schrift in dreifacher Hinsicht hinführt: zum Gnadenleben, zum gerechten Leben und zum Leben in der Herrlichkeit. In der Ausformung dieser drei Bereiche sah Thomas den Zweck von Theologie: Diese soll den Menschen sittlich bessern, aber mehr noch eine Lebensgemeinschaft mit Gott bewirken, hier auf Erden in der Dimension der Gnade, die bereits anfänglich eröffnet, was in der Ewigkeit der vollen Gemeinschaft mit Gott das Ziel und die Erfüllung jeglichen Lebens ist. Die Heilige Schrift steht ganz im Dienst dieser Fundamentalzwecke der Theologie und eröffnet dieses Leben unter doppelter Hinsicht: sowohl »vorschreibend« als auch »helfend«. Damit meinte Thomas zunächst die beiden Testamente, die jedoch als Teile der Schrift Sinnbild, als einzelne Bücher und Texte hingegen Konkretionen der beiden Gottesgaben von Gesetz und Gnade darstellen.

42 THOMAS *Rigans montes*; vgl. auch die englische Übersetzung dieses kürzeren Principiums des Aquinaten in *Albert & Thomas*, S. 355–360.

43 THOMAS *Rigans montes*, S. 442 (§§ 1212–1213).

44 THOMAS *Hic est liber*. Der Herausgeber, R. Verardo, stellte die historisch korrekte Reihenfolge der beiden *Principia* um. Die *Partitio canonis* war normalerweise Bestandteil des zweiten *Principiums*. Zur *Inceptio* des Aquinaten siehe TORRELL 1993, S. 73–78; SPATZ 1992, S. 108–111.

In bezug auf das AT favorisierte Thomas die Einteilung des Hieronymus in Gesetz, Propheten und Hagiographen. Thomas erwähnte auch die Apokryphen, die ihre Autorität nicht von ihren Autoren her bezögen, sondern *ex receptione Ecclesiae.* Da sie dem Stil nach (*modus loquendi*) die dritte Gruppe der alttestamentlichen Schriften, die *hagiographi,* imitieren, seien sie am besten diesen zuzuordnen.[45] Das Gesetz teilte Thomas in ein »öffentliches« und ein »privates« ein. Letzteres wähnte er besonders in der Genesis mit den dort offenbarten Individualvorschriften verkörpert, während die anderen Bücher Mose die *lex publica* enthielten, die dem gesamten Volk anheimgegeben wurde. Die Propheten wurden zunächst nach den *divina edicta,* die sie mitzuteilen haben, unterschieden, wobei sich die vier großen Propheten in grundsätzlicher Weise an das gesamte Volk wandten, wohingegen die kleinen Propheten zu speziellen Kommunitäten gesandt waren. Die Kanonerklärung des Thomas legte also zunächst die großen Hauptinhalte fest, gleichsam das Was, und wandte sich danach dem Wie zu, dem *modus loquendi* und der Feinunterscheidung. Jedes Buch der Bibel erhielt dabei eine besondere Charakterisierung und gleichzeitig eine unverwechselbare Rolle zugewiesen, die es im Kanon und seinem Gesamtzusammenhang zu spielen hat. Dabei versuchte Thomas eine möglichst textnahe, dem Literalsinn verpflichtete Charakterisierung der biblischen Bücher vorzutragen. Nur einmal bediente er sich einer typologischen Erklärung, nämlich bei der Charakterisierung der vier großen Propheten als Vorbilder für die vier Evangelien. Demzufolge spiegeln die Propheten auch die vier christologischen Hauptgeheimnisse wider: Jesaja, der im Advent gelesen wird, die Inkarnation, Jeremia, der in der Fastenzeit gelesen wird, die Passion, Ezechiel die Auferstehung, und Daniel die Gottheit Christi. In der dritten Gruppe des AT, den Hagiographen, entdeckte Thomas eine implizite Tugendethik eingewoben, namentlich die vier Kardinaltugenden, aber auch eine Einteilung der Tugenden nach Plotin. Die Gerechtigkeit komme demzufolge besonders im Buch der Sprichwörter zum Tragen, Jdt verkörpere ein Beispiel der *temperantia,* 1–2 Makk und Tob verträten die Tapferkeit, während Esra und Est die Klugheit repräsentieren. Die plotinischen Tugenden spezifizierte Thomas als *praecepta sapientiae* und wies sie den Sprüchen, Kohelet und dem Hohelied zu.[46] Oberflächlich betrachtet, mag man versucht sein, die Parallelisierungen von Teilen des Schriftkanons mit den

45 »Unde ex auctoritate auctorum robur non habent, sed magis ex Ecclesiae receptione. Quia tamen idem modus loquendi in eis et in agiographis observatur, ideo simul cum eis computentur.« THOMAS *Hic est liber,* S. 437 (§ 1204). Zuvor verwies Thomas auf HIERONYMUS *Prologus galeatus*; vgl. oben Anm. 7. – Auch Matthäus von Acquasparta erwähnte die Apokryphen und daß sie ihre Autorität der kirchlichen Rezeption verdankten. Er verriet auch seine Quelle: »ut dicit Augustinus«; MATTHAEUS AB AQUASPARTA *De excellentia sacrae Scripturae,* S. 21; vgl. AUGUSTINUS *De doctrina christiana,* II, 8 (12), S. 39.

46 »... et hoc in tribus libris Salomonis: qui quidem distinguuntur secundum tres gradus virtutum quos Plotinus distinguit; quia praecepta sapientiae non nisi de actibus virtutum esse debent. In primo gradu, secundum eum, sunt virtutes politicae ... (Prov). In secundo gradu sunt virtutes purgatoriae ... (Eccles). In tertio gradu sunt virtutes purgati animi ... (Cant).« THOMAS *Hic est liber,* S. 438 (§ 1207).

bekannten antiken Tugendkatalogen als gewagt, ja naiv abzutun. Man ginge jedoch fehl, in diesem Versuch nur eine exegetische Grobbestimmung der betreffenden Bücher zu erblicken. Viel wichtiger erscheint mir, daß Thomas damit schon zu Beginn seiner Laufbahn der Tugendethik, die er später in der *Secunda Secundae* so großartig entfaltete, einen wesentlichen Platz im Aufriß seiner Theologie eingeräumt hatte. Er sah diese Ethik nicht als ein heidnisches Erbe und als ein der Theologie wie der Heiligen Schrift fremdes Spezifikum rechten Lebens an, sondern wie Gesetz und Gnade auch als Hilfsmittel, die Gott dem Menschen zu dessen Vervollkommnung und Vollendung anvertraut. So gesehen wird die Tugendlehre als originärer Bestandteil des theologischen Wissenskanons akzentuiert.

Das NT, das ganz unter dem Aspekt der Gnade steht, imitiert die Einteilung des AT. Die Evangelien handeln demnach vom Ursprung der Gnade, die Briefe des Apostels Paulus von der Macht der Gnade, die übrigen Bücher des NT von der »Ausführung« (*executio*) der in Paulus dargelegten machtvollen Gnade. Der handschriftliche Text der *Principia* des Aquinaten weist nun eine eigenartige Lücke auf. Der »Ursprung der Gnade« in den Evangelien (*Origo autem gratiae Christus est.*) wird zwar – parallel zur allegorischen Auslegung der vier großen Propheten – hinreichend beschrieben, jedoch nicht der zweite Teil, die »Macht der Gnade«, die anhand des paulinischen Briefcorpus spezifiziert werden sollte. Stattdessen schloß Thomas (oder der Kopist) den Vortrag mit einem kurzen Absatz über die *executio gratiae* ab, worin die Apostelgeschichte, die katholischen Briefe und die Johannesoffenbarung als der Kirche Anfang, Fortschritt und Ende vorgestellt wurden. Wo blieb also die Einteilung der Paulusbriefe? Der Herausgeber der *Opuscula theologica* des Aquinaten, P. Verardo, neigte der Auffassung zu, es liege eine Auslassung in der Handschrift vor, die andernorts nachgeholt wurde. Thomas hat nämlich in der Tat eine Einteilung der Paulinen entworfen, die dem Schema seines *Principium* voll entspricht. Diese ist aber nicht im Rahmen der *Principia* überliefert, sondern findet sich im Prolog zum Römerbriefkommentar, wo Thomas, wie im *Principium* angekündigt, das gesamte paulinische Schrifttum als eine geschlossene, großartige Abhandlung über die Gnade interpretierte. Jeder Brief im *Corpus Paulinum* hebt demzufolge einen besonderen Aspekt von Gnade hervor.[47] Die Konsequenz dieser Einteilung sowie die offenkundige Lücke in dem zweiten *Principium* scheint mir ein Hinweis darauf zu sein, daß Thomas die Paulinen zeitlich sehr nahe am *Principium* zu kommentieren

47 Die Einteilung der einzelnen Briefe findet sich im Prolog zum Römerbriefkommentar: »Scripsit enim quatuordecim epistulas quarum novem instruunt Ecclesiam Gentium; quatuor praelatos et principes Ecclesiae, id est reges; una populum Israel, scilicet quae est ad Hebraeos. Est enim haec doctrina tota de gratia Christi, quae quidem potest tripliciter considerari. Uno modo secundum quod est in ipso capite, scilicet Christo, et sic commendatur in epistula ad Hebraeos. Alio modo secundum quod est in membris principalibus corporis mystici, et sic commendatur in epistulis quae sunt ad praelatos. Tertio modo secundum quod est in ipso corpore mystico, quod est Ecclesia, et sic commendatur in epistulis quae mittuntur ad Gentiles.« THOMAS *Super epistulas Pauli,* I, S. 3 (§ 11).

begann. Zumindest hatte er bereits im Frühjahr 1256, zum Zeitpunkt seiner *Inceptio*, eine sehr konkrete Vorstellung für diesen Kommentar. Wenn Thomas womöglich seine Lehrtätigkeit als ordentlicher Professor mit einer Paulusvorlesung begann, so würde die Auslassung im *Principium* sogar Sinn machen, da er diesen Teil bei dem Vortrag anläßlich der *Resumptio* (vielleicht aus Zeitgründen) nicht auszuführen, sondern nur auf die nächste, d.h. seine erste reguläre, Vorlesung zu verweisen brauchte, wo er den Auslegungsrahmen der Paulusbriefe im größeren Zusammenhang darlegte.[48]

Mit seiner Einteilung des Kanons gab sich der Aquinate nicht nur ein verbindliches Schema der Heiligen Schrift, an das er sich im Großen und Ganzen auch in seinen Schriftkommentaren hielt, er fand darüber hinaus im Gedanken der Gnade einen Leitbegriff, der zu einem wichtigen, vielleicht sogar zu *dem* Leitbegriff seiner Theologie wurde. Im dritten Buch der *Summa contra Gentiles* legte er die heilsgeschichtliche und theologische Abfolge von Gesetz und Gnade als aufeinander aufbauende *adiutoria* für das Glaubensleben seinem Verständnis von göttlicher Vorhersehung zugrunde. Gesetz und Gnade als Aspekte des göttlichen Planes und seiner providenziellen Zuwendung zum Menschen wurden in der Tat zu bestimmenden Parametern der thomasischen Theologie.[49] Auf diesem Hintergrund gewinnt die Identifizierung von *theologia* und *sacra scriptura* bei Thomas eine neue, tiefere Qualität. Theologie muß die Bewegung der Heiligen Schrift nachvollziehen, muß den großen Bogen der Offenbarung einsichtig machen und ihn entsprechend nachzeichnen.

Zusammenfassung

Schriftauslegung und Theologie werden im Mittelalter nicht nur als komplementär, sondern geradezu als synonym verstanden, denn der dichte Begriff von *Sacra Scriptura* umfaßt einen weit größeren Bedeutungsinhalt als nur den philologisch-literarischen Aspekt von Exegese und einer Erhebung der ersten Textebene. *Sacra Scriptura* zielt nicht nur auf ein Wissen um den Text, sondern auch auf ein Verstehen seiner Intention, auf eine Einsicht in die tiefere Struktur, die mit der Struktur von Offenbarung übereinkommt. Dies mag vom heutigen Standpunkt eher als Eisegese denn als Exegese abgetan werden, für den mittelalterlichen Theologen bildete es den Kern der Theologie.

Die Kanonerklärungen der *Principia* mittelalterlicher Theologieprofessoren stellten eine Fingerübung dar, den konkreten Schrifttext, hier in der Gestalt des biblischen Kanons, in diese tiefere theologische Sinnstruktur einzupassen. Man könnte das Verfahren eine ›Kartierung‹ der Heiligen Schrift nennen, die dem Theologen die Chance bot, eine eigene Systematik vorzustellen, die sich nicht an den Sentenzen zu orientieren brauchte, sondern Alternativen anbot,

48 Die Gründe für diese Hypothese, daß Thomas das *Corpus Paulinum* während seines ersten Pariser Lehraufenthaltes kommentierte, habe ich breiter dargelegt in Prügl 2005. Zum Problem der Datierung des Paulinenkommentars des Aquinaten siehe Bataillon 1994, S. 586f.

49 Pesch 1988, v.a. S. 284–317 (= Kap. 12: »Gesetz und Gnade, oder Theologie der Geschichte«); Kühn 1965, v.a. S. 82–91; O'Meara 1988; kritisch dazu Cessario 1993.

den theologischen Stoff zu gruppieren. So konnten eigene Schwerpunkte gesetzt oder Zusammenhänge hergestellt werden, die in den ›traditionellen‹ Einteilungen der Theologie zu wenig oder gar nicht berücksichtigt wurden. Freilich wurde dabei das Rad nicht ständig neu erfunden, und dennoch nutzten nicht wenige Theologen die Gelegenheit, ein theologisches Programm zu skizzieren, dem sie sich in ihren weiteren exegetischen wie systematischen Schriften verpflichtet sahen.

Darin zeigt sich aber ein wichtiger Wesenszug mittelalterlicher Theologie: die Suche nach dem *ordo* der geschaffenen und offenbarten Realität. Wenn es stimmt, daß die Heilige Schrift die Summe der Offenbarung enthält, dann muß dieser Offenbarung auch eine innere Ordnung zugrunde liegen, die sich dem Glaubenden als einsichtig und nachvollziehbar erschließt. Der mittelalterliche Theologieprofessor sah in der Suche nach dieser Ordnung der Offenbarungsdaten das Zentrum seines Forschens und seiner Lehre. Die uns womöglich künstlich anmutenden Versuche mittelalterlicher Theologen, in jedem Buch, Kapitel und Vers, ja im einheitlich konzipierten Schriftkanon solche Ordnung aufzuspüren, sollten daher als Versuch verstanden werden, die Struktur von Theologie abzubilden und ihre innere Erkenntnisbewegung zu rekonstruieren.

Bibliographie

Quellen

Abaelardus *Ad Romanos*

Petrus Abaelardus: *Expositio in Epistolam ad Romanos*, ed. Eligius M. Buytaert (CChr.CM 11), Turnhout 1969.

Abaelard *Römerbriefkommentar*

Abaelard: *Römerbriefkommentar*, übers., eingel. von Rolf Peppermüller (FC 26), I-III, Freiburg u.a. 2000.

Albert & Thomas

Albert & Thomas. Selected Writings, transl., ed., introd. by Simon Tugwell (The Classics of Western Spirituality), New York/Mahwah 1988.

Albertus Magnus *Principium*

Albertus Magnus: *Principium super totam Bibliam*, in Albertus Magnus *Quaestiones*, ed. Albert Fries, Wilhelm Kübel, Henryk Anzulewicz (Sancti Doctoris Alberti Magni Opera Omnia, 25/2), Münster 1993, 242–254.

Matthaeus ab Aquasparta *De excellentia sacrae Scripturae*

Matthaeus ab Aquasparta: *Tractatus de excellentia sacrae Scripturae*, in Matthaeus ab Aquasparta *Quaestiones disputatae selectae*, I: *Quaestiones de fide et de cognitione* (BFSMA 1), Quaracchi 1903, 1–22.

Augustinus *Contra Adimantum*

Augustinus Hipponensis: *Contra Adimantum*, ed. Josephus Zycha (CSEL 25/1), Prag/Wien/Leipzig 1891.

AUGUSTINUS *De doctrina christiana*
AUGUSTINUS HIPPONENSIS: *De doctrina christiana*, edd. IOSEPHUS MARTIN, KLAUS-DIETER DAUR (CChr.SL 32), Turnhout 1962, 1–167.
Biblia Vulgata
Biblia Sacra iuxta Vulgatam Versionem, recensuit ROBERTUS WEBER, editionem quartam praeparavit ROGER GRYSON, Stuttgart 1969, [4]1994.
BONAVENTURA *In Sent. I*
BONAVENTURA: *In Primum Librum Sententiarum*, in *Opera Omnia*, ed. PP. Collegii a S. Bonaventura, I, Quaracchi 1882.
BONAVENTURA *Breviloquium*
BONAVENTURA: *Breviloquium*, in *Opera Omnia*, ed. PP. Collegii a S. Bonaventura, V, Quaracchi 1891, 201–291.
BONAVENTURA *Breviloquium* (dt.)
BONAVENTURA: *Breviloquium*, übertr., eingel. u. mit einem Glossar versehen von MARIANNE SCHLOSSER, Freiburg 2002.
HIERONYMUS *Prologus galeatus*
HIERONYMUS: *Prologus in Libro Regum*, in *Biblia Vulgata*, 364–366.
HUGO *De scripturis*
HUGO DE SANCTO VICTORE: *De scripturis et scriptoribus sacris* (PL 175) 9–29.
HUGO *Didascalicon*
HUGO VON SANKT VIKTOR: *Didascalicon. De studio legendi* [lat.-dt.] = *Studienbuch*, übers. u. eingel. von THILO OFFERGELD (FC 27), Freiburg u.a. 1997.
ISIDORUS *Sententiae*
ISIDORUS HISPALENSIS: *Sententiae*, ed. PIERRE CAZIER (CChr.SL 111), Turnhout 1998.
RUPELLA *Introitus*
JOHANNES DE RUPELLA: *Generalis introitus ad sacram doctrinam*, ed. F. M. DELORME: »Deux leçons d'ouverture de cours biblique données par Jean de La Rochelle«, in *La France Franciscaine 16* (1933) 345–360.
THOMAS *Hic est liber*
THOMAS DE AQUINO: *De commendatione et partitione sacrae scripturae. Principium 'Hic est liber mandatorum Dei'*, in *S. Thomae Aquinatis Opuscula Theologica*, I-II, ed. RAYMUNDI A. VERARDO, Torino/Roma 1954, I, 435–439.
THOMAS *Rigans montes*
THOMAS DE AQUINO: *Principium 'Rigans montes de superioribus suis'*, in S. THOMAE AQUINATIS *Opuscula Theologica*, I-II, ed. RAYMUNDI A. VERARDO, Torino/Roma 1954, I, 441–443.
THOMAS *Summa contra gentiles*
THOMAS DE AQUINO: *Summa contra gentiles*, I-III, ed. C. PERA, P. MARC, P. CARAMELLO, Torino/Roma 1961.
THOMAS *Super epistulas Pauli*
THOMAS DE AQUINO: *Expositio et Lectura super Epistulas Pauli Apostoli*, ed. RAPHAEL CAI, I-II, Torino/Roma [8]1953.

Abhandlungen

Bataillon 1994

Louis J. Bataillon: »La diffusione manoscritta dei commenti biblici di San Tommaso d'Aquino« in *Ang. 71* (1994) 579–590.

Cessario 1993

Romanus Cessario: »Is Aquinas's Summa only about Grace?«, in *Ordo Sapientiae et Amoris. Image et message de saint Thomas d'Aquin à travers les récentes études historiques, herméneutiques et doctrinales.* Hommage à J.-P. Torrell à l'occasion de son 65e anniversaire, éd. par Carlos-Josaphat Pinto de Oliveira (Studia Friburgensia, n.s. 78), Fribourg 1993, 197–209.

Chenu 1969

Marie-Dominique Chenu: *La théologie comme science au* xiiie *siècle* (BiblThom 33), Paris 31969.

Cloes 1958

Henri Cloes: »La systématisation théologique pendant la première moitié du xiie siècle«, in *EThL 34* (1958) 277–329.

Denifle 1894

Heinrich Denifle: »Quel livre servait de base à l'enseignement des maîtres en théologie dans l'université de Paris?«, in *RT 2* (1894) 149–161.

Donohoo 1999

Lawrence Donohoo: »The Nature and Grace of 'Sacra Doctrina' in St. Thomas's 'Super Boethium de Trinitate'« in *Thom. 63* (1999) 343–401.

Falque 2000

Emmanuel Falque: *Saint Bonaventure et l'entrée de Dieu en théologie. La Somme théologique du Breviloquium, prologue et première partie* (EPhM 81), Paris 2000.

Fries 1950

Albert Fries: »Eine Vorlesung Alberts des Großen über den biblischen Kanon«, in *DT 28* (1950) 195–213.

Fries 1951

Albert Fries: »Der Schriftkanon bei Albert dem Großen«, in *DT 29* (1951) 345–368, 402–428.

Fries 1952

Albert Fries: »Principium Biblicum Alberti Magni«, in *Studia Albertina.* Festschrift für Bernhard Geyer zum 70. Geburtstag, hg. von Heinrich Ostlender (BGPhMA Suppl. 4), Münster 1952, 128–147.

Heinzmann 1974

Richard Heinzmann: »Die Theologie auf dem Weg zur Wissenschaft. Zur Entwicklung der theologischen Systematik in der Scholastik«, in *MThZ 25* (1974) 1–17.

Heinzmann 1995

Richard Heinzmann: »Die Entwicklung der Theologie zur Wissenschaft«, in *Aufbruch, Wandel, Erneuerung. Beiträge zur ›Renaissance‹ des 12. Jahrhunderts,* hg. von Georg Wieland, Stuttgart/Bad Cannstatt 1995, 123–138.

Hödl 1991

Ludwig Hödl: »Johannes de Rupella«, in *LMA V* (1991) 598.

HUNING 1993
ALOIS HUNING: »Matthäus von Acquasparta«, in *LMA VI* (1993) 397f.
HUNT 1948
R. W. HUNT: »The Introductions to the 'artes' in the Twelfth Century«, in *Studia mediaevalia in honorem Raymundi Josephi Martin*, Brügge 1948, 85–112.
JOHNSON 1999
MARK F. JOHNSON: »God's Knowledge in Our Frail Mind. The Thomistic Model of Theology« in *Ang. 76* (1999) 25–45.
JOHNSTONE 2002
BRIAN JOHNSTONE: »The Debate on the Structure of the Summa Theologiae of St. Thomas Aquinas from Chenu (1939) to Metz (1998)«, in *Aquinas as Authority*. A collection of studies presented at the 2nd conference of the Thomas Instituut te Utrecht, December 14–16, 2000, ed. by PAUL J. J. VAN GEEST (Publications of the Thomas Instituut te Utrecht, n.s. 7), Leuven 2002, 187–200.
KELLY 1992
D. KELLY, L.G.: »Accessus ad Auctores«, in *Historisches Wörterbuch der Rhetorik I* (1992) 27–36.
KLAUCK 1974
HANS-JOSEF KLAUCK: »Theorie der Exegese bei Bonaventura«, in *S. Bonaventura 1274–1974*, Grottaferrata 1974, IV, 71–128.
KÖPF 1974
ULRICH KÖPF: *Die Anfänge der theologischen Wissenschaftstheorie im 13. Jahrhundert* (BHTh 49), Tübingen 1974.
KÜHN 1965
ULRICH KÜHN: *Via Caritatis. Theologie des Gesetzes bei Thomas von Aquin* (Kirche und Konfession 9), Göttingen 1965.
LEPPIN 1997
VOLKER LEPPIN: »Matthäus von Acquasparta«, in *LThK³ VI* (1997) 1482.
MERCKER 1971
HANS MERCKER *Schriftauslegung als Weltauslegung. Untersuchungen zur Stellung der Schrift in der Theologie Bonaventuras* (VGI 15), München/Paderborn/Wien 1971.
MEWS 2003
CONSTANT J. MEWS: »Peter Abelard on Dialectic, Rhetoric and the Principles of Argument«, in *Rhetoric and Renewal in the Latin West, 1110–1540.* Essays in Honour of John O. Ward, ed. by CONSTANT MEWS, CARY J. NEDERMAN, RODNEY M. THOMSON (Disputatio 2), Turnhout 2003, 37–53.
MINNIS 1984
ALASTAIR J. MINNIS: *Medieval Theory of Authorship. Scholastic literary attitudes in the later Middle Ages*, Aldershot 1984, ²1988.
MONTI 1979
DOMINIC MONTI: *Bonaventure's Interpretation of Scripture in his Exegetical Works*, Ph. Diss., University of Chicago 1979.

Ofilada Mina 2000
MACARIO OFILADA MINA: »The role of the teacher as a condescending mediator as viewed from Aquinas' notion of 'sacra doctrina' and its bearing on the nature of the theological enterprise«, in *Ang. 77* (2000) 373–396.

Olszewski 2001
MIKOLAJ OLSZEWSKI: »St. Albert the Great's Theory of Interpretation of the Bible«, in *Albertus Magnus. Zum Gedenken nach 800 Jahren: Neue Zugänge, Aspekte und Perspektiven,* hg. von WALTER SENNER (QFGDO. NF 10), Berlin 2001, 467–478.

O'Meara 1988
THOMAS F. O'MEARA: »Grace as a Theological Structure in the 'Summa theologiae' of Thomas Aquinas«, in *RThAM 55* (1988) 130–153.

Perkams 2001
MATTHIAS PERKAMS: *Liebe als Zentralbegriff der Ethik nach Petrus Abaelard* (BGPhThMA. NF 58), Münster 2001.

Pesch 1988
OTTO HERMANN PESCH: *Thomas von Aquin. Grenze und Größe mittelalterlicher Theologie. Eine Einführung,* Mainz 1988.

Prügl 2005
THOMAS PRÜGL: »Thomas Aquinas as a Scriptural Exegete«, in *The Theology of Thomas Aquinas,* ed. by RIK VAN NIEUWENHOVE, JOSEPH WAWRYKOW, Notre Dame 2005 (im Druck).

Riedlinger 1984
HELMUT RIEDLINGER: »Die geschichtlich-geistliche Auslegung der Heiligen Schrift nach dem Prolog zum Breviloquium Bonaventuras«, in *WiWei 47* (1984) 163–179.

Riedlinger 1987
HELMUT RIEDLINGER: »Zur buchstäblichen und mystischen Schriftauslegung Bonaventuras«, in *Grundfragen christlicher Mystik,* hg. von MARGOT SCHMIDT (MyGG I, 5), Stuttgart 1987, 139–156.

Shanley 1997
BRIAN J. SHANLEY: »'Sacra doctrina' and the Theology of Disclosure« in *Thom. 61* (1997) 163–187.

Spatz 1992
NANCY K. SPATZ: *Principia. A study and edition of inception speeches delivered before the faculty of theology at the University of Paris, ca. 1180–1286,* Ph. Diss., Cornell University 1992.

Spatz 1994a
NANCY K. SPATZ: »A newly identified text: The inception speech of Galdericus, first Cluniac Regent Master of Theology at the University of Paris«, in *AHDL 61* (1994) 133–147.

Spatz 1994b
NANCY K. SPATZ: »Inception Ceremonies in the Schools of Paris«, in *History of Universities 13* (1994) 3–19.

TORRELL 1993
JEAN-PIERRE TORRELL: *Initiation à saint Thomas d'Aquin: Sa personne et son œuvre* (Pensée antique et médiévale), Fribourg/Paris 1993.
TORRELL 1996
JEAN-PIERRE TORRELL: »Le savoir théologique chez saint Thomas« in *RT 96* (1996) 355–396 [Nachdruck in IDEM: *Recherches Thomasiennes. Études revues et augmentées* (BiblThom 52), Paris 2000, 121–157].
TROTTMANN 1999
CHRISTIAN TROTTMANN: *Théologie et noétique au XIIIe siècle. À la recherche d'un statut* (EPhM 78), Paris 1999.
VOSTÉ 1932/1933
JACQUES-M. VOSTÉ: *S. Albertus Magnus Sacrae Paginae Magister*, I-II, Roma 1932–1933.
WEIJERS 1987
OLGA WEIJERS: *Terminologie des universités au XIIIe siècle* (Lessico Intellettuale Europeo 39), Roma 1987.

Archa Verbi 1 (2004) 67–90

La questione *De raptu* nel ms. Assisi, Biblioteca Comunale, Fondo antico 186

a cura di Barbara Faes de Mottoni

Il ms. Assisi, Biblioteca Comunale, Fondo antico 186 è noto da anni.[1] Come è indicato nel verso del foglio di guardia anteriore, contiene *questiones multe*, tra cui quella *De raptu* al f. 14ra-vb della quale si dà la trascrizione. Henquinet, che per primo lo ha descritto,[2] osserva che è tutto di una stessa mano, tranne quella delle due ultime questioni (f. 128ra–129va) e delle due tavole (rispettivamente a f. 33va–34ra e f. 76v); sulla base degli autori citati lo data intorno al 1250 o forse anche prima;[3] lo ritiene inoltre un brogliaccio autografo di Bonaventura. Prove ne sarebbero: le numerose questioni e il prologo al libro IV delle Sentenze del Lombardo contenuti in questo ms., ripresi letteralmente da Bonaventura nel suo Commento alle Sentenze;[4] il fatto che la mano di 35

1 Tutta la mia gratitudine a Padre Torrell che generosamente ha accettato di leggere questo lavoro; un vivo ringraziamento al Sig. Stefano Cannelli della Biblioteca di Assisi per la sollecita cura nell'apprestare il materiale fotografico e bibliografico, e a Padre Victor Sánchez OFM che, con la consueta disponibilità e informalità, mi ha permesso di collazionare la trascrizione con quella di Henquinet depositata a Grottaferrata presso gli Editori di Quaracchi.

2 Henquinet 1932–1933. Lo studioso afferma (p. 636) che il ms. è costituito di 16 pecie o fascicoli di 8 fogli. In realtà i fascicoli sono 18 e non sempre di 8 fogli. Infatti la loro composizione e successione è attualmente la seguente: I^{8-3} (2–6); II^{8} (7–14); III^{12-2} (15–24); IV^{14-3} (25–35); V^{8} (36–43); VI^{6-1} (44–48); VII^{8-1} (49–55); VIII^{6-2} (56–59); IX^{12} (60–71); X^{10-2} (72–79); XI^{14-3} (80–90); XII^{8-3} (91–95); XIII^{8} (96–103); XIV^{10-3} (104–110); XV^{8-3} (111–115); XVI^{6-3+1} (116–119); XVII^{4} (120–123); XVIII^{8-1} (124–130). L'errore di Henquinet nasce dal basarsi sulle indicazioni della tabula dei f. 33va–34ra che segnala 16 pecie sotto ognuna delle quali raggruppa i titoli delle questioni del ms. (il termine 'pecia', che si legge anche nella seconda tavola incompleta, non ha il significato tecnico attribuito dagli stazionari, ma come giustamente ritiene Henquinet semplicemente quello di fascicolo sciolto). Ora esaminando la successione attuale dei fascicoli con quella delle questioni in ogni singola pecia, risulta che i fascicoli I-XIV corrispondono alle pecie I-XIV. Risulta inoltre che i fascicoli XV e XVI originariamente costituivano un fascicolo unico, più precisamente un settenione, che la tavola designa come '⟨petia⟩ XVI', la cui successione dei fogli è la seguente: 116–119, 111 (non 112 come indica Henquinet) – 115. Risulta infine che anche i fascicoli XVII e XVIII originariamente costituivano un fascicolo unico, più precisamente un senione, che la tavola designa come '⟨petia⟩ XV', la cui successione dei fogli è la seguente: 120–121, 124–129, 122–123.

3 Segnala che sono citati Alessandro di Hales, Guglielmo di Melitone, Giovanni della Rochelle, Guerrico di S. Quintino, Guiardo di Laon.

4 Più precisamente Henquinet 1932–1933, p. 77 distingue tra questioni letteralmente riprodotte nel Commento alle Sentenze di Bonaventura, in particolare nel suo libro IV; questioni appena delineate o lasciate incomplete; questioni finora sconosciute, origi-

marginalia, correzioni al testo e schemi di questioni di un altro ms. – ovvero di Assisi, Biblioteca Comunale, Fondo antico 138 – sia la medesima di Assisi 186, e che tale mano in Assisi 138 sigli una nota marginale con «fB», che Henquinet scioglie in «fr. Bonaventura».[5] Mentre Doucet e Lio concordano con Henquinet,[6] Brady sostiene che Assisi 186 non è autografo di Bonaventura.[7]

Di recente Padre Torrell, che ha edito la questione sulla profezia da questo ms.,[8] nella prima parte della sua accurata introduzione ha presentato gli argomenti di Henquinet[9] e la critica a essi di Brady, notando che le osservazioni critiche rivolte alla posizione di Henquinet (di cui riconosce la fragilità) circa il problema dell'autografo, «lasciano tuttavia intatta la questione dell'autenticità bonaventuriana del materiale riunito in questa raccolta». Essa è riconosciuta senza difficoltà per ciò che concerne il Commento alle Sentenze e la questione *De superfluo*[10] edita da Lio. Torrell però si chiede se ciò valga anche per la questione sulla profezia: in altre parole se anche quest'ultima possa essere attribuita a Bonaventura. Egli non avanza una conclusione definitiva circa questa paternità, ma offre un'ampia base documentaria, rintracciando e fornendo nell'apparato di note al testo dottrine similari e numerosi punti di contatto in nozioni e temi discussi precedentemente. Più precisamente egli adotta questo metodo: nell'introduzione presenta in dettaglio le due più significative questioni sulla profezia – ovvero quella che si interroga se la profezia sia un *habitus* e quella circa la visione *in speculo* – per delineare lo stile e il pensiero dell'autore; nell'apparato delle fonti, riporta i passi di Bonaventura che possono considerarsi paralleli a quelli del *De prophetia* e, sempre nell'in-

nariamente destinate a far parte, sembra, del Commento alle Sentenze, ma che per qualche motivo non hanno trovato posto in esso e tra queste ultime segnala la questione sulla profezia e quella sul rapimento.

5 Henquinet 1932, p. 553.

6 Doucet 1948, p. CXLVI n. 43; Lio 1966; Distelbrink 1975, p. 8 nota 1, indica tutti gli studiosi favorevoli e contrari alla tesi di Henquinet.

7 Brady 1973. Per Brady il fatto che in Assisi 138 vi siano anche questioni di Riccardo Rufo di Cornovaglia disputate quando era 'magister regens', ovvero a partire dal 1256 circa, significa «che tali questioni sono arrivate a Parigi solo nel 1259–60 circa, se non nel decennio 1260–1270» (Brady 1973, p. 73). Ciò indicherebbe che Bonaventura non ha utilizzato questo ms., contrariamente a quanto ritiene Henquinet, il quale – secondo Brady – daterebbe questo codice al 1250 circa (in realtà Henquinet afferma soltanto che è «un prezioso testimone dello stato delle dottrine teologiche tra il 1235–1250»). Pertanto la mano degli interventi di Assisi 138 non sarebbe quella di Bonaventura e di conseguenza neppure la mano di Assisi 186: dunque per Brady quest'ultimo ms. non è autografo di Bonaventura. Per questo studioso Assisi 186 rappresenta «il lavoro di uno studente universitario che raccoglie materiale per il suo commentario sul Lombardo, che cerca questioni da discutere, che fa abbozzi di molte questioni» è «il laboratorio di uno studente che copia molto da S. Bonaventura» (Brady 1973, p. 71).

8 Torrell 1992.

9 Henquinet ripete e amplia i suoi argomenti anche in un articolo successivo cf. Henquinet 1947.

10 Torrell 1992, p. 254.

troduzione, esamina tre punti supplementari di confronto fra la trattazione di Bonaventura e il *De prophetia*: da essi risulta che l'attribuzione della questione al Francescano ha basi esili.

Dalla sua indagine conclude inoltre che autore della questione e copista possano essere la stessa persona, tuttavia ancora senza nome.[11] Infatti alcune particolarità segnalate da Henquinet per Assisi 186 nella sua globalità per indicare che è un brogliaccio autografo,[12] Torrell le ritrova nella questione sulla profezia: per esempio spazi bianchi, frasi incomplete, schemi, e soprattutto una seconda redazione di un passo che egli ipotizza d'autore. Questi elementi sembrano indicare – a suo giudizio – che il testo più che una *reportatio* «è il lavoro di una persona che si documenta, uno studente oppure un maestro che sta preparando una disputa sulla profezia e che fa l'inventario delle posizioni in presenza».[13] Lo studioso propende per un maestro, dal momento che pochi studenti potevano disporre simultaneamente di tanti testi cui attingere. L'autore della questione infatti ne aveva davanti a sé almeno quattro: quello di Alessandro di Hales, di Filippo il Cancelliere, di Ugo di Saint-Cher, probabilmente di Alberto Magno e forse una fonte complementare.[14] Spirito vigoroso e chiaro, ma non originale – infatti non prende posizione nei confronti delle varie dottrine che presenta, ma spesso si limita ad adottare un differente ordine di esposizione di esse – l'autore, conclude Torrell, è verosimilmente un italiano, come denunciano alcune particolarità della sua scrittura, che lavora «senza dubbio» a Parigi intorno alla metà del secolo XIII, poiché «utilizza soltanto contemporanei che insegnano a Parigi e le questioni sulla profezia di alcuni di essi (Ugo e Alberto) non sembrano aver avuto una grande diffusione».[15]

Torrell ha notato che il *raptus* «è la questione obbligatoriamente complementare nei *De prophetia* del secolo XIII»[16] e ha addotto come esempio la trattazione di Tommaso sia nel *De veritate* (q. 13) che nella *Summa Theologiae* (*II II^{ae}*, q. 175). Ora una testimonianza ulteriore è fornita proprio da Assisi 186, poiché anche in questo ms. la questione sul *raptus* segue immediatamente quella sulla profezia.[17] Può sembrare allora un passaggio obbligato applicare

11 Dunque limitatamente al fatto che la questione possa essere autografa, concorda con Henquinet.

12 Per Henquinet 1932–1933, pp. 639–640 sono: spazi bianchi tra gruppi di questioni o all'interno di esse; incompletezza di molte questioni; profondi rimaneggiamenti nelle questioni sui sacramenti; segni di rinvii per raggruppare questioni sparse, schemi, 'vacat'; 'marginalia' con modificazoni dottrinali; variazioni nell'impiego di fogli per lo più a due colonne, ma anche in un caso a linee continue; correzioni di contenuto dottrinale di un passo cancellato e segnato da un 'vacat'.

13 Torrell 1992, p. 270.

14 Torrell non nomina Guglielmo di Auxerre, ma lo segnala più volte nell'apparato delle note dottrinali.

15 Torrell 1992, p. 271.

16 Torrell 1992, p. 238.

17 Il testo sulla profezia finisce a f. 13va a due terzi della colonna; il f. 13vb è bianco; la questione sul *raptus*, come detto, inizia a f. 14ra.

alla questione sul *raptus* le conclusioni di Torrell, considerato che anche la scrittura, il modo di abbreviare e certe particolarità linguistiche,[18] sono le medesime nelle due questioni. Tuttavia, anziché estendere indebitamente tali conclusioni, è sembrato più prudente seguire il suo metodo, ossia cercare di ricostruire la base documentaria della questione sul *raptus*; confrontare quest'ultima con i passi sul *raptus* del Commento alle Sentenze di Bonaventura per accertarne la presunta paternità; infine, vedere se le conclusioni che se ne traggono siano conciliabili con quelle di Torrell.

Gli argomenti affrontati in una serie di sottoquestioni sono i seguenti: 1 se il *raptus* comporti separazione dell'anima dal corpo; 2 quale sia la potenza conoscitiva coinvolta durante esso; 3 se dipenda dall'uomo provocarlo; 4 che cosa significhi terzo cielo; 5 in che cosa differisca la visione per rapimento da quella *in patria*; 6 in che cosa differisca da quella che ha luogo durante la profezia, durante la contemplazione e da quella di Mosè; 7 quale sia la differenza tra *raptus* e sopore. Il contenuto e l'articolazione di questi argomenti non sono originali, ma espressione del genere letterario delle questioni sul *raptus* che a partire già dalla seconda metà del secolo XII vengono costruite sul medesimo apparato di autorità – ovvero principalmente sulla Glossa del Lombardo a 2 Cor 12,2–4, Agostino, Dionigi e Gregorio Magno – e le cui soluzioni in linea di massima concordano, tranne nell'approfondimento di singoli dettagli.

Più in particolare, è risultato che l'autore ha dinnanzi a sè due modelli di riferimento cui attinge ampiamente: la *Summa aurea* di Guglielmo di Auxerre e la questione sul *raptus* delle *Quaestiones 'antequam esset frater'* di Alessandro di Hales. Non è da escludere inoltre che possa essersi avvalso anche di fonti complementari a me ignote. Diversamente che nella questione sulla profezia, invece, ho trovato riferimenti troppo generici e individuabili già prima di Ugo,[19] per poter ipotizzare una dipendenza da costui. Anzi su un punto ho riscontrato dissomiglianza non di soluzione ma di impostazione del medesimo tema. Per l'autore, infatti, l'anima è unita al corpo in tre modi: come perfezione a ciò che deve perfezionare, come motore al mobile, come conoscente

18 Ad esempio 'Agustinus' anziché 'Augustinus'.

19 Per esempio la dottrina secondo la quale lo *speculum aeternitatis* è volontario, ossia rivela ciò che vuole, diversamente da quello naturale (infra lin. 39–40). Per questa dottrina, presente anche nel *De prophetia* di Assisi 186 (Torrell 1992, p. 299, lin. 526–527), Torrell (p. 299) molto opportunamente rimanda ad un passo del *De prophetia* di Ugo e inoltre segnala la stretta parentela con Bonaventura. Prima di Ugo però – almeno per la questione sul *raptus* – mi sembra si possa segnalare Guglielmo di Auxerre, sebbene usi un linguaggio differente, come emerge da un confronto tra l'anonimo di Assisi e Guglielmo: «Item, quomodo potuit hoc ignorare, cum videret in speculo eternitatis aperte in quo omnia relucent? Ergo et hoc videbat, ut videtur» (lin. 18–19); «Quod obicitur de speculo, dicendum quod representat voluntarie que vult, et ideo non oportet quod omnia» (lin. 39–40); cf. «Non enim quicumque legit in speculo eternitatis, legit ibi omnis (*sic pro*: omnia), sed tantum illa quorum Deus se ostendit exemplar esse, sicut patet in prophetis, qui non videbant omnia in speculo eternitatis, sed tantum illa quae Deus illis revelabat» (GA, p. 702,42–46).

all'organo con il quale conosce, e l'anima di Paolo nel rapimento fu unita al corpo quanto ai primi due modi, astratta invece quanto al terzo.[20] Per Ugo invece l'anima è unita al corpo soltanto in due modi, come forma e come motore, e durante il rapimento fu unita a esso in quanto forma, non in quanto motore.[21]

La presenza dei due modelli è la seguente: nella questione 1 la base documentaria è costituita soprattutto da Alessandro di Hales, tranne in un caso; nella 2 esclusivamente da Alessandro; nella 3 esclusivamente da Guglielmo; ugualmente nella 4, tranne in un punto; nelle 5, 6 e 7 esclusivamente da Alessandro. L'autore attinge ora all'uno ora all'altro non perché operi delle scelte di campo, ma più semplicemente perché alcuni argomenti sono trattati esclusivamente da Guglielmo, per esempio se l'uomo possa indurre il rapimento,[22] altri da Alessandro, per esempio il diverso grado di chiarezza rispettivamente della visione paolina, della gloriosa e della angelica,[23] oppure la tipologia delle visioni intellettuali (visione per rapimento, mosaica, profetica e contemplativa).[24] Tuttavia in una stessa questione nella quale si richiama prevalentemente a un autore, non esita ad attingere anche all'altro, quando trova argomentazioni ritenute interessanti, come appare appunto nelle questioni 1 e 4. La questione 1 è infatti in massima parte una rielaborazione che sintetizza motivi già presenti in Alessandro e anche la soluzione che individua un triplice rapporto di unione dell'anima con il corpo, si muove nella stessa direzione di costui.[25] Presenta però anche il motivo dello *speculum aeternitatis*, assente nel contesto della discussione sul *raptus* di Alessandro e presente invece nella *Summa aurea*.[26]

Le questioni più significative sono la 4 e la 5: la 4, che è la più estesa, appunto perché permette di cogliere come l'autore usi le sue fonti, e più in generale il suo modo di lavorare; la 5, perché illustra le sue doti di chiarezza. E' opportuno pertanto soffermarsi su queste.

Nella questione 4 egli riporta le tre principali interpretazioni del terzo cielo tratte dalla *Glossa* del Lombardo, ossia quelle che lo identificano rispettivamente con l'empireo, con la visione intellettuale e con la terza gerarchia angelica. A ognuna di queste fa seguire una breve questione costituita di obiezioni che negano valore all'identificazione e la cui soluzione attinge nel primo caso ad Alessandro, nel secondo a Guglielmo, nel terzo parzialmente a quest'ultimo.

20 Infra lin. 20–24.

21 «Duobus enim modis est anima in corpore, ut forma et ut motor. Primo modo fuit anima Pauli in corpore suo, non secundo, unde corpus eius fuit quasi mortuum ullo sensus officio utens, non tamen mortuum» (Ms. Douai, Bibl. mun., 434, II, f. 130vb). La più recente e completa descrizione di questo ms. miscellaneo è in Quinto 1996, pp. 233–361.

22 Infra lin. 55–63 e 82–92.

23 Infra lin. 163–172.

24 Infra lin. 184–197.

25 Infra lin. 20–25.

26 Infra lin. 18–19 e 39–40.

La prima micro questione è così costruita: all'identificazione del terzo cielo con l'empireo si obietta che al momento del *raptus* l'anima di Paolo era unita al corpo, pertanto essa non mutò luogo, appunto dal corpo all'empireo; dunque il terzo cielo non può essere intenso in senso locale. Ancora, affermando che il *raptus* all'empireo fu mentale (*secundum cogitationem*), si dovrebbe affermare di essere rapiti a Roma, quando si vedono o pensano cose che avvengono in questa città, il che invece non si dice.[27] La soluzione propone in forma più sintetica, ma con linguaggio proprio, quella di Alessandro e come costui si appella alla medesima citazione scritturaria: il rapimento dell'anima dell'Apostolo all'empireo non va inteso in senso locale, ovvero non comporta da parte di essa l'abbandono di un luogo (= corpo) per ascendere a un altro (= empireo), ma riguarda la qualità della sua contemplazione: l'anima ha visto infatti con tale chiarezza le cose che erano lì, come se fosse stata presente localmente. Il rapimento all'empireo, dunque, non va inteso in senso proprio, ma traslato e iperbolico, come quando nelle Scritture si afferma: «Ubi est thesaurus tuus, ibi est cor tuum» (Mt 6,21).[28]

La seconda microquestione non contesta tanto l'identificazione del terzo cielo con la visione intellettuale, ma l'esplicitazione di Agostino secondo il quale questo genere di visione contiene «eas res que videntur per similitudines, que non sunt aliud quam ipse res»,[29] in altre parole che caratteristica di tale genere di visione è l'immediatezza dell'oggetto percepito, ossia il non vederlo attraverso un'immagine o similitudine quando queste sono altre dall'oggetto stesso. Su come intendere il passo di Agostino, che riferito a quella visione intellettuale che ha come oggetto Dio, introduceva al tema se la visione paolina di Dio durante il rapimento fu mediata o facciale, si era soffermato a lungo Guglielmo nella *Summa aurea*, al quale l'autore di Assisi attinge, riprendendo in forma più concisa alcune argomentazioni e soluzioni.

All'esplicitazione di Agostino, l'autore oppone tre obiezioni, che convergono nell'affermazione che la visione di Paolo rapito fu mediata da un'immagine. Esse sono le seguenti: come il sensibile sta al senso, così l'intelligibile all'intelletto; ma come il sensibile si vede sempre tramite un'altra immagine, così è dell'intelligibile; pertanto anche nella visione intellettuale l'oggetto è visto tramite un'immagine, che è altro dall'oggetto stesso. Ancora, Paolo durante il rapimento vedeva gli angeli; in questa visione però essi non erano

27 Infra lin. 100–102.

28 «Responsio. Dicendum quod non intelligitur raptus fuisse ad celum empyreum quod anima illuc localiter ascenderit, set quod contemplabatur. Clare videbat ea que ibi erant, sicut si localiter esset presens. Et per hoc quod non valet quod obicit; et est similis modus dicendi, sicut cum dicitur «Ubi est thesaurus tuus, ibi et cor tuum» (lin. 100–107); cf. «Dico ergo quod raptus est ad tertium caelum, id est ad empyreum caelum: non quod anima tunc localiter fuerit in caelo empyreo, immo adhuc corpori uniebatur; nihilominus tamen quantum ad modum actus sui fuit in caelo empyreo, id est comprehendit ut exsistens in caelo empyreo: non quod definitive esset ibi, sed secundum hunc modum loquendi, sicut ibi: Ubi thesaurus tuus, ibi cor tuum» (AH, p. 1351 n. 18, lin. 14–20).

29 Infra lin. 110–111 per Agostino cf. *De Gen. ad litt.* 12, 6, 15.

in lui secondo la loro essenza, dunque li vedeva attraverso qualche cosa d'altro da essa. Infine, se la sua visione non fu per immagine o similitudine, ritornato allo stato normale dopo il rapimento, nulla gli rimase della visione avuta.[30]

La risposta dell'autore è netta e inequivocabile. Mentre Guglielmo si limita ad allinearsi alla posizione di Agostino,[31] egli afferma chiaramente che l'anima di Paolo rapito ebbe visione di Dio facciale e non mediata da un'altra immagine o similitudine e che vide gli angeli attraverso se stessa.[32] Diversa però rispetto a Guglielmo è la soluzione della prima obiezione. Per l'autore è errato il parallelismo senso-intelletto rispetto ai loro rispettivi oggetti, perché il primo ha a che fare con il luogo e una certa distanza del suo oggetto e dunque può vedere il sensibile solo attraverso una specie (o immagine) e non in se stesso, poiché non può riflettere su di sè, dal momento che è materiale.[33] Per Guglielmo, che non parla genericamente di senso e intelletto, ma di forme visibili e di forme intelligibili rispetto ai loro rispettivi organi (vista e intelletto), si deve distinguere: intesa in senso generale la proposizione «come le forme visibili stanno alla vista, così le forme intelligibili stanno all'intelletto», è falsa. Le forme visibili infatti non sono presenti alla stessa vista, poiché non sono nell'occhio, pertanto è necessaria un'immagine, mentre alcune forme intelligibili sono presenti all'intelletto, quindi non la richiedono. Invece intesa in senso particolare, la proposizione è vera; ma poiché *ex particularibus* non si può costruire un sillogismo, la conclusione tratta dall'obiezione non ha valore.[34] Come si può notare, l'autore assume solo la prima alternativa indicata

30 «Obicitur contra hoc sic: sicut se ⟨habet⟩ sensibile ad sensum, ita intelligibile ad intellectum. Set sensibile semper videtur per speciem aliam; ergo etc. Item, apostolus videbat angelos et cognoscebat. Set constat quod angeli non erant essentialiter in ipso; ergo videbat per aliud quod non erat essentia angeli, cum videret per aliquid quod esset in ipso. Item, si non vidit per ymagines vel similitudines, ergo nichil remansit in cognitione post reversionem ad corpus; nulla ergo fuit visio talis» (lin. 112–118); cf. «Sicut forme visibiles se habent ad visum, ita forme intelligibiles ad intellectum; sed forme visibiles videntur per ymagines, que non sunt quod ipse; ergo forme intelligibiles intelliguntur per ymagines, que non sunt quod ipse. Item, intellectus humanus in futuro intelliget angelum et non per sui presenciam, quoniam angelus non erit essencialiter in humana anima; ergo intelliget ipsum per ymaginem, que non est quod ipse angelus; eadem ratione proprietates angelicas, scilicet virtutes et scientias, intelliget per ymagines, que non sunt idem quod ipse. Item, si in patria videntur res sine ymaginibus, ergo Apostolus in raptu suo vidit Deum et alia archana non per ymagines, sed per presentiam ipsarum rerum; ergo quando rediit ad priorem statum, nulle ymagines rerum, quas viderit, remanserunt in eo ...» (GA, p. 706,68–80).

31 «Quod concedimus cum Augustino» (GA, p. 707,98).

32 Infra lin. 119–121.

33 «Quod obicit de sensu, dicendum quod non est simile, quia sensus concernit situm et distantiam aliquam respectu obiecti, quia sensibile supra sensum etc.; et ideo non potest videre ipsum sive cognoscere sensibile nisi per speciem, nec se ipso, quia non reflectitur supra se, cum sit materialis» (lin. 122–125).

34 «... dicimus quod hec est falsa: 'sicut forme visibiles se habent ad visum, ita' etc., si intelligatur generaliter, quoniam non omni eodem modo se habent, quia forme visibiles non sunt presentes ipsi visui, non enim sunt in ipso oculo, et propter hoc ymago est

da Guglielmo, che approfondisce ed esplicita chiamando in causa il luogo e la distanza dell'oggetto rispetto all'organo che li percepisce, non mostrando interesse per la seconda e per le errate conseguenze che sul piano logico Guglielmo individua in essa. Questa mancanza di interesse per un'interpretazione di natura logica potrebbe essere in linea con l'omissione da parte dell'autore della trattazione – sempre che tale omissione sia volontaria e non accidentale – su come intendere il termine 'uomo' nella proposizione che da l'avvio al racconto del rapimento paolino: «Scio hominem in Christo» (2 Cor 12,2). Dall'interpretazione di questo termine, infatti, che poteva intendersi o in senso proprio ('uomo' in quanto composto di anima e corpo) oppure improprio ovvero per sineddoche ('uomo' in quanto anima soltanto), dipendeva la questione se il rapimento di Paolo aveva investito soltanto la sua anima, oppure l'uomo nella sua totalità: discussione questa, appunto del tutto assente nel nostro autore in questi termini, e invece diventata un *topos* nelle questioni sul *raptus* tra la fine del secolo XII inizio del XIII.[35]

La soluzione delle altre due obiezioni è del tutto in linea con quella di Guglielmo di cui riprende anche i termini tecnici. Come costui, infatti, anche l'autore ritiene che l'anima dell'Apostolo abbia visto gli angeli attraverso un'immagine e similitudine che non sono altro che la stessa sua anima; che come esistano più tipi di immaginazione, che chiama al pari di Guglielmo *recolens, assimilans e confingens,* così esista un'intelligenza *recolens* ed una assimilante, e che con quest'ultima un angelo conosca un altro angelo.[36]

Come Guglielmo, risolve l'obiezione che se la visione di Paolo fu senza immagine, nel ritorno allo stato normale niente rimase di essa, distinguendo tra conoscenza reale e nominale di un oggetto. La prima si ha o per la presenza stessa dell'oggetto o per l'immagine che proviene da esso; la seconda si

necessaria; sed quedam forme intelligibiles sunt presentes intellectui. Si autem intelligatur particulariter, vera est, sed argumentatio sequens non valet, quoniam ex particularibus non est sillogizandum» (GA, p. 707,99–105).

35 Cf. per esempio GA, p. 700,59–64; AH, p. 1346 n. 3, lin. 7–13.

36 «Tamen de angelis dici potest quod vidit per ymaginem vel similitudinem, que non est aliud quam ipsa anima. Unde notandum quod ymaginatio dicitur tripliciter, scilicet recolens quod receptum est, assimilans, ut quando per hominem quem vidi cognosco hominem quem non vidi, et confingens, ut in cimera. Similitudo dupliciter dicitur, est enim intelligentia recolens et est intelligentia assimilans. Intelligentia assimilante intelligit unus angelus alterum, dum se intelligendo intelligit illum» (lin. 127–134); cf. «... humanus intellectus intelliget angelum per ymaginem, sed non per ymaginem que procedit ex ipso angelo, sed per animam, que est ymago ipsius angeli, anima enim per se ipsam intelligit se et omnia sibi similia, quia sicut multiplex est ymaginatio, ita multiplex est intelligentia. Est autem ymaginatio recolens, qua ymaginatur illud quod prius fuit in sensu nostro et quod scimus fuisse in sensu nostro; et est ymaginatio assimilans, qua ymaginamur illud quod non fuit in sensu, sed cuius simile fuit, sicut ymaginor Herculem per aliquem similem ei, qui fuit in sensu nostro; et est ymaginatio confingens, qua ymaginor chimeram. Similiter est intelligencia recolens, et est intelligencia assimilans et secundum hanc intelligenciam intelligit anima angelum, per hoc quod intelligit se, que est similis angelo» (GA, pp. 707–708,106–117).

ha attraverso i nomi che lo esprimono, come avviene del colore per il cieco nato. Dopo il rapimento Paolo non ebbe più la prima, ma la seconda.[37]

L'ultima breve questione infine è così costruita: intendere il rapimento al terzo cielo come rapimento alla terza gerarchia angelica significa: o Paolo vide quest'ultima, e allora quando vide Dio, che è infinitamente oltre a tutto, fu rapito oltre a questa; oppure vide come gli angeli di questa gerarchia somma. Ma ciò era impossibile dal momento che la sua anima era ancora unita al corpo, quindi non del tutto libera; pertanto la sua visione in quel momento non fu così limpida come quella dell'ultima gerarchia angelica.[38] La prima obiezione sembra – almeno a mia conoscenza – originale, la seconda invece riunisce due motivi già reperibili nella *Summa aurea*: da un lato l'affermazione della *Glossa* del Lombardo a 2 Cor 12,2–4 secondo cui l'Apostolo vide gli *archana Dei* come li vedeva la suprema gerarchia angelica; dall'altro l'interpretazione a essa fornita da Guglielmo, secondo il quale la *Glossa* non afferma che l'Apostolo vide così chiaramente come questa gerarchia, ma nel medesimo modo di questa:[39] in altre parole che il 'medesimo modo' non concerne la limpidezza della visione, ma altre caratteristiche, ossia l'immediatezza di essa, la conformità di ardore, scienza e giudizio di Paolo con i Serafini, Cherubini e Troni, la sua eccellenza in quanto sommo gerarca. Ora due punti della soluzione del nostro autore toccano proprio il motivo dell'immediatezza della visione e dell'eccellenza di Paolo come sommo gerarca avanzati da Guglielmo.[40]

Le doti di chiarezza dell'autore emergono con evidenza nella questione 5, che affronta un tema ricorrente nelle discussioni su *raptus* a partire almeno dalla fine del secolo XII,[41] riproposto all'inizio del XIII anche da Guglielmo di

37 «… dicendum quod est cognitio realis quando aliquis cognoscit rem per sui presentiam vel ymaginem illius, et est cognitio nominalis que ponit altera nomina, sicut cecus natus cognoscit quod color est quod sentitur per oculum. Sic apostolus post⟨ea⟩ de illa visione non habuit cognitionem realem, set nominalem» (lin. 135–139); cf. «Est enim cognitio realis et cognitio nominalis, liceat sic loqui. Realis est, que fit per ipsam presenciam rei, vel per ymaginem que procedit ab ipsa; huiusmodi cognitio non remansit in Apostolo de eis, que vidit in raptu. Nominalis est, que fit per nomina aliquo modo exponencia rem, sicut cecus natus cognoscit colorem per rationem istam, color est qui cognoscitur per sensum, cecus autem natus cognoscit colorem per tactum et sic cecus natus habet cognitionem aliquam de colore, sed longe minorem quam ille qui videt. Consimilem cognitionem habuit Apostolus, postquam rediit ad priorem statum, quoniam scivit se vidisse archana Dei, et scivit dicere diffinitionem illius visionis, que aliquo modo exponebat per nomina illam visionem; unde cognitionem nominalem habuit de illa visione et non realem» (GA, p. 708,121–133).

38 Infra lin. 142–146.

39 «Glosa non asserit quod Apostolus viderit ita clare sicut illi qui sunt de suppremis ordinibus, sed quod eodem modo vidit, sicut illi vident. Et hoc dicit tribus de causis. Una est propter immediationem visionis … Secunda causa … est propter conformitatem quam habebat cum illis suppremis ordinibus … Tertia causa est, quoniam ipse erat summus ierarcha …» (GA, p. 709,11–24).

40 Infra lin. 147–151.

41 Cf. Wicki 1954, pp. 162–174.

Auxerre e da Alessandro di Hales:[42] si tratta della natura della visione paolina, ovvero se fu la visione di un comprensore e, nel caso affermativo, se fu del tutto assimilabile a quest'ultima. L'autore sottoscrive la soluzione della visione *mediastina*, vale a dire quella di una visione che non fu né semplicemente del viatore né del comprensore, ma appunto intermedia, specificando che ciò emerge sia considerando il soggetto che la detiene, sia il modo di vedere di costui. Chi vede, infatti, può essere o comprensore e nello stato del comprensore, o viatore e nello stato di viatore, oppure in un modo medio, ossia viatore, che temporaneamente si trova ad essere nello stato di comprensore: e questo è appunto il caso di Paolo, la cui visione pertanto era compatibile con l'*habitus* della fede.[43] Il suo modo di vedere fu intermedio, perché sebbene non mediato – e pertanto in ciò molto simile a quello dei comprensori – tuttavia non fu così chiaro come il vedere di questi ultimi e a causa dell'*habitus* della fede, che comportava una certa conoscenza enigmatica, e perché la sua anima era unita a un corpo corruttibile, non ancora in gloria, né libera da ogni pena. E ancora tra i comprensori, come già sosteneva Alessandro di Hales sulla falsariga di Agostino, la visione non è la stessa: meno chiara è infatti quella dell'anima in gloria, perché frenata a volgersi con tutte le sue forze verso il cielo dalla sua tendenza verso il corpo; più chiara quella dell'angelo che è del tutto privo di qualsiasi corpo.[44]

Dal breve esame delle questioni 4 e 5, ma ciò vale anche per le altre, emerge che l'autore non cita mai alla lettera – tranne in un caso[45] – le argomentazioni

42 GA, pp. 701–702 e AH, pp. 1353–1356 n. 24–32.

43 Infra lin. 161–166. Il motivo dell'*habitus fidei* nella discussione sul *raptus* si ritrova in AH, p. 1354 n. 28, lin. 26–27. E' invece assente in GA.

44 «Media fuit a parte modi videndi, quamvis enim videret immediate, et quantum ad hoc esset simillima cognitioni comprehensionis, tamen sicut dicit Agustinus XII super Genesim quod retardatur anima glorificata nec totaliter tendat in summum celum, multo fortius retardabatur anima unita corpori corruptibili. Non igitur erat ita clara sicut cognitio anime glorificate, quoniam actu unita, nec ⟨cognitio⟩ anime glorificate ita clara ut angelorum» (lin. 166–172); cf. «... In parte est convenientia, in parte autem differentia. Unde Augustinus: Angeli vident Deum abstracti ab omni corporali forma et corpore; anima autem glorificata videt, habet tamen quamdam intentionem ad suum corpus, propter quam intentionem cognitio sua est inferioris gradus quam angelorum quoad hoc. Unde dicit: 'Minime tamen dubitandum est, et raptam hominis mentem a carnalibus sensibus, et post mortem ipsa carne deposita, non sic videre Deum sicut angeli vident' etc. Si ergo intentio ad corpus retardat, ita quod non ita clara est visio sicut angelorum, multo fortius unio ad corpus non glorificatum retardat; unde non fuit ita clara visio ipsius Pauli sicut angelorum, vel etiam animae glorificatae» (AH, p. 1359 n. 42, lin. 13–25).

45 L'unica citazione alla lettera è la definizione del *raptus*. L'autore la inserisce in un contesto che ripropone efficacemente, grazie a un altro ordine espositivo e ad alcune selezioni, il pensiero di Alessandro su come intendere che il *raptus* è un fenomeno «sopra la natura»: «Raptus proprie dicitur 'ab eo quod est secundum naturam in id quod est preter naturam in insensibili tempore'; ad similitudinem huiusmodi dicitur hic raptus, ut dicatur raptus est elevatio quoad cognitivam ab eo quod est secundum naturam in id quod est supra naturam. Supra naturam dico, quia non est contra naturam, nisi

e soluzioni dottrinali dei suoi due modelli di riferimento, ma piuttosto le filtra, semplifica e rielabora, rendendole così più chiare e concise.[46] Inoltre spesso riporta le medesime *auctoritates* già utilizzate da Guglielmo e da Alessandro.[47] La sua questione ha la configurazione di una raccolta di materiale forse ancora da completare[48] selezionato in base a criteri logici e di chiarezza. Ciò non significa tuttavia che all'occorrenza l'autore non intervenga con riformulazioni più personali, che pur ispirandosi alle sue fonti, comportino integrazioni e conclusioni assenti in esse. Ciò appare soprattutto nella questione sulla differenza tra visione durante il *raptus*, visione mosaica, profetica e contemplativa, questione all'interno della quale egli inserisce una distinzione della visione intellettuale in quattro generi. Come si è accennato, ispiratore di tale questione e anche dei vari tipi di visione intellettuale è Alessandro, che però diversamente dall'autore di Assisi, tratta questi ultimi quando si interroga

dicatur contra naturam, idest contra solitum cursum, set nichil deperiit de natura. Supra naturam dico, quia anima, dum est corpori unita, nata est videre per speculum et enigma vel per ymaginem, non facie ad faciem, sicut est in raptu» (lin. 64–71); cf. «Raptus dicitur hic per quamdam similitudinem respectu eius ubi proprie dicitur; dicitur enim proprie raptus 'ab eo quod est secundum naturam, in id quod est praeter naturam in insensibili tempore'. Supra naturam enim animae exsistentis in corpore corruptibili est, quod videat immediate et sine phantasmate et imaginatione Deum suum. Unde raptus dicitur elevatio ab eo quod est secundum naturam, ad id quod est supra naturam quoad cognitivam. Hoc autem quod est 'supra naturam' dicitur, quia non *per speculum in aenigmate* neque imagine, quia per hoc naturaliter potest videre. Ad hoc quod obicitur quod contra naturam elevabatur, dico quod contra naturam, id est contra solitum cursum naturae; non proprie contra naturam, quia non erat ibi destructa natura aliqua, licet esset usus alter, quia fuit supra naturam» (AH, pp. 1346–1347 n. 5–6, lin. 24–9).

46 Ancora un esempio di concisione e di massima chiarezza dell'autore rispetto alla sua fonte emerge da: «Quod queritur a quo actu sensitive fiat abstractio, dicendum quod quidam est actus continuus, sicut vivificare corpus et ab hoc non fiebat abstractio, quidam est actus eius interior in cognoscendo qui recipit interpolationem, sicut est actus phantasie, et tam ab hoc quam a sensibus exterioribus fiebat abstractio» (lin. 77–81); cf. «Ego autem dico quod duplex est actus phantasiae. Unus enim est actus qui continuus est in cerebro, quod est organum illius, et quantum ad illum agit continue; et quantum ad illum non fuit abstractio, quia sic non fuisset ultra in corpore. Sicut quaedam infirmitates sunt, ubi deperit sensus et motus, et tamen vitalis motus permanet. Duplex enim est unio in corpore: una per hoc quod anima est in corpore; alia secundum quod secundum suum actum est in corpore. Non autem abstrahitur quoad actum illum, secundum quem vivit corpus secundum actum sensibilem et vegetabilem. Alius autem actus intelligitur, secundum quem phantasia in somno magis operatur quam in vigilia: respectu huius fit abstractio; quia abstrahitur a phantasia in contemplatione, ergo multo fortius in raptu» (AH, p. 1357 n. 35, lin. 8–21).

47 Per esempio, Aug. *De Gen. ad litt.*, 12, 27, 55: lin. 28, cf. AH, p. 1348 n. 9, lin. 15; Mt 6,21: lin. 106, cf. AH, p. 1351 n. 18, lin. 20; Aug. *De Gen. ad litt.*, 12, 35, 68: lin. 168–169, cf. AH, p. 1359 n. 42, lin. 14; Richardus a S. Victore *Beniamin maior*, I, 4: lin. 182, cf. AH, p. 1360 n. 46, lin. 18; *XII Num.*, 8: lin. 185, cf. AH, p. 1361 n. 49, lin. 20.

48 Come potrebbe indicare l'interruzione improvvisa del testo all'inizio, poco dopo l'inizio del f. 14va.

se la visione paolina fu *sub imagine* oppure intellettuale. Anche in questo caso, dunque, l'autore adotta un differente ordine di esposizione rispetto all'Halense; non solo, con incisività e precisione distingue e caratterizza queste visioni: quella *per raptum* è *secundum speciem*, le altre tre sono o in *aliqua ymagine* o *in aliquo effectu;*[49] inoltre in ogni tipo di visione intellettuale enuclea due differenze.[50] Alessandro invece nel passo parallelo, ovvero in quello che ha come oggetto la differenza tra visione per rapimento, visione profetica e visione contemplativa, si limita a osservare che «aliud est videre Deum» e qui si riferisce alla visione per rapimento, e «aliud est videre aliqua in Deo, quia hec visio est sub imaginibus ad enuntiandum» e qui si riferisce alla profezia, oppure vedere in Dio «quae sunt operabilia, cum affectione eorum», e qui si riferisce alla contemplazione;[51] inoltre in questo specifico contesto non parla di visione in qualche effetto. Ne accenna invece, ma molto di sfuggita, nell'altra questione quando, dopo aver sostenuto che la visione paolina fu di natura intellettuale e con Agostino che fu «sub similitudinibus quae non sunt aliud quam ipsae res», in connessione a ciò tratta dei vari tipi di visione intellettuale e tra questi annovera la conoscenza di Dio per grazia, grazia che è effetto nell'anima,[52] senza però specificare chi sia detentore di questo tipo di visione.

49 Infra lin. 188–191.

50 «Primum est cum aliquod intelligibile videtur se ipso, et hoc habet duas differentias, prima et summa cum videtur se ipso et a se, sicut Deus intelligit se; secunda cum aliquid se ipso videtur ab alio, ut Deus a beatis et iustitia ab eo qui habet eam. Secundum genus est cum aliquod intelligibile videtur per aliud quod est eius similitudo, et hoc habet duas differentias, quia illa similitudo aut est ipsa essentia videntis, ut cum anima videt aliam per se ipsam; secunda differentia cum similitudo est essentialiter in vidente, ut cum video caritatem tuam per meam. Tertium genus visionis est cum aliquod intelligibile videtur per aliud quod est eius effectus, et hoc habet duas differentias, prima est cum effectus est essentialiter in vidente, ut anima per gratiam videt Deum sive ⟨per⟩ irradiationem; secunda differentia est cum effectus est extra, ut anima per creaturas videt Deum. Quartum genus est cum aliquod sensibile videtur per speciem intelligibilem, et hoc habet duas differentias, prima est quia illa species intelligibilis prius imprimitur ipsi intelligibili, sicut est in tertio genere visionis intellectualis; alia differentia est cum recipitur ab inferiori vi, et hec est ultima differentia. Visio igitur raptus est secundum tres primas differentias, visio autem intellectualis prophetie est in effectu qui est irradiatio, visio contemplationis in effectu qui est gratia vel creatura» (infra lin. 199–219).

51 Cf. AH, pp. 1360–1361 n. 48, lin. 27–29 e 10–11.

52 «Est ergo visio intellectualis large dicta per imaginem, sicut in corporalibus rebus; item per similitudinem quae est aliud quam res, et hoc a posteriori; item per similitudinem quae est aliud quam res in aequali, ut anima per se sui similem et angelus angelum; item per similitudinem quae non est aliud quam ipsa res, sicut anima cognoscit suam iustitiam et suam prudentiam et Deum. Cognoscit etiam Deum per gratiam in anima exsistentem, quae est eius effectus; item cognoscit anima prudentiam et iustitiam per rationem aeternam. Non ergo omnis intellectualis visio est per similitudinem quae non est aliud quam ipsa res. Visio autem Apostoli fuit intellectualis et praeterea fuit per similitudinem quae non est aliud quam ipsa res; sed non omnis visio intellectualis est huiusmodi» (AH, p. 1353 n. 23, lin. 7–19).

Confrontando la tipologia delle visioni intellettuali delineata dall'autore con quella più faticosa di Alessandro,[53] emergono notevoli differenze. Tra queste le più importanti sono le seguenti: la visione intellettuale che Dio ha di se stesso è assente in Alessandro; assente è soprattutto la distinzione di un intelligibile che viene visto non per se stesso, ma attraverso altro, altro che non è la sua *similitudo*, ma il suo effetto. Tale effetto a sua volta può essere duplice: può essere o essenzialmente in chi vede, come quando l'anima per grazia ovvero per irradiazione vede Dio, oppure può essere esteriore, come quando l'anima attraverso le creature vede Dio. Il primo è proprio della visione profetica, il secondo della contemplativa. L'autore, dunque, allarga la nozione di effetto: mentre infatti Alessandro accenna genericamente a una conoscenza di Dio per effetto, ma considera solo quell'effetto che è la grazia nell'anima, l'autore specifica che questa è un'irradiazione ed è detenuta dal profeta e la distingue dall'effetto esteriore o da quella grazia che è la creatura, appannaggio del contemplativo quando conosce Dio.

Dottrinariamente la concezione del *raptus* del ms. Assisi 186 è così riassumibile: durante esso Paolo era in vita, inattivi invece erano i suoi organi corporei per sentire (lin. 20–25); la sua intelligenza si è elevata da ciò che è secondo natura a ciò che è sopra di essa, poiché, essendo la sua anima unita al corpo, poteva vedere Dio solo *per speculum et in aenigmate*, invece in quel momento lo vide faccia a faccia (lin. 64–71, 119–121). La sua visione di Dio, dunque, fu sì quella di un viatore, ma che per un momento si trovò nello stato di comprensore. Tuttavia benché molto simile a quella di quest'ultimo, in quanto immediata, era meno limpida di quella dell'anima in gloria e ancor meno di quella dell'angelo, poiché frenata dall'unione dell'anima con il corpo corruttibile (lin. 166–172). La visione per rapimento si distingue da quella profetica quanto al suo aspetto intellettuale, da quella contemplativa e da quella di Mosè (che sono tutte dello stesso genere in quanto intellettuali), per il fatto di essere una visione *per speciem*, ovvero facciale, mentre le altre colgono Dio mediatamente, ossia in qualche immagine, o in qualche effetto. A parte la visione per rapimento, delle tre la più alta e chiara è quella di Mosè, la cui visione di Dio non comporta né operazione, come invece avviene per la contemplazione, né comunicazione di ciò che si è visto, come invece accade nella profezia.

Resta ora da affrontare il problema della paternità della questione. E' di Bonaventura? Va osservato a questo proposito che i passi del suo Commento alle Sentenze che accennano al rapimento sono scarsi e non permettono un confronto molto fruttuoso. Tuttavia alcuni sporadici elementi dottrinali e stilistici e soprattutto il contesto in cui il Francescano inserisce il motivo del *raptus* permettono se non proprio di caratterizzare, almeno di tratteggiare la sua posizione e su taluni punti di verificarla con quella del ms. di Assisi.

Bonaventura accenna a esso incidentalmente e – tranne in un caso[54] – sempre in connessione con l'*excessus mentis* o estasi, che per lui è fenomeno dis-

53 Cf. supra note 50 e 52.

54 «... sicut Dominus gratiam raptus alicui dat ad unam horam ...» (*In IV Sent.* 6, p. II, *dub.* 1, t. IV, p. 160).

tinto dal *raptus*.[55] Pur avendo un denominatore comune – l'alienazione percettiva – *excessus mentis* e *raptus* si differenziano per il tipo di visione, per i fruitori, per la loro frequenza. L'*excessus mentis* non comporta una conoscenza chiara di Dio nella sua essenza; è una conoscenza sì immediata, perché non speculare, ma in caligine, caratterizzata dal sentire, sperimentare, intimamente Dio; appannaggio di Mosè nella sua ascesa al Sinai e dei sommi contemplativi, deve essere cercata e perseguita da ogni uomo *in via*, poiché rientra in una legge comune: è infatti la più alta delle conoscenze *in via*. Il rapimento invece, ritiene Bonaventura manifestando una certa perplessità ed esitazione a parlare di esso, è una conoscenza superiore: è infatti visione di Dio nella sua essenza, ha carattere del tutto eccezionale, è un privilegio speciale accordato da Dio che fa oltrepassare al rapito lo stato di viatore; è del tutto indipendente dalla iniziativa di costui che infatti è del tutto passivo, è appannaggio di Paolo e di pochissimi contemplativi.[56] Bonaventura, dunque, accennando al *raptus* qualifica la visione di Dio che si ha durante esso come visione di Lui nella sua essenza; parla di privilegio speciale, sottolinea la sua eccezionalità rispetto ad altre esperienze, in primo luogo rispetto a quella dell'*excessus mentis*.

L'autore di Assisi 186, invece, anziché di conoscenza di Dio nella sua essenza, usa l'espressione 'faccia a faccia', non parla né di stato comune, né di privilegio speciale, non sottolinea la passività del soggetto quando è rapito, soprattutto – e questo mi sembra l'elemento veramente distintivo – non accenna in un solo punto all'*excessus mentis*, che in realtà è ben più del *raptus* l'elemento primario focalizzante l'interesse di Bonaventura. Per questi motivi ritengo la paternità bonaventuriana fragile.

55 Ciò peraltro è affermato esplicitamente in *Hex.* III, 30, V, pp. 347–348: «Sexta est visio intelligentiae per raptum in Deum absorptae ... Haec enim sublevatio facit animam Deo simillimam, quantum potest in statu viae – nec est idem ecstasis et raptus – unde, ut dicunt, non habent habitum gloriae, sed actum; et sicut illa visio est in confinio viae et patriae, sic illa est in confinio unionis et separationis a corpore ...»

56 «Unde si quae auctoritates id dicere inveniantur quod Deus in praesenti ab homine videtur et cernitur, non sunt intelligendae quod videtur in sua essentia, sed quod in aliquo effectu interiori cognoscitur ...; nisi fortassis in his qui rapiuntur, sicut credimus fuisse in Paulo, qui specialitate privilegii statum viatorum supergrediuntur, nec ibi aliquid agunt, sed solum aguntur» (*In II Sent*, 23, 2, 3, *resp.*, II, p. 544); «Concedo tamen nihilominus quod oculi aspectus in Deum figi potest, ita quod ad nihil aliud aspiciat; attamen non perspiciet vel videbit ipsius lucis claritatem, immo potius elevabitur in caliginem et ad hanc cognitionem elevabitur per omnium ablationem, sicut Dionysius dicit in libro De Mystica Theologia et vocat istam cognitionem doctam ignorantiam. Haec enim est in qua mirabiliter inflammatur affectio, sicut eis patet, qui aliquoties consueverunt ad anagogicos elevari excessus. Hunc modum cognoscendi arbitror cuilibet viro iusto in via ista esse quaerendum; quodsi Deus aliquid ultra faciet, hoc privilegium est speciale, non legis communis» (*In II Sent*, 23, 2, 3, ad 6, p. 546); «... sapientia non potest essa nimia, quia excessus in experimento divinae dulcedinis potius est laudabilis quam vituperabilis, secundum quod patet in viris sanctis et contemplativis, qui prae nimia dulcedine modo elevantur in ecstasim, modo sublevantur usque ad raptum, licet hoc contingat paucissimis» (*In III Sent*, 35, un., 1, *resp.*, III, p. 774).

Esaminando la questione sul *raptus*, emerge che il ricorso ad autori quali Guglielmo di Auxerre e ancor più Alessandro di Hales, il modo di usare queste fonti non citandole quasi mai alla lettera, ma piuttosto rielaborandole e semplificandole,[57] le doti di chiarezza e di concisione, le formule introduttive,[58] le particolarità linguistiche[59] e, dal punto di vista codicologico, la scrittura, sono i medesimi di quelli dell'autore del *De prophetia*. Ciò, insieme alla contiguità delle due questioni, induce a ritenere che unico sia l'autore di esse, che però allo stato attuale resta ancora anonimo. Le indagini sulla questione *De raptu* mi sembra confermino le conclusioni di Torrell; che però l'autore lavori a Parigi intorno alla metà del secolo XIII, non vi sono motivi sufficienti per stabilirlo se ci si basa sulle fonti del *De raptu*. Poiché l'autore ricorre unicamente a Guglielmo e ad Alessandro, tale data infatti si potrebbe forse anticipare di un decennio.

***

57 La semplificazione a volte diventa incompletezza, effetto forse di una certa fretta. Significativo per esempio a tal proposito il termine 'Gregorius' (lin. 27–28) che nel ms. di Assisi resta sospeso e la cui presenza isolata si comprende soltanto individuando la sua base documentaria, come emerge confrontando il luogo del ms. di Assisi ove il termine e presente e la fonte da cui è tratto, ovvero Alessandro di Hales: «Quod obicit 'Non videbit me' etc., intelligitur de vivente qui est in statu viventis quoad cognitionem sensibilium et affectionem carnalium, unde Gregorius … Agustinus Nisi ab hac vita quisque quodammodo moriatur sive exiens a corpore sive alienatus sive aversus ita a carnalibus, ut nesciat utrum in corpore sit an extra corpus, non in illam rapitur visionem» (lin. 26–30); cf. «Ad hoc quod obicitur: *Non videbit me homo et vivet*, dico quod sic intelligitur: non videbit me et carnaliter vivet. Dicit enim Gregorius ibi: 'A quibusdam in hac carne viventibus, sed inaestimabili virtute crescentibus, contemplationis acumine potest Dei claritas videri; sed tunc, cum videtur, huic vitae funditus moritur'. Sed non propter hoc separatur a corpore, sed tanta est delectatio quod vita haec non reputatur nisi mors. Unde dicit: 'quibusdam in hac carne viventibus moritur' et hoc quoad cognitionem sensibilem sive inferiorem, vel inferiorum, et quoad affectionum carnalium desideriorum. Unde super hoc Augustinus: 'Nisi ab hac vita quisque quodam modo moriatur, sive exiens de corpore, sive ita alienatus et aversus a carnalibus sensibus ut nesciat *sive in corpore sive extra corpus* sit, non in illam rapitur visionem'» (AH, p. 1348 n. 9, lin. 5–18). Come appare chiaramente da quest'ultimo testo, a 'Gregorius' segue il passo di costui, omesso invece in Assisi, il cui luogo corrispondente non ha pertanto senso compiuto.

58 Alcuni esempi: »Si dicas quod« (lin. 60), cf. *De prophetia* (Torrell 1992, p. 297, lin. 482); »Quod obicit … dicendum quod« (lin. 74, 122), cf. *De prophetia* (p. 278, lin. 80); »Quod queritur … dicendum quod« (lin. 90, 126), cf. *De prophetia* (p. 279, lin. 89; p. 281, lin. 122–123; »Responsio. Dicendum quod« (lin. 103, 161), cf. *De prophetia* (p. 277, lin. 64; p. 282, lin. 158).

59 Appunto 'Agustinus' anziché 'Augustinus'; la soppressione di 'h' in 'abstrahere' (lin. 57).

Edizione

Poiché l'apparato critico è esiguo, non lo si riporta in un registro distinto, ma con quello delle fonti. Si riproduce la grafia del ms. nelle sue peculiarità: 'Agustinus' per 'Augustinus', 'testus' per 'textus', 'cimera' per 'chimera', 'austum' per 'haustum'.

Sigle

...	omissioni nel ms.
⟨ ⟩	addenda
(?)	lettura dubbia

Assisi, Biblioteca comunale, Fondo antico 186

⟨Quaestio de raptu⟩

⟨q. 1⟩ ⟨f. 14ra⟩ De raptu queritur utrum attendatur quantum ad separationem anime a corpore. Quod sit patet sic: visio que fuit in raptu Pauli fuit facie ad faciem, sicut dicitur Cor. XII «Raptus est apostolus ad videndum Deum in ea claritate qua in eternum videndus est.» Set de hac visione Exo. XXXIII, dixit Dominus ad Moysen «Non videbit me homo et vivet»; ergo Paulus non fuit vivens; set inter vitam et mortem non est medium.

Item, prima Io. «Deum nemo vidit unquam», Glosa «Nemo purus homo existens in carne vidit Deum ut est.» Set Paulus fuit purus homo et vidit Deum ut est; non ergo fuit existens in carne.

Contra: si separatio esset anime a carne secundum substantiam, tunc fuisset mortuus et postea resuscitatus, quod tamen non dicitur. Preterea fuisset beatus, sicut anime aliorum sanctorum, quod non dicitur.

Item, Glosa ibidem «Facta est ab ipsis sensibus quedam vehementissima intentionis aversio,» non dicit anime a corpore separatio.

Item, videtur quod non sit nostrum nec alicuius sancti determinare, quia ipse dicit quod nescit utrum in corpore an extra corpus. Set ipse multius (?) hoc novit improportionaliter quam aliquis alter; ergo etc.

Item, quomodo potuit hoc ignorare, cum videret in speculo eternitatis aperte in quo omnia relucent? Ergo et hoc videbat, ut videtur.

Responsio. Anima dicitur tripliciter unita corpori, vel sicut perfectio perfectibili, vel sicut motor mobili, vel sicut cognoscens organo mediante quo cognoscit. Primis duobus modis unita fuit corpori, set tertio modo abstracta,

1–5 Cf. AH, p. 1346, n. 4, lin. 14–18 **2** Pauli *add. mg.* **3–4** Cf. *Glossa Lombardi in II Cor.*, 12, 2, c. 80B, 82C **4** Ex 33,20 **7–9** Cf. AH, p. 1348, n. 10, lin. 19–25 **7** 1 Joh 4,12 **7–8** *Glossa in Io.*, 1, 18 (Rusch *Biblia*, I, p. 225) **10–11** Cf. AH, p. 1346, n. 4, lin. 18–20 **13–14** Cf. *Glossa Lombardi in II Cor.*, 12, 2, c. 83A et AH, p. 1346, n. 4, lin. 20–23 **15–17** Cf. AH, p. 1346, n. 3, lin. 7–13 **18–19** Cf. GA, p. 701, lin. 22–25 **20–22** Cf. AH, p. 1347, n. 8, lin. 22–26

quia non utebatur corporis organo in sentiendo, sicut patet per Glosam quod «Facta est a sensibus vehementissima aversio.» Simpliciter igitur vivebat, set mortuus erat quoad cognitionem inferiorum et affectionem carnalium.

Quod obicit «Non videbit me» etc., intelligitur de vivente qui est in statu viventis quoad cognitionem sensibilium et affectionem carnalium, unde Gregorius … Agustinus «Nisi ab hac vita quisque quodammodo moriatur, sive exiens a corpore sive alienatus sive aversus ita a carnalibus, ut nesciat utrum in corpore sit an extra corpus, non in illam rapitur visionem.»

Similiter patet sequens, quia non fuit ut existens in carne quoad cognitionem sensibilium etc.

Quod queritur quod apostolus nescivit, dicendum quod tunc nescivit utrum aliquid cognosceret secundum potentiam sensitivam aut nichil, quia intelligentia tota erat ad Deum conversa, et quantum ad hoc dicit «sive in corpore,» non quantum ad separationem. Exemplum Agustini: sicut multi qui dormiunt sompniantes credunt se vere videre, quia conversio est ad ymaginem quasi ad rem.

Quod obicitur de speculo, dicendum quod representat voluntarie que vult, et ideo non oportet quod omnia.

Queritur secundum quam potentiam attenditur abstractio raptus. Quod ⟨q. 2⟩
quantum ad intelligentiam, videtur quia in raptu videtur Deus immediate. Set intelligentia est cuius est videre Deum immediate; ergo etc.

Contra: raptus est ab eo quod est secundum naturam in id quod est preter naturam. Set intelligentia de se nata est ad videndum Deum; ergo non attenditur quantum ad intelligentiam.

Item, raptus est aversio a sensibus. Set illius est aversio cuius est conversio, ergo illius vis est aversio que est nata converti ad sensus. Set hoc est intellectus vel ratio; ergo etc.

Item, cum avertatur potentia intellectiva a sensibus, aut intelligitur quantum ad sensus exteriores tantum, aut quantum ad exteriores et interiores. Si quantum ad exteriores solum, set tunc maxime viget phantasia; ergo in raptu maxime vigebat phantasia. Si quantum ad omnes, cum igitur animal esse non possit sine omni actu sensitive, redit tunc quod esset mortuus.

Queritur etiam tertio utrum in potestate nostra sit rapi. Quod non, videtur ⟨q. 3⟩
quia est supra naturam, cum sit ibi violentia.

Set contra: anima potest se abstraere a sensibilibus ut in ⟨…⟩ consoletur quantum ad affectionem et quantum ad cognitionem, quia potest cogitare de intelligibilibus; ergo etc.

23–24 Cf. *Glossa Lombardi in II Cor.*, 12, 2, c. 83A **26–30** Cf. AH, p. 1348, n. 9, lin. 5–18 **27–28** Gregorius cf. supra nota 57 **28–30** Agustinus] Augustinus *De Gen. ad litt.*, 12, 27, 55, p. 422 **31–32** Cf. AH, p. 1348, n. 10, lin. 19–25 **33–36** Cf. AH, p. 1347, n. 8, lin. 31–33 **36–38** Cf. AH, p. 1349, n. 11, lin. 3–5 ex Augustino *De Gen. ad litt.*, 12, 2, 3, et 12, 20, 42–43 **39–40** Cf. GA, p. 702, lin. 42–46 **41–43** Cf. AH, p. 1349, n. 14, lin. 17–23 **44–46** Cf. AH, pp. 1345–1346, n. 2, lin. 15–6 **47–48** Cf. AH, p. 1349, n. 13, lin. 12–16 **50–54** Cf. AH, pp. 1356–1357, n. 33–34, lin. 17–2 **53** animal] anime *praem. d. del.* **57–59** Cf. GA, p. 703, lin. 63–67

Si dicas quod in raptu videtur Deus immediate, set hoc non est in potestate anime, contra in Canticis «Paululum cum pertransissem, inveni quem diligit anima mea»; cum ergo possit anima omnes creaturas ut apostolos qui immediate adherent Deo pertransire, potest igitur videre Deum immediate.

Responsio. Raptus proprie dicitur «ab eo quod est secundum naturam in id quod est preter naturam in insensibili tempore»; ad similitudinem huiusmodi dicitur hic raptus, ut dicatur raptus est elevatio quoad cognitivam ab eo quod est secundum naturam in id quod est supra naturam. Supra naturam dico, quia non est contra naturam, nisi dicatur contra naturam, idest contra solitum cursum, set nichil deperiit de natura. Supra naturam dico, quia anima, dum est corpori unita, nata est videre per speculum et enigma vel per ymaginem, non facie ad faciem, sicut est in raptu.

Quod queritur cuius potentie, dico quod intelligentie; quod optime (?) patet, quia hoc est supra naturam intelligentie sic videre, dum est in corpore.

Quod obicit quod non convertitur nec est unita sensibus, dicendum quod dum est unita corpori, et recipit a sensibus et unitur ipsis non tamen immediate set mediate, set omnino abstrahit quantum ad actum.

Quod queritur a quo actu sensitive fiat abstractio, dicendum quod quidam est actus ⟨f. 14rb⟩ continuus, sicut vivificare corpus et ab hoc non fiebat abstractio, quidam est actus eius interior in cognoscendo qui recipit interpollationem, sicut est actus phantasie, et tam ab hoc quam a sensibus exterioribus fiebat abstractio. Et sic patet illud.

Ad illud quod queritur utrum sit in potestate nostra rapi, dicendum quod non. Quod obicit quod in potestate nostra est abstrahi, dicendum quod etsi quis possit se abstrahere a sentiendo, non tamen ⟨a⟩ cognoscendo. Non enim possumus in hac vita cognoscere nisi per speculum et sub velamine creature; est enim velamen peccati, scripture et creature.

Set obicies quod creatura non intrat ⟨in⟩ intellectum nostrum, Deus intrat; ergo non velatur a creatura. Dicendum quod occultatio non est ab ipsis creaturis, set a defectu intellectus propter sui imperfectionem et parvitatem.

Quod queritur de pertransitione, dicendum quod est pertransitio immediationis et est pertransitio translationis. Prima non est in hac vita in potestate nostra, secunda sic.

⟨q. 4⟩ Queritur de termino (?) raptus qui dicitur tertium celum et exponitur tripliciter. Primo de celo empireo, ut dicatur primum celum aereum, de quo in Matheo «Volucres celi comedebant illud»; secundum sidereum, de quo in principio Genesis «Fiant luminaria»; tertium empireum, de quo «In principio creavit Deus celum.»

Contra hoc, est quia anima fuit unita corpori; ergo non mutavit locum; ergo non potest exponi de celo localiter.

60–63 Cf. GA, p. 703, lin. 73–81 **61** Cant 3,4 **62** anima] *interl.* **64–71** AH, pp. 1346–1347, n. 5–6, lin. 24–9 **74–76** Cf. AH, p. 1350, n. 15, lin. 8–11 **74** est *iter.* **77–81** Cf. AH, p. 1357, n. 35, lin. 9–12, 18–21 **80** tam *interl.* **82–85** Cf. GA, p. 703, lin. 86–92 **86–89** Cf. GA, pp. 705–706, lin. 33–52 **90–92** Cf. GA, p. 704, lin. 93–97 **93–97** Cf. *Glossa Lombardi in II Cor.*, 12,2, c. 80A–82B **95** Mt 13,4 **96** Gen 1,14 **96–97** Gen 1,1

Item, si dicas quod rapta fuit illuc secundum cogitationem, similiter posset dici quod ego essem raptus Rome, si viderem sive cogitarem que fiunt Rome, quod tamen non dicitur.

Responsio. Dicendum quod non intelligitur raptus fuisse ad celum empyreum quod anima illuc localiter ascenderit, set quod contemplabatur. Clare videbat ea que ibi erant, sicut si localiter esset presens. Et per hoc, quod non valet quod obicit; et est similis modus dicendi, sicut cum dicitur «Ubi est thesaurus tuus, ibi et cor tuum.»

Secunda expositio est ut dicatur tertium celum, idest tertium genus visionis, que quidem est visio intellectualis, que tertia est respectu visionis corporalis et ymaginarie. Hoc autem genus visionis continet eas res «que videntur per similitudines, que non sunt aliud quam ipse res.»

Obicitur contra hoc sic: sicut se ⟨habet⟩ sensibile ad sensum, ita intelligibile ad intellectum. Set sensibile semper videtur per speciem aliam; ergo etc.

Item, apostolus videbat angelos et cognoscebat. Set constat quod angeli non erant essentialiter in ipso; ergo videbat per aliud quod non erat essentia angeli, cum videret per aliquid quod esset in ipso.

Item, si non vidit per ymagines vel similitudines, ergo nichil remansit in cognitione post reversionem ad corpus; nulla ergo fuit visio talis.

Responsio. Dicendum quod anima Pauli in raptu vidit Deum facie ad faciem et non per similitudinem vel ymaginem aliam; vidit autem spirituales substantias per se ipsam.

Quod obicit de sensu, dicendum quod non est simile, quia sensus concernit situm et distantiam aliquam respectu obiecti, quia sensibile supra sensum etc.; et ideo non potest videre ipsum sive cognoscere sensibile nisi per speciem, nec se ipso, quia non reflectitur supra se, cum sit materialis.

Quod queritur qualiter videbat angelos, dicendum quod illud Agustini de visione intelligit⟨ur⟩ respectu divine nature, non de omnibus que vidit. Tamen de angelis dici potest quod vidit per ymaginem vel similitudinem, que non est aliud quam ipsa anima. Unde notandum quod ymaginatio dicitur tripliciter, scilicet recolens quod receptum est, assimilans, ut quando per hominem quem vidi cognosco hominem quem non vidi, et confingens, ut in cimera. Similitudo dupliciter dicitur, est enim intelligentia recolens et est intelligentia assimilans. Intelligentia assimilante intelligit unus angelus alterum, dum se intelligendo intelligit illum. Et sic patet etc.

Quod queritur postea, dicendum quod est cognitio realis quando aliquis cognoscit rem per sui presentiam vel ymaginem illius, et est cognitio nominalis que ponit altera nomina, sicut cecus natus cognoscit quod color est quod sentitur per oculum. Sic apostolus post⟨ea⟩ de illa visione non habuit cogni-

103–107 Cf. AH, p. 1351, n. 18, lin. 14–20 **106–107** Mt 6,21 **110–111** Augustinus *De Gen. ad litt.*, 12, 6, 15, p. 387 **112–113** Cf. Aristoteles *De an.*, III, 4, 429a, 16–18 et cf. GA, p. 706, lin. 68–71 **117–118** Cf. GA, p. 706, lin. 77–80 **122–125** Cf. GA, p. 707, lin. 99–105 **127–134** Cf. GA, pp. 707–708, lin. 106–117 **135–141** Cf. GA, p. 708, lin. 118–129 **137–138** sicut cecus ... oculum] cf. Aristoteles *Phys.*, II, 1, 193a, 7–9

tionem realem, set nominalem. Alia vero que vidit sub ymaginibus adhuc cognoscebat, set visionem illam cognoscebat vel per altera nomina vel per privationem. Exemplum de ceco qui vidit lucem.

Tertia expositio «usque ad tertium celum,» idest ad tertiam ierarchiam, pro quanto dicitur illuc raptus aut quia vidit illam et tunc ultra illam raptus est, vidit enim Deum qui est ultra in infinitum. Si quia vidit sicut illi, hoc nichil est, quia anima eius uniebatur corpori, ergo non erat omnino expedita; non ergo videbat ita limpide ut illi.

Responsio. Raptus dicitur usque ad tertiam ierarchiam tum ratione obiecti, quia ultra illam non erat aliqua creatura, et inclusive dicitur non exclusive nisi ratione creature; ⟨tum⟩ ratione modi cognoscendi, quia sine omni medio et sine adiutorio spiritus creati; set inferiores ierarchie recipiunt a superioribus … ; ⟨tum⟩ ratione subiecti, quia fuit summus ierarcha.

⟨q. 5⟩ ⟨f. 14va⟩ Questio est qualiter differat visio raptus Pauli a visione patrie, et queritur utrum fuerit visio comprehensoris. Et quod sit videtur: visio que est facie ad faciem non est viatoris, ergo aliquo modo est comprehensoris, quia non est media ut videtur.

Item, Agustinus in Glosa «Raptus est ad videndum Deum in illa claritate in qua videndus est in eternum.» Set hec est visio comprehensionis; ergo etc.

Contra: visio comprehensionis compatitur secum nec actum nec habitum fidei. Set in Paulo erat fidei habitus; ergo etc. Nec viatoris fuit; queritur ergo cuiusmodi fuit.

Responsio. Dicendum quod hec visio nec simpliciter fuit viatoris nec simpliciter comprehensoris, set mediastina, tum a parte videntis, tum a parte modi. A parte videntis, quia videns potest esse comprehensor et in statu comprehensoris, vel viator et in statu viatoris, vel medio modo viator, set in statu comprehensoris ad tempus. Et talis fuit Paulus, et ideo visio sua compatiebatur habitum fidei, non tamen actum secundum statum illum. Media fuit a parte modi videndi, quamvis enim videret immediate, et quantum ad hoc esset simillima cognitioni comprehensionis, tamen sicut dicit Agustinus XII super Genesim quod retardatur anima glorificata nec totaliter tendat in summum celum, multo fortius retardabatur anima unita corpori corruptibili. Non igitur erat ita clara sicut cognitio anime glorificate, quoniam actu unita, nec ⟨cognitio⟩ anime glorificate ita clara ut angelorum. Et sic dicendum quod erat media scientia. Et sic patet responsio ad obiecta.

Quod non ita clara tripliciter ostenditur, tum ratione habitus fidei qui dicit aliquod enigma, tum ratione unionis, tum quia non erat gloriosa, quamvis esset grata, nec libera ab omni pena, elevabatur autem per gratiam increatam.

144–146 Cf. GA, p. 709, lin. 11–16 **151** Cf. GA, p. 709, lin. 24 **154** modo] ergo **156–157** Cf. *Glossa Lombardi in II Cor.*, 12, 2, c. 80B, 82C et AH, p. 1359, n. 41, lin. 9–11 **163** videntis] videns **163–172** Cf. AH, p. 1359, n. 42, lin. 13–25 **168–169** Augustinus *De Gen. ad litt.*, 12, 35, 68, pp. 432–433

Queritur quomodo differat a visione prophetali, quantum ad visionem intellectualem. Et videtur quod sit eadem specie, quia idem genus et eadem differentia. ⟨q.6⟩

Set contra: prophete non videbant Deum facie ad faciem, sicut est in raptu. Item, de differentia ad visionem contemplationis, cum illa sit visio intellectualis. Dicit enim Ricardus «Contemplatio est liber et perspicax animi intuitus ad res perspiciendas.»

Item queritur qualiter differat a visione Moysi. Et videtur quod fuerit secundum modum raptus. Dicitur enim XII Numerorum ⟨8⟩ «Ore ad os loquor ei» et item ibi «palam et non per enigmata» etc. Set constat quod Moyses erat viator; ergo etc. Contrarium habetur in Glosa.

Responsio. Visio raptus differt a visione mosayca et prophetali et contemplationis, quia cum in raptu funditus moriebatur Paulus huic vite, ut dicit Gregorius, videbat Deum secundum speciem; iste autem visiones aut sunt in aliqua ymagine aut in aliquo effectu, non quod viderent Deum in sua specie. Differt autem, quia visio contemplationis est ad videndum Deum quantum ad operanda, prophetie quantum ad enuncianda, Moysi neutro modo, et ideo clarior et sublimior. Unde posset poni gradus quod visio contemplationis non est ita clara ut visio prophetalis quoad intellectualem, nec visio prophetalis fuit ita clara ut Moysi et hoc vult testus dicere in Numeris quod Moyses clarius vidisset aliis.

Quod obicitur de visione intellectuali, notandum quod quadruplex est genus intellectualis visionis. Primum est cum aliquod intelligibile videtur se ipso, et hoc habet duas differentias, prima et summa cum videtur se ipso et a se, sicut Deus intelligit se; secunda cum aliquid se ipso videtur ab alio, ut Deus a beatis et iustitia ab eo qui habet eam.

Secundum genus est cum aliquod intelligibile videtur per aliud quod est eius similitudo, et hoc habet duas differentias, quia illa similitudo aut est ipsa essentia videntis, ut cum anima videt aliam per se ipsam; secunda differentia cum similitudo est essentialiter in vidente, ut cum video caritatem tuam per meam.

Tertium genus visionis est cum aliquod intelligibile videtur per aliud quod est eius effectus, et hoc habet duas differentias, prima est cum effectus est essentialiter in vidente, ut anima per gratiam videt Deum sive ⟨per⟩ irradiationem; secunda differentia est cum effectus est extra, ut anima per creaturas videt Deum.

Quartum genus est cum aliquod sensibile videtur per speciem intelligibilem, et hoc habet duas differentias, prima est quia illa species intelligibilis prius imprimitur ipsi intelligibili, sicut est in tertio genere visionis intellectua-

177–179 Cf. AH, p. 1360, n. 44, lin. 8–13 et n. 46, lin. 18–19 **181–183** Cf. AH, p. 1360, n. 44, lin. 8–13 et n. 46, lin. 18–19 **182–183** Richardus a S. Victore *Ben. maior*, I, 4, c. 67D **184–187** Cf. AH, p. 1361, n. 49, lin. 18–22 **185** xii] xvii **188–193** Cf. AH, pp. 1360–1361, n. 48, lin. 26–14 **190** Gregorius Magnus *Mor.*, 18, 54, 89, p. 952 **193–196** Cf. AH, p. 1362, n. 51–52, lin. 4–18 **198–210** Cf. AH, p. 1353, n. 23, lin. 7–19 **201** ab *iter.* **210** sive] vel *d. del.*

lis; alia differentia est cum recipitur ab inferiori vi, et hec est ultima differentia. Visio igitur raptus est secundum tres primas differentias, visio autem intellectualis prophetie est in effectu qui est irradiatio, visio contemplationis in effectu qui est gratia vel creatura. Et sic patent quesita.

⟨f. 14vb⟩ Queritur de differentia soporis ad raptum. Et videtur quod idem modus sit videndi, quia nec in sopore nec in raptu est operatio cognitive.

Item, super illud Genesim II «Immisit Dominus soporem» etc. Glosa «Extasis illa ad hoc immissa est ut mens ⟨Ade⟩ intrans in sanctuarium Dei novissima intelligeret» etc.; set hoc est in raptu etc.

Item, de visione Ioannis cum dormivit supra pectus Domini, utrum fuerit raptus vel sopor questio est.

⟨q. 7⟩ Queritur etiam quis limpidius viderit, utrum Paulus vel Ioannes. Quod Ioannes videtur Agustinus «Transcendit nebulam qua omnis terra tegitur et pervenit ad celum,» scilicet deitatis claritatem. Videtur ergo quod consimilis.

Item, quod limpidior «Divinitatis potentiam sublimius omnibus contemplans, cum Domino ad celum volans, celestis sapientie austum de dominici pectoris fonte limpidius ceteris potavit»; ergo limpidius vidit quam Paulus.

Contra: Paulus fuit raptus usque ad tertiam ierarchiam, que limpidius ceteris videt etc. …

220–232 Cf. AH, pp. 1362–1363, n. 53–54, lin. 23–6 **222–224** Cf. *Glossa in Gen*, 2, 21 (Rusch *Biblia*, I, p. 24b) ex Augustino *De Gen. ad litt.*, 9, 19 **222** Gen 2,21 **225** Cf. Joh 13,23 **228–229** Augustinus *De consensu Evang.*, I, 4, 7, 43, p. 6 **230–232** Augustinus *In Ioan.*, praefatio incerti auctoris, c. 1378

BIBLIOGRAFIA

Manoscritti

Assisi, Biblioteca comunale, Fondo antico 138.
Assisi, Biblioteca comunale, Fondo antico 186.
Douai, Bibliothèque municipale, 434, III.

Fonti

AH
Magistri Alexandri de Hales Quaestiones disputatae ‹Antequam esset frater›, q. LXVIII: *De raptu Pauli*, ed. PP. Collegii S. Bonaventurae (Bibl. Franc. schol. Medii Aevi 21), 19, Quaracchi 1960, 1345–1363.

AUGUSTINUS *De Gen. ad litt.*
AUGUSTINUS HIPPONENSIS: *De Genesi ad litteram libri duodecim*, ed. IOSEPHUS ZYCHA (CSEL 28/1), Pragae/Vindobonae/Lipsiae 1894.

AUGUSTINUS *De consensu Evang.*
AUGUSTINUS HIPPONENSIS: *De consensu evangelistarum libri quattuor*, ed. FRANCISCUS WEIHRICH (CSEL 43), Vindobonae/Lipsiae 1904.

AUGUSTINUS *In Ioan.*
AUGUSTINUS HIPPONENSIS: *In Ioannis Evangelium tractatus CXXIV. Praefatio incerti auctoris* (PL 35) 1377–1380.

BONAVENTURA DE BALNEOREGIO
S. Bonaventurae Opera omnia, I-X, ed. PP. Collegii a S. Bonaventura, Ad Claras Aquas 1882–1902.

GREGORIUS MAGNUS
Sancti Gregorii Magni Moralia in Iob, ed. MARCUS ADRIAEN (CChr.SL 143A), Turnhout 1979.

GA
Magistri Guillelmi Altissiodorensis Summa aurea liber III, *tomus* II, *tract.* XXXVII: *De raptu in Deum*, ed. JEAN RIBAILLIER (SpicBon 18B), Paris/Grottaferrata 1986, 698–712.

PETRUS LOMBARDUS
Petri Lombardi Collectaneorum in Epistolas S. Pauli, In Epistolam II ad Corinthios (PL 192) 9–94.

RICHARDUS A S. VICTORE
RICHARDUS A S. VICTORE: *Beniamin maior* (PL 196) 64–202.

RUSCH *Biblia*
Biblia latina cum glossa ordinaria, Facsimile reprint of the Editio Princeps, Adolph Rusch of Strassburg 1480–1481, I-IV, introduction by MARGARET GIBSON, KARL FROEHLICH, Turnhout 1992.

Letteratura secondaria

DISTELBRINK 1975
BALDUINUS DISTELBRINK: *Bonaventurae scripta authentica dubia vel spuria critice recensita*, Roma 1975.

DOUCET 1948
Alexandri de Hales ... Summa Theologica ... IV/3 (*Prolegomena cur.* VICTORIN DOUCET), Quaracchi 1948.

BRADY 1973
IGNATIUS BRADY: «S. Bonaventura alunno della scuola francescana di Parigi», in *L'uomo Bonaventura.* Atti del XIII Incontro al Cenacolo bonaventuriano dell'Oasi Maria Immacolata di Montecalvo Irpino (Incontri Bonaventuriani 9), Montecalvo Irpino 1973, 63–74.

HENQUINET 1932
FRANÇOIS-MARIE HENQUINET: «Un recueil de questions annoté par S. Bonaventure», in *AFH 25* (1932) 553–555.

HENQUINET 1932–1933
FRANÇOIS-MARIE HENQUINET: «Un brouillon autographe de S. Bonaventure sur le Commentaire des Sentences», in *EtFr 44* (1932) 633–655; *45* (1933) 59–81.

HENQUINET 1947
FRANÇOIS-MARIE HENQUINET: «Trois petits écrits théologiques de Saint Bonaventure à la lumière d'un quatrième inédit», in *Mélanges Auguste Pelzer*, Louvain 1947, 195–216.

LIO 1966
ERMENEGILDO LIO: *S. Bonaventura e la questione autografa «De superfluo» contenuta nel ms. di Assisi, Bibl. Com. 186, citata al Conc. Vat. II*, Roma 1966.

QUINTO 1996
RICCARDO QUINTO: «Il codice 434 di Douai, Stefano Langton e Nicola di Tournai», in *SE 36* (1996) 233–361.

TORRELL 1992
JEAN-PIERRE TORRELL: «Un ‹De Prophetia› de saint Bonaventure? (Assise, Bibl. com. 186). Édition critique, avec introduction et notes», in IDEM: *Recherches sur la théorie de la prophétie au Moyen Âge* XIIe-XIVe *siècles. Études et textes* (Dokimion 13), Fribourg/Suisse 1992, 251–317.

WICKI 1954
NIKOLAUS WICKI: *Die Lehre von der himmlischen Seligkeit in der mittelalterlichen Scholastik von Petrus Lombardus bis Thomas von Aquin*, Freiburg (Schweiz) 1954 (Studia Friburgensia NF 9).

Archa Verbi 1 (2004) 91–118

Die glossierten Bibeln des Bamberger Doms im 12. und 13. Jahrhundert

von Matthias M. Tischler

Die Erforschung der vornehmlich hochmittelalterlichen glossierten Bibeln, der neben den frühesten theologischen Summen wohl wichtigsten Neuentwicklung der frühscholastischen Schulpraxis in den nordfranzösischen Dom- und Stiftsschulen des ausgehenden 11. und früheren 12. Jahrhunderts, steckt trotz erster Ergebnisse etwa durch Beryl Smalley[1] und Margaret Gibson[2] noch in den Anfängen. Eine schrittweise Erschließung einzelner zentraler Bestände glossierter Bibeln nach kodikologischen, paläographischen, kunst- und textgeschichtlichen Kriterien ist daher wünschenswert, vermag doch erst diese eine wesentliche Grundlage der hochmittelalterlichen Exegesepraxis zum Sprechen zu bringen. Daher sollen in unregelmäßigen Abständen kritisch gesichtete Überblicke über die Verteilung, Provenienzen und Entstehungszeiten glossierter Bibelbücher in herausragenden europäischen Handschriftensammlungen veröffentlicht werden, deren Ergebnisse in eine gemeinsame internationale Datenbank zur sog. ›Glossa ordinaria‹ einfließen können.

Eine vorzüglich überlieferte Sammlung wie die des Bamberger Doms, deren hoher Stellenwert für die Erforschung der Bibelglosse etwa in Friedrich Stegmüllers *Repertorium biblicum* noch nicht erkannt ist,[3] kann zudem einen beispielhaften Eindruck davon vermitteln, mit welcher Intensität, aber auch mit welcher zeitlichen Verzögerung vor allem gegenüber den Pariser Schulen in Saint-Victor oder Notre-Dame ein Bildungszentrum der deutschsprachigen Peripherie zeitgenössische glossierte Bibelcodices hauptsächlich französischer Provenienz bis zum Anfang des 13. Jahrhunderts rezipierte und die eigene Sammlung etwa ab dem 3. Viertel des 12. Jahrhunderts durch heimische Produkte ergänzte.[4]

Die Bamberger Handschriften sind im folgenden nach dem heute gültigen Bibelkanon sowie bei Mehrfachüberlieferung pro Bibelbuch nach chronologischen Kriterien angeordnet. Die Bestimmung ihrer Provenienzen und Entstehungszeiten ergibt sich aus dem Vergleich mit gesichertem nordfranzösi-

1 Vgl. Smalley 1935–1936; Smalley 1937; Smalley 1984.

2 Vgl. Gibson 1992a; Gibson 1992b.

3 Vgl. Stegmüller 1977, S. 465–556 Nr. 11781–11854, wo kein einziger Bamberger Codex verzeichnet ist. Erwähnt ist lediglich Msc. Bibl. 123 in Stegmüller 1954, S. 337 Nr. 6654–6668.

4 Die folgende Übersicht ist das Teilergebnis eines von der DFG 1999–2001 finanzierten Forschungsprojektes zur Bamberger Domschule im 12. und 13. Jahrhundert. Die Autopsie führte zur partiellen Revision der nahezu ausschließlich mit kunstgeschichtlichen Argumenten unterfütterten Forschungsergebnisse von Suckale-Redlefsen 1995.

schen bzw. Pariser, ferner italienischem sowie originär Bamberger Handschriftenmaterial; die Datierungen leiten sich von der von Christopher de Hamel[5] und Guy Lobrichon[6] rekonstruierten Entwicklungsgeschichte der Seitengestaltung der glossierten Bibeln des 12. und 13. Jahrhunderts und ihrer Kriterien ab.[7]

ALTES TESTAMENT[8]

Gn Msc. Bibl. 29 * Paris * 1160–1180[9]
Ex Msc. Bibl. 31 * Paris * 1160–1180[10]
Lv Msc. Bibl. 32 * Paris * 1160–1180[11]

5 Vgl. DE HAMEL 1984, S. 14–27.

6 Vgl. LOBRICHON 1984, S. 97–103.

7 Hinsichtlich der Seitenschemata wird im folgenden vom ›Laoneser Modell‹ (1.), vom ›Pariser Modell seit 1130‹ (2.) und vom ›System der alternierenden Zeilen‹ (3.) die Rede sein. Zu (1.): Hier ist der Bibeltext in größerer Schrift als Haupttextkolumne in der Seitenmitte geschrieben, während die Glosse in kleinerer Schrift marginal in den beiden Seitenspalten, deren Liniierungsschemata sich nicht am Zeilenspiegel der Haupttextkolumne orientieren, sowie auch interlinear eingebracht ist. Da die Randglossen manchmal sehr lang sind, müssen sie auf dem nicht vorausberechneten Glossenraum oft zusammengequetscht und vom seitlichen Rand zum unteren Seitenbereich weitergeführt werden. Bei kurzen Marginalglossen bleiben größere Bereiche des Randes unbeschrieben, die allenfalls für spätere Ergänzungen genutzt werden können. Zu (2.): Dieses Seitenmodell ist der Versuch, die oftmals unästhetische und vor allem unökonomische Seitengestaltung des älteren ›Laoneser Modells‹ zu überwinden, indem die Marginalglosse innerhalb der Glossenspalten aus Platzersparnisgründen immer häufiger auf mehrere schmale Kolumnen aufgeteilt wird. Der Haupttext wird unverändert links und rechts von jeweils einem Glossenraum umrahmt, jedoch pendeln sich die Zeilenzahlen von Haupt- und Glossentexten nun auf ein Verhältnis von 1 : 2 ein. Zu (3.): Unter dem Einfluß der Neuorganisation der *magna glosatura* des Petrus Lombardus in den Pariser Buchwerkstätten (vgl. unten Anm. 45) entsteht ein Liniierungssystem, bei dem die Zeilenziehung für den Haupttext und die Glossenspalten in einem einzigen Arbeitsgang vorgenommen wird. Auch der Schreibvorgang wird ökonomisiert und erfolgt in einem Zuge. Der in größerer Schrift kopierte Bibeltext von unterschiedlicher Länge und Kolumnenbreite wird nun immer zwischen zwei Zeilen gesetzt, während die nach wie vor in kleinerer Schrift angefertigte Glosse auf jeder dieser Zeilen zu stehen kommt, so daß das maximale Zeilenverhältnis zwischen Haupt- und Glossentext 1 : 2 beträgt.

8 Die Bibelbücher sind mit den Siglen der Vulgata-Ausgabe von *Biblia Vulgata*, S. XXXI, gekennzeichnet. Die römischen Ziffern I und II hinter der Signatur zeigen den Handschriftenteil an. Eine nähere Untersuchung der jeweiligen Textzustände der einzelnen Glossae mußte aus Zeitgründen unterbleiben. Erst sie kann die Textgenese aufdecken und die chronologische Ordnung der einzelnen Überlieferungsträger sichern.

9 Vgl. SUCKALE-REDLEFSEN 1995, S. 87 Kat. Nr. 84 und Tafel VI (von f. 4r). Schriftraum: ca. 21,5 x 12 cm * Zeilenverhältnis Haupttext : Glosse = 1 : 2 (max. 22 : 44 Zeilen) * Seitenschema: ›System der alternierenden Zeilen‹.

10 Vgl. SUCKALE-REDLEFSEN 1995, S. 84 f. Kat. Nr. 80 und S. 169 Abb. 199 (von f. 1r). Schriftraum: ca. 21,5 x 13 cm * Zeilenverhältnis Haupttext : Glosse = 1 : 2 (max. 22 : 44 Zeilen) * Seitenschema: ›System der alternierenden Zeilen‹.

11 Vgl. SUCKALE-REDLEFSEN 1995, S. 85 Kat. Nr. 81 und S. 169 Abb. 200 (von f. 2r). Schriftraum: ca. 21,5 x 12,5 cm * Zeilenverhältnis Haupttext : Glosse = 1 : 2 (max. 22 : 44 Zeilen) * Seitenschema: ›System der alternierenden Zeilen‹.

Dt	Msc. Bibl. 35 * Paris * 1160–1180[12]
Ios	Msc. Bibl. 36 * Nordfrankreich * 1160–1180
Idc	Msc. Bibl. 36 * Nordfrankreich * 1160–1180[13]
I Sm–IV Rg	Msc. Bibl. 39 * Bamberg * 1. Viertel des 13. Jahrhunderts[14]
Iob	Msc. Bibl. 15, I * Bamberg * 3. Viertel des 12. Jahrhunderts[15]
Ps	Msc. Bibl. 46 * Italien (vermutlich Pisa) * 1170–1180[16]
Prv	Msc. Bibl. 69 * Laon * vor 1135–1140[17]
Ecl	Msc. Bibl. 69 * Laon * vor 1135–1140[18]
Is	Msc. Bibl. 77 * Nordfrankreich * 2. Viertel des 12. Jahrhunderts[19]
Ier	Msc. Bibl. 82 * Paris * letztes Viertel des 12. Jahrhunderts[20]
Lam	Msc. Bibl. 82 * Paris * letztes Viertel des 12. Jahrhunderts[21]
	Msc. Bibl. 81 * Bamberg * 1. Viertel des 13. Jahrhunderts[22]
Ez	Msc. Bibl. 83 * Paris * letztes Viertel des 12. Jahrhunderts[23]
Dn	Msc. Bibl. 86 * Paris * 1. Viertel des 13. Jahrhunderts[24]

12 Vgl. SUCKALE-REDLEFSEN 1995, S. 86 f. Kat. Nr. 83 und S. 170 Abb. 203 und 207 (von f. 1r und 74v). Schriftraum: ca. 20 x 13 cm * Zeilenverhältnis Haupttext : Glosse = 1 : 2 (max. 21 : 42 Zeilen) * Seitenschema: ›System der alternierenden Zeilen‹.

13 Schriftraum: ca. 19 x 13 cm * Zeilenverhältnis Haupttext: Glosse = 1 : 2 (max. 22 : 44 Zeilen) * Seitenschema: ›System der alternierenden Zeilen‹. Msc. Bibl. 36 ist bei SUKKALE-REDLEFSEN 1995, nicht berücksichtigt.

14 Schriftraum: ca. 21 x 13,5 cm * Zeilenverhältnis Haupttext : Glosse = 1 : 2 (max. 23 : 46 Zeilen) * Seitenschema: ›System der alternierenden Zeilen‹.

15 Vgl. SUCKALE-REDLEFSEN 1995, S. 37 Kat. Nr. 37. Haupttext max. 21 Zeilen * Seitenschema: ›Laoneser Modell‹.

16 Vgl. SUCKALE-REDLEFSEN 1995, S. 96 f. Kat. Nr. 92, Tafel VIII (von f. 1v) und S. 174 Abb. 224–229 (von f. 236r, 202v, 243r, 251v, 125r und 169v). Haupttext max. 15 Zeilen * Seitenschema: ›Pariser Modell seit 1130‹.

17 Vgl. SUCKALE-REDLEFSEN 1995, S. 79 Kat. Nr. 75 und S. 167 Abb. 188 f. (von f. 1v und 3v).

18 Vgl. SUCKALE-REDLEFSEN 1995, S. 79 Kat. Nr. 75. Haupttext max. 20 Zeilen * Seitenschema: ›Laoneser Modell‹.

19 Haupttext max. 15 Zeilen * Seitenschema: ›Pariser Modell seit 1130‹. Diese Handschrift ist bei SUCKALE-REDLEFSEN 1995, nicht berücksichtigt, da sie nicht illuminiert wurde.

20 Vgl. FRIED 1986, S. 173 Anm. 64; SUCKALE-REDLEFSEN 1995, S. 87 f. Kat. Nr. 85 und S. 170 Abb. 202 (von f. 2v).

21 Vgl. SUCKALE-REDLEFSEN 1995, S. 87 f. Kat. Nr. 85 und S. 170 Abb. 205 f. (von f. 143v und 156r). Schriftraum: ca. 21,5 x 13,5 cm * Zeilenverhältnis Haupttext : Glosse = 1 : 2 (max. 21 : 42 Zeilen) * Seitenschema: ›System der alternierenden Zeilen‹.

22 Vgl. FRIED 1986, S. 173 mit Anm. 64. Schriftraum: ca. 22,5 x 15,5 cm * Zeilenverhältnis Haupttext : Glosse = 1 : 3 (max. 13 : 39 Zeilen) * Seitenschema: ›System der alternierenden Zeilen‹.

23 Vgl. SUCKALE-REDLEFSEN 1995, S. 88 f. Kat. Nr. 86 und S. 170 Abb. 204 (von f. 1r). Schriftraum: ca. 21,5 x 13 cm * Zeilenverhältnis Haupttext : Glosse = 1 : 2 (max. 23 : 46 Zeilen) * Seitenschema: ›System der alternierenden Zeilen‹.

24 Schriftraum: ca. 17,5 x 12,5 cm * Zeilenverhältnis Haupttext : Glosse = 1 : 2 (max. 17 : 34 Zeilen) * Seitenschema: ›System der alternierenden Zeilen‹.

NEUES TESTAMENT

Mt	Msc. Bibl. 107 * Nordfrankreich (Paris?) und Italien * Mitte des 12. Jahrhunderts[25]
	Msc. Bibl. 15, II * Bamberg * 3. Viertel des 12. Jahrhunderts[26]
	Msc. Bibl. 108 * Bamberg * 3. Viertel des 12. Jahrhunderts[27]
	Msc. Bibl. 106 * Paris * 1. Viertel des 13. Jahrhunderts[28]
Mc	Msc. Bibl. 99, I * Italien * 3. Viertel des 12. Jahrhunderts[29]
	Msc. Bibl. 98, I * Bamberg * 1. Viertel des 13. Jahrhunderts[30]
Lc	Msc. Bibl. 112 * Bamberg * 3. Viertel des 12. Jahrhunderts[31]
	Msc. Bibl. 113 * Paris * 1. Viertel des 13. Jahrhunderts[32]
Io	Msc. Bibl. 117 * Nordfrankreich * 2. Viertel des 12. Jahrhunderts[33]
	Msc. Bibl. 99, II * Bamberg * 3. Viertel des 12. Jahrhunderts[34]
	Msc. Bibl. 98, II * Bamberg * 1. Viertel des 13. Jahrhunderts[35]
Rm–Hbr	Msc. Bibl. 122 (ohne Glosse) * Bamberg * 3. Viertel des 12. Jahrhunderts[36]
	Msc. Bibl. 123 (Petrus Lombardus) * Paris * 1. Viertel des 13. Jahrhunderts[37]

25 Vgl. SUCKALE-REDLEFSEN 1995, S. 98 Kat. Nr. 93 und S. 173 Abb. 220 (von f. 5r). Bei WEISWEILER 1960, S. 365, S. 368 Anm. 17, S. 376 Anm. 9 und S. 529 f., ist die Handschrift zu spät ins 13. Jahrhundert datiert. Haupttext max. 14 Zeilen * Seitenschema: ›Laoneser Modell‹.

26 Vgl. SUCKALE-REDLEFSEN 1995, S. 37 Kat. Nr. 37 und S. 135 Abb. 91 (von f. 76r). Haupttext max. 20 Zeilen * Seitenschema: ›Laoneser Modell‹.

27 Haupttext max. 23 Zeilen * Seitenschema: ›Laoneser Modell‹. Diese Handschrift ist bei SUCKALE-REDLEFSEN 1995, nicht berücksichtigt, da sie nicht illuminiert wurde.

28 Vgl. WEISWEILER 1960, S. 368 Anm. 17 und S. 376 Anm. 9. Schriftraum: ca. 21 x 14,5 cm * Zeilenverhältnis Haupttext : Glosse = 1 : 2 (max. 21 : 42 Zeilen) * Seitenschema: ›System der alternierenden Zeilen‹.

29 Haupttext max. 20 Zeilen * Seitenschema: ›Pariser Modell seit 1130‹ (vgl. mehrspaltige Marginalglosse auf f. 12r und 15v).

30 Schriftraum: ca. 19 x 13 cm * Zeilenverhältnis Haupttext : Glosse = 1 : 2 (max. 22 : 44 Zeilen) * Seitenschema: ›System der alternierenden Zeilen‹.

31 Vgl. SUCKALE-REDLEFSEN 1995, S. 26 Kat. Nr. 25 und S. 128 Abb. 65 f. (von f. 3v und 4r). Haupttext max. 18 Zeilen * Seitenschema: ›Laoneser Modell‹.

32 Schriftraum: ca. 19,5 x 14,5 cm * Zeilenverhältnis Haupttext : Glosse = 1 : 2 (max. 17 : 34 Zeilen) * Seitenschema: ›System der alternierenden Zeilen‹.

33 Vgl. SUCKALE-REDLEFSEN 1995, S. 80 f. Kat. Nr. 77 und S. 167 Abb. 192 f. (von f. 3r und 1r). Haupttext max. 13 Zeilen * Seitenschema: ›Pariser Modell seit 1130‹.

34 Haupttext max. 27 Zeilen * Seitenschema: ›Laoneser Modell‹. Msc. Bibl. 99 ist bei SUCKALE-REDLEFSEN 1995, nicht berücksichtigt, da beide Handschriftenteile nicht illuminiert wurden.

35 Schriftraum: ca. 19,5 x 13 cm * Zeilenverhältnis Haupttext : Glosse = 1 : 2 (max. 22 : 44 Zeilen) * Seitenschema: ›System der alternierenden Zeilen‹.

36 Vgl. SUCKALE-REDLEFSEN 1995, S. 48 f. Kat. Nr. 52 und S. 139 f. Abb. 107–111 (von f. 2v, 4r, 97r, 163v und 177r). Vorgesehener Schriftraum: ca. 20 x 15 cm * max. 20 Zeilen Haupttext.

37 Schriftraum: ca. 24,5 x 16,5 cm bzw. 24,5 x 7,5–8 cm * Zeilenverhältnis Haupttext : Glosse = 1 : 2 (max. 25 : 50 Zeilen).

Iac–Iud Msc. Bibl. 135 * Laon * 1. Drittel des 12. Jahrhunderts[38]
Msc. Bibl. 134 * Nordfrankreich (Paris?) * Mitte des 12. Jahrhunderts.[39]

Die Geschichte der glossierten Bibeln des Bamberger Doms war lange Zeit kaum näher zu skizzieren, da die frühesten Exemplare ausnahmslos nordfranzösischer Provenienz aufgrund der Ende des 19. Jahrhunderts noch unzureichenden Kenntnisse über die Entwicklung und Verbreitung gotischer Minuskeln von dem Bamberger Bibliothekar Friedrich Leitschuh allesamt irrtümlich ins 13. Jahrhundert gewiesen wurden.[40] Dabei sind noch heute sechs frühe, bis zur Mitte des 12. Jahrhunderts entstandene glossierte Bibeln des Bamberger Doms mit zum Teil prominenter Herkunft nachweisbar. Die schönste Neuentdeckung dürfte sicher Msc. Bibl. 135, ein handlicher Codex mit den glossierten Kanonischen Briefen, sein, der, nach dem frühgotischen Schrifttyp zu schließen, mit hoher Wahrscheinlichkeit während des 1. Drittels des 12. Jahrhunderts in Laon entstanden ist.[41] Aufgrund des zeitgenössischen Besitzeintrags auf f. 1r oben (*Iste liber est ⟨domnorum maioris ecclesie in babenberga⟩*) muß die Handschrift recht bald an den Bamberger Dom gekommen sein (Abb. 1). Auch Msc. Bibl. 69, ein Codex mit glossierten Prv und Ecl, ist in der nordfranzösischen Kathedralstadt entstanden. Jedoch kam für seine Herstellung, die Patricia Stirnemann auf vor 1135–1140 ansetzt,[42] bereits der auch aus anderen Laoneser Handschriften bekannte, stilisierte jüngere Schrifttyp zur Anwendung. Die Handschrift ist in Bamberg schon recht bald benutzt worden, wie die ausführlichen marginalen Ergänzungen z. B. auf f. 2r, 3r, 14v, 61v–62r, 66r, 67r und 72v, dann auch bisweilen in der Glosse des Haupttextschreibers (z.B. f. 3v–4r) zeigen. Beide Laoneser Handschriften weisen noch das traditionelle heimische Seitenschema glossierter Bibeln ohne Feingliederung der Marginalglosse auf.

Aus dem zweiten Jahrhundertviertel stammen ferner zwei noch nicht näher lokalisierbare nordfranzösische Codices: zum einen der glossierte Is Msc. Bibl. 77, der noch in seinem nichtilluminierten Rohzustand vorliegt, und zum anderen das glossierte Io-Evangelium Msc. Bibl. 117. Das kleine Format dieses Evangeliums und die exquisiten, mit Tinte und Feder gezeichneten Initialen *H* (f. 1r) und *I* (f. 3r) verweisen auf ein vorzügliches Skriptorium. Datierung

38 Haupttext max. 18 Zeilen * Seitenschema: ›Laoneser Modell‹. Diese Handschrift ist bei Suckale-Redlefsen 1995, nicht berücksichtigt, da sie nicht illuminiert wurde.

39 Vgl. Suckale-Redlefsen 1995, S. 35 Kat. Nr. 34 und S. 134 Abb. 86 f. (von f. 3r und 17r). Haupttext max. 15 Zeilen * Seitenschema: ›Laoneser Modell‹.

40 Vgl. Leitschuh 1887.

41 Die Handschrift weist nämlich noch den älteren, gedrungenen Laoneser Schrifttyp mit einer links eingekerbten *ct*-Ligatur als Ohrmarke auf. Zum Vergleich können herangezogen werden die wohl etwas älteren Laoneser glossierten Handschriften Paris, Bibliothèque nationale de France, Ms. lat. 14625, f. A–C (Iob-Fragmente) und Laon, Bibliothèque municipale, Ms. 74, I–II (Mt und Ct).

42 Vgl. Stirnemann 1994, S. 260–262; Stirnemann 1997, S. 85 mit Anm. 5.

und Lokalisierung dieser beiden zuletzt genannten Handschriften lassen sich insofern verfeinern, als sie bereits die mehrspaltige Gliederung der Marginalglosse aufweisen, die seit den 1130er Jahren offensichtlich in Paris entwickelt wurde (Msc. Bibl. 77 noch zögerlich nur auf f. 1v; Abb. 2). Zur Gruppe der frühesten auswärtigen glossierten Bibeln am Bamberger Dom treten schließlich noch das um die Jahrhundertmitte vielleicht in Paris geschriebene rohe Textkorpus der glossierten Kanonischen Briefe Msc. Bibl. 134, das erst nach seiner Ankunft in Bamberg illuminiert wurde, und das glossierte Mt-Evangelium Msc. Bibl. 107 (mit dem auf f. 1va–3ra überlieferten sog. Matthäuskommentar von Valenciennes). Größe und Anlage der Seiten (bereits mit Bleiliniierung) nähern Msc. Bibl. 134 dem eben behandelten Msc. Bibl. 117 an. Auffallend ist hier die für Haupttext und Glosse verwendete leicht linksschräge frühe gotische Minuskel, die auch bisweilen im Bestand der zeitgleichen glossierten Viktoriner Bibeln anzutreffen ist.[43] Die Glosse des Codex ist noch nach dem konservativen ›Laoneser Modell‹ organisiert. Auch bei Msc. Bibl. 107 sprechen das Quartformat, die frühe gotische Minuskel des Haupttextes und das gleichfalls anzutreffende ›Laoneser Modell‹ der Seitengestaltung für ein vermutlich Pariser Skriptorium der Jahrhundertmitte. Im Gegensatz zu Msc. Bibl. 134 wurden hier die Initialen etwas später in Italien eingebracht, bevor die Handschrift in die Bamberger Domkapitelbibliothek gelangte, wo sie mit Sicherheit im 13. Jahrhundert lag (vgl. f. 1r oben: ¶ *Matheus glosatus . et est domnorum maioris ecclesie in Babenberga .*).

Wir sind mit unseren Betrachtungen an der Mitte des 12. Jahrhunderts angekommen. Eine bemerkenswerte Momentaufnahme der traditionellen Glossierungspraxis in Bamberg noch während des 3. Viertels des 12. Jahrhunderts liefert Msc. Bibl. 122. Diese in Bamberg in einer spätromanischen Minuskel anfertigte Handschrift mit den Paulusbriefen sollte nämlich links bzw. rechts des jeweils in einer Innenspalte mit großem Zeilenabstand geschriebenen Haupttextes die Marginalglosse in einem genauso breiten unliniierten Schriftraum aufnehmen (Abb. 3).[44] Dieses für die Entstehungszeit des Codex relativ antiquierte Modell der Seitengestaltung ist noch dem traditionellen Glossierungsschema der reorganisierten Gilbert Porreta-Handschriften verpflichtet und verrät keine Kenntnis der durch die *magna glosatura* des Petrus Lombardus in Paris ausgelösten Neuorganisation der glossierten Psalter- und Paulinenhandschriften seit etwa 1160.[45]

Dieser Befund einer recht konservativen Glossierungspraxis gilt auch für alle weiteren wohl in Bamberg während des 3. Viertels des 12. Jahrhunderts hergestellten, auffallend kleinerformatigen glossierten Bibeln, so etwa für Msc. Bibl. 15, I und Msc. Bibl. 15, II, eine von Friedrich Leitschuh zu spät ins 13. Jahrhundert datierte glossierte Iob-Handschrift, hinter die ein ebenso zu

43 Vgl. Paris, Bibliothèque nationale de France, Ms. lat. 14399, 14403, 14406, 14408, 14771, 14772, II, 14780, 14784 und 14789.

44 Das Doppelblatt f. 1r–2v ist eine nahezu zeitgleiche Ergänzung, die auf f. 1r das Argument, auf f. 1r–2r den Prolog des Hieronymus zu den Paulusbriefen und auf f. 2v eine ganzseitige Federzeichnung mit Paulus und den Empfängern seiner Briefe enthält.

45 Vgl. hierzu de Hamel 1984, S. 18–24.

spät angesetztes glossiertes Mt-Evangelium derselben Zeitstellung gebunden wurde. Der auf f. 73v–74v stehende Prolog zu Mt und die dazugehörige Glosse auf f. 73v–75r sind von einer einzigen frühgotischen Hand des 3. Viertels des 12. Jahrhunderts geschrieben. Diese hat auch den Beginn und weitere einzelne Passagen der Mt-Glosse geschrieben, während der Haupttext und die übrige Glosse von einer spätromanischen Bamberger Hand stammen. Die beiderseitige Glossierung endet auf f. 100r (Abb. 4); ab hier wird nur noch die Interlinearglosse weitergeführt. Die auf f. 76r am Anfang des Evangeliums stehende, mit brauner und roter Tinte federgezeichnete Ranken-Initiale mit dem Evangelisten Matthäus, der auf einem Hund steht, gehört in dieselbe Zeit. Zu dieser Gruppe traditionell glossierter Bamberger Bibelbücher aus dem 3. Viertel des 12. Jahrhunderts zählen ferner Msc. Bibl. 108, ein von Friedrich Leitschuh erneut zu spät ins 13. Jahrhundert datiertes, bis heute ungeschmücktes Mt-Evangelium (Abb. 5), dann Msc. Bibl. 112, ein glossiertes Lc-Evangelium, und Msc. Bibl. 99, II, ein von Leitschuh ebenso ins 13. Jahrhundert verwiesenes glossiertes Io-Evangelium (Abb. 6; mit dem Prolog und dem Beginn des Argumentum zum Mc-Evangelium auf f. 86r–87v), das hinter ein im 3. Viertel des 12. Jahrhunderts in Italien kopiertes glossiertes Mc-Evangelium (Abb. 7) gebunden worden ist.

Die bislang genannten Handschriften zeugen von den frühscholastischen Bemühungen am Bamberger Dom, ab dem dritten Viertel des 12. Jahrhunderts wie in den großen französischen Buchzentren eine eigene glossierte Bibelausgabe herzustellen. Dieses Projekt wird vermutlich seinen Befürworter in dem frühscholastisch gebildeten Bischof Eberhard II. von Bamberg (1146–1170)[46] gehabt haben. Dieser bei Johannes Fried 1986 noch nicht erkannte Aspekt der Bamberger Frühscholastik[47] ist das komplementäre Element zu den seit dieser Zeit verstärkt beobachtbaren Importen glossierter auswärtiger, vor allem nordfranzösischer Bibeln nach Bamberg. Ein interner Innovationsschub in der Bamberger Glossierungstechnik ist freilich während der frühen zweiten Jahrhunderthälfte noch nicht erkennbar. Dieser wurde anscheinend durch die Beschaffung neuester ausländischer Handschriftenmodelle ermöglicht, wie sie etwa die glossierte italienische Ps-Handschrift Msc. Bibl. 46 oder Msc. Bibl. 29, 31, 32 und 35, eine eigene Untergruppe glossierter Pentateuch-Bücher, repräsentieren. Der exquisite Psalter, der noch die ursprüngliche Glossa aufweist, stammt vermutlich aus Pisa und ist zwischen 1170 und 1180 entstanden. Seine Marginalglosse ist jedoch bereits nach Pariser Vorbild mehrspaltig organisiert. Nach dem auf f. 1v oben eingetragenen zeitgenössischen Exlibris (*Liber domnorum maioris ecclesie* .) gehörte der Codex schon recht bald

46 Vgl. Guttenberg 1937, S. 142; Hausmann 1959, S. 226; Meyer 1964, S. 346–353; Guth 1972, S. 342–360; Fried 1986, S. 172 mit Anm. 59 und S. 174 mit Anm. 71.

47 Fried 1986, S. 173 Anm. 64, berücksichtigt mit Msc. Bibl. 81 und 82 überhaupt nur zwei glossierte Bibeln des Doms. Ansonsten erwähnt Fried 1986, S. 189, »die ›Glossa ordinaria‹ zu den Biblischen Büchern, die im 13. Jahrhundert neben anderen Glossen recht vollständig zu greifen ist«, nur kursorisch. Daß dieses auch durch die zahlreichen Fehldatierungen Friedrich Leitschuhs verursachte Bild chronologisch wie inhaltlich ungenau ist, ergibt sich aus den vorliegenden Beobachtungen.

dem Bamberger Domkapitel. Friedrich Leitschuh hat die genannten Msc. Bibl. 29, 31, 32 und 35 ausnahmslos zu spät ins 13. Jahrhundert datiert. Diese vier Bücher sind wohl in einem professionellen Pariser Skriptorium schon zwischen 1160 und 1180 geschrieben und im sog. ›Channel-Style‹ illuminiert worden. Derselbe Haupttext- und Glossenschreiber dürfte auch Rouen, Bibliothèque municipale, Ms. 40 (A. 203) hergestellt haben, das der Magister Stephan von Reims († 1221), wahrscheinlich der Pariser Dekan von 1216–1221, der normannischen Abtei Lyre vermachte.[48] Vermutlich ist die gesamte Bamberger Pentateuch-Gruppe geschlossen angeschafft worden, und man muß nicht mit Gude Suckale-Redlefsen für Msc. Bibl. 35 ein etwas späteres Datum (›4. Viertel 12. Jh.‹) annehmen, da in dieser Handschrift zudem die tintenfarbige (!) Federverzierung bei den Textmajuskeln auf f. 69v (*D*), 71v (*D*) und 74v (*O*) erst nachträglich und nicht besonders professionell vorgenommen wurde. Es ist daher zu fragen, ob diese exquisite Sammlung glossierter Pentateuch-Bücher, der lediglich der Nm-Band fehlt (oder abhanden gekommen ist?), noch unter Bischof Eberhard II. angeschafft worden ist. Bemerkenswert ist in unserer Liste das Fehlen eines glossierten Nm-Bandes (neben Act) auch deshalb, weil nach dem gegenwärtigen Forschungsstand die älteste Überlieferung von Nm (und Act) überhaupt noch nicht näher bestimmt ist. Selbst in einer so vorzüglich erhaltenen Sammlung wie der von Saint-Victor zu Paris stammen beispielsweise die ältesten glossierten Nm-Codices erst vom Anfang bzw. 1. Viertel des 13. Jahrhunderts (Paris, Bibliothèque Mazarine, Ms. 81 und Paris, Bibliothèque Mazarine, Ms. 132).

An den eben behandelten Pentateuch schließt sich die von Friedrich Leitschuh zu spät ins 13. Jahrhundert datierte glossierte Ios- und Idc-Handschrift Msc. Bibl. 36 an. Sie ist in einem dem Pariser Pentateuch-Skriptorium zeitgleichen Schreibermilieu entstanden, das jedoch noch den älteren Schrifttypus einer frühen gotischen Minuskel mit karolingischem *g* für Haupt- und Glossentext zum Einsatz bringt (eine gotische Hand schreibt hingegen den Haupttext f. 68v Z. 4 Mitte – Ende der Seite). Auffallend sind bei dieser Schrift zudem die unten glatt abgeschnittenen Schäfte etwa bei *m* und *n*, die bereits auf die später entwickelte gotische *littera praecisa* verweisen. Die vorgeschlagene Datierung auf 1160–1180 wird durch die blau-rote Silhouetten-Initiale *P* mit frühgotischer rot-blauer Fiederung auf f. 1ra bestätigt. Den ursprünglich unfertig illuminierten Zustand der Handschrift unterstreichen die erst im früheren 13. Jahrhundert wohl in Bamberg hinzugefügte goldene *E*-Initiale auf f. 3r (wo nur die blau-rote Fiederung zeitgenössisch ist; Abb. 8) und die auf f. 61r nachträglich mit Mennige eingefügte *P*-Initiale.

Die Variationsbreite gotischer Schriftformen in den Pariser Skriptorien des letzten Viertels des 12. und des frühen 13. Jahrhunderts bei gleichzeitiger großer Ähnlichkeit der Illuminationsleistungen demonstrieren eindrucksvoll die drei folgenden, kunstgeschichtlich verwandten glossierten Pariser Bibelhandschriften, die jeweils einen großen Propheten des Alten Testaments ent-

48 Vgl. de Hamel 1984, S. 13 und 51 sowie Tafel 15 (von f. 1r); zu vergleichen mit Suckale-Redlefsen 1995, S. 169 Abb. 199.

halten: Während Msc. Bibl. 82 einen in noch relativ runder, gotischer Minuskel geschriebenen glossierten Ier (mit Lam) überliefert, sind der glossierte Ez in Msc. Bibl. 83 und der glossierte Dn in Msc. Bibl. 86 in einer stark gebrochenen gotischen Minuskel bzw. in einer archaisierenden, steif ausgeführten Minuskelschrift (Abb. 9) geschrieben. Alle diese Handschriften weisen selbstverständlich das damals moderne ›System der alternierenden Zeilen‹ auf.

Der Bestand an neuesten glossierten Bibeln in Bamberg ist dann auch im früheren 13. Jahrhundert durch drei weitere Pariser Handschriften aus dem 1. Viertel des 13. Jahrhunderts bereichert worden. Dabei ist bemerkenswert, daß alle drei Bücher mehr oder weniger im nichtilluminierten Rohzustand geliefert wurden, was ihre Anfertigung beschleunigt und auch erschwinglich gehalten haben dürfte. Es handelt sich zum einen um das in einer ausgebildeten gotischen Minuskel geschriebene glossierte Mt-Evangelium Msc. Bibl. 106, bei dem lediglich die roten und blauen Textmajuskeln des Haupttextes ausgeführt worden sind (Abb. 10), ferner um das in einer *littera praecisa* angefertigte glossierte Lc-Evangelium Msc. Bibl. 113, das neben den roten und blauen Textmajuskeln im Haupttext lediglich eine rot-blaue Silhouetten-Initiale *P* mit roter Federverzierung am Anfang des *Pater noster* auf f. 80v aufweist (Abb. 11), und eine partiell bereits mit Tinte liniierte Handschrift mit der *magna glosatura* des Petrus Lombardus zu den Paulinen, Msc. Bibl. 123, bei welcher der Haupttext – wie bereits seit etwa 1170 üblich – jeweils am linken Rand der beiden Spalten portionsweise verteilt und von der umfangreichen Glosse umrahmt ist (Abb. 12).[49] Auch in diesem Codex sind nur im Haupttext und in der Marginalglosse die vergrößerten roten und blauen Textmajuskeln ausgeführt worden, während die Initialen am Beginn eines jeden neuen Paulusbriefes unausgeführt blieben.

Die genannten nordfranzösischen glossierten Bibeln des späten 12. und frühen 13. Jahrhunderts scheinen nach 1200 auch die Bamberger Glossierungspraxis neu befruchtet zu haben. Zu nennen ist in diesem Zusammenhang eine markante Bamberger Hand des 1. Viertels des 13. Jahrhunderts, die zuerst in dem schon erwähnten Msc. Bibl. 36 auf f. 13v Z. 3 Ende–Z. 8, f. 37r Z. 14f., f. 40r Z. 9–15, f. 44v Z. 7f., f. 49r Z. 14–Ende der Seite, f. 51v Z. 22–52r Z. 5, f. 63v Z. 1–7, f. 90v Z. 14–91r Z. 5, f. 96v Z. 1–10 und f. 110r Z. 23–110v Z. 1 sowie an weiteren kleinen Stellen den Haupttext auf Rasur neu geschrieben hat. Diese Hand hat auch im Glossenbereich hier und da Ergänzungen angebracht (vgl. etwa f. 91r oben). Offenkundig bestand zu dieser Zeit das Bedürfnis, auch eine glossierte Handschrift mit den vier Königsbüchern zu besitzen, da der eben genannte Bamberger Schreiber mit Msc. Bibl. 39 ein komplettes rohes Textkorpus hiervon anfertigte (Die Auszeichnung mit rotblauen Silhouetten-Initialen und mit roten und blauen Textmajuskeln ist erst im Spätmittelalter hinzugefügt worden; Abb. 13). Mit fortschreitender Übung tendiert seine Hand in Msc. Bibl. 39 zu verstärkt gotischer Formung des *g* ab f. 89v. Die Tätigkeit dieses interessanten gotischen Bamberger Schreibers, dem man noch seine Suche nach festen Buchstabenformen anmerkt, verbin-

49 Vgl. zu diesem Modell DE HAMEL 1984, S. 22 f. mit Abb. 14 und S. 25.

det die bereits beschriebenen nordfranzösischen Handschriftenimporte mit der heimischen Produktion. Zu letzterer zählt auch Msc. Bibl. 98, eine von Leitschuh bereits korrekt ins 13. Jahrhundert datierte glossierte Mc- und Io-Handschrift, die wohl auch von der Nachtragshand von Msc. Bibl. 36 bzw. von dem Kopisten von Msc. Bibl. 39 in Bamberg während des 1. Viertels des 13. Jahrhunderts geschrieben worden ist. Der Stand der gotischen Schriftentwicklung spricht für eine Herstellung des Mc-Evangeliums vor der Schreibarbeit an Msc. Bibl. 39 (Abb. 14) und für eine Entstehung des Io-Evangeliums eher nach Beendigung von Msc. Bibl. 39 (Abb. 15; das als vordere Schmutzblätter eingebundene Doppelblatt f. 1–2 ist eine Doublette zum Doppelblatt f. 104/107). Ebenso wie bei Msc. Bibl. 39 lag das wohl schon zeitgenössisch zusammengestellte Textkorpus der beiden Evangelien zunächst nur im nichtilluminierten Rohzustand vor. Es besitzt so gut wie keine Lesespuren (vgl. aber f. 15v und 52r).

Weniger prachtvoll und in handlicherem Format ist die glossierte Lam-Handschrift Msc. Bibl. 81 jedoch gleichfalls etwa zu Beginn des 13. Jahrhunderts von einem einzigen Schreiber in Bamberg hergestellt worden. Auch sie war im Haupttext zunächst gänzlich ungeschmückt. Erst im 13. Jahrhundert wurden die rot gestrichelten oder ganz in Rot geschriebenen Rubriken, die rot-blaue Spaltleisten-Initiale *A* auf f. 1v (Abb. 16) und die blaue Textmajuskel *Q* auf f. 28v nachgetragen.

Bibliographie

Biblia Vulgata

Biblia Sacra iuxta Vulgatam Versionem, recensuit Robertus Weber, editionem quartam praeparavit Roger Gryson, Stuttgart 1969, [4]1994.

Fried 1986

Johannes Fried: »Die Bamberger Domschule und die Rezeption von Frühscholastik und Rechtswissenschaft in ihrem Umkreis bis zum Ende der Stauferzeit«, in *Schulen und Studium im sozialen Wandel des hohen und späten Mittelalters* (Vorträge und Forschungen 30), hg. von Johannes Fried, Sigmaringen 1986, 163–201.

Gibson 1992a

Margaret T. Gibson: »The Glossed Bible«, in *Biblia latina cum glossa ordinaria. Facsimile reprint of the editio princeps Adolph Rusch of Strassburg 1480/81* 1, ed. by Karlfried Froehlich/Margaret T. Gibson, Turnhout 1992, VII–XI.

Gibson 1992b

Margaret T. Gibson: »The place of the Glossa ordinaria in medieval exegesis«, in *Ad litteram. Authoritative texts and their medieval readers* (Notre Dame Conferences in Medieval Studies 3), ed. by Mark D. Jordan, Notre Dame (Ind.) 1992, 5–27 [wieder abgedruckt in eadem: *'Artes' and bible in the medieval West* (Collected Studies Series 399), Aldershot 1993, Nr. XV].

Guth 1972

Klaus Guth: »Bischof Eberhard II. (1146–1170) und die Aufnahme der Frühscholastik in Bamberg«, in *FZPhTh 19* (1972) 331–360 [wieder abgedruckt in idem: *Kultur als Lebensform. Aufsätze und Vorträge* 2: Kontinuität und Wandel, St. Ottilien 1997, 13–47].

Guttenberg 1937

Erich von Guttenberg: *Das Bistum Bamberg* 1 (Germania sacra II, 1, 1), Berlin/Leipzig 1937, 141–154.

de Hamel 1984

Christopher F. R. de Hamel: *Glossed books of the bible and the origins of the Paris booktrade*, Woodbridge 1984.

Hausmann 1959

Friedrich Hausmann: »Eberhard II., Bischof von Bamberg«, in *Neue Deutsche Biographie* 4, Berlin 1959, 226f.

Leitschuh 1887

Friedrich Leitschuh: *Katalog der Handschriften der Königlichen Bibliothek zu Bamberg* 1, Bamberg 1887.

Lobrichon 1984

Guy Lobrichon: »Une nouveauté: les gloses de la Bible«, in *Le moyen âge et la Bible* (Bible de tous les temps 4), éd. par Pierre Riché/Guy Lobrichon, Paris 1984, 95–114 [wieder abgedruckt in idem: *La Bible au moyen âge* (Les médiévistes français 3), Paris 2003, 158–172].

Meyer 1964
Otto Meyer: *Bischof Eberhard II. von Bamberg (1146–1170). Mittler im Wandel seiner Zeit* (Neujahrsblätter der Gesellschaft für fränkische Geschichte 29), Würzburg 1964 [wieder abgedruckt als »Bischof Eberhard II. von Bamberg«, in idem: *Varia Franconiae Historica* 1 (MFSt 24/I), Würzburg 1981, 330–356].

Smalley 1935–1936
Beryl Smalley: »Gilbertus Universalis, bishop of London (1128–34), and the problem of the Glossa ordinaria«, in *RThAM 7* (1935) 235–262; *8* (1936) 24–60.

Smalley 1937
Beryl Smalley: »La Glossa ordinaria. Quelques prédécesseurs d'Anselme de Laon«, in *RThAM 9* (1937) 365–400.

Smalley 1984
Beryl Smalley: »Glossa ordinaria«, in *TRE* 13, Berlin/New York 1984, 452–457.

Stegmüller 1954
Friedrich Stegmüller: *Repertorium biblicum medii aevi* 4, Madrid 1954.

Stegmüller 1977
Friedrich Stegmüller: *Repertorium biblicum medii aevi* 9, Madrid 1977.

Stirnemann 1994
Patricia Stirnemann: »Où ont été fabriqués les livres de la glose ordinaire dans la première moitié du xiie siècle?«, in *Le xiie siècle. Mutations et renouveau en France dans la première moitié du xiie siècle* (Cahiers du Léopard d'Or 3), éd. par Françoise Gasparri, Paris 1994, 257–301 [mit 23 Abbildungen].

Stirnemann 1997
Patricia Stirnemann: »Gilbert de la Porrée et les livres glosés à Laon, à Chartres et à Paris«, in *Monde médiéval et société chartraine. Actes du colloque, Chartres, 8–10 septembre 1994*, éd. par Jean-Robert Armogathe, Paris 1997, 83–96 [mit 18 Abbildungen].

Suckale-Redlefsen 1995
Gude Suckale-Redlefsen: *Die Handschriften des 12. Jahrhunderts der Staatsbibliothek Bamberg* (Katalog der illuminierten Handschriften der Staatsbibliothek Bamberg 2), Wiesbaden 1995.

Weisweiler 1960
Heinrich Weisweiler: »Paschasius Radbertus als Vermittler des Gedankengutes der karolingischen Renaissance in den Matthäuskommentaren des Kreises um Anselm von Laon«, in *Scholastik 35* (1960) 363–402. 503–536.

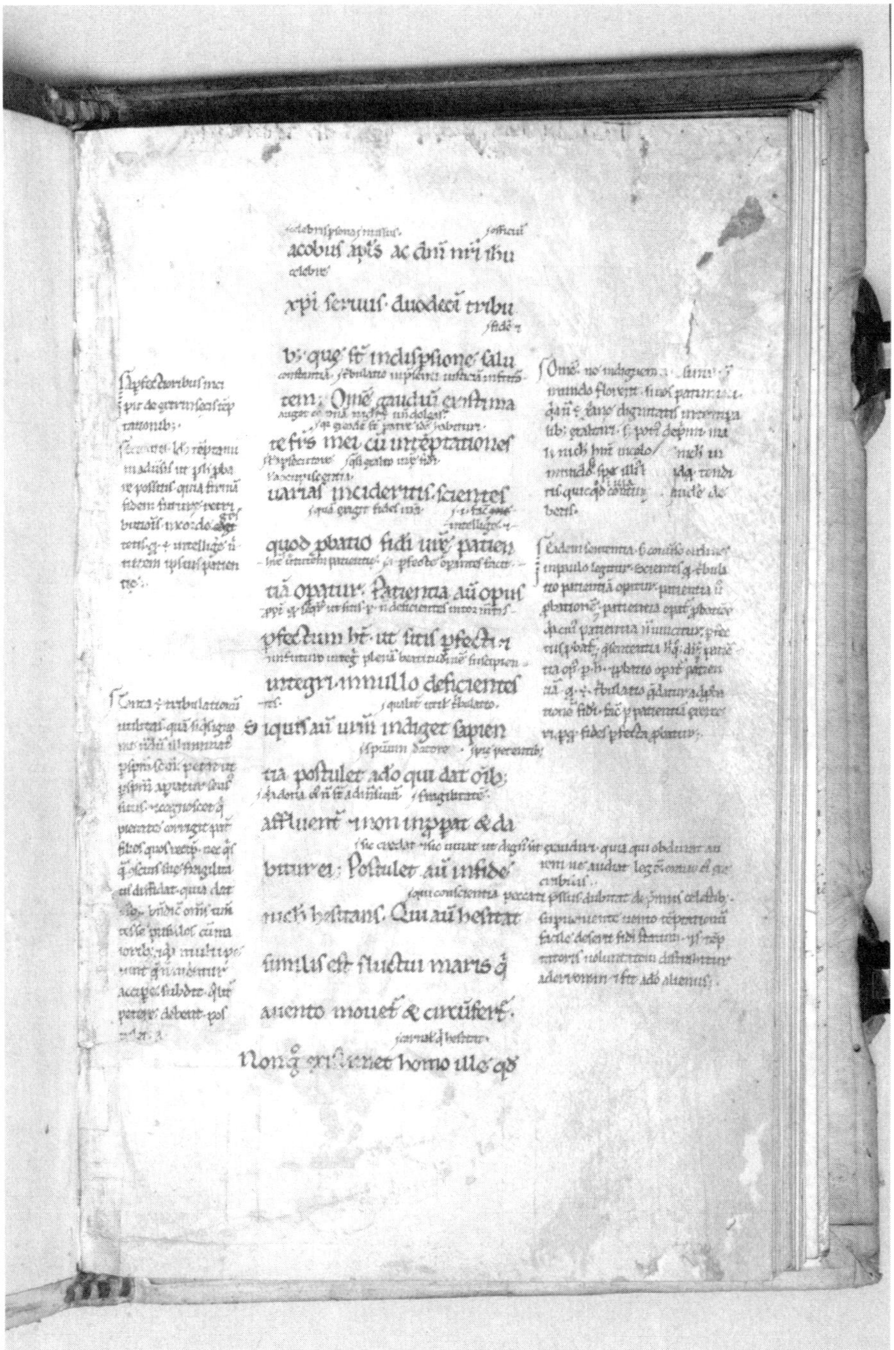

Abbildung 1: Msc. Bibl. 135, f. 1r

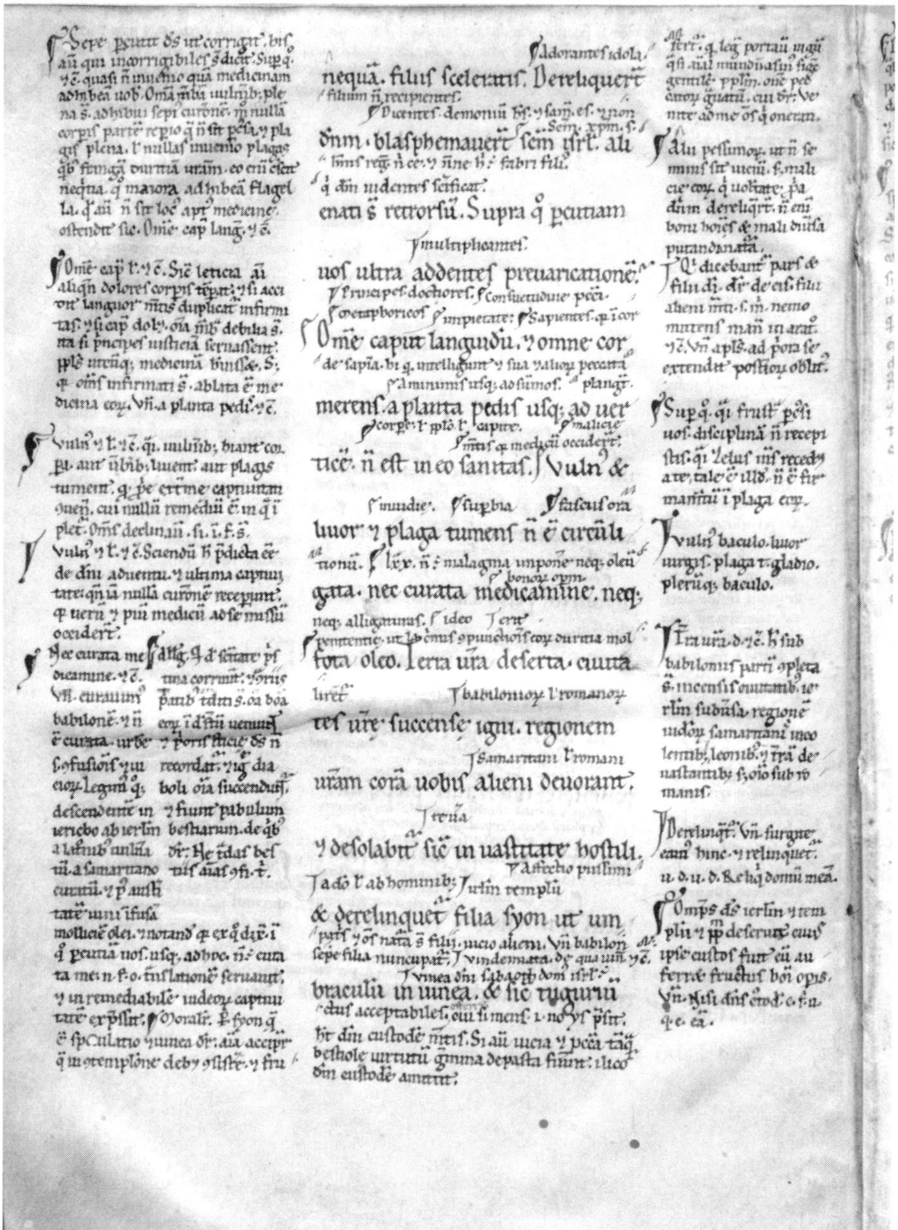

Abbildung 2: Msc. Bibl. 77, f. 1v

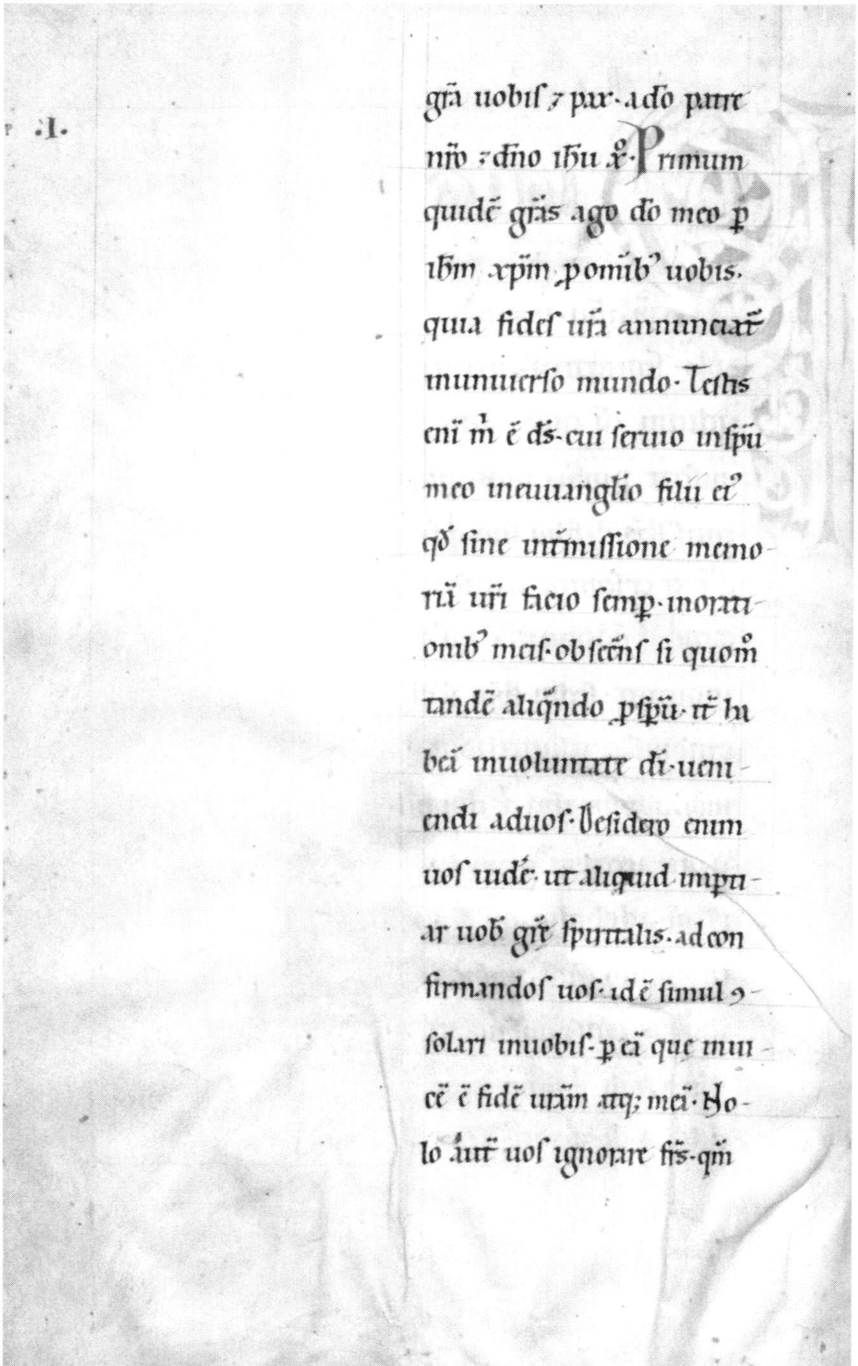

Abbildung 3: Msc. Bibl. 122, f. 4v

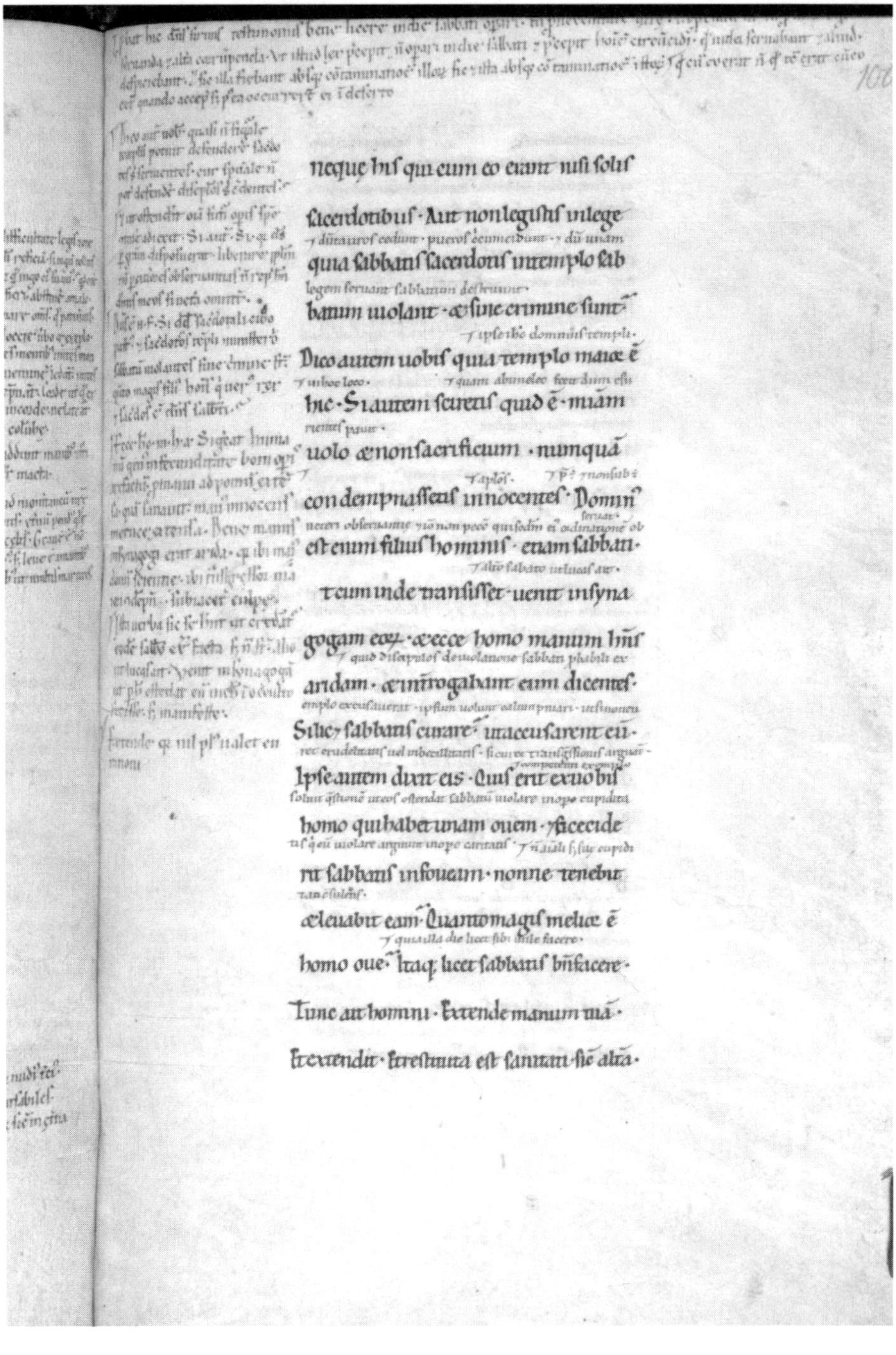

Abbildung 4: Msc. Bibl. 15, f. 100r

Abbildung 5: Msc. Bibl. 108, f. 3v

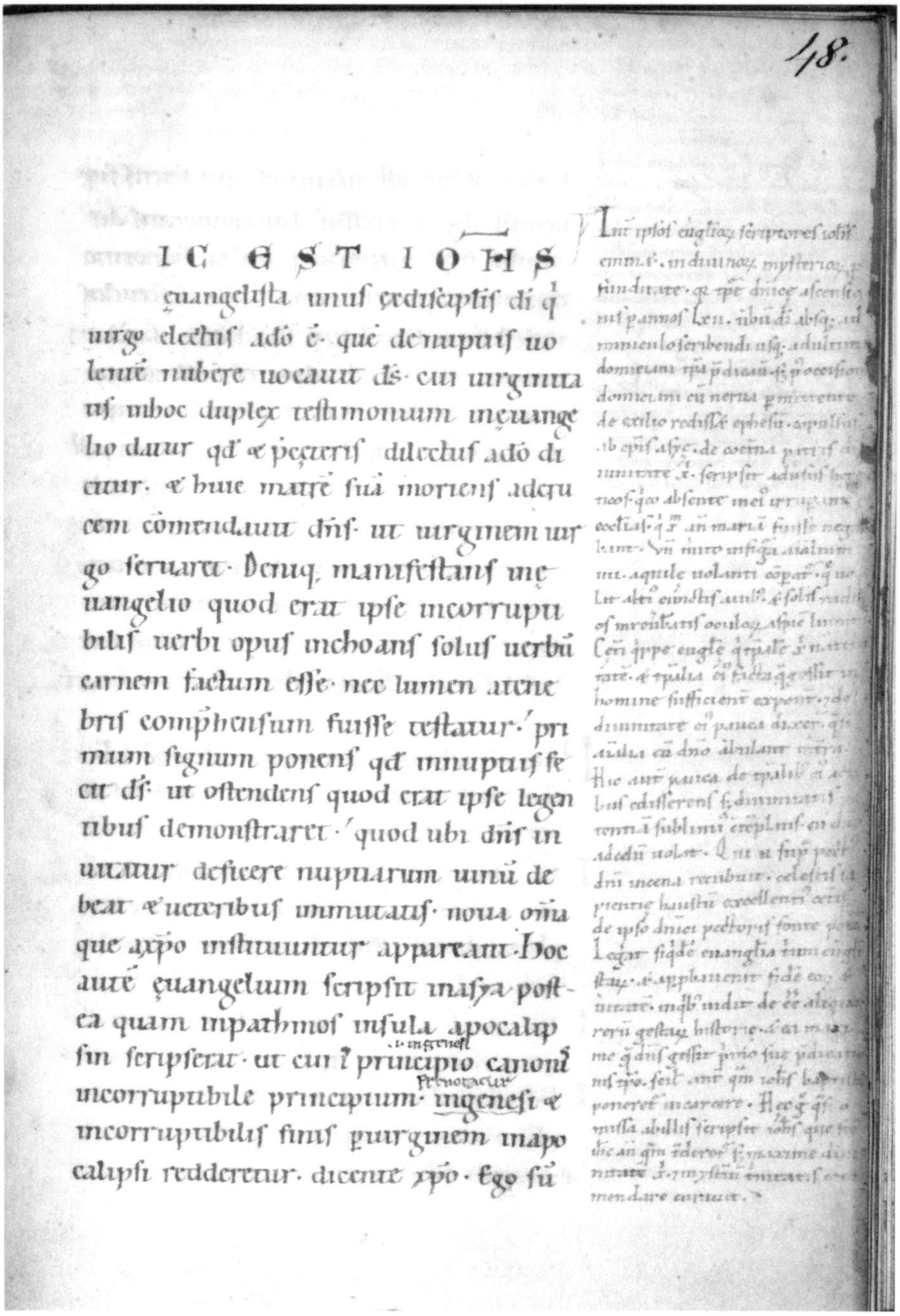

Abbildung 6: Msc. Bibl. 99, f. 48r

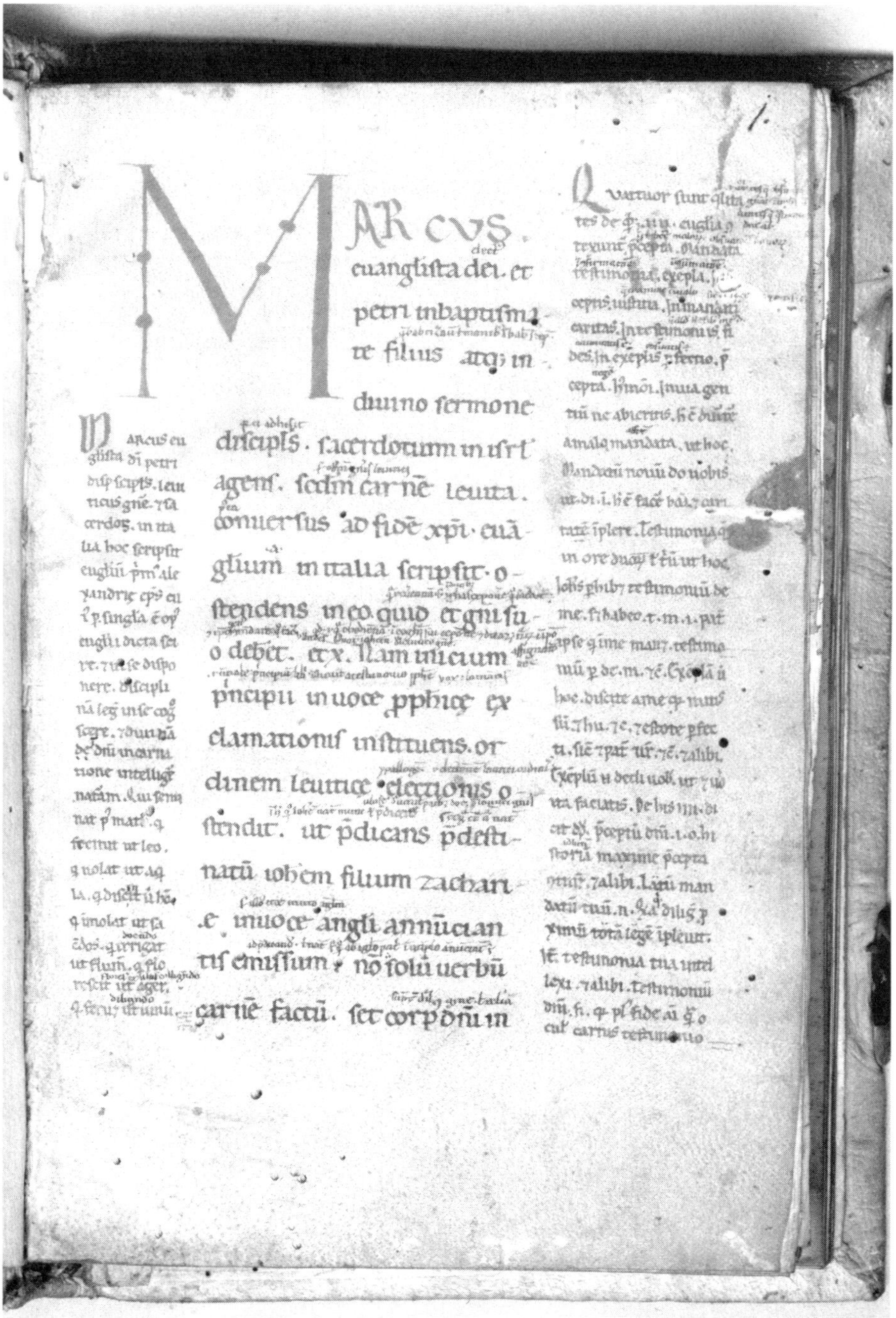

Abbildung 7: Msc. Bibl. 99, f. 1r

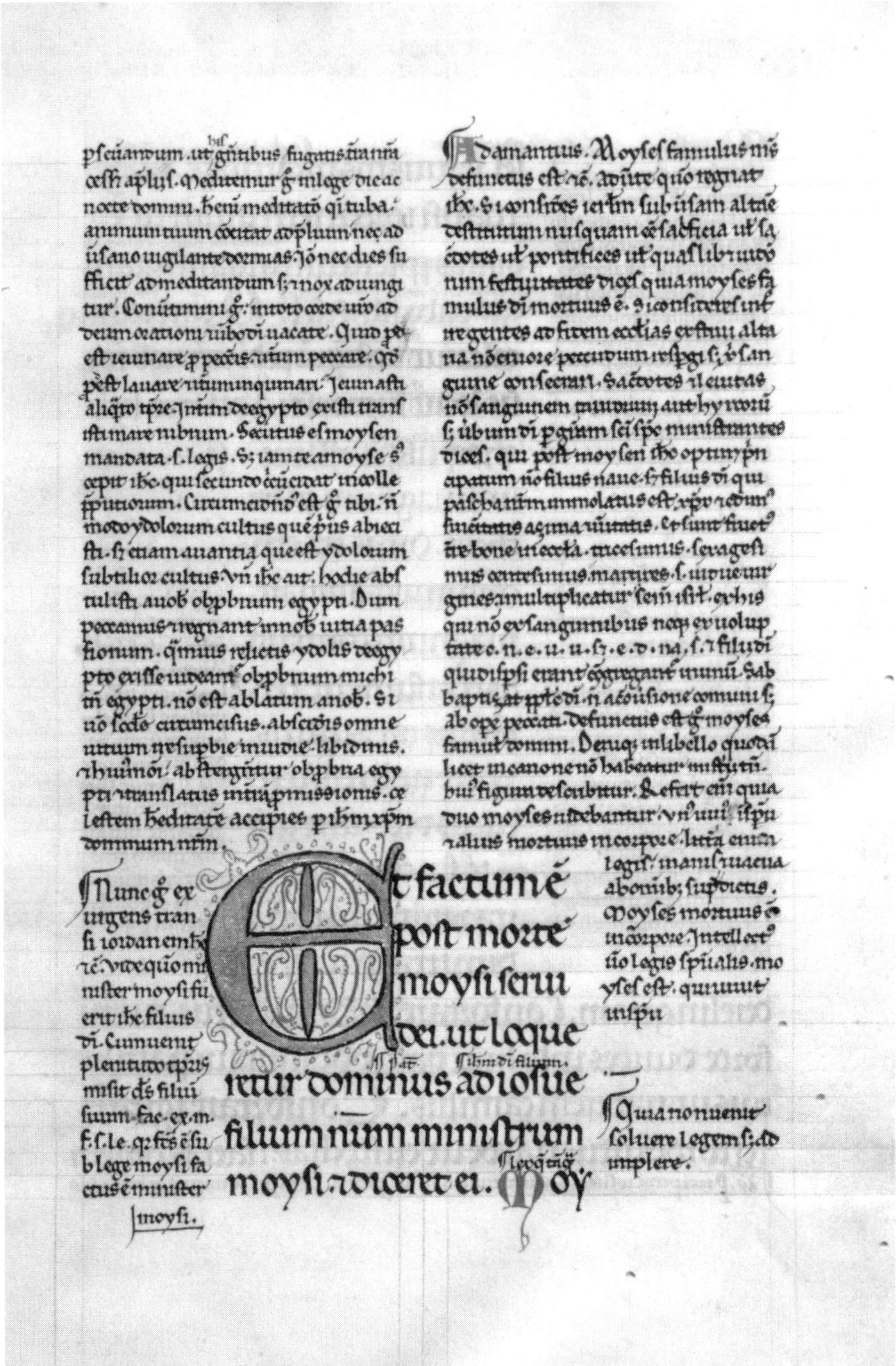

Abbildung 8: Msc. Bibl. 36, f. 3r

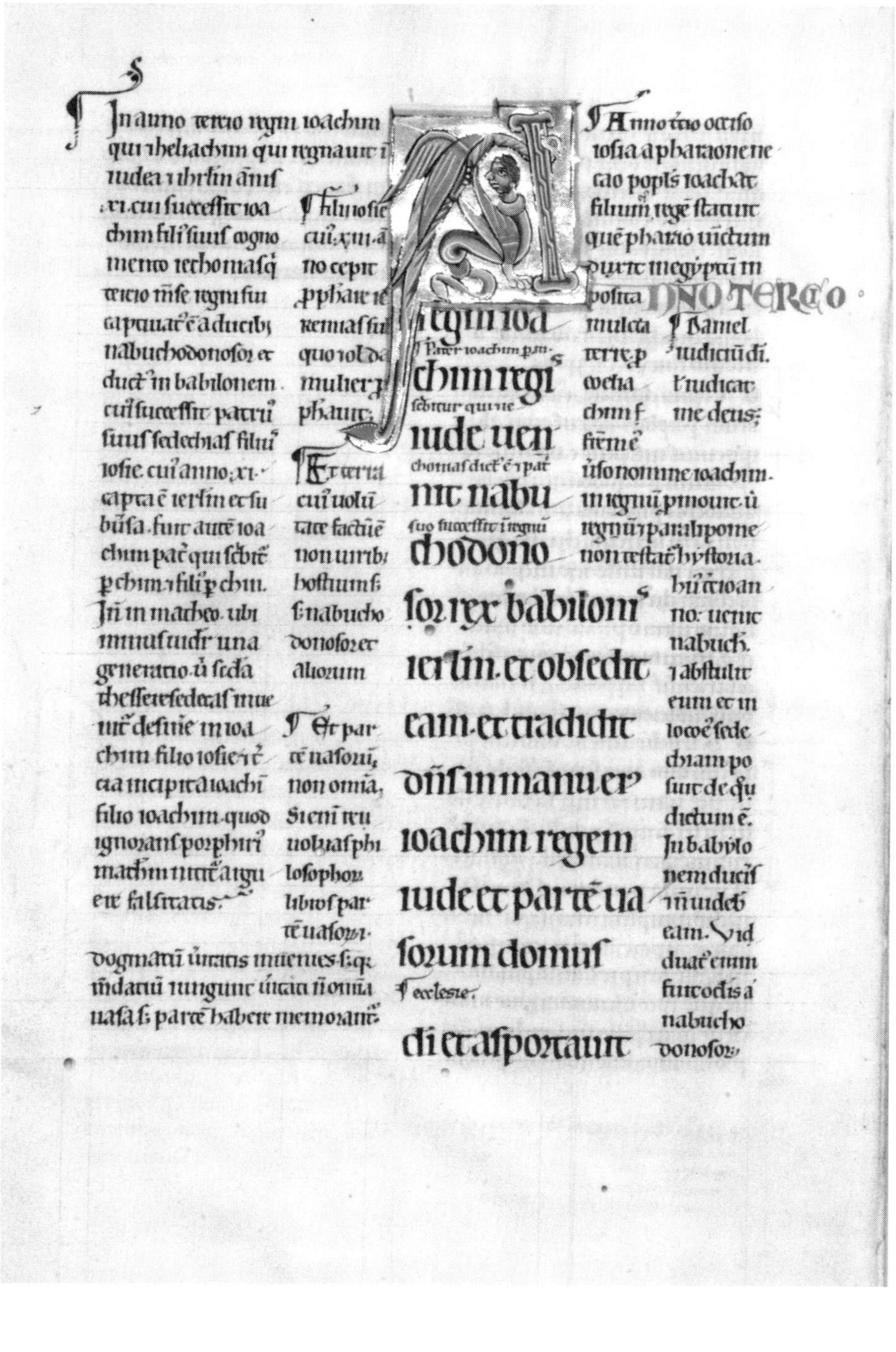

Abbildung 9: Msc. Bibl. 86, f. 3v

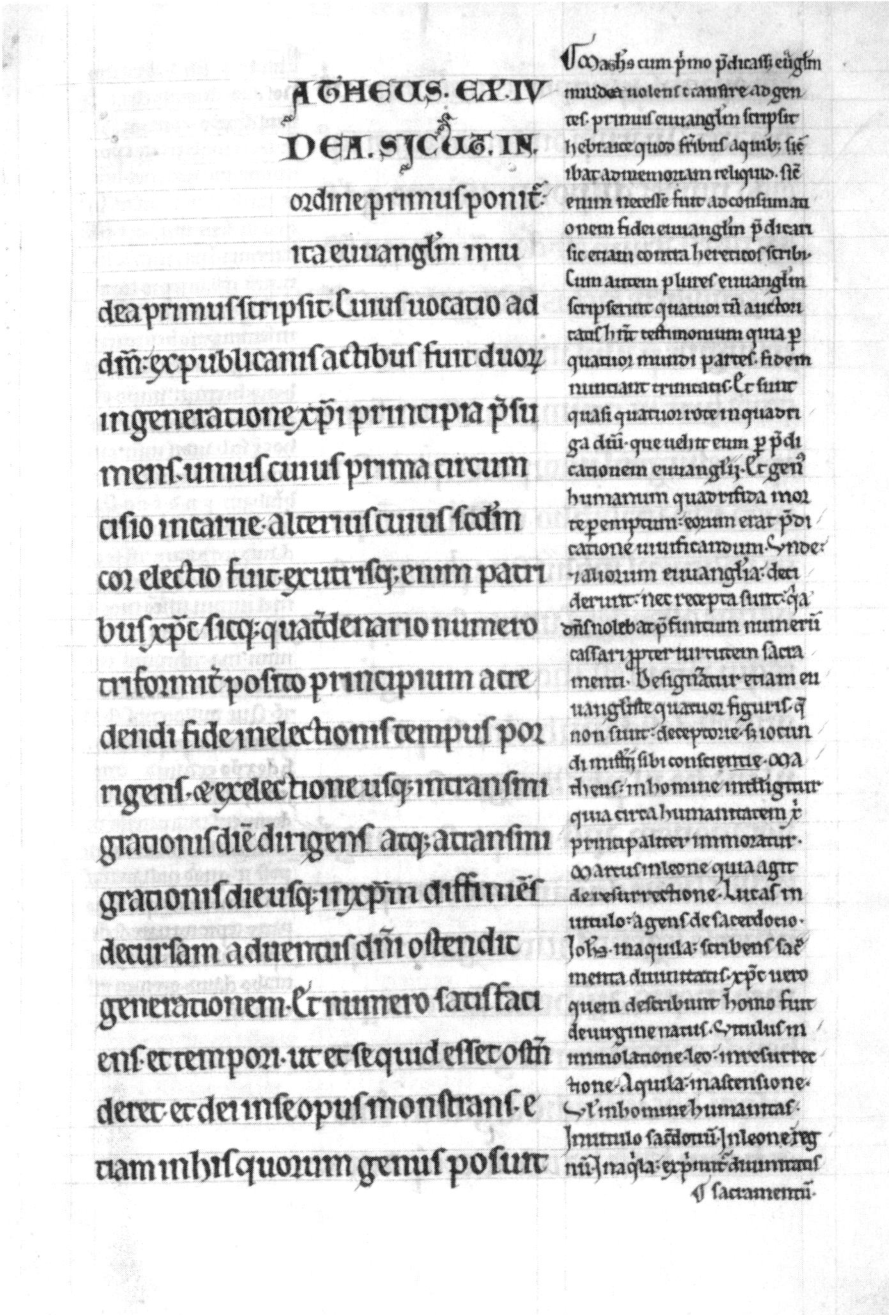

Abbildung 10: Msc. Bibl. 106, f. 1r

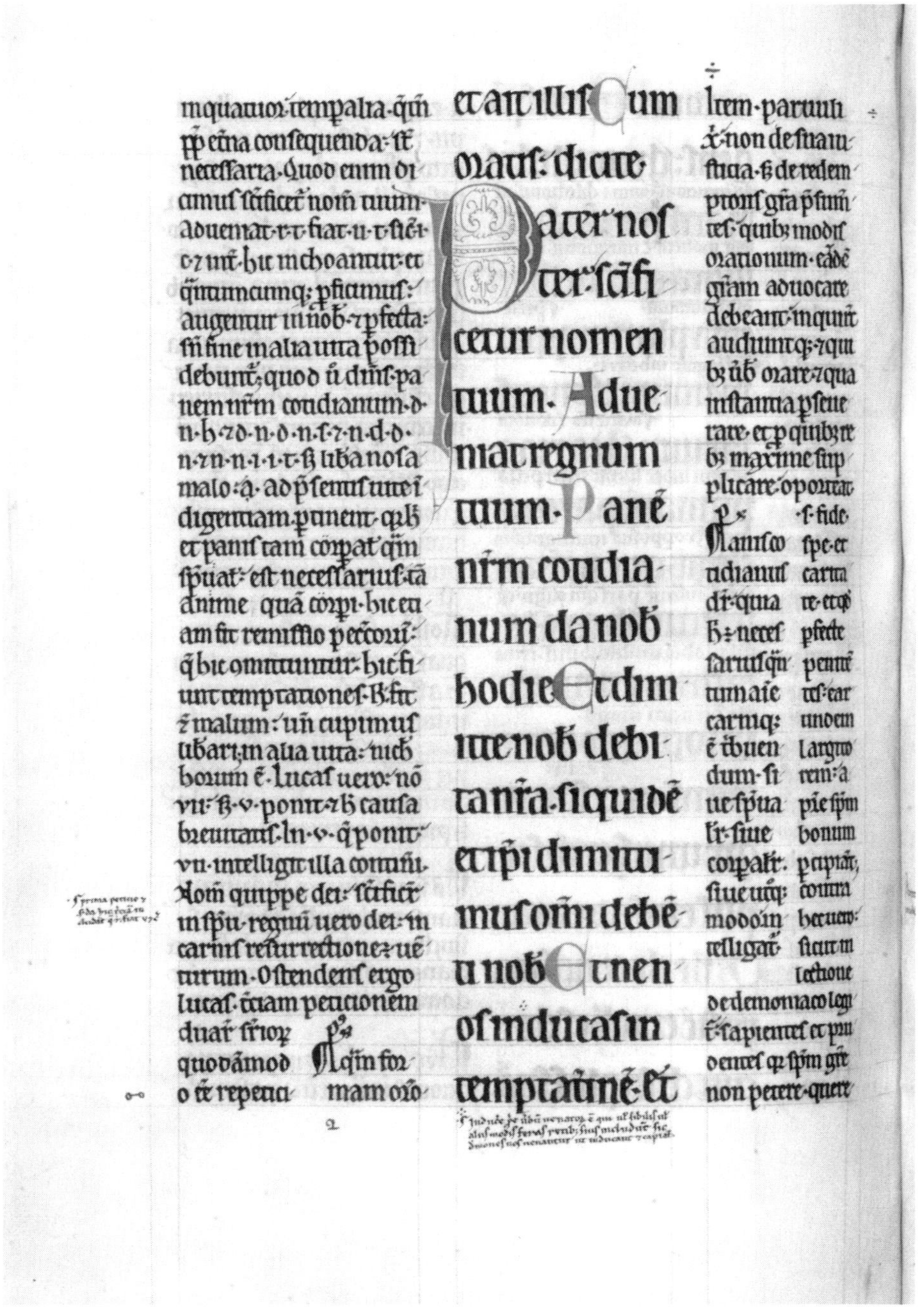
et ait illis Cum
oratis: dicite
Pater nos
ter: sancti
ficetur nomen
tuum. Adue
niat regnum
tuum. Panē
nr̄m cotidia
num da nob
hodie Et dim
itte nob debi
ta nr̄a. siquidē
et ipsi dimitti
mus omni debē
ti nob Et ne n
os inducas in
temptatīnē. et

Abbildung 11: Msc. Bibl. 113, f. 80v

Abbildung 12: Msc. Bibl. 123, f. 186r

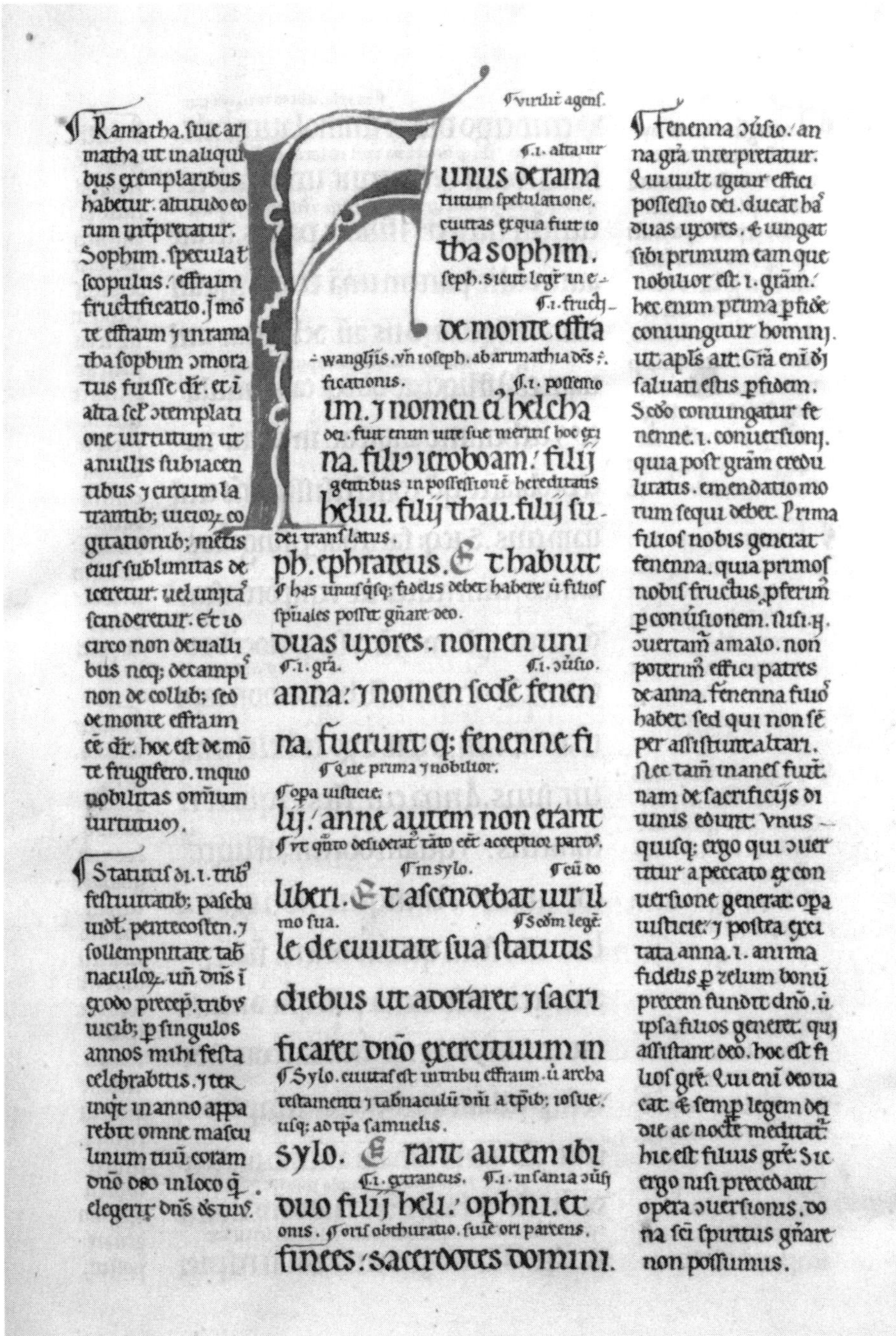

Abbildung 13: Msc. Bibl. 39, f. 4r

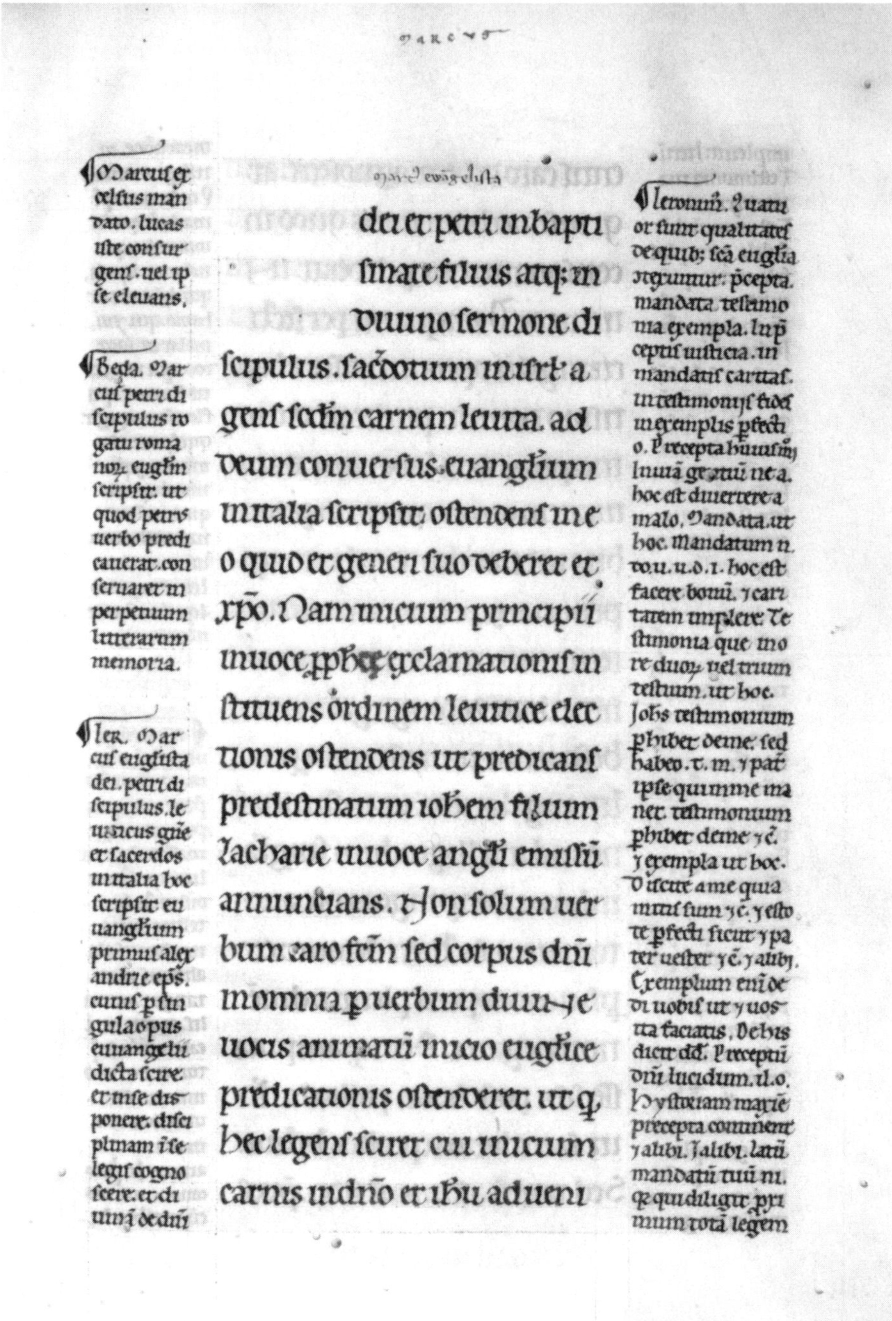

Abbildung 14: Msc. Bibl. 98, f. 3r

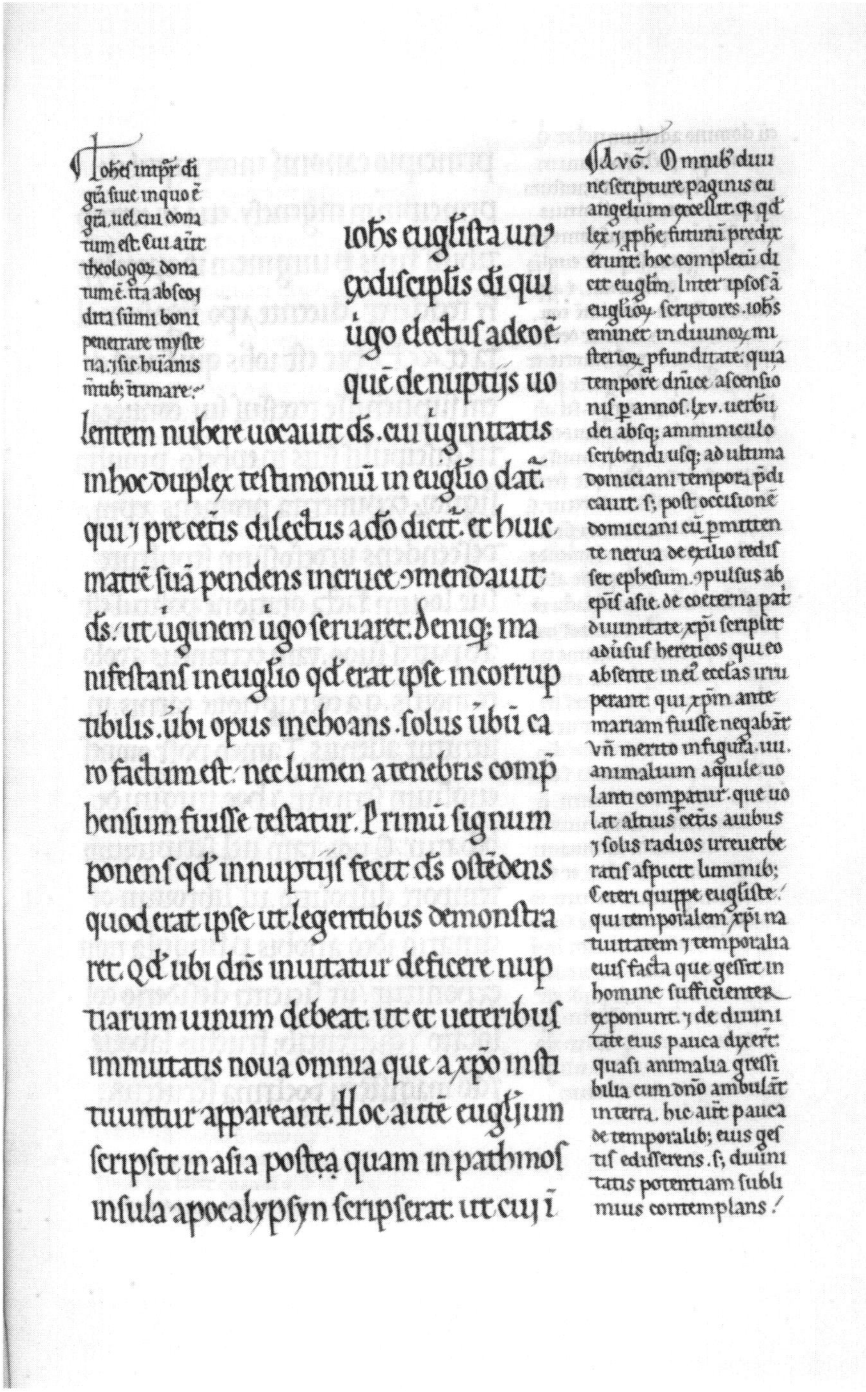
Iohes interpretatur dei gratia sive in quo est gratia vel cui donatum est. Cui autem theologorum donatum est ita absconditam summi boni penetrare mysteria et sic humanis mentibus intimare.

Iohs euglista unus ex discipulis di qui uirgo electus a deo ē. quē de nuptijs uolentem nubere uocauit ds. cui uirginitatis in hoc duplex testimoniū in euglio datr. qui 7 pre ceťis dilectus a dō dicit. et huic matrē suā pendens in cruce cōmendauit ds. ut uirginem uirgo seruaret. Deniq; manifestans in euglio qđ erat ipse incorruptibilis. ubi opus inchoans. solus uerbū caro factum est. nec lumen a tenebris cōprehensum fuisse testatur. Primū signum ponens qđ in nuptijs fecit ds ostēdens quod erat ipse ut legentibus demonstraret. qđ ubi dns inuitatur deficere nuptiarum uinum debeat. ut et ueteribus immutatis noua omnia que a xpo instituuntur appareant. Hoc autē euglium scripsit in asia postea quam in pathmos insula apocalypsyn scripserat. ut cui i

Aug. Omnibus diuine scripture paginis euangelium excellit. quod lex 7 prophete futurum predixerunt: hoc completum dicit euglm. Inter ipsos autem euangeliorum scriptores iohs eminet in diuinorum misteriorum profunditate: qui a tempore dnice ascensionis per annos .lxv. uerbum dei absq; amminiculo scribendi usq; ad ultima domiciani tempora predicauit. sed post occisionem domiciani cum permittente nerua de exilio redisset ephesum. compulsus ab episcopis asie. de coeterna patri diuinitate xpi scripsit aduersus hereticos qui eo absente in eius ecclesias irruperant. qui xpm ante mariam fuisse negabant. Unde merito in figura .iiii. animalium aquile uolanti comparatur. que uolat altius ceteris auibus 7 solis radios irreuerberatis aspicit luminibus. Ceteri quippe euangelistę qui temporalem xpi natiuitatem 7 temporalia eius facta que gessit in homine sufficienter exponunt. 7 de diuinitate eius pauca dixerunt: quasi animalia gressibilia cum dno ambulant in terra. hic autem pauca de temporalibus eius gestis edisserens. sed diuinitatis potentiam sublimius contemplans.

Abbildung 15: Msc. Bibl. 98, f. 70r

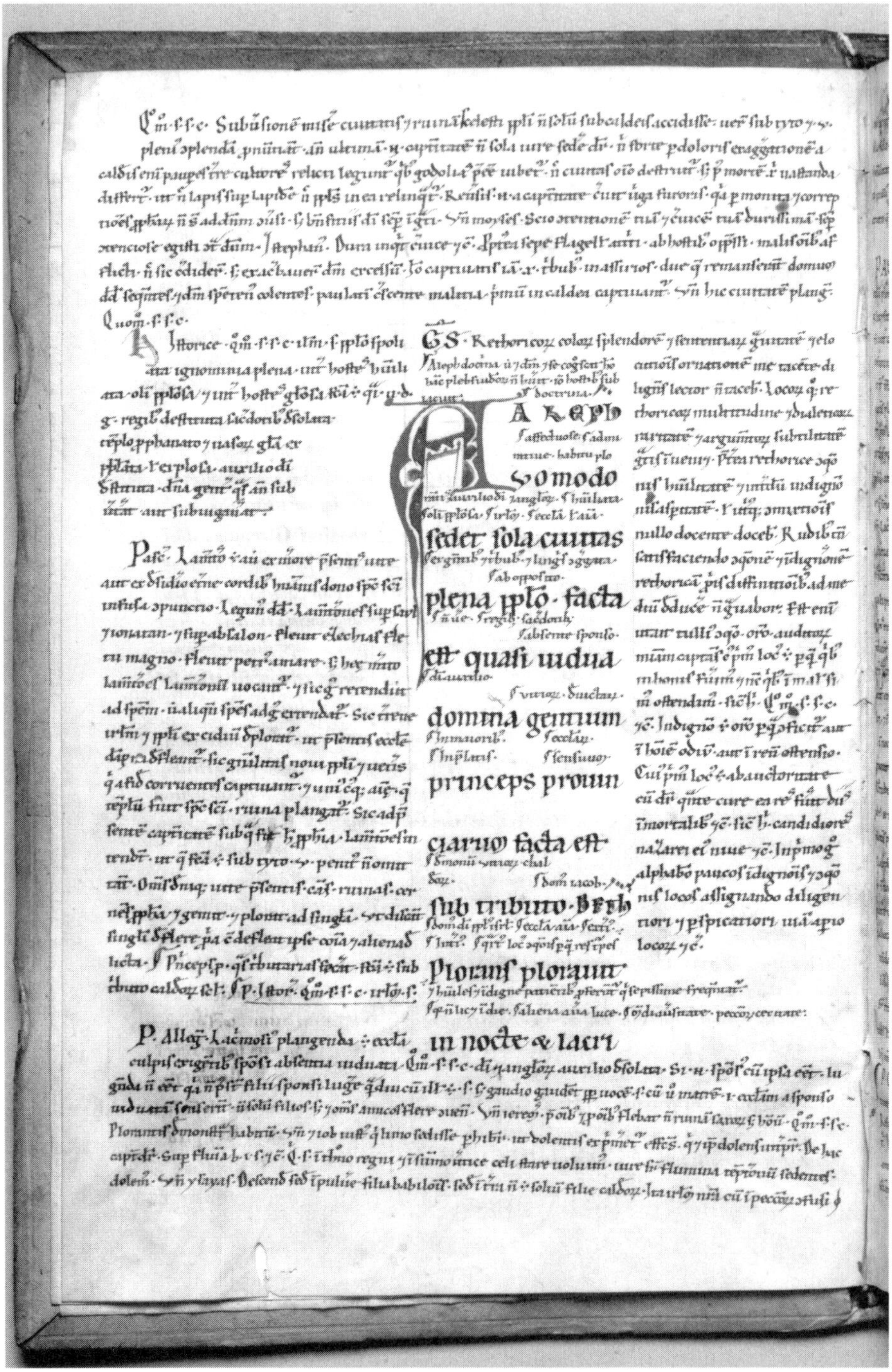

Abbildung 16: Msc. Bibl. 81, f. 1v

Archa Verbi 1 (2004) 119–127

On some recent publications relating to Peter Abelard

by CONSTANT J. MEWS

PETER ABELARD: *Collationes*, ed. and transl. JOHN MARENBON, GIOVANNI ORLANDI (Oxford Medieval Texts), Oxford: Clarendon Press 2001. – 368 pp. – ISBN 0–19–820579–1. – £ 55.00.

ABAELARDUS: *Scito te ipsum*, ed. RAINER M. ILGNER (Petri Abaelardi Opera Theologica 4 = CChr.CM 190), Turnhout: Brepols 2001. – LXIX, 107 pp. – ISBN 2–503–04901–X (hardback), € 85,00. – ISBN 2–503–04902–8 (paperback), € 75,00.

MATTHIAS PERKAMS: *Liebe als Zentralbegriff der Ethik nach Peter Abaelard* (BGPhThMA. NF 58), Münster: Aschendorff 2001. – xi, 395 S. – ISBN 3–402–04009–3. – € 51,20.

STEPHAN ERNST: *Petrus Abaelardus* (Zugänge zum Denken des Mittelalters 2), Münster: Aschendorff 2003. – 213 S. – ISBN 3–402–04631–8. – € 14,80.

Peter Abaelard. Leben – Werk – Wirkung, hg. v. URSULA NIGGLI (Forschungen zur europäischen Geistesgeschichte 4), Freiburg/Basel/Wien: Herder 2003. – 432 S. – ISBN 3–451–28172–4. – € 49,90.

Over the last few years, there as has been no shortage of new publications and critical editions relating to Peter Abelard. There are many reasons that his writings continue to fascinate modern readers. There is the dramatic story of his life as told in the letters he exchanged with Heloise. The accusations of heresy made by Bernard of Clairvaux at the Council of Sens in 1141, continue to provoke discussion about Abelard's orthodoxy. Is he a rationalist who anticipates the values of Enlightenment philosophy, or is he simply a loyal, catholic Christian, misunderstood by his critics? Ever since his philosophical writings were first identified by Victor Cousin in the nineteenth century, historians of philosophy have been intrigued by the acuity with which he analyses language. There is also the question of how we are to relate both Abelard's expertise in logic and his fascination with theological exploration to his thinking about ethics. In 1997, Cambridge University Press published JOHN MARENBON's richly detailed analysis of Abelard's logical and ethical theories, *The Philosophy of Peter Abelard*. In the same year, Blackwell published MICHAEL T. CLANCHY's biography, *Abelard. A Medieval Life*, a volume that has since been translated into both French[1] and German[2].

1 *Abélard*; trad. de l'anglais par PIERRE-EMMANUEL DAUZAT, Paris: Flammarion 2000.

2 *Abaelard. Ein mittelalterliches Leben*; aus dem Engl. übers. v. RAUL NIEMANN, RALF M. W. STAMMBERGER, Darmstadt: Wissenschaftliche Buchgesellschaft 2000.

Of particular importance for our understanding of Peter Abelard's ethical thought have been new critical editions of the *Collationes* and *Scito teipsum*. For many decades, the Latin text of the *Collationes* had been accessible through an edition prepared by Rudolf Thomas, under the title *Dialogus inter Philosophum, Judaeum et Christianum* (Stuttgart, Bad Cannstatt: Frommann 1970), marred by many serious errors of transcription, coupled by a tendency to follow the readings of the Vienna manuscript, ÖNB 819, when they were at variance with those preserved in the important fourteenth-century manuscript of Abelard's writings, Oxford, Balliol College 296. Thomas's faulty text was reprinted and translated into German by H.-W. KRAUTZ, *Gespräch eines Philosophen, eines Juden und eines Christen* (Frankfurt am Main: Suhrkamp 1995). GIOVANNI ORLANDI can only be congratulated for producing a more reliable critical edition, the value of which is greatly enhanced not just by John Marenbon's accurate and fluent translation, but by his detailed introduction to Abelard's ethical thought, as presented in the *Collationes*. Of particular interest in this volume is Marenbon's careful analysis of how Abelard draws on, but also differentiates himself from his pagan sources, notably Cicero and Seneca. One of the great enigmas of the *Collationes* is the extent to which the Stoic ideas presented by the philosopher reflect Abelard's own perspective. This dialogue is a philosophical comparison between religious and philosophical ethical theories, not between different religious systems. By comparing initially the arguments of the Jew and the philosopher, and then of the Christian and the philosopher, Abelard urges his reader to come to his or her own judgement about the common ground between their different traditions. Marenbon suggests that the *Collationes* were written, not at the end of Abelard's life (as used to be thought), but in the period between 1123 and the mid 1130s, most likely between 1127 and 1132, the early years of the new foundation of the Paraclete under Heloise. While the dating of the *Collationes* is one of the most enigmatic questions in Abelard's output, the thematic parallels between this work and his *Historia calamitatum*, as well as with some of the early sermons delivered to the Paraclete, make it quite likely that the work marks a new stage in his intellectual evolution. In the *Collationes* he starts to develop ethical ideas with greater sophistication than in the *Theologia Christiana* (from the early 1120s), but before he elaborates his analyses of sin and redemption in his commentary on Romans, and of vice and sin in the *Ethics*, which circulated under the title *Scito teipsum*.

Given that the critical edition of Abelards' *Ethics*, published by DAVID E. LUSCOMBE (Oxford: Clarendon Press 1971) is markedly superior in quality to the 1970 edition of the *Dialogus*, it might seem surprising that a new critical edition should have been prepared by RAINER ILGNER within the series *Corpus Christianorum Continuatio Mediaevalis*. The central premise of this new edition, however, is not without interest. Ilgner presents impressive philological arguments for judging that the manuscript which Luscombe preferred to follow in cases of disagreement between textual witnesses (Munich, Bayerische Staatsbibliothek, Clm 14160) is itself the product of a scribe correcting Abelard's original text. Ilgner prefers to follow the witness of another twelfthcentury manuscript (Munich, Bayerische Staatsbibliothek, Clm 28363), whose text often agrees with that preserved in the Oxford, Balliol College MS 296. Ilgner largely confines himself to philological matters within his introduction, not reproducing the detailed description of manuscripts provided by Luscombe, whose overview of ethical reflection in the twelfth century is still helpful. It is clear, however, that any new translation of the *Scito teipsum* needs to take account of the new edition.

Unfortunately neither of these two editions were available to MATTHIAS PERKAMS (now at the University of Jena), in his monograph, *Liebe als Zentralbegriff der Ethik nach Peter Abaelard*, published by Aschendorff, within the *Beiträge zur Geschichte der Philosophie und Theologie des Mittelalters*. This does not detract, however, from the value of this important survey of Abelard's ethical thought, which Perkams originally presented as a dissertation within the Philosophy Faculty at the University of Bonn within the winter semester of 2000/2001. Whereas Marenbon pays close attention to the philosophical dimension of Abelard's arguments about virtue, Perkams concentrates on the centrality for Abelard of the concept of love, understood in different contexts as passionate longing (*amor*), as selfless love for another (*dilectio*), and above all simply as *caritas*, a term weakly translated into English as 'charity'.

From the outset of his monograph, Perkams declares his interest in the concept of love as a philosophical concept. The great problem with discussing the word "love" (or *amour*, or *Liebe*) is that modern languages do not convey the subtle distinction conveyed in Latin by the terms *amor*, *dilectio* and *caritas*, just as do their parallel terms in Greek. To his credit, Perkams introduces his reader to the subtle differences between these terms in relation to Abelard's writings. These are terms, of course, that have an enormously rich and complex history, not just in terms of philosophy, but also in the context of theology and spiritual writing. To do full justice to Abelard's discussion of love one would first need to examine the complex variety of intellectual currents, both Christian and philosophical (not to mention poetic) that he inherited from his reading.

Perkams is at his best in the close reading that he offers of the major texts in which Abelard speaks about the ideal of love as the basis of an ethical life: the *Theologia Christiana*, the *Collationes*, the *Commentary on Romans*, the *Theologia 'Scholarium'*, and the *Ethica*. By following these texts in chronological sequence, he is able to trace in some detail how Abelard develops his ethical thinking from relatively crude attempts in the early 1120s to trace the common ground shared by Christian and pagan (largely Stoic) ethical thought to a far more sophisticated analysis of the difference between vice, sin and virtue, that he develops in the *Ethica*. Perkams rightly argues that through this evolving body of writing, Abelard emphasizes the importance of good intention and conformity to God's will as essential to right behaviour. Without knowing the Marenbon-Orlandi edition of the *Collationes*, Perkams presents a helpful analysis of the text (sometimes correcting the faulty Thomas/Krautz edition), in which he argues that Abelard's ethical ideas are founded on his right recognition of the meaning of "supreme good" and "supreme evil". Rejecting the accusation that Abelard's ethics are purely subjective, Perkams holds that Abelard's emphasis on right intention must be related to his sense of doing the will of God, and his sense of the fundamental compatibility of philosophical and theological concerns. There are significant disagreements between the philosopher and the Christian in the *Collationes*, such as about the identity of the virtues. Whether Abelard himself agrees with what the philosopher has to say is not necessarily clear. Nonetheless, it is clear that Abelard puts forward *caritas* as the philosophical foundation of the virtues, as well as the goal of the Christian life.

With the *Commentary on Romans*, Abelard has to confront a great body of theological tradition, shaped above all by St Augustine, about original sin, the weakness of the flesh, and our need for divine grace. In looking for ethical insights within the *Commentary on Romans*, Perkams does not engage in great depth with the theories of redemption with which Abelard has to engage. Nonetheless, Perkams rightly gives weight to the importance that Abelard attaches to the free exercise of the will in accepting the freely offered love of God, manifest in Christ, as the basis of right behaviour. Abelard presents his reading of Romans as fully consistent with the teaching both of St Paul and the best of what the ancient philosophers had to say. Perkams also uses the final book of *Theologia 'Scholarium'*, completed after the *Commentary on Romans*, to follow up Abelard's thinking about the ethical basis of his understanding of God's action in the world as the product of his benignity, another way of talking about God's love. At the outset of this version of the *Theologia*, Abelard formulates his very original definition of *caritas* as *amor honestus*, passionate desire that loves the other, only for the sake of God, not for any selfish end. He concludes the treatise by arguing that *caritas* is also the basis of God's action in the world, and that humanity should simply strive to conform that underlying will of God.

Perkams emphasizes the significance of the new ideas developed in the *Ethics*, transmitted in manuscripts under the title *Scito teipsum*. In particular Abelard develops the idea that sin is not simply a wrong will, but consent to a wrong will in contempt of God. While there is much that one could say about how notions of consent are found in the teaching of Anselm of Laon and William of Champeaux, the original feature of Abelard's mature thinking is not so much his use of the term *consensus*, as his consideration that simply experiencing a wrong will, such as sexual temptation, is not in itself a sin. Christian tradition had always emphasized that intention is an integral part of any sin. Nonetheless, Abelard was unusual for arguing that even those who crucified Christ did not themselves commit a wrong action, if they were acting out of a right intention and genuine love for God.

One text missing from Perkam's analysis is the *Sic et Non*, important not just for its prologue (in which *caritas* provides a norm for evaluating contrasting patristic and scriptural testimonies), but for its vast dossier of patristic, and occasional pagan authorities relating to *caritas*. The third and final part of the *Sic et Non* (assembled either before or at the same time as the *Theologia Christiana* in the 1120s) begins with a set of questions about *caritas*, such as whether charity once acquired could ever be lost, or whether we ought to love all people equally, of great interest, because they show how carefully Abelard mined patristic and occasional pagan ideas for his understanding of *caritas*. To his credit, however, Perkams does explore the rich contribution of two other texts, often ignored in discussions of Abelard's thought: the various collections of *sententiae*, taken down by students from his oral teaching (which often comment on questions presented in the *Sic et Non*), and the *Commentarius Cantabrigiensis*, a vast commentary on all the Pauline epistles. Perkams rightly points out that the teaching presented both in the most immediate sentence collections and in this *reportatio* of lectures on St Paul is fully consistent with the thought of Abelard, and is in many ways more detailed than his writings. We have here a rich insight into Abelard's most mature thought.

Perkams concludes with a chapter on notions of ethics and love in Abelard's epistolary exchange with Heloise. He points out that even in the *Historia calamitatum*, we can see Abelard's presentation of his love for Heloise in moralistic terms as a love that was not directed to its rightful end. While Perkams rightly demonstrates the fundamental continuity between Abelard's interest in right intention in his writing for Heloise and in the *Scito teipsum*, he acknowledges the chronological problem that his exchanges with Heloise occur before his more mature reflections on ethical theory. The traditional assumption is that Heloise must have gained her interest in the role of intention from Abelard. An alternative view, which I suggest in *The Lost Love Letters of Heloise and Abelard. Perceptions of Dialogue in Twelfth-Century France* (New York: Palgrave 1999), is that Heloise provided Abelard with the major stimulus for thinking about the ethics of love in the early years of his relationship, when his expertise was still very much only in ethics. When I wrote that monograph, unfortunately not available to Perkams, I had not realized that when the male lover in the *Epistolae duorum amantium* endeavours to respond to his student's question about the nature of love, he paraphrases the one sentence of Cicero's *De amicitia* that Abelard includes within the *Sic et Non* (138:21), about true love only existing between the closest of friends. This Ciceronian text is quoted in the *Sic et Non* alongside many other Augustinian passages to justify the idea that *caritas* once acquired, can never be lost. There is a very close relationship between the discussion of love as the foundation of a virtuous life in these love letters and the driving emphasis on the centrality of love to ethical behaviour, as presented by Perkams. If the *Epistolae duorum amantium* are an authentic record of an early exchange, then it would seem that the young Heloise was pushing Abelard to think about love even during these years. While the young Abelard was a dialectician, fascinated by the intention behind words, she forced him to think about the intention behind behaviour.

Perkams is to be commended for drawing attention to the centrality of the conception of love in Abelard's ethical thought in a way that brings together philosophical and theological perspectives. This is a vast subject on which so much more work needs to be done, not least by relating Abelard's reflection on the subject to the discussion of his contemporaries, most notably Heloise, William of St-Thierry and Augustine. Abelard was not the only figure in the twelfth century to try to bring together the ideas about *amor* and *caritas* of Ovid, Cicero, and St Paul (not to mention Augustine) into a coherent fusion. Perkams has laid a helpful foundation for such research.

While Perkams focuses on Abelard's ethical thought, a slim volume by STEPHAN ERNST provides a compact introduction to his thought as a whole, that will be of great value to students beginning to get to know a difficult and complex thinker. Even though Ernst makes no major claims to originality of perspective, he provides a reasonably thorough overview of Abelard's career and short summaries of all of his major writings, followed by a briefer chapter on the significance of Abelard's contribution to philosophy, theology and ethics. The biggest challenge confronting any general survey of Abelard is the sheer diversity of the topics and literary genres of his writing. Students will be grateful for his compact, but still substantive summaries of all of his major writings on logic, theology and ethics (with rather briefer attention given to his poetry and other writing for the Paraclete). It is informed by wide reading within the secondary literature. The volume also includes German translations of extracts from a variety of his more significant writings. Ernst provides a reasonably complete listing of recent editions of Abelard's works, in which the only serious omission is the Marenbon-Orlandi edition of the *Collationes* (although the Ilgner edition of the *Scito teipsum* is mentioned). There is also a good bibliography, particularly thorough with reference to recent German scholarship.

Ernst offers a measured interpretation of Abelard's originality. He argues that Abelard does offer an original ontology and theory of knowledge, but (following arguments put forward over twenty years ago by Jean Jolivet) argues that his nominalism is not as radical as that of Ockham in the fourteenth century. Ernst gives particular attention to Abelard's contribution to philosophical and theological ethics, supported by strong interest in pagan theory (without particularly arguing the case in detail). Perhaps the most remarkable absence from this monograph is the near complete omission of any discussion of the ideas of Heloise about ethics in the evolution of Abelard's thought. While the monograph provides a sober and useful introduction to his writings, students will need to work out for themselves the complex issues of how Abelard developed ideas in response to questions raised by his students (like Heloise) and other contemporaries.

By comparison, the volume of essays edited by URSULA NIGGLI under the ambitious title *Peter Abaelard. Leben – Werk – Wirkung* is less unified in its perspective. It also focuses much more on Abelard than on Heloise. Six of the ten chapters include contributions by Ursula Niggli herself, many originally written in the 1980s. Her perspective, as presented in both her introduction and conclusion, focuses on Abelard as protomodern individualist, coupled with the rather general assertion that he remained "ein mittelalterlicher Mensch" in being a theist with a theocentric image of the world and of humanity (p. 24). The difficulty with such generalisations is that they involve very broad claims about both medieval and modern thought. Her essay on the exchange with Heloise, "Erotische Konfession und klösterliche Instruktion,", traces what she sees as an unresolved tension between erotic and monastic elements in the correspondence, without fully doing justice to the tension between the protagonists in the exchange. In another chapter, "Philosophischer Scharfsinn in der theologischen Kritik," she investigates whether or not the accusations of heresy levelled against Abelard were justified. Her conclusion, that they failed to understand the philosophical acuity of his theological method, is valid, without being particularly profound. Her essay on Abelard's ideas about Judaism in the *Dialogus* (*Collationes*), like that of Hans-Wolfgang Krautz, "Zwischen Boethius, Lullus, Cusanus und Lessing – Streiflichter auf Abaelards Collationes," focuses on Abelard as a proto-Enlightenment figure, transcending religious dogmatism, paying particular attention to the comments made by the figure of the philosopher as a critic of both Judaism and Christianity. This interpretation tends to underplay the significance of the contrasting ethical ideas between the philosopher and the Christian that Abelard is wanting to work out in the second part of the work. Unfortunately, neither Niggli nor Krautz were able to draw on the Marenbon-Orlandi edition in their discussion.

The essay of Hans-Jürgen Müller on Abelard's dialectical method, offers a helpful reading of Abelard's logical thinking as about language rather than about ontology. He explores the way Abelard develops his critique of both Roscelin's vocalism and William of Champeaux's realism into an *ars sermocinalis*. By focusing on Abelard's dialectic as an exploration of the causes behind the imposition of language, Müller develops a perspective that can be easily extended to theology.

The difficulty with any collection of essays looking at Abelard from different disciplines is that it is often very difficult for the reader to arrive at any synthetic overview. Rolf Peppermüller, for example, offers a solid summary of Abelard's theology of redemption through love, as presented in the Commentary on Romans, but with little connection to Abelard's other writings. Matthias Perkams provides an interesting extended comparison of Abelard's ethical principles to those of Immanuel Kant, developing ideas he had raised at the end of his monograph. He concludes that, although there are evident divergences between the two thinkers, there are also parallels in the way that they give priority to an ethical dimension. His observation that Abelard offers a very original variant on medieval thought is more nuanced than simply saying that Abelard is "a medieval man" or that he is theocentric in his concerns. Nonetheless, one must ask about the usefulness of attempting such comparisons, when the historical circumstances of these two thinkers are so different. Certainly Abelard deserves respect as a thinker, but within the framework of his own time, rather than within that of a future quite foreign to him.

There are also three essays in this volume by Werner Robl, an indefatigable researcher into neglected historical aspects of Abelard's career. In one, he summarizes research that he has published elsewhere more fully into the family of Heloise, which he identifies as coming from the Loire valley, rather than the Île-de-France. In particular, he identifies her mother, Hersinde, recorded in the Paraclete obituary as having died on 1 December, with Hersinde, first prioress of Fontevrault (recorded as having died on 30 November). The coincidence is intriguing, particularly given that the death of Hersinde of Fontevrault is recorded as occurring on 29 November and 1 December by two obituaries from Chartres (Saint-Père-en-Vallée and Saint-Jean-en-Vallée). Inevitably such arguments rely on surmise. Nonetheless, they help provide a cultural and religious context for Heloise, and explain Abelard's ambiguous attitude towards Fontevrault. He both admired Robert of Arbrissel, but also questioned the submission of men to an abbess at that abbey. Robl's research is always backed up by close attention to historical sources, more than that of any other author in this volume. He is intrigued by the parallels between the life of Hersinde and Heloise. His arguments confine themselves to historical questions, however, and thus intersect relatively little with the philosophical and theological studies (strongly focused on Abelard rather than on Heloise) in this volume.

Robl also provides a detailed commentary on the life of Goswin of Anchin, who sparred with Abelard at the Mont Ste-Geneviève and later at St-Médard, Soissons, and two letters of Peter the Venerable to "master Peter", very likely indeed to be addressed to Abelard. While it is helpful to reprint the original Latin text, with accompanying translation and commentary, of these sections of the *Vita Goswini*, there is an urgent need for a new critical edition of the whole text, not just those little extracts relevant to Abelard. This *Vita* begins with an enigmatic salutation (*Suo suus seipsum*) such as one would find at the beginning of a letter. This suggests that the author of the entire *Vita* is Goswin himself, offering his reader nothing less than himself. While Robl dismisses the possibility that Goswin is himself its author, Rupert of Deutz and Otloh of St Emmeram both write autobiographical texts in the third person. The *Vita Goswini* demands attention, not simply for the information it provides about Abelard, but as a remarkable literary work of the twelfth century. Robl performs a valuable service in bringing this text to our attention. Its account, for example, of how Goswin was copying "piece by piece" a famous and controversial commentary (undoubtedly the *Glosule*) on Priscian is of great significance for appreciating the intellectual context in which Abelard developed his early thought.

The volume also contains Robl's commentary on two letters of Peter the Venerable, addressed to master Peter, very likely indeed to be Abelard himself, while Niggli provides translation (with little analysis) of Berengar's writings in defence of Peter Abelard. While these are significant documents, these commentaries do not connect closely to the argument of the other chapters. This volume's title suggests that it includes a survey of Abelard's influence, no chapter is actually devoted to his *Wirkung*. It is also unfortunate that there is such great inconsistency within the volume about such basic matters as the date of the Council of Sens, correctly assigned to 25 May 1141 by Robl, but given as 1 June 1140 by a number of authors, or the date of Abelard's *Collationes* (assigned by Krautz to the end of Abelard's life). These are small details, but they give an unfortunate impression of disconnectedness from recent scholarship. The task of drawing together recent research into Abelard from a range of different disciplines, and of situating him in a wider intellectual and cultural context, is left to the reader.

Bibliography

Sources

PETRUS ABAELARDUS: *Dialogus inter Philosophum, Judaeum et Christianum*, ed. RUDOLF THOMAS, Stuttgart 1970.

PETRUS ABAELARDUS: *Gespräch eines Philosophen, eines Juden und eines Christen.* Lateinisch und deutsch, übers. und ed. HANS-WOLFGANG KRAUTZ, Frankfurt am Main 1995.

Peter Abelard's Ethics, ed. and transl. DAVID E. LUSCOMBE, Oxford 1971.

Studies

MICHAEL T. CLANCHY: *Abelard. A Medieval Life* , Oxford [Blackwell] 1997.

MICHAEL T. CLANCHY: *Abélard,* trad. PIERRE-EMMANUEL DAUZAT, Paris 2000.

MICHAEL T. CLANCHY: *Abaelard. Ein mittelalterliches Leben,* übers. RAUL NIEMANN und RALF M. W. STAMMBERGER, Darmstadt 2000.

JOHN MARENBON: *The Philosophy of Peter Abelard,* Cambridge 1997.

CONSTANT MEWS: *The Lost Love Letters of Heloise and Abelard. Perceptions of Dialogue in Twelfth-Century France,* New York 1999.

Archa Verbi 1 (2004) 128–142

Biographie und Theologie am Beispiel Wilhelms von Ockham

von Volker Leppin[1]

»De nobis ipsis silemus«. Diese Aussage von Francis Bacon hat Immanuel Kant bekanntlich der zweiten Auflage der *Kritik der reinen Vernunft* vorangestellt:[2] »Was uns selbst angeht, so schweigen wir.« Eben das tun auch wir heute oft und gerne in unserer Wissenschaftsprosa, und die Altvorderen des Mittelalters, mit denen wir uns zu beschäftigten pflegen, haben es offenkundig auch immer wieder getan. Die Ausnahmen sind rasch aufgezählt: Jener Briefwechsel Abaelards mit Heloise, jene auf Augustin zurückzuführende Tradition plötzlicher Bekehrung, deren sich noch Thomas Bradwardine bedient,[3] oder auch der Bericht persönlich erfahrener Visionen in den Texten großer Mystikerinnen. Ausnahmen, bei denen sich dann durchaus auch die Frage stellt, ob und inwieweit sie eigentlich noch in den Bereich theologischer Mediävistik gehören, ob sie nicht eher Randphänomene, Umfeldphänomene dessen berühren, das uns als Theologen und Theologinnen interessiert: die Auseinandersetzung mit den theologischen Inhalten.

So unbestreitbar es auch für solche Loslösung des textlichen Produktes von seinem Autor argumentative Gründe geben kann, so sehr hat doch die jüngere internationale mediävistische Forschung gezeigt, daß Inhalte und Umfeld, Text und Kontext in einer Weise zusammen gehören, die sehr fruchtbringend aufeinander bezogen werden können. Ich erwähne nur Richard W. Southerns Einzeichnung Anselms in seine Landschaft,[4] die mentalitätsgeschichtlichen Anstöße Alain de Liberas,[5] die institutionengeschichtlichen Analysen William J. Courtenays[6] oder auch die permanente Polemik Kurt Flaschs gegen eine vereinseitigende Geistesgeschichte.[7] Die Anwendung kontextueller, erst recht spezifisch biographischer Fragestellungen auf unseren Untersuchungsgegenstand ist uns freilich in der Regel schon allein dadurch erschwert, daß wir von unseren Autoren nur sehr wenig konkrete Personkenntnis besitzen. Die unter Historikern so beliebten ›Ego-Dokumente‹ fehlen oft völlig, und die vorliegenden theologischen Traktate, Kommentare und Summen scheinen allesamt von jenem Satz Francis Bacons inspiriert: »De nobis ipsis silemus«.

1 Der vorliegende Artikel ist ein Vortrag, der im Rahmen der Jahrestagung der IGTM e.V. am 03. Mai 2003 in Frankfurt am Main gehalten wurde.

2 Kant *Kritik*, S. 7.

3 Oberman 1968, S. 424.

4 Southern 1990.

5 De Libera 1991.

6 Courtenay 1987.

7 Besonders: Flasch ³1994; Flasch ²2000.

Will man also etwas über den Zusammenhang von Biographie und Theologie erfahren, muß man methodische Wege gehen, die unter Umständen nicht den Grad philologischer Absicherung besitzen, wie es beim Nachweis geistiger Abhängigkeiten über das wörtliche Zitat der Fall ist. Ich will daher im Folgenden anhand des englischen Franziskaners Wilhelm von Ockham experimentell solche methodisch unterschiedlichen Tiefenbohrungen vorstellen, von denen ich meine, daß sie unser Bild des *Venerabilis Inceptor* ein klein wenig konkreter und plastischer machen können, als es die traditionellen Zugänge der Forschung ermöglicht haben. Sie reichen dabei allesamt in das Zentrum seines philosophisch-theologischen Denkens: Anhand der Universalienlehre werde ich versuchen, den argumentativen Duktus von Ockhams Ausführungen biographisch auszuwerten. Sodann werde ich seine *potentia*-Lehre vor ihrem Entstehungs- bzw. Entfaltungskontext profilieren. Und drittens werde ich verstreute Selbst-Äußerungen Wilhelms von Ockham im Blick auf sein prophetisches Selbstverständnis deuten.

1. Die Universalienlehre und ihr theologischer Entdeckungshorizont

Diejenige Lehre, mit der Ockham wohl am meisten verbunden wird, ist seine Lehre von den Universalien. Ich will nicht die Frage behandeln, ob es sich hier nun um Nominalismus handelt oder nicht – es mag der Hinweis reichen, daß ich diese Bezeichnung für verkürzend halte.[8] Wichtiger ist, daß es sich hierbei nicht, wie es gemeinhin scheint und rezipiert wird, ausschließlich um ein philosophisches Problem handelt: denn gerade der Entdeckungszusammenhang verweist auf die theologische Bedingtheit dieses denkerischen Konzeptes. Wenn also in diesem Abschnitt von ›Biographie‹ die Rede ist, so geht es um die ›innere Biographie‹, und diese Überlegungen bewegen sich auch noch relativ nahe an traditioneller geistesgeschichtlicher Methodik, sofern diese nicht nur systematisch, sondern auch genetisch arbeitet.

Dabei wurde bislang wenig beachtet, daß es sich nun wirklich um eine Entdeckung, auch im biographischen Sinne, handelt,[9] und zwar um eine solche Entdeckung, die dem Franziskaner und Theologen Wilhelm von Ockham überhaupt wohl erstmals den Blick dafür geöffnet hat, daß er aus theologischen Notwendigkeiten heraus eine eigenständige philosophische Position vertreten muß und kann.

Auf diesen Zusammenhang verweist schon die bloße Tatsache, daß das Universalienproblem im Kontext seines Œuvres chronologisch erstmals in der vierten bis neunten *quaestio* zur zweiten *distinctio* des Ersten Buches des Sentenzenkommentars erscheint, also in seinem theologischen Hauptwerk, das er gegen Ende des zweiten Jahrzehnts des vierzehnten Jahrhunderts in Oxford

8 Die massivste Kritik hieran, freilich aus erkennbar apologetischen Gründen bei Boehner 1958, S. 156–174; vgl. meine eigenen Ausführungen in Leppin 1995, S. 59–63; eine positive Aufnahme des Begriffs findet sich bei Kaufmann 1994, S. 100; Beckmann 1995, 120–126. Einen differenziert-distanzierten Gebrauch des Begriffs ›Nominalismus‹ schlägt Schulthess 1992, S. 274, vor.

9 Vgl. hierzu demnächst auch Leppin 2004.

verfaßt hat. Ausgangspunkt seiner breit angelegten Überlegungen zu einem grundlegenden sprachphilosophischen Thema ist dann auch die theologische Frage: »Gibt es irgend etwas, was Gott und Geschöpf gemeinsam ist und univok und unter Bezug auf das Wesen von beiden ausgesagt werden kann?«[10] Es ist also das Problem von Univokation und Äquivokation, das Ockham noch einmal, wieder einmal, aufrollt.

Um sich dieser Frage zu nähern, mußte Ockham den Umweg über die Universalienlehre gehen: Um überhaupt zu wissen, ob wir unsere Begriffe univok oder äquivok verwenden, müssen wir zunächst wissen, in welchem Verhältnis unsere Begriffe zur Realität stehen. Es ist dieses Thema, das nun in überraschender Gründlichkeit die folgenden Seiten des Sentenzenkommentars füllt: Die Frage nach Univozität und Äquivokation wird in der auf sie ausgerichteten Frage gar nicht wirklich beantwortet, sondern Ockham mäandert die folgenden Fragekomplexe durch das Universalienproblem hindurch, ehe er in der neunten Frage neu ansetzt: »Ich frage, ob irgend etwas Allgemeines für Gott und Geschöpf univok sei«.[11] Schon dieser lange Umweg zeigt, wie sich das Problem gewissermaßen unter der Hand verselbständigte.

Das für die Universalienlehre entscheidende Ergebnis findet sich dabei schon in der *quaestio septima*: Das *universale*, der Allgemeinbegriff ist keine Realität außerhalb der Seele,[12] positiv formuliert: Das Allgemeine existiert allein im menschlichen Verstand: zwar nicht im bloßen Namen, aber eben doch im Begriff.[13] Die Bedeutung dieser Quästionen des Ockhamschen Sentenzenkommentars aber geht über eine solche lehrhaft faßbare Definition weit hinaus. Die weitgehend systematisch ausgerichtete philosophische und theologische Forschung beachtet zu wenig, daß hier nicht nur gewichtige Erkenntnisse inhaltlicher Art zu gewinnen sind, sondern daß es sich hier im Verlauf der intellektuellen Biographie Ockhams um eine Art Umbruch- oder Durchbruchstelle handelt. Hier geschieht in der akademischen Vita des etwa dreißigjährigen Franziskaners etwas höchst Bedeutsames: Es scheint, daß er zum ersten Mal von seinem eigenen Tun und Denken den Eindruck gewinnt, es sei etwas wirklich Neues.

Äußeres Indiz hierfür ist, daß die Gliederung des Sentenzenkommentars an dieser Stelle geradezu aus den Fugen bricht – die eigentliche Frage nach Äquivokation und Univokation wird fast verdrängt durch die gewichtigere Frage nach dem Status der Universalien, sie verschwindet thematisch geradezu aus diesem Vorlesungszusammenhang. Den Grund für die überraschende Breite der Behandlung der Universalienfrage aber gibt Ockham selbst an, wenn er erklärt, hier an eine Stelle gelangt zu sein, an der er von der *opinio communis* abweicht. Die Diskussionslage zur Universalienlehre nämlich stellt sich nach Ockham so dar:

10 »An Deo et creaturae sit aliquid commune univocum praedicabile essentialiter de utroque«; Guillelmus de Ockham *Sentenzenkommentar,* I d. 2 q. 4 (II 99,10f).

11 »... quaero utrum aliquod universale sit univocum Deo et creaturae«; Guillelmus de Ockham *Sentenzenkommentar* I d. 2 q. 9 (II 292,9f).

12 Guillelmus de Ockham *Sentenzenkommentar,* I d. 2 q. 7 (II 248,23–249,1).

13 Zu der gleichwohl gegebenen realen Fundierung der Allgemeinbegriffe s. Leppin 1998.

> In der abschließenden Beantwortung dieser Frage stimmen alle, die ich eingesehen habe, überein, insofern sie sagen, daß die Natur, die auf irgendeine Weise allgemein ist – wenigstens der Möglichkeit nach und unvollständig –, real im Einzelding ist.[14]

Dem aber setzt er seine schon erwähnte klare Position entgegen: »Ich sage hierzu, daß keine Entität außerhalb der Seele … allgemein ist«[15] Man wird diesen Vorgang in einer Zeit, in der Kriterien für theologisch und wissenschaftlich angemessenes Denken nicht unbedingt Kreativität und Originalität waren, nicht unterschätzen dürfen. Ockham entdeckt sich selbst als einen Neuerer – und wird damit geradezu zur intensiveren Auseinandersetzung mit der Philosophie gezwungen, und das hieß angesichts der am Begrifflichen orientierten Universalientheorie Ockhams: Er mußte sich von nun an intensiver als bislang mit der sprachlich orientierten terministischen Logik auseinandersetzen. Auch wenn Ockham hier Vorläufer für sein eigenes Denken fand, bleibt die Feststellung bemerkenswert, daß wir hier eine Selbstwahrnehmung der kompletten Abweichung vom Konsens und damit der völligen Neuerung haben. Und es scheint angesichts dessen, daß der Sentenzenkommentar ja das älteste erhaltene Werk Ockhams ist, durchaus plausibel, an dieser Stelle überhaupt erst den Anstoß für eine eigenständige Auseinandersetzung mit philosophischen Themen zu sehen.

Wenn wir heute Ockham als Gestalt der Philosophiegeschichte kennen und würdigen, dürfen wir dabei nicht vergessen, daß seine eigene Ausbildung in den *artes* eher kümmerlich war: Er dürfte die *artes* nicht an der Universität Oxford studiert haben, sondern an einem Ordensstudium,[16] vermutlich in London. Also verfügte er, als er mit der Theologie anfing, nicht einmal über den Abschluß eines *Magister artium* – das war aufgrund einer allerdings sehr umstrittenen Sonderregelung der Oxforder Statuten für Angehörige von Bettelorden möglich.[17] Und erst später – nach Abschluß seiner Sentenzenvorlesung – konnte er sich intensiver der Philosophie des Aristoteles zuwenden. Die derzeit plausibelste Annahme über die chronologische Reihenfolge seiner Schriften nämlich besagt, daß er hier den Auftrag eines philosophischen Lehrers für die nachwachsenden Franziskaner der Londoner Kustodie hatte.[18] Diesem ist er dann mit großem Engagement nachgekommen: In diesen Jahren, etwa 1320 bis 1324, hat er neben der allgemeinen Vorlesungstätigkeit sein logisches Hauptwerk, die *Summe der Logik* abgefaßt.

Versucht man, diese biographischen Beobachtungen zusammenzufassen, so ergibt sich ein Gesamtbild für das Verständnis Ockhams, das durchaus Folgen für sein inhaltliches Verständnis hat: Wenn es stimmt, daß Ockham an einem

14 »In conclusione istius quaestionis omnes quos vidi concordant, dicentes quod natura, quae est aliquo modo universalis, saltem in potentia et incomplete, est realiter in individuo«; Guillelmus de Ockham *Sentenzenkommentar,* I d. 2 q. 7 (II 225,17–19).

15 »Ideo aliter dico ad quaestionem quod nulla res extra animam … est universalis«; Guillelmus de Ockham *Sentenzenkommentar,* I d. 2 q. 3 (II 248,23–249,1).

16 Vgl. hierzu Miethke 1969, S. 7f.

17 Zu den Streitigkeiten s. *Friars Preachers,* S. 195–215, sowie Leppin 1995, S. 246–254.

18 Eine – im Ergebnis allerdings skeptische – Zusammenfassung der einschlägigen Argumente bietet Courtenay 1990, S. 327–337.

theologischen Problem die Entdeckung gemacht hat, daß sein eigenes Denken so neu und ungewöhnlich ist, daß er von hier aus die Philosophie neu zu durchdenken hatte; wenn es weiterhin stimmt, daß er tatsächlich erst nach den ersten theologischen Schriften seine philosophischen geschrieben hat, dann bedeutet dies auch etwas für die Zuordnung der philosophischen und theologischen Teile seines Werkes: Sie sind nicht, wie es ein an Thomas oder der Neuscholastik orientierter Zugriff oder eine einfache Nachzeichnung des Aufbaus der mittelalterlichen Universität vermuten lassen könnte, im Sinne der Zuordnung von Propädeutik und materialer Durchführung, von *ancilla* und *domina* zu verstehen, sondern das Modell ist noch schärfer zu fassen: Theologie ist die den Erkenntnishorizont ganz bestimmende Wissenschaft, auf die hin die Philosophie zu ordnen ist. Anders ausgedrückt: Wenn die vorgestellten Beobachtungen zu Ockhams innerer Biographie stimmen, dann ist Ockham, der im allgemeinen Bewußtsein wenn überhaupt, so eher als Philosoph präsent ist, primär als Theologe zu verstehen und auch so zu deuten.

2. Die *potentia*-Lehre als papomorphes Gottesbild

Kaum weniger prominent als die Universalienlehre ist im Werk Ockhams die Lehre von der Allmacht Gottes. Immer wieder erscheint in seinen Überlegungen der Satz, dieses oder jenes könne Gott wohl nach seiner absoluten Macht, setze es aber nicht in Wirklichkeit um.[19] Wollte man seine Philosophie und Theologie systematisch rekonstruieren, so wäre ein durchaus denkbarer Weg der, eben mit der Unterscheidung von *potentia absoluta* und *potentia ordinata* einzusetzen und von hier aus den Rest zu entfalten. Ockham aber argumentierte nicht wie ein moderner Systematiker, sondern setzte das Argument der beiden *potentiae* zunächst stillschweigend voraus.[20] Dies konnte er, da er sie keineswegs erfunden, sondern übernommen hat: Vor ihm hatte sich insbesondere Duns Scotus ihrer bedient und dabei selbst schon auf einen älteren Gebrauch zurückgegriffen.[21]

Erst als Ockham seit den frühen zwanziger Jahren sowohl von seinen franziskanischen Brüdern als auch von seinem ehemaligen Oxforder Universitätskanzler, Johannes Lutterell, unter Häresieverdacht gestellt wurde, sah er sich genötigt, klärend Stellung zu dieser Frage zu nehmen. Und es zeigte sich dabei tatsächlich, daß seine Definition der *potentia*-Lehre etwas anders erfolgte, als es bei Duns Scotus der Fall gewesen war. Seine eigene Erklärung bot er in der ersten Quaestio des sechsten Quodlibets, bezeichnenderweise im Zusammenhang einer Frage, die dem Heil des Menschen gilt: »Kann ein Mensch ohne geschaffene Liebe erlöst werden?«[22] Die entscheidenden Passagen seiner Antwort lauteten:

19 Iserloh 1956, S. 279, spricht daher in seiner kritischen Gesamtwürdigung Ockhams geradezu von einer »Theologie des Als-Ob«.

20 Zur Abfolge der Äußerungen zur *potentia*-Frage s. jetzt grundlegend Schröcker 2003, S. 29–33.

21 Vgl. hierzu Randi 1987, S. 43–50.

22 Zum gnadentheologischen Kontext s. zuletzt Biard 1998, S. 107–113.

Zum ersten Punkt sage ich, daß Gott gewisse Dinge nach seiner anordnungsgemäßen Macht tun kann und einige nach seiner absoluten Macht. Diese Unterscheidung ist nicht so zu verstehen, als gebe es in Gott real zwei Mächte, deren eine anordnungsgemäß sei und die andere absolut. Denn in Gott gibt es nach außen nur eine einzige Macht, die ganz und gar mit Gott selbst identisch ist. Die Unterscheidung ist aber auch nicht so zu verstehen, daß Gott manches anordnungsgemäß machen kann, manches hingegen absolut und nicht-anordnungsgemäß. Denn Gott kann nichts nicht-anordnungsgemäß machen. Vielmehr ist diese Unterscheidung so zu verstehen, daß ›etwas können‹ manchmal im Blick auf die von Gott angeordneten und eingesetzten Gesetze verstanden wird. Dann wird gesagt, Gott könne das gemäß der anordnungsgemäßen Macht tun. Anders wird ›können‹ in folgendem Sinne verstanden als: alles machen können, was nicht impliziert, daß ein Widerspruch entstünde – unabhängig davon, ob Gott angeordnet hat, daß er dies tun werde oder nicht. Denn Gott kann, gemäß dem Sentenzenmeister, Buch 1 distinctio 43, vieles machen, was er doch nicht machen will. Hiervon heißt es, das mache Gott gemäß der absoluten Macht. Ebenso kann ja der Papst manches nach den von ihm angeordneten Rechten nicht, was er gleichwohl absolut kann.[23]

Diese Ausführungen sind in mancherlei Hinsicht bemerkenswert. Wichtig ist zunächst, daß Ockham nicht zwei Mächte in Gott unterschieden wissen will, sondern nach außen nur eine Macht sieht. Ja, er betont, daß Gott nichts *inordinate*, nicht-anordnungsgemäß tun kann. Gottes absolute und anordnungsgemäße Macht also unterscheiden sich nicht anhand zweier unterschiedlicher Handlungsbezirke, sondern sie sind eher als der Unterschied zwischen Möglichkeit und Wirklichkeit zu verstehen: Die *potentia absoluta* drückt aus, was Gott alles tun ›kann‹, nämlich alles, was logisch nicht ausgeschlossen ist. Hierfür steht die Bindung an das Widerspruchsprinzip. Die *potentia ordinata* hingegen steht für das, was Gott aus diesen Möglichkeiten tatsächlich macht. In der Tat entsprach die Verwendung des *potentia-absoluta*-Argumentes im Sentenzenkommentar immer wieder dieser Unterscheidung: Mit seiner Hilfe lotete Ockham die Möglichkeiten Gottes aus, die gewissermaßen die denkerischen Rahmenbedingungen der tatsächlich existierenden Schöpfung und Heilsordnung darstellen. Und eben hierin liegt auch die entscheidende,

23 »Circa primum dico quod quaedam potest Deus facere de potentia ordinata et aliqua de potentia absoluta. Haec distinctio non est sic intelligenda quod in Deo sint realiter duae potentiae quarum una sit ordinata et alia absoluta, quia unica potentia est in Deo ad extra, quae omni modo est ipse Deus. Nec sic est intelligenda quod aliqua potest Deus ordinate facere, et aliqua potest absolute et non ordinate, quia Deus nihil potest facere inordinate.
Sed est sic intelligenda quod 'posse aliquid' quandoque accipitur secundum leges ordinatas et institutas a Deo, et illa dicitur Deus posse facere de potentia ordinata. Aliter accipitur 'posse' pro posse facere omne illud quod non includit contradictionem fieri, sive Deus ordinaverit se hoc facturum sive non, quia multa potest Deus facere quae non vult facere, secundum Magistrum Sententiarum, lib. I, d. 43; et illa dicitur Deus posse de potentia absoluta. Sicut Papa aliqua non potest secundum iura statuta ab eo, quae tamen absolute potest.« GUILLELMUS DE OCKHAM *Quodlibeta*, VI q. 1 [IX, 585,14–586,30]; Übersetzung nach LEPPIN/MÜLLER 2000, S. 69.

von Ockham selbst in dieser Schärfe nicht markierte Differenz zu Duns Scotus.[24] Während für Ockham die Unterscheidung der beiden *potentiae* gerade nicht unterschiedliche Handlungsketten oder Handlungsräume Gottes bezeichnete, waren für Duns Scotus durch die absolute Macht einerseits, die geordnete Macht andererseits zwei verschiedene Handlungsräume bezeichnet. *De potentia ordinata* handelte Gott demnach im regulären Weltablauf, *de potentia absoluta* hingegen bei einzelnen speziellen Handlungen, durch die er diesen Weltablauf unterbrach.[25]

Ockham hatte ein deutliches Gespür dafür, daß so die einheitliche Welterklärung in Gefahr geriet: Wer in dieser Weise zwei Handlungsebenen Gottes unterschied, lief irgendwann Gefahr, auch zwei Realitätsebenen zu unterscheiden. Erst Ockham gewann die Möglichkeit, Gottes Handeln als einheitlich zu interpretieren und dennoch den sinnvollen Sachgehalt der Unterscheidung von *potentia absoluta* und *potentia ordinata* aufrechtzuerhalten. Allerdings handelte er sich ein anderes Problem ein: Wenn tatsächlich alles Handeln Gottes *ordinate* erfolgt, dann gilt diese Bestimmung auch für die Durchbrechung der Ordnung. Selbst Wunder erfolgen nach diesem Schema ›*ordinate*‹: In Quodl. IV q. 32[26] bringt Ockham die drei Männer im Feuerofen aus Dan 3 als Beispiel dafür, daß Gott natürliche Kausalverhältnisse aufheben kann. Dies ist geradezu der typische Anwendungsfall des Gedankens der *potentia absoluta* bei Ockham, und damit wird der geistige Hintergrund der Betonung dieser Art von Allmacht bei Ockham deutlich: Zu den problematischen Lehren jener konsequenten Aristoteliker, auf deren Herausforderung Ockham mit seinem theologischen Denken reagiert hat, gehört auch die Lehre von dem notwendigen Kausalzusammenhang aller Dinge.[27] Theologisch-philosophisch korrekt gesprochen, bedeutete Ockhams Lösung nun, daß Gott nicht mehr nur durch und mit Hilfe der einmal in Gang gesetzten Kausalketten, der Ketten von Zweitursachen, agierte, sondern daß er als Erstursache jederzeit diese Kausalketten durchbrechen konnte. Damit war das Kausalprinzip keineswegs grundsätzlich bestritten – und doch in seiner generellen Bedeutung aufgehoben oder mindestens relativiert: Die innerweltlich feststellbaren Kausalitäten wurden in ihrer Bedeutung auf den Status überholbarer Ketten von Zweitursachen reduziert, jede Aussage über Kausalität war letztlich nur noch unter Vorbehalt zu treffen. Obwohl also Gott niemals unmittelbar *de potentia absoluta* handelt, erreicht er durch sein Handeln Wirkungen auf Erden, die als Durchbrechung der normalerweise gültigen, verläßlichen und naturwissenschaftlich nachvollziehbaren Ordnung zu gelten haben.

Es ist kaum erstaunlich, daß dieses Verständnis von Gottes Allmacht nicht nur Zeitgenossen irritiert, sondern auch längerfristig dazu geführt hat, daß dem Ockhamschen Gott eine ›Willkürfreiheit‹ zugeschrieben wurde.[28] Hans

24 S. hierzu im Einzelnen Leppin 1995, S. 47–51; Leppin 1998, S. 169–180; Schröcker 2003, S. 72.

25 Ioannes Duns Scotus *Opera*, VI, 364,11–19; 366,8–19.

26 Guillelmus de Ockham *Quodlibeta*, IV q. 32 [IX, 455,18–456,21].

27 Tempier *Verurteilung*, S. 17 u.ö.

28 Blumenberg ²1983, S. 171. Etwas moderater folgt ihm Heinzmann 1992, S. 247.

Blumenberg hat gerade wegen dieses Gedankens Ockham eine entscheidende Schlüsselstellung für die Entwicklung der Neuzeit zugerechnet: Es sei gerade die in Gottes Willkür begründete Ent-Sicherung des Gottesverhältnisses, die den Menschen in die eigene Verantwortung ruft. Diese allgemeine Auseinandersetzung ist aber für meinen vorliegenden Gedankengang weit weniger entscheidend als die Tatsache, wo und wie Ockham diese Definition seiner *potentia*-Lehre vorgetragen hat. Aus verschiedenen Erwägungen heraus kann man meines Erachtens wahrscheinlich machen, daß wenigstens das sechste Quodlibet, wenn nicht die gesamten Quodlibeta in Avignon entstanden sind.[29] Hierher war Ockham 1324 wegen der erwähnten Anklagen Lutterells geraten, der sich die Erlaubnis vom König geholt hatte, sein Anliegen an den Papsthof zu tragen.[30] Ockham hatte sich dem Prozeß gestellt und auch einen sehr peniblen, fairen Prozeß bekommen.[31] Die Zensoren haben es sich nicht leicht gemacht – was man schon daran sieht, daß der Prozeß vier Jahre nach Ockhams Ankunft in Avignon noch nicht beendet war: Die Exkommunikation Ockhams erfolgte im Jahre 1328 nicht wegen eines entsprechenden Prozeßergebnisses, sondern weil Ockham sich mit seinen Gefährten der Jurisdiktion des Papstes entzogen hatte und aus Avignon geflohen war. Diese vier Jahre dürfte Ockham im Franziskanerkloster in Avignon verbracht haben, wohl in einer faktischen Arrestsituation[32] – und: mit reichlich Zeit. Nachdem er in sieben akademischen Jahren in Oxford und London eine überaus reiche Textproduktion vorgelegt hatte, hat er nun Muße, sich grundlegend mit anderen Fragen zu befassen. Es läßt sich, wie gesagt, wahrscheinlich machen, daß in dieser Situation, die ich bei anderer Gelegenheit als Ockhams »virtuelle Universität« bezeichnet habe,[33] auch die Quodlibeta entstanden: als rein literarische Fiktion jener universitären Gespräche, auf deren reale Durchführung er, wie er hoffte, zeitweise, letztlich aber für den Rest seines Lebens verzichten mußte.

Das heißt nun auch: Sie entstanden in direkter Konfrontation mit einem avignonesischen Papsttum, dessen früher übliche negative Wertung durch die jüngere französische Forschung ganz erheblich korrigiert worden ist:[34] Es handelt sich um ein Papsttum auf der Höhe seiner kulturellen Entfaltung, ein modernes, strahlendes Papsttum – bei aller theologischen Problematik.

Vor diesem Hintergrund ist nun eine vorhin zitierte Formulierung mehr als auffällig: »Ebenso kann ja der Papst manches nach den von ihm angeordneten Rechten nicht, was er gleichwohl absolut kann.« In Avignon, als Gefangener des Papstes geäußert, gewinnt diese Aussage ein ganz anderes Gewicht, als wenn man sie in theoretischer Allgemeinheit stehen läßt: Ockham war ja mit dem gegenwärtigen Papst gerade in Rechtsdingen konfrontiert. Und er

29 S. Leppin 2003, S. 133–139; abwägend, mit einer gewissen Tendenz zur Datierung in Avignon jetzt auch Schröcker 2003, S. 33–35.

30 S. zu ihm Hoffmann 1959.

31 S. Koch 1935, S. 353–380; Koch 1936, S. 79–93. 168–197.

32 S. Leppin 2003, S. 132f.

33 Leppin 2003, S. 139.

34 S. insbesondere Guillemain 2000; Vingtain 1998.

hat zu diesem Zeitpunkt keinerlei kritische Folgerungen aus dieser seiner Situation für das Papstverständnis gezogen: Die zitierte Passage macht deutlich, daß Ockham die papalistischen Theorien seiner Zeit[35] in erheblichem Maße internalisiert hatte. Für ihn, den Angeklagten in Avignon, bestand kein Zweifel daran, daß der Papst über eine Macht in der Kirche verfügte, die alles rechtliche Maß sprengte. Die Aussage, daß der Papst absolut gesehen einen weiteren Spielraum hätte als nach den von ihm gegebenen Gesetzen, ist schwerlich anders zu verstehen als so, daß der Papst unhinterfragt als oberster Gesetzgeber der Kirche angesehen wird. Die Analogie mit Gott, die Ockham hier völlig unproblematisch andeutet, zeigt, daß er noch weit davon entfernt war, den Papst durch Hinweis auf irgendwelche anderen Größen kirchlichen Rechts in seiner Macht einzuschränken. Das Vertrauen in den Papst war ungebrochen, und zwar gerade das Vertrauen in jenen zentralistisch agierenden und regierenden Papst, den er in Avignon erleben konnte. Denkt man an die Auswirkungen, die der Gedanke der *potentia*-Unterscheidung in der Gotteslehre hat: daß nämlich Gott durch Wunder permanent in der Lage ist, seine eigenen regulären Bestimmungen zu durchbrechen, so wird die Analogie noch deutlicher. Päpstlicherseits bedeutet dies nichts anderes als die *potestas directa*, die Aegidius Romanus dem Papst zugesprochen hatte.

Mit dieser Analogie erweist sich dann aber jenes Denkmodell Ockhams, die starke Betonung der *potentia absoluta*, die Blumenberg und andere dazu geführt hat, die Modernität Ockhams herauszustreichen, als zutiefst in den spätmittelalterlichen Zeitumständen verhaftet: Gott ist in diesem Modell nicht mehr als ein überdimensionierter Papst. Gerade dadurch, daß sich das Papsttum in der Entwicklung von Innozenz III. zu Bonifaz VIII. wenigstens ideologisch zur allein bestimmenden Macht der Christenheit entwickelt hatte, wurde nun auch ein Gott denkbar, der mit Machtmitteln ausgestattet war, die letztlich durch nichts und niemanden als sich selbst kontrolliert waren, und der jederzeit in das innerweltliche Geschehen hineinregieren konnte. Geistesgeschichtlich bedeutet dies eine ungeheure Dynamisierung des Gottesbildes: Gott war nun der durchaus papomorph gedachte freie Souverän, der Gesetze zwar erlassen hatte, an diese aber eben in dem Sinne, wie wir heute naturwissenschaftliche Gesetze verstehen, also in dem Sinne der Allgemeinheit, nicht gebunden war. Mehr als sein jeweils notfalls auch spezielles Dekret war nicht erforderlich, um sein Handeln rechtens zu machen. Wenn meine Überlegungen stimmen, so hätte man an dieser Stelle einen ganz ähnlichen Fall wie das schon lange diskutierte Phänomen der Abhängigkeit von *Cur Deus homo?* von der sozial fundierten *honor* Vorstellung des Mittelalters: Der Gott Ockhams wäre der an den Himmel projizierte Papst – für einen als Papstkritiker bekannt gewordenen Theologen vielleicht eine überraschende Einsicht, in jedem Falle aber eine, die etwas von der Zeitgebundenheit von Theologie erahnen läßt.

35 Zur Diskussion s. jetzt grundlegend MIETHKE 2000.

3. Der Philosoph als Prophet

Mit diesen Überlegungen bin ich auch schon an der Schwelle der letzten – und längsten Lebensphase Ockhams angelangt: 1328 floh er vor dem nun in seinen Augen eindeutig als häretisch erkannten Papst aus Avignon und kam auf Umwegen über Pisa nach München, wo er fortan bis zu seinem Tod im Jahr 1347 als Berater des vom Papst gebannten Kaisers Ludwig des Bayern fungierte,[36] zusammen mit so illustren Gestalten wie dem ehemaligen Franziskanergeneral Michael von Cesena und Marsilius von Padua. In dieser Lebensphase liegt es auf der Hand, daß allein schon die neuen Themenstellungen: franziskanische Armut, Stellung von Papst und Kaiser, Ausdruck des tiefen biographischen Bruchs sind, den das Leben des englischen Franziskaners genommen hat. Ich will mich aber im Folgenden auf einen Aspekt konzentrieren, der in der bisherigen Forschung meines Erachtens noch nicht zureichend beachtet worden ist: Ockham, der scharfsinnige Theologe und Philosoph, interpretiert sich selbst nämlich in diesen Schriften seiner letzten Lebensphase, als Prophet. Daß diese Stellen bislang noch keine ausreichende Deutung erfahren haben, liegt nicht nur daran, daß sie rar sind, sondern auch daran, daß der wichtigste Belegtext hierfür, das *Compendium errorum Joannis* XXII. erst seit Kurzem innerhalb der kritischen Ausgabe von Ockhams politischen Werken zugänglich ist.

Im Prooemium dieses Werkes nun heißt es: »Durch diese (, die Päpstlichen) bin ich zusammen mit anderen Verehrern Christi ungerechterweise nach Patmos verbannt worden.«[37] Anders ausgedrückt: Ockham identifiziert sich metaphorisch mit dem endzeitlichen Seher der Johannes-Apokalypse – ein Vergleich, der natürlich allein schon aufgrund der Isolierung in München naheliegt. Doch wird man das Zitat hiermit allein nicht begründen können, denn es wird durch andere apokalyptische Passagen gerahmt: Ockham erklärt von zwei Bibelstellen, sie seien nun erfüllt: 2 Tim 4,3–4 und Dan 13,5. An der Stelle aus dem zweiten Timotheusbrief ist der intendierte Zeitbezug überdeutlich: »Denn es wird eine Zeit kommen, in der man die gesunde Lehre nicht erträgt, sondern sich nach eigenen Wünschen immer neue Lehrer sucht, die den Ohren schmeicheln; und man wird der Wahrheit nicht mehr Gehör schenken, sondern sich Fabeleien zuwenden«. Offenkundig ist Ockham in seiner Selbstwahrnehmung derjenige, der die Zeit erlebt, in der die Wahrheit beiseite geschoben wird, der gleichsam ins Leere, in die Verstockung hinein zu predigen beauftragt ist.

Interessanter und zugleich komplexer ist die Erwähnung von Dan 13,5 aus der Geschichte von Susanna im Bade. In diesem eher novellesken Zusammenhang heißt es in Vers 5: »Ungerechtigkeit ging von Babylon aus, von den Ältesten, von den Richtern, die als Leiter des Volkes galten«,[38] und Ockham erklärt in offenkundiger Anwendung des *sensus anagogicus*, eben dieser Vers sei nun erfüllt. Die Ältesten und Richter sind dabei deutlich aufschlüsselbar:

36 Zu ihm Thomas 1993.

37 Guillelmus de Ockham *Compendium*, IV, S. 15, 25f.

38 Guillelmus de Ockham *Compendium*, IV, S. 15, 24f.

Nach dem Kontext im Vorwort sind damit die Kardinäle gemeint, die Benedikt XII. umgeben; Ockham hatte sie schon vorher massiv angegriffen, als *sequaces*, Gefolgsleute des Papstes, und auch jetzt scheint er mehr sie im Blick zu haben als den Papst. Besonders raffiniert ist nun aber die Verwendung von Babylon, bekanntlich schon innerhalb des Neuen Testamentes ein Deckname für Rom: In Ockhams Zeit wurde noch deutlicher, daß es hier nicht um eine geographische Größe ging, sondern um eine theologische oder kirchenpolitische: um Rom als Papstsitz, das hieß: Avignon. Aufgrund der klaren apokalyptischen Konnotation dieser Babylon-Identifikation Roms wird man kaum umhin können, auch in dieser Zitation apokalyptische Obertöne mitschwingen zu hören.

Daß dies keineswegs abwegig ist, zeigt auch das persönlichste Dokument aus Ockhams Feder, das uns erhalten ist: ein Brief, den er 1334 an das Generalkapitel seines Ordens in Assisi geschrieben hat, um sein Verhalten, insbesondere sein Abweichen von der päpstlichen Kirche zu legitimieren. In diesem Schreiben nun nimmt er als Vorbild für seine eigene, vereinsamte Situation in München nicht den Johannes auf Patmos, sondern Elia, also eine zentrale Gestalt des Endzeitszenarios. Ockham begründet diese Analogie nun nicht mit eigenem prophetischen Anspruch, sondern mit dem Modell der Restkirche, also jenem aus der Kanonistik übernommenen Gedanken, nach dem es möglich wäre, daß die wahre Kirche Jesu Christi nur in einigen Wenigen erhalten bliebe: Dies war, so Ockham, bei Elia der Fall – und es ist nun, im Jahre 1334 wieder der Fall: Die Wenigen sitzen, so läßt sich erschließen, in München, auf jenem Patmos, das der Verkündigung der Wahrheit dient.

Die darin inszenierte prophetische Selbstdarstellung ist – das habe ich an anderer Stelle versucht auszuarbeiten[39] – gewiß nicht in charismatischem Sinne zu verstehen: Der Philosoph und Theologe wird hier gerade dadurch zum Propheten, daß er, im Unterschied zum Papst und seinen *sequaces*, an der Heiligen Schrift und, darin eingeschlossen, den legitimen kirchlichen Lehrentscheidungen festhält. Ockhams Prophetie ist also, gewissermaßen, eine Schreibstubenprophetie. Und doch bleibt es meines Erachtens bemerkenswert für ein Verständnis Ockhams, daß wir hier ein sonst kaum zu beobachtendes Ineinander von theologischer und kirchenjuristischer Begründung – im Restkirchenmodell – und biographischem Selbstverständnis haben: Das Selbstbewußtsein zum Protest gegen die real existierende Papstkirche von Avignon zieht Ockham aus seinen akademisch gewonnenen theologischen Überzeugungen – aber er bleibt nicht akademisch: Er sieht sich zugleich als Verwirklichung eines biblischen Patterns, als Realisierer des prophetischen Amtes in seiner Gegenwart des vierzehnten Jahrhunderts. Zumindest im Blick auf solche Gesamtdarstellungen der Philosophiegeschichte, die Ockham vornehmlich als den Erfinder des Ockhamschen Rasiermessers, als radikalen ontologischen Reduktionisten verstehen wollen, gewinnt Ockham dadurch, so denke ich, einen anderen Kontext – und letztlich auch für jene, die ihn unter der Perspektive heutiger analytischer Sprachphilosophie in die Gegenwart

39 LEPPIN 2001.

ziehen wollen: Dieser Wilhelm von Ockham ist, auch wenn ihm Buchtitel wie *Das Risiko modern zu denken*[40] oder *Die Gegenwart Ockhams*[41] gewidmet sind, ein zutiefst mittelalterlicher Mensch.

Fazit

Die an einzelnen Stellen einhakende biographische Relecture hat natürlich zunächst jenen antiquarischen Wert, auf den wir Kirchenhistoriker immer stolz sind: Wir wissen etwas genauer, wie wir uns einen Menschen der Vergangenheit vorstellen sollen – auch wenn wir ebenso gut wissen, daß wir niemals wissen werden, ›wie es eigentlich gewesen ist‹. Doch scheint mir die biographische Herangehensweise auch noch etwas mehr zu bewirken: Gerade die biographische Aufschlüsselung etwa der Universalienlehre legt in Wilhelm von Ockham eben jenen Kontext frei, ohne den meines Erachtens ein mittelalterlicher Denker gar nicht zu begreifen ist: den theologischen oder, allgemeiner: den kirchlichen Kontext.

Wilhelm von Ockham ist ein Denker, dessen Wirkungsgeschichte ganz überwiegend eine philosophische gewesen ist. Dafür gibt es Gründe in beiden großen Konfessionen: Auf katholischer Seite sein Konflikt mit dem Papst und die daraus resultierende Exkommunikation, auf evangelischer Seite das Verdikt der Humanisten und Martin Luthers über die Spitzfindigkeiten der Scholastik, ja, beim Reformator ausdrücklich über Wilhelm von Ockham. So haben Theologen und Theologinnen sich in der Ockham-Forschung eher zurückhaltend gezeigt. Blättert man die einschlägige Bibliographie durch, so findet man in großer Zahl Werke zu Themen der Wissenschaftslehre der Logik oder der Ontologie, kaum etwas zur Gotteslehre, zur Christologie oder zur Eucharistielehre. Eine solche Verselbständigung der Philosophie gegenüber der Theologie wird durch die neuscholastische Trennung seiner Werkausgabe in philosophische und theologische Opera sogar noch unterstützt. Hier kann meines Erachtens eine konsequent biographische Lektüre nicht nur zur Historisierung führen, deren Nutzen für die Theologie immer ein fraglicher ist, sondern auch zur konsequenten Re-Theologisierung: Wer auf die biographischen Motive Ockhams schaut, entdeckt einen frommen Franziskaner und engagierten Theologen. Und diese Entdeckung ist im Rahmen der Jahrestagung einer Internationalen Gesellschaft für ›theologische‹ Mediävistik vielleicht nicht die unangemessenste.

40 Aicher/Greindl/Vossenkuhl u.a. 1986.
41 Vossenkuhl/Schönberger 1990.

Bibliographie

Quellen

Guillelmus de Ockham

Opera Theologica
Guillelmus de Ockham: *Opera Theologica,* ed. Juvenalis Lalor u.a., i-x, N.Y. 1967–1986.

Compendium
Guillelmus de Ockham: *Compendium errorum Joannis* xxii, in *Opera Politica,* ed. by Hilary S. Offler, iv, Oxford 1997, 14–77.

Quodlibeta
Guillelmus de Ockham: *Quodlibeta vi,* in *Opera Theologica,* ix.

Sentenzenkommentar
Guillelmus de Ockham: *Sentenzenkommentar,* in *Opera Theologica,* i-vii.

Leppin/Müller 2000
Wilhelm von Ockham. Texte zur Theologie und Ethik. Lateinisch-Deutsch. Ausgewählt, übersetzt und hg. von Volker Leppin, Sigrid Müller, Stuttgart 2000.

Andere Quellen

Ioannes Duns Scotus *Opera*
Doctoris Subtilis et Mariani Ioannis Duns Scoti Ordinis Fratrum Minorum Opera Omnia, ed. Karl Balic, vi, Vatikan 1963.

Friars Preachers
The Friars Preachers vs. the University, ed. Hastings Rashdall, in *Collectanea 2,* hg. von Montagu Burrows, Oxford 1890, 193–273.

Kant *Kritik*
Immanuel Kant: *Kritik der reinen Vernunft,* in *Werke in sechs Bänden,* ed. Wilhelm Weischedel, ii, Darmstadt [5]1983.

Tempier *Verurteilung*
Aufklärung im Mittelalter? Die Verurteilung von 1277, Das Dokument des Bischofs von Paris eingel., übers. u. erkl. von Kurt Flasch (Excerpta classica 6), Mainz 1989.

Abhandlungen

Aicher/Greindl/Vossenkuhl 1986
Wilhelm von Ockham. Das Risiko modern zu denken, hg. von Otl Aicher, Gabriele Greindl, Wilhelm Vossenkuhl, München 1986.

Beckmann 1995
Jan P. Beckmann: *Wilhelm von Ockham,* München 1995.

Biard 1998
Joël Biard: *Guillaume d'Ockham et la théologie,* Paris 1998.

BLUMENBERG ²1983
HANS BLUMENBERG: *Säkularisierung und Selbstbehauptung.* Erweiterte und überarbeitete Neuausgabe von *»Die Legitimität der Neuzeit«*, erster und zweiter Teil, Frankfurt ²1983.
BOEHNER 1958
PHILOTHEUS BOEHNER: »The Realistic Conceptualism of William Ockham«, in *Collected Articles on Ockham*, hg. von ELIGIUS M. BUYTAERT (FIP.P 12), N.Y. u.a. 1958 (= 1992), 156–174.
COURTENAY 1987
WILLIAM J. COURTENAY: *Schools and Scholars in Fourteenth-Century England*, Princeton 1987.
COURTENAY 1990
WILLIAM J. COURTENAY: »Ockham, Chatton, and the London studium. Observations on Recent Changes in Ockham's Biography«, in *Die Gegenwart Ockhams*, hg. von WILHELM VOSSENKUHL/ROLF SCHÖNBERGER, Weinheim 1990, 327–337.
DE LIBERA 1991
ALAIN DE LIBERA: *Penser au Moyen Âge*, Paris 1991.
FLASCH ³1994
KURT FLASCH: *Einführung in die Philosophie des Mittelalters*, Darmstadt ³1994.
FLASCH ²2000
KURT FLASCH: *Das philosophische Denken im Mittelalter. Von Augustin zu Machiavelli*, Stuttgart ²2000.
GUILLEMAIN 2000
BERNARD GUILLEMAIN: *Les papes d'Avignon 1309–1376*, Paris 2000.
HEINZMANN 1992
RICHARD HEINZMANN: *Philosophie des Mittelalters* (Grundkurs Philosophie 7), Stuttgart u.a. 1992.
HOFFMANN 1959
FRITZ HOFFMANN: *Die Schriften des Oxforder Kanzlers Iohannes Lutterell. Texte zur Theologie des vierzehnten Jahrhunderts* (EThSt 6), Leipzig 1959.
ISERLOH 1956
ERWIN ISERLOH: *Gnade und Eucharistie in der philosophischen Theologie des Wilhelm von Ockham. Ihre Bedeutung für die Ursachen der Reformation* (VIEG 8), Wiesbaden 1956.
KAUFMANN 1994
MATTHIAS KAUFMANN: *Begriffe, Sätze, Dinge. Referenz und Wahrheit bei Wilhelm von Ockham* (STGMA 40), Leiden u.a. 1994.
KOCH 1935
JOSEF KOCH: »Neue Aktenstücke zu dem gegen Wilhelm Ockham in Avignon geführten Prozeß«, in *RThAM 7* (1935) 353–380.
KOCH 1936
JOSEF KOCH: »Neue Aktenstücke zu dem gegen Wilhelm Ockham in Avignon geführten Prozeß«, in *RThAM 8* (1936) 79–93. 168–197.
LEPPIN 1995
VOLKER LEPPIN: *Geglaubte Wahrheit. Das Theologieverständnis Wilhelms von Ockham* (FKDG 63), Göttingen 1995.

LEPPIN 1998
VOLKER LEPPIN: »Does Ockham's Concept of Divine Power Threaten Man's Certainty in His Knowledge of the World?«, in *FrS 55* (1998) 169–180.

LEPPIN 2001
VOLKER LEPPIN: »Ockham und die Prophetie. Beobachtungen zur Selbstwahrnehmung eines philosophischen Theologen«, in *FZPhTh 48* (2001) 470–476.

LEPPIN 2003
VOLKER LEPPIN: *Wilhelm von Ockham. Gelehrter – Streiter – Bettelmönch*, Darmstadt 2003.

LEPPIN 2004
VOLKER LEPPIN: »Gotteslehre und Logik bei Wilhelm von Ockham«, in *Theologie und Logik. Das Organon im Mittelalter*, hg. von DOMINIK PERLER, (im Druck).

MIETHKE 1969
JÜRGEN MIETHKE: *Ockhams Weg zur Sozialphilosophie*, Berlin 1969.

MIETHKE 2000
JÜRGEN MIETHKE: *De potestate papae* (SuR.NR 16), Tübingen 2000.

OBERMAN 1968
HEIKO AUGUSTINUS OBERMAN: »›Iustitia Christi‹ und ›Iustitia Dei‹. Luther und die scholastischen Lehren von der Rechtfertigung«, in *Der Durchbruch der reformatorischen Erkenntnis bei Luther*, hg. von BERNHARD LOHSE, Darmstadt 1968, 413–444.

RANDI 1987
EUGENIO RANDI: »A Scotist Way of Distinguishing between God's Absolute and Ordained Powers«, in *From Ockham to Wyclif*, ed. by ANNE HUDSON, MICHAEL WILKS, Oxford/New York 1987, 43–50.

SCHRÖCKER 2003
HUBERT SCHRÖCKER: *Das Verhältnis der Allmacht Gottes zum Kontradiktionsprinzip nach Wilhelm von Ockham* (VGI 49), Berlin 2003.

SCHULTHESS 1992
PETER SCHULTHESS: *Sein, Signifikation und Erkenntnis bei Wilhelm von Ockham*, Berlin 1992.

SOUTHERN 1990
RICHARD W. SOUTHERN: *Saint Anselm. A portrait in a landscape*, Cambridge 1990.

THOMAS 1993
HEINZ THOMAS: *Ludwig der Bayer (1282–1347). Kaiser und Ketzer*, Regensburg 1993.

VINGTAIN 1998
DOMINIQUE VINGTAIN: *Avignon. Le palais des papes*, [Saint-Léger-Vauban 1998].

VOSSENKUHL/SCHÖNBERGER 1990
Die Gegenwart Ockhams, hg. von WILHELM VOSSENKUHL, ROLF SCHÖNBERGER, Weinheim 1990.

Archa Verbi 1 (2004) 143–162

Basilisken und ägyptische Frösche
Alte und neue Theologie im bayerisch-österreichischen Raum im 12. Jahrhundert

von CHRISTOPH EGGER[1]

In der um 1200 von einem Mönch des oberösterreichischen Benediktinerstiftes Lambach abgefaßten Vita des 1090 verstorbenen Bischofs Adalbero von Würzburg findet sich folgende Beschreibung der Studienzeit des Bischofs:

> Als er das Jünglingsalter erreicht hatte ... kam er mit einigen Gefährten nach Paris, wo damals, so wie auch heutzutage, die Kenntnis aller Wissenschaften in Blüte stand, und nachdem er sich dort in reichem Maße an den süßen Früchten des Wissens erquickt hatte, kehrte er voll von Weisheit nach Würzburg zurück.

Gemeinsam mit ihm hätten sich der spätere Erzbischof von Salzburg, Gebhard, und der spätere Bischof Altmann von Passau in Frankreich aufgehalten.[2] Allerdings weiß man aus den Lebensbeschreibungen Altmanns und Gebhards nichts über ein Studium in Paris und wäre ein solches bald nach der Mitte des 11. Jahrhunderts auch einigermaßen überraschend, da die Schulen dieser Stadt erst gegen Ende des Jahrhunderts ihre große Anziehungskraft zu entwickeln begannen. Die Schilderung der *Vita Adalberonis* sagt daher wohl weniger über die Verhältnisse während der Lebenszeit ihres Helden als über die Zeit ihres Autors aus,[3] in der ein Studium an einer der großen Schulen – Laon, Chartres, Reims, Orléans und immer mehr vor allem Paris und Bologna – zu einem festen Bestandteil kirchlicher Karrieremuster geworden war.[4]

1 Der vorliegende Artikel ist ein Vortrag, der im Rahmen der Jahrestagung der IGTM e.V. am 03. Mai 2003 in Frankfurt am Main gehalten wurde. Da es sich um die Vorstellung eines im Laufen befindlichen Forschungsvorhabens handelt, wurde die Vortragsform im wesentlichen beibehalten und nur die notwendigste Literatur angeführt. Einen ersten Überblick über das Vorhaben habe ich gegeben in EGGER 2004, S. 87–97.

2 *Vita sancti Adalberonis*, c. 1: »Ubi vero annos adolescentie intravit ... assumptis aliquibus sodalibus Parisius pervenit, ubi tunc, sicut et nunc, omnium floruit peritia artium, ibique dulcibus habundanter theorye refectus fructibus, sapientia plenus Herbipolym est regressus.« *Vita sancti Adalberonis*, S. 18f, zu Gebhard und Altmann ebd., c. 2–3, S. 18–22. Ein gemeinsames Studium von Adalbero, Gebhard und Altmann erwähnt auch die um 1140 in Göttweig verfaßte *Vita Altmanni prior*, c. 7, S. 231, jedoch ohne eine Ortsangabe; ansonsten wird nur in c. 2 erwähnt, daß Altmann sich lange in Paderborn aufgehalten und dort die Schule geleitet hätte (ebd. S. 229). Für Gebhard von Salzburg ist ebenfalls kein Studium in Paris belegt. LOSEK 2001, S. 67–69.

3 Vermutlich dem selben Muster folgt der englische Chronist des 13. Jahrhunderts Matthew Paris, der den späteren Papst Hadrian IV. in Paris studieren läßt, was aus keiner der nahzeitigen Quellen belegt werden kann: vgl. EGGER 2003, S. 19f.

4 Zu nennen wären etwa die Bischöfe Otto von Freising, Hartwig von Bremen, Adalbert II. von Mainz oder Daniel von Prag. Vgl. EHLERS 1996.

Indem ein Studium in Paris für einen bedeutenden kirchlichen Funktionär als selbstverständlich unterstellt wird, zeigt sich, welch tiefgreifenden Bewußtseinswandel die bildungsgeschichtlichen Entwicklungen des 12. Jahrhunderts auch im bayerisch-österreichischen Raum bewirkt hatten. Für die Beschäftigung mit dieser »Renaissance«, wie der amerikanische Historiker Charles H. Haskins den kulturellen Aufbruch im 12. Jahrhundert, den verstärkten Rückgriff auf antikes Bildungsgut, die Blüte von Dichtung und Literatur, die Entwicklung der »scholastischen Methode« und ihrer Anwendung in Theologie und Kanonistik, beschrieben hat,[5] bietet der bayerisch-österreichische Raum trotz seiner in bezug auf die nordfranzösischen und oberitalienischen Bildungszentren anscheinend peripheren Lage ausgezeichnete Voraussetzungen.

Das hatte bereits in den dreißiger Jahren des 20. Jahrhunderts der Historiker Konrad Josef Heilig erkannt und festgestellt, »daß die von C. H. Haskins vielfach nachgewiesene Renaissance of the twelfth century in Österreich eine Filiale besonderer Art aufgemacht hat.«[6] Zur Abfassung einer Arbeit, in der er dies »an Hand der fast noch völlig unbekannten Theologie in den österreichischen Klöstern« zeigen wollte, ist Heilig jedoch nicht mehr gekommen.[7] Auch der österreichische Historiker Alphons Lhotsky, der sich in verschiedenen Arbeiten mit der »Geschichte der Wissenschaftspflege« in österreichischen Klöstern befaßte, hat früh auf den Reichtum der einschlägigen handschriftlichen Überlieferung und die Bedeutung ihrer Auswertung hingewiesen.[8] Von theologiegeschichtlicher Seite erstmals unter einem bestimmten Gesichtspunkt systematisch gesichtet und erfaßt wurde die handschriftliche Überlieferung durch Heinrich Weisweiler in seinem Buch über Werke aus dem Bereich der Schule von Laon im deutschsprachigen Raum.[9] Seine Arbeit, die immer noch von großem Wert für die Literargeschichte ist, zeigt besonders deutlich den Reichtum der einschlägigen Überlieferung in bayerisch-österreichischen Bibliotheken; eine Einordnung der Ergebnisse in den bildungsgeschichtlich-allgemeinhistorischen Zusammenhang konnte Weisweiler allerdings nicht geben. Einen wesentlichen Schritt in diese Richtung bedeutete die Identifizierung eines bereits durch Heinrich Weisweiler bekanntgemachten Magister Petrus mit einem sich um die Mitte des 12. Jahrhunderts am Babenbergerhof in Wien aufhaltenden Franzosen und Schülers des Gilbert von Poitiers durch Heinrich Fichtenau.[10] Nach und nach kamen eine

5 Haskins 1927. Obwohl der Begriff nicht unumstritten ist (vgl. etwa Schimmelpfennig 1989), hat seine Verwendung doch eine Berechtigung, solange man sich seiner Grenzen bewußt ist. Vgl. auch Benson/Constable/Lanham 1982, sowie Classen 1983.

6 Heilig 1944, hier S. 271 Anm. 1, unter Verweis auf Heilig 1935, bes. S. 17.

7 Heilig 1944, S. 271. Heilig ist in den letzten Kriegsmonaten 1945 in Kroatien verschollen.

8 Lhotsky 1961; Lhotsky selbst war vor allem am Spätmittelalter und am historiographisch-literarischen Schrifttum interessiert; zur frühscholastischen Theologie enthalten seine Arbeiten daher nur wenig.

9 Weisweiler 1936.

10 Fichtenau 1944/48.

Reihe von Texten – Briefe,[11] Sammlungen von Autoritäten,[12] Traktate[13] – zutage, die mit diesem Magister Petrus von Wien und seinen Auseinandersetzungen mit dem Regularkanoniker Gerhoch von Reichersberg und seinem Kreis zusammenhängen. Diese Texte zeigen deutlich, daß man fern der Zentren schon sehr früh durchaus gut über die neuesten Entwicklungen informiert war, sich aktiv für sie interessierte und sich mit ihnen auseinandersetzte. Zugleich gewann auch eine Schlüsselpersönlichkeit der bayerisch-österreichischen Bildungsgeschichte des 12. Jahrhunderts deutlichere Gestalt: Peter Classen verfaßte eine ausführliche Biographie Gerhochs, die in mustergültiger Weise die allgemeinhistorische und theologiegeschichtliche Sicht zu einer detaillierten und bis heute nicht überholten Darstellung vereinigt, deren Bedeutung weit über ihr engeres Thema hinausreicht.[14] Classen ist auch der erste und bisher einzige Versuch eines Überblickes über die Geschichte der Frühscholastik in Bayern und Österreich im Spiegel der handschriftlichen Überlieferung zu verdanken.[15] Wie ein solcher Überblick in detaillierter und methodisch zuverlässiger Form auszusehen hätte, hat schließlich Winfried Stelzer am Beispiel der Rezeption des gelehrten Rechts in Österreich gezeigt.[16] Auch wenn sich der Bereich des Rechtswesens von dem der Theologie in mancher Hinsicht unterscheidet, sind doch die Rezeptionswege und auch die rezipierenden Personen in beiden Bereichen oft die selben, was auch nicht verwunderlich ist, da im 12. Jahrhundert keinesfalls von einer scharfen Trennung zwischen Theologie und Kanonistik ausgegangen werden kann. Vor allem aber ist Stelzers Buch exemplarisch für die methodische Vorgangsweise bei der Erforschung von überlieferungsgeschichtlichen Zusammenhängen und Rezeptionsvorgängen im bildungsgeschichtlichen Bereich. Parallel zu den Bemühungen um einzelne Personen fand natürlich eine stetige Nutzung bayerisch-österreichischer Handschriftenbestände im Rahmen von problemgeschichtlichen Arbeiten oder für die Erstellung kritischer Editionen statt,[17] eine neuere Untersuchung, die die Überlieferungs- und Rezeptionsvorgänge an sich, die dafür verantwortlichen und daran beteiligten Personen und Institutionen und ihr jeweiliges Interesse in den Blick nimmt und in den historischen Zusammenhang zu stellen versucht, fehlt aber. Zudem ist auf ein gewisses Ungleichgewicht hinsichtlich der chronologischen Verteilung der unter-

11 Z. B. Weisweiler 1938a; Weisweiler 1938b; Weisweiler 1939; Günster 1955.

12 Z. B. Häring 1966; oder die unten Anm. 61 erwähnten Exzerptsammlungen aus Werken des Hilarius von Poitiers.

13 Z.B. Häring 1965.

14 Classen 1960. Einen wesentlichen Beitrag zur Kenntnis Gerhochs hatte bereits Heinrich Fichtenau geleistet: Fichtenau 1938.

15 Classen 1959b.

16 Stelzer 1982.

17 Stellvertretend für viele sei die von Dominique Poirel erstellte Edition von Hugo von St. Viktor *De tribus diebus*, genannt, in der zwei Textfamilien herausgearbeitet sind, die wesentlich von Handschriften aus dem bayerisch-österreichischen Raum getragen werden: Hugo de Sancto Victore *De tribus diebus*.

suchten Autoren hinzuweisen: im Mittelpunkt des bisherigen Forschungsinteresses stand die Zeit bis bald nach der Mitte des 12. Jahrhunderts, die spätere Frühscholastik hingegen, mit Autoren wie Praepositinus von Cremona, Petrus von Poitiers oder Alanus von Lille und Textcorpora wie den Glossen zu den biblischen Büchern, hat bisher nur wenig Beachtung gefunden.

Wie kommt es nun zu der reichhaltigen Tradition einschlägiger Texte in bayerischen und österreichischen Bibliotheken? Es ist gut möglich, daß durch das aktive Interesse Gerhochs von Reichersberg und seines Kreises schon im Mittelalter die Voraussetzungen für diese reiche Überlieferung geschaffen wurden – letztlich ist die Richtigkeit dieser Vermutung Teil meiner Fragestellung. Daß sich aber so viele Handschriften bis zur Gegenwart und oft am oder doch nahe dem Ort ihrer mittelalterlichen Aufbewahrung erhalten haben, ist sicher vor allem ein Verdienst der günstigen Überlieferungsumstände. Im Gegensatz zu anderen Teilen des deutschsprachigen Raumes waren in Österreich und Bayern keine großen Schäden durch Reformation und Dreißigjährigen Krieg zu beklagen.[18] Die Säkularisierungen Ende des 18. und am Beginn des 19. Jahrhunderts führten kaum zur Vernichtung von Bibliotheksbeständen, sondern zu ihrer Verwahrung in staatlichen Bibliotheken wie der Österreichischen Nationalbibliothek in Wien oder der Bayerischen Staatsbibliothek in München. In der Inflationszeit der Dreißigerjahre des 20. Jahrhunderts waren einige österreichische Klöster gezwungen, Handschriften zu verkaufen; mit der Ausnahme von Lambach, wo dies zu einer gravierenden Verringerung des Bestandes führte, hielten sich die Verluste aber in Grenzen. Zum Teil wurden sie auch dadurch erträglicher, daß wichtige Handschriften in den Besitz öffentlicher Bibliotheken gelangten und so für die Forschung zugänglich blieben.[19] Unbedingt wären Untersuchungen der frühscholastischen Textüberlieferung und Rezeption aber auch für andere, unter Umständen weniger begünstigte, geographische Bereiche, etwa für Norddeutschland[20] oder Flandern, anzustreben, um so durch die vergleichende Perspektive zusätzliche Einblicke gewinnen zu können.

Der Reichtum der Überlieferung verursacht allerdings auch eine Reihe von grundsätzlichen, zum Teil sehr schwerwiegenden Problemen. Schon die Grundvoraussetzung für die Arbeit mit Handschriften, die inhaltliche Erschließung, fehlt für viele der Bibliotheken im bayerisch-österreichischen Raum weitgehend. So existiert für die sehr reiche und wichtige Bibliothek des

18 Schwer wiegt allerdings der Verlust der Stiftsbibliothek von Reichersberg 1624 durch einen Brand: Plante 1977; von großem Wert dürfte auch die 1633 durch die Schweden zerstörte Bibliothek des Stiftes von St. Mang in Stadtamhof bei Regensburg gewesen sein: vgl. Fuchs 1989.

19 So etwa die ehemals Admonter Handschriften 382 und 729: Cod. 382 (Thierry von Chartres, Abaelard) befindet sich heute in Oxford, Bodleian Library, Lyell Ms 49; Cod. 729 (Schule von Laon, Abaelard) in Princeton, University Library, Garrett Ms 169.

20 Es sei nur an die Bücherschenkung des Bischofs Hartwig von Bremen an seine Domkirche erinnert; oder an den Buchbesitz, den der Hildesheimer Kanoniker Harderardus an Halberstadt schenkte: vgl. Stammberger 2001.

Benediktinerstiftes Admont kein gedruckter Katalog; zur Orientierung helfen nur die Angaben aus dem 1880 bis 1889 von Jakob Wichner verfaßten handschriftlichen Verzeichnis, das übrigens, verglichen mit manchem zeitgenössischen Katalog, als durchaus qualitätvoll bezeichnet werden kann. Für die österreichischen Zisterzienserstifte finden sich die notwendigsten Angaben in einer 1891 veröffentlichten Katalogserie, deren einzelne Teile allerdings von recht unterschiedlicher Qualität sind.[21] Ein Großteil der Bestände der Österreichischen Nationalbibliothek und der Bayerischen Staatsbibliothek sind durch Kataloge aus der zweiten Hälfte des 19. Jahrhunderts nur sehr unzureichend erschlossen. Die Erstellung von Katalogen, die in kodikologisch-paläographischer und in inhaltlicher Hinsicht alle Ansprüche erfüllen, ist zwar im Gange, nimmt aber viel Zeit in Anspruch und schreitet dementsprechend langsam voran.[22]

Die unzureichende Erschließung vergrößert aber nicht nur den Zeitaufwand der selbst zu leistenden Forschungsarbeit, sie bringt noch weitere Probleme mit sich. Zur Untersuchung der Überlieferung frühscholastischer Literatur in einem bestimmten geographischen Bereich reicht eine rein listenmäßige Erfassung der in Frage kommenden Handschriften keinesfalls aus. Vielmehr ist es ganz wesentlich, daß zwischen Provenienz und Bibliotheksheimat einer Handschrift unterschieden wird. Die Provenienz bezeichnet den Ort, wo die Handschrift geschrieben worden ist, die Bibliotheksheimat hingegen den Ort (oder die Orte), an dem (oder an denen) sie in der weiteren Folge ihres Lebenslaufes aufbewahrt wurde.[23] Die Beachtung dieser Unterscheidung ist sehr wichtig, da ansonsten die Gefahr schwerer Fehlschlüsse besteht. An zwei Beispielen sei dies kurz vorgeführt.

Die Bibliothek des Museums für Angewandte Kunst in Wien besitzt eine Handschrift des 13. Jahrhunderts, die die Summe des Praepositinus von Cremona enthält. Es wäre nun aber völlig verfehlt, aus dem österreichischen Aufbewahrungsort auch auf eine Entstehung in Österreich schließen zu wollen. Vielmehr stammt die 1865 erworbene Handschrift aus dem Besitz des Dominikanerklosters in Metz; geschrieben wurde sie in Nordfrankreich. Ihre weitere Geschichte ist unbekannt.[24] Für die – im hochmittelalterlichen Österreich

21 Die Handschriftenverzeichnisse der Cistercienser-Stifte (*Xenia Bernardina* 2/1–2, Wien 1891); einzig die Bibliothek des Stiftes Zwettl besitzt einen vollständigen modernen Katalog, der aber leider nur mit Vorbehalten zu benützen ist.

22 Erfaßt ist etwa ein Teilbestand des Regularkanonikerstifts Klosterneuburg und ein Großteil des Bestandes des Benediktinerstiftes Kremsmünster. Für die Handschriften des Benediktinerstiftes Melk vor etwa 1400 liegt ein Kurzinventar vor. Zum Stand der Katalogisierung der österreichischen Handschriften vgl. die Homepage der Kommission für Schrift- und Buchwesen des Mittelalters der Österreichischen Akademie der Wissenschaften, http://www.oeaw.ac.at/ksbm/k3.htm#k3_bm1 [16.10.2004].

23 Vgl. Garand 1980, hier S. 10 (wobei darauf hinzuweisen ist, daß dem französischen Wort »provenance« der deutsche Ausdruck »Bibliotheksheimat« entspricht).

24 Wien, Museum für Angewandte Kunst, Cod. S 24. Für den Hinweis auf diese Handschrift (die in der einschlägigen Literatur, soweit ich sehe, bisher nicht berücksichtigt ist) und eine Beschreibung danke ich Dr. Franz Lackner (Kommission für Schrift- und Buchwesen des Mittelalters der Österreichischen Akademie der Wissenschaften in Wien).

und Bayern durchaus gegebene[25] – Praepositinus-Rezeption kann dieser Codex somit nicht als Zeuge herangezogen werden.

Noch deutlicher wird die Wichtigkeit einer konsequenten Unterscheidung zwischen Provenienz und Bibliotheksheimat am Beispiel des Cod. 312 der Stiftsbibliothek Klosterneuburg. Die Handschrift, aus dem späten 12. Jahrhundert stammend, enthält den Text der *Summa sententiarum* mit gewissen Einschüben, weiters den Brief des Walter von Mortagne an Hugo von St. Victor und dessen Antworttraktat *De sapientia animae Christi* sowie einen anonymen *Tractatus de caritate*.[26] Von großem Interesse ist die enge Verwandtschaft der Handschrift mit dem aus dem 12. Jahrhundert stammenden ersten Teil eines Codex, der der Zisterzienserabtei Heilsbronn gehörte und sich heute in der Universitätsbibliothek Erlangen befindet.[27] Doch bevor man sich auf weitergehende Spekulationen über etwaige Austauschbeziehungen zwischen Heilsbronn und Klosterneuburg im 12. Jahrhundert einläßt, tut man gut daran, die Klosterneuburger Handschrift sorgfältig zu untersuchen.[28] Auf dem letzten Blatt findet sich unter dem Textende wohl von der Texthand der zum Teil radierte Vermerk »Explicit liber s(ancte) m(arie) vualtsassen«; daneben steht »Cedeliz«.[29] Die Handschrift befand sich also um 1200 nicht in Klosterneuburg, sondern im Zisterzienserkloster Waldsassen in der Oberpfalz.

Von dort gelangte sie, wie der zweite Vermerk zeigt, in die Waldsassener Tochtergründung Sedlec (Sedlitz) in Mittelböhmen. Als 1421 die Hussiten das Kloster bedrohten, flüchtete der Konvent unter Mitnahme der Bibliothek nach Klosterneuburg, wo er bis 1454 Unterschlupf fand.[30] Beim Klosterneuburger Cod. 312 handelt es sich offenbar um eine bei dieser Gelegenheit aus unbekannten Gründen zurückgelassene Handschrift. Sie darf daher nicht als Zeuge für die Überlieferung der *Summa sententiarum* und anderer zeitgenössischer Texte im niederösterreichischen Raum im ausgehenden 12. Jahrhundert herangezogen werden, sondern ist vielmehr wertvoll für die Kenntnis der Verhältnisse in Franken und der Oberpfalz. Aus diesen beiden Beispielen leuchtet unmittelbar ein, welche Bedeutung der Feststellung von Provenienz und Bibliotheksheimat zukommt und welches methodische Prinzip für die Erforschung von Überlieferung und Rezeption des frühscholastischen Schrifttums im bayerisch-österreichischen Raum zu beachten ist. Keine Handschrift,

25 Die Summe ist in Österreichische Nationalbibliothek, Cod. 1409 und Cod. 1501, beide aus der Dombibliothek Salzburg stammend, überliefert; außerdem in Erlangen, Universitätsbibliothek, Cod. 260 und in einer späten Handschrift der Bayerischen Staatsbibliothek in München, Clm 6985.

26 Eine weitgehend zutreffende Beschreibung des Inhalts findet sich in Pfeiffer/Černík 1931, S. 74f. Zum *Tractatus de caritate* vgl. Wielockx 1982/1983 (die Handschrift ist erwähnt im ersten Teil, S. 56).

27 Erlangen, Universitätsbibliothek, Cod. 229. Beschreibung in Fischer 1928, S. 276–278.

28 Es sei aber am Rande angemerkt, daß Beziehungen zwischen Heilsbronn und dem österreichischen Raum, wenn vielleicht auch indirekt, sehr wohl bestehen; darauf wird an anderer Stelle einzugehen sein.

29 Klosterneuburg, Stiftsbibliothek, Cod. 312, f. 150r.

30 Vgl. Černík 1910; allgemein zu Sedlec vgl. Bahlcke/Eberhard/Polívka 1998, S. 563f.

auch wenn der in ihr enthaltene Text noch so interessant ist, darf für entsprechende Überlegungen herangezogen werden, wenn ihre Anwesenheit im bayerisch-österreichischen Raum, und unter Umständen näherhin sogar an einem bestimmten Ort, in der fraglichen Zeit nicht erwiesen ist. Die Befolgung dieses methodischen Prinzips erfordert nicht nur eine gewisse Disziplin und Aufrichtigkeit sich selbst gegenüber, wenn es darum geht, nicht eindeutig bestimmbare Handschriften aus der Untersuchung auszuscheiden, sondern mitunter auch erheblichen Aufwand an Scharfsinn und Ausdauer, denn leider liegen die Dinge in nur wenigen Fällen so eindeutig wie beim Klosterneuburger Cod. 312. Sehr oft bieten die Handschriften selbst keine offensichtlichen Anhaltspunkte für die Feststellung ihrer Provenienz; sehr oft fehlen auch Besitzvermerke, die ihre frühe Besitzgeschichte nachvollziehbar machen.

Welche Hilfsmittel und Vorgangsweisen kommen nun für die Bestimmung von Provenienz und Bibliotheksheimat in Frage? Gewisse Anhaltspunkte können mittelalterliche Bibliotheksverzeichnisse und Bibliothekskataloge liefern.[31] Freilich ist bei ihrer Benützung große Sorgfalt angebracht, denn oft sind die in ihnen enthaltenen Angaben so wortkarg, daß eine sichere Identifizierung nicht möglich ist. Häufig kann nicht einmal sicher gesagt werden, ob die jeweilige Liste den gesamten Buchbesitz einer Institution beschreibt oder einen Teilbestand. Schließlich sind die Editionen mittelalterlicher Bibliothekskataloge mitunter unzulänglich, weil sie allfällige chronologische Schichtungen in einer Buchliste – spätere Korrekturen, Streichungen, Nachträge und Ergänzungen – gar nicht oder nicht klar erkennen lassen. Für manche Klöster fehlen für das 12. und frühe 13. Jahrhundert Bibliotheksverzeichnisse überhaupt.[32]

Zur Bestimmung von Provenienz und Bibliotheksheimat kommen somit vor allem paläographische und kodikologische Kriterien in Frage, die aus Beobachtungen an den Handschriften selbst und durch Vergleich mit anderen Handschriften gewonnen werden müssen. So fruchtbringend diese Vorgangsweise ist, so schwierig ist sie, zumindest zum gegenwärtigen Zeitpunkt, in der Praxis durchzuführen. Für kaum ein bayerisches oder österreichisches Kloster liegen zuverlässige Untersuchungen des Skriptoriums vor, die als Grundlage und Bezugspunkt entsprechender Analysen dienen könnten.[33] Dementsprechend wären in vielen Fällen so umfangreiche, zeitaufwendige und schwierige Vorarbeiten zu leisten, daß eine Lösung der eigentlichen Fragestellung in weite Ferne rückt. Für die gegenwärtige Praxis bedeutet das, daß auch auf paläographisch-kodikologische Argumentationen nur in Einzelfällen zurück-

31 Derolez 1979; Nebbiai-Dalla Guarda 1992.

32 Besonders bedauerlich ist das im Fall des Benediktinerstiftes Admont, dessen erster bekannter Bibliothekskatalog bald nach 1376 zusammengestellt wurde: Möser-Mersky 1961, S. 17–34.

33 An Studien über monastische Skriptorien im bayerisch-österreichischen Raum sind derzeit vor allem folgende Arbeiten zu nennen: Pfaff 1967; Dengler-Schreiber 1979; Frioli 1990; Frioli 1999; Wind 1996; Wind 1998/1999; Wind 2003. Manche der in den genannten Arbeiten vorgebrachten Ergebnisse können auch noch nicht als völlig gesichert gelten.

gegriffen werden kann. Die erfolgreiche Anwendung einer solchen Argumentation soll im folgenden Beispiel vorgeführt werden. Immer wieder ist auf die reiche Überlieferung verschiedener Werke des Petrus Abaelardus im bayerisch-österreichischen Raum hingewiesen worden.[34] Darunter sind auch wenig verbreitete Schriften wie die *Collationes* (bekannt auch unter dem Titel *Dialogus inter Philosophum, Iudaeum et Christianum*). Die Überlieferung des Textes ist auf einen englischen Zweig, vertreten durch zwei mittelalterliche Handschriften, und einen bayerisch-österreichischen Zweig, vertreten durch den Cod. 819 der Österreichischen Nationalbibliothek, beschränkt.[35] Als Herkunftsort dieses gegen Ende des 12. Jahrhunderts geschriebenen Codex, der keine Schreiber- oder Besitzvermerke enthält, wird traditionell Stift Klosterneuburg angenommen, weil der Titel des Werkes in der Handschrift – »Dialogus Petri Baiolardi«[36] – übereinstimmt mit einem Eintrag in einer um 1200 zu datierenden Bücherliste aus dem Stift.[37] Diese Zuordnung ist zwar plausibel, mangels anderer Anhaltspunkte aber keineswegs zwingend. Dies gilt um so mehr, als, bisher unbeachtet, eine weitere Erwähnung einer heute mutmaßlich verlorenen Handschrift existiert. Dieser Codex dürfte sich im Benediktinerstift St. Peter in Salzburg befunden haben, wo ihn in den Vierziger- oder Fünfzigerjahren des 16. Jahrhunderts ein Mitarbeiter des an der Wiener Hofbibliothek beschäftigten Bücherjägers Kaspar Niedbruck eingesehen und, mit anderen Büchern, möglicherweise für eine Entlehnung ausgewählt hat. Über den Vorgang existiert eine knappe, in einer sehr mühsam zu lesenden Konzeptschrift geschriebene Aufzeichnung.[38] Unter der Überschrift »Ad D. Petrum in Salzburg gen Wien zu fueren« finden sich 22 Titel genannt, darunter an vierter Stelle »Dialogus petri Bayolardi Inter christianum et philosophum«. Am Rand des Eintrags ist hinzugefügt »habeo restituendus«.[39] Da viele der von Niedbruck durchgeführten ›Entlehnungen‹ nie wieder in ihre Heimatbibliotheken zurückkehrten, sondern sich zum Teil heute noch in der Österreichischen Nationalbibliothek befinden,[40] wäre es also nicht ausgeschlossen, daß die Wiener Handschrift der *Collationes*, die sich mit Sicherheit bereits 1576 in der kaiserlichen Hofbibliothek befand, gar nicht aus Klosterneuburg, sondern aus St. Peter in Salzburg stammt. Diese Vermutung läßt sich nun aber durch eine Untersuchung der Schrift des Cod. 819 entkräften. Auf f. 23v stechen aus dem Schriftbild wenige Zeilen hervor, die mit ziemlich spitzer Feder in einer sehr

34 Classen 1959, S. 254–258; Mews 1988.

35 Abaelardus *Collationes*, über die Handschriften S. xci-ci.

36 Wien, Österreichische Nationalbibliothek, Cod. 819, f. 1r.

37 Klosterneuburg, Stiftsbibliothek, Cod. 161, f. 118r Z. 3: »… Dialogus petri baiolardi …« Vgl. Gottlieb 1915, S. 99 Z. 2.

38 Wien, Österreichische Nationalbibliothek, Cod. 9737k, f. 291–291a. Vgl. Möser-Mersky/Mihaliuk 1966, S. 62 mit Anm. 25–27.

39 Die Bearbeiterinnen der mittelalterlichen Bibliothekskataloge lasen »restitutus«.

40 Besonders schön läßt sich das an einer umfangreichen Entlehnung aus Stift Melk zeigen: sogar die Entlehnquittung befindet sich heute in der Nationalbibliothek. Vgl. die Objektbeschreibung von Niederkorn-Bruck 1989, S. 273–275 sowie, zu den Handschriften, Glassner 1997, besonders S. 313f.

aufrechten, etwas manieriert wirkenden Schrift geschrieben sind. Genau diese Hand findet sich nun auch in verschiedenen Klosterneuburger Codices; vor allem steht sie in unmittelbarem Zusammenhang mit der Bücherliste von um 1200, auf deren Versoseite sie eine Kurzfassung eines Briefes Bernhards von Clairvaux eingetragen hat.[41] Damit kann als erwiesen angesehen werden, daß der Wiener Codex von Abaelards *Collationes* tatsächlich in Klosterneuburg geschrieben worden ist. Der Salzburger Codex scheint, da der in ihm enthaltene Text mit der Klosterneuburger Handschrift in der Hofbibliothek bereits vorhanden war, wieder an St. Peter zurückgegeben worden zu sein, wie der oben zitierte Randvermerk »habeo restituendus« vermuten läßt; diese Handschrift muß heute als verschollen gelten.[42]

Nachdem nun ausführlich einige mit der Erforschung der Überlieferung der frühscholastischen Theologie im bayerisch-österreichischen Raum verbundene methodische Probleme dargestellt worden sind, sollen nun auch noch – in aller Vorläufigkeit, die dem Charakter des »work in progress« entspricht – einige inhaltliche Beobachtungen vorgestellt werden. Die vielleicht auffälligste Entwicklung auf dem Gebiet des Buchwesens im 12. Jahrhundert, die nicht zu trennen ist von der gleichzeitigen Entwicklung der Lehrtätigkeit in den Schulen, ist das Aufkommen glossierter Bibeln mit charakteristischem Layout und sich zusehends verfestigendem Glossenbestand.[43] Ihr Vorkommen in bayerischen und österreichischen Bibliotheken ist daher von besonderem Interesse, da sie Zeugen früher Kontakte in die Studienzentren in Nordfrankreich und Oberitalien sein können. Sind sie außerdem auch noch mit alten – Besitz- oder Schenkungsvermerken versehen, können sie unter Umständen Hinweise auf einen ehemaligen Scholaren sein und so einen Ausgangspunkt für prosopographische Nachforschungen bieten. Ein Beispiel für mit Schenkungsvermerken versehene glossierte Bibelhandschriften sind sechs Codices, die aus der Salzburger Dombibliothek in die Österreichische Nationalbibliothek gelangt sind und alle von einer Hand des 12. Jahrhunderts eingetragene Vermerke »Iste liber est domni Chonradi Salzburgen(sis) archiepiscopi« enthalten.[44] Leider ist die Identität des »Chonradus archiepiscopus« ein gewisses Problem, denn für das 12. Jahrhundert stehen drei Personen dieses Namens

41 Klosterneuburg, Stiftsbibliothek, Cod. 161, f. 117v–118r (Bücherliste), 118v–119r (Bernhard von Clairvaux, Ep. 238). Vgl. die Beschreibung der Handschrift in Haidinger 1991, S. 101–104, besonders 101 unter Sigle S über die Hand, die den Bernhardbrief schrieb. Zusätzlich zu den von Haidinger genannten weiteren Vorkommen in den Klosterneuburger Cod. 638, 809, 1037 und 1243 wäre auch noch der Cod. 777 zu nennen. Interessanterweise können alle diese Handschriften auch in der Bücherliste von um 1200 identifiziert werden. Dieser Zusammenhang wird an anderer Stelle behandelt werden.

42 In St. Peter muß noch zumindest eine weitere Handschrift vorhanden gewesen sein, die mit Abaelard oder seiner Schule in Verbindung zu bringen ist. Eine aus der 2. Hälfte des 12. Jahrhunderts stammende Liste von Büchern nennt »Sententie Petri Bailardi« (Möser-Mersky/Mihaliuk 1966, S. 71 Z. 1), hingegen fehlt eine Erwähnung der Collationes. Zu den Sententie vgl. Mews 1986, bes. S. 137.

43 de Hamel 1984; Lobrichon 1984.

44 Cod. 1081 (Markus, Lukas, Deuteronomium), 1236 (Leviticus und Numeri), 1250 (Exodus), 1251 (Katholische Briefe), 1260 (Paulusbriefe), 1673 (Daniel).

zur Auswahl. Nicht wirklich in Betracht kommt Erzbischof Konrad I. (1106–1147). Konrad II. war, nachdem er bereits Bischof von Passau gewesen war (1148–1164), von 1164 bis 1168 Erzbischof von Salzburg. Er war ein Sohn Markgraf Leopolds III. und damit ein Bruder Ottos von Freising. Während für diesen aber ein Studium in Frankreich gesichert ist,[45] ist von Konrad nichts dergleichen bekannt. Trotzdem werden die genannten Handschriften gewöhnlich ihm zugeschrieben,[46] was natürlich auch nicht zwingend ausgeschlossen werden kann, da der Erwerb der Codices ja auch unabhängig von einem Studium erfolgt sein kann. Als weiterer Schenker kommt schließlich Erzbischof Konrad III. (1177–1183, dann bis 1200 Erzbischof von Mainz) in Frage. Der Angehörige der Familie der Wittelsbacher war Salzburg eng verbunden – er hatte bereits als junger Mann ein Kanonikat an der Domkirche innegehabt – und hatte in Paris und vielleicht auch in Bologna studiert. In der Zeit des Schismas entzog er sich dem Zugriff Friedrichs I. und hielt sich bei Alexander III., somit zeitweilig auch in Frankreich auf. Als Schenker der sechs glossierten Bibelhandschriften käme auch er in Frage. Zur Klärung des Problems sind noch weitere eingehende Untersuchungen erforderlich.[47]

Einen ebenfalls sehr interessanten Bestand glossierter Bibelhandschriften besitzt beziehungsweise besaß das Benediktinerstift Admont. Der besondere Wert der drei Codices[48] besteht in ihren romanischen Blindstempeleinbänden, die durch Stempelvergleiche eine relativ genaue chronologische Einordnung und Identifizierung der Buchbinderwerkstätte ermöglichen. Diese Untersuchungen führen zu einer um 1165 in Frankreich tätigen, sogenannten »Dritten Pariser Werkstatt« und konnten eine Reihe nahe verwandter Einbände aufzeigen.[49] Ob die Vermutung zutrifft, daß der Ankauf der Bände für Admont durch den Abt Gottfried (gest. 1165) erfolgte, kann gegenwärtig noch nicht gesagt werden. Nähere Untersuchungen, vor allem von Einbandmakulaturen, werden vielleicht noch weitere Erkenntnisse über den Weg der Handschriften nach Admont ergeben.[50] Jedenfalls aber wird eine systematische Erfassung der zahlreichen Vorkommen dieses für das Schulmilieu so charakteristischen Handschriftentyps in österreichischen und bayerischen Bibliotheken ein deutlicheres Bild den Verbindungen zu den Bildungszentren des

45 Vgl. zuletzt Deutinger 2002.

46 So etwa in Mazal 1982, hier S. 83. Jedenfalls unzutreffend ist die Zuschreibung an Erzbischof Konrad IV. (1290–1312), wie sie sich bei Foltz 1877, S. 39 findet.

47 In diesem Zusammenhang ist es auch bemerkenswert, daß die Ausstattung der Cod. 1251 und 1260 nach Italien weist. Hermann 1927, S. 84–86 Nr. 61f.

48 Admont, Stiftsbibliothek, Cod. 415 (Klagelieder); Madrid, Privatsammlung (olim Admont, Cod. 418; Apokalypse); Stuttgart, Württembergische Landesbibliothek, Cod. theol. et phil. 4° 646 (olim Admont Cod. 537; kanonische Briefe). Zur letzten Handschrift vgl. Boese 1977.

49 Schmidt-Künsemüller 1985, S. 77, 79f. Nr. 26, 28f. sowie allgemein S. 25–28.

50 In diese Überlegungen einzubeziehen sind zwei weitere ehemals Admonter Codices (Cod. 347 und 568), die Schmidt-Künsemüller (ebd. 58f. Nr. 11f.) der um 1150 in Paris tätigen Werkstatt des »ersten Prinz Heinrich-Binders« zuordnet: Oxford, Bodleian Library, Broxbourne Ms 83.1; Cambridge (Mass.), Harvard University Library, Ms Typ. 204. Zu Gottfried vgl. den Überblick von Braun 1981.

12. Jahrhunderts ergeben. Die in der zweiten Hälfte des Jahrhunderts einsetzende Nachahmung des Layouts durch einheimische Schreiber zeigt schließlich den Erfolg eines neuen Buchtyps und der mit ihm verbundenen neuen Weise des Zugangs zu und der Benützung von biblischen Texten.[51]

Ebenfalls unmittelbar in den Bereich der Wissensvermittlung in den Schulen führt die Befassung mit Textzusammenstellungen, Exzerpt- und Sentenzensammlungen. Auch hier sind mitunter Probleme sehr grundsätzlicher Art zu bedenken. Oft finden sich in solchen Sammlungen nämlich Auszüge aus Werken von Autoren vereint, die nach dem herkömmlichen Verständnis von »Schulen« nichts miteinander zu tun haben. So vereint etwa die Handschrift der *Sententiae Florianenses* neben diesem, eindeutig der Schule des Petrus Abaelardus zuzurechnenden Text, auch Exzerpte aus den (oder Textparallelen zu den) *Sententiae Divinitatis*, die dem Umkreis des Gilbert von Poitiers angehören, sowie aus Werken des Hugo von St. Victor.[52] Eine andere Sammlung dieser Art vereint Texte aus den Bereichen Abaelards, der Schule von Laon und Hugos von St. Victor. Sie ist besonders interessant, weil sie aus zwei Handschriften bekannt ist und sich so die Möglichkeit bietet, zu untersuchen, wie Textzusammenstellungen als solche tradiert und dabei verändert werden. Überdies führt das Vorkommen einer frühen Textform von Abaelards *Theologia Scholarium* in beiden Codices vermutlich unmittelbar in den Entstehungszusammenhang der Textsammlung in den Schulen.[53] Ein wesentlicher Gesichtspunkt ist natürlich das Interesse, wohl auch die Neugier der Person, die hinter einer solchen Sammlung steht. Unter den Arbeitsbedingungen eines mittelalterlichen Gelehrten waren Interesse und Neugier allerdings wohl meist eingeschränkt durch so nüchterne Kriterien wie Erreichbarkeit und Verfügbarkeit. Daß manche der in den Bibliotheken Österreichs oder Bayerns zu findenden Zusammenstellungen wesentlich von dieser Spannung geprägt sind, ist zu vermuten, macht die Befassung mit ihnen aber auch besonders interessant. Ausdrücklich angesprochen wird das Dilemma zwischen Erreichbarkeit eines Textes und Wißbegier im Prolog des *Horreum formicae* des Liebhard von Prüfening, der von einem durchreisenden Scholaren die *Distinctiones Abel* des Petrus Cantor geliehen bekommt und nun unter großem Zeitdruck diesen Text kopiert und adaptiert.[54]

Der Schritt von der Analyse von Textzusammenstellungen zur Untersuchung der lokalen Nutzung rezipierter Texte ist naheliegend und folgerichtig. Leider können zum gegenwärtigen Zeitpunkt zu dieser Fragestellung nur

51 Vgl. Rouse 1991.

52 St. Florian, Stiftsbibliothek, Cod. XI, S. 264. Eine genaue Analyse dieser Zusammenstellung werde ich an anderer Stelle liefern. Zu den *Sententiae Florianenses* vgl. die Edition von Ostländer 1929; Luscombe 1969, S. 153–158; zu den *Sententiae Divinitatis* siehe Geyer 1951 sowie die Nachträge in *Sententiae Divinitatis*.

53 Fulda, Bibliothek des Priesterseminars, Cod. 1; Heiligenkreuz, Stiftsbibliothek, Cod. 153. Vgl. Mews 1985, hier S. 138–147.

54 Überliefert in München, Bayerische Staatsbibliothek, Clm 13107 und in Salzburg, St. Peter, Cod. a.VII.21. Der Prolog ist gedruckt in Grabmann 1911, S. 485–487. Vgl. auch Hödl 1960, S. 336–338; Schmitz 1975, S. 187f.; Hödl 1985.

ganz vereinzelte und knappe Angaben gemacht werden. Die wohl deutlichste Form der Rezeption ist die der wörtlichen Wiedergabe in Übersetzung. Dies ist, zum Teil auch in bearbeiteter Form, mit zwei Predigten des Gottfried Babion geschehen, die in deutscher Sprache in eine im Klosterneuburger Cod. 1118 enthaltene lateinische Predigtsammlung eingefügt worden sind. Weder der Autor der Übersetzung noch das intendierte Publikum sind bekannt.[55] Ebenfalls im Bereich der Predigtliteratur findet sich eine Rezeption von Texten der Schultheologie des 12. Jahrhunderts bei dem Zisterzienser Hermann von Rein. In seinen *Sermones festivales* läßt sich etwa die Verwendung von Werken Hugos von St. Victor oder der exegetischen Schriften des Petrus Lombardus nachweisen.[56]

Die interessanteste Form der Rezeption ist aber die der aktiven Auseinandersetzung, mitunter auch – so eigenartig das klingen mag – der Ablehnung. Dies soll abschließend am Beispiel des Gerhoch von Reichersberg vorgeführt werden, wobei auch die im Titel erwähnten Basilisken und ägyptischen Frösche zu ihrem Recht kommen werden. Ein Kennzeichen Gerhochs von Reichersberg ist neben einer beachtlichen Tatkraft auch eine gewisse Hartnäckigkeit (manche würden es Sturheit nennen). Dies gilt ebenso für seine Aktivitäten zugunsten der Anliegen der Kirchenreform und seines Stiftes Reichersberg wie für seine mitunter etwas eigenwilligen theologischen Ansichten, die er in einer umfangreichen literarischen Tätigkeit entfaltete.[57] Mit besonderem Nachdruck vertrat er eine christologische Auffassung, derzufolge der menschlichen Natur Christi, dem Menschen Jesus, die Verehrung als Gott zukomme. Mit den christologischen Lehren der verschiedenen französischen Schulen war diese Sicht natürlich nicht vereinbar, und so finden sich bei Gerhoch umfangreiche und heftige Auseinandersetzungen mit Anhängern etwa des Petrus Abaelardus oder des Gilbert von Poitiers.[58] Dabei zeigt Gerhoch sich über die Ansichten seiner Gegner meist ausgezeichnet informiert. Gelegentlich sind wir sogar in der Lage, ihn bei der Arbeit zu beobachten; so etwa bei seiner Lektüre von Gilberts Kommentar zu den Paulusbriefen. Im Cod. 1562 der Österreichischen Nationalbibliothek liegt wahrscheinlich ein aus der Bibliothek von Reichersberg stammendes Exemplar vor, das mit umfangreichen Glossen versehen ist, die zum Teil von Gerhoch selbst, zum Teil von seinen Mitarbeitern stammen.[59] Als nun mit dem bereits oben erwähnten Magister Petrus von Wien, der sich wahrscheinlich ab den Vierzigerjahren des

55 Palmer 1989.

56 Hermannus de Runa *Sermones festivales.*

57 Vorbildlich und maßgeblich ist weiterhin die Biographie von Classen 1960.

58 Vgl. z. B. Gerhohus de Reichersberg *De novitatibus*, XLII, 2: »Vt nouerint illum sapientiorem qui nichil se scire fatebatur nisi Christum Iesum et hunc crucifixum quam coaceruatos illos magistros de quorum doctrina non fulget ecclesia sed fumant scole plures in Francia et aliis terris, permaxime a duabus caudis ticionum fumigantium: uidelicet Petri Abaiolardi et episcopi Gilliberti. Qurum discipuli eorum dictis et scriptis inbuti hominem Verbo dei unitum negant esse filium dei deum dicendum nisi accidentali, ut aiunt, connexione.«

59 Classen 1960, S. 435–438.

12. Jahrhunderts am Babenbergerhof in Wien aufhielt, ein unmittelbarer Schüler Gilberts beginnt, Gerhochs Christologie zu attackieren, wird für den Reichersberger Propst die Beschäftigung mit der gilbertinischen Argumentationsweise noch dringlicher. Bemerkenswert ist vor allem die Intensität, mit der Gerhoch und seine Umgebung sich mit dem bevorzugten Autor der Gilbertiner, mit Hilarius von Poitiers, auseinandersetzen. Dieser Vorgang hat in der handschriftlichen Überlieferung deutliche Spuren hinterlassen. Einerseits findet sich eine mit Glossen versehene Handschrift mit Hilarius Werken in der Stiftsbibliothek Klosterneuburg,[60] andererseits hat sich in mehreren Handschriften der Text von *De synodis*, begleitet von einer Exzerptsammlung aus *De Trinitate*, erhalten, die ebenfalls mit einigen Randglossen versehen ist.[61] Überdies waren beide Kontrahenten bemüht, zur Stützung ihrer Argumente neue Autoritäten anzuführen. Auf gegenwärtig noch nicht bekannte Weise gelangte Gerhoch in den Besitz einer von einem Venezianer namens Cerbanus angefertigten Übersetzung eines kleinen Teils von *De fide orthodoxa* des Johannes von Damaskus. Dieser Text, der in zwei voneinander direkt abhängigen österreichischen Handschriften überliefert ist, von denen der Admonter Codex eng mit der Tätigkeit Gerhochs und seines Kreises zusammenhängt, wird von Gerhoch in seinen Schriften oft verwendet – allerdings gibt er den Autor lange Zeit fälschlich als Basilius an.[62] Ein solches Zitat war es, das den Magister Petrus von Wien in einem leider verlorenen Brief an Gerhoch zur polemischen Verballhornung des Autorennamens »Basilius« zu »Basiliscus« veranlaßte – was Gerhoch entrüstet kommentiert: »sanctus Basilius quem tu ore profano Basiliscum nominas.«[63] Allerdings blieben Gerhoch und seine Mitarbeiter dem Gegner, was Gehässigkeiten betrifft, nichts schuldig. So findet sich in einem Brief, den an Stelle von Gerhoch sein Bruder Rüdiger von Klosterneuburg an Magister Petrus richtete, ein Vergleich der Äußerungen der scholastischen Gelehrten, mithin auch des Adressaten, mit dem Quaken der ägyptischen Frösche – mit einer der ägyptischen Plagen gleichgesetzt zu werden, muß für einen bibelkundigen, die Anspielung daher sofort in ihrer ganzen Schärfe verstehenden mittelalterlichen Menschen und Intellektuellen doch eher beleidigend gewesen sein.[64]

60 Cod. 206; vgl. Classen 1960, S. 441; Classen 1959b, S. 268.

61 Klosterneuburg, Stiftsbibliothek, Cod. 777 (vgl. zu dieser Handschrift oben, Anm. 41); Bibliotheca Apostolica Vaticana, Cod. Vat. lat. 254 (diese Handschrift, die keinen mittelalterlichen Besitzvermerk trägt, ist sicher im bayerisch-österreichischen Raum geschrieben worden. Dr. Friedrich Simader [Österreichische Nationalbibliothek, Wien] verdanke ich den Hinweis, daß die Gestaltung der Initialen auf eine Ausstattung der Handschrift im Benediktinerkloster Göttweig schließen läßt); zum Teil auch in Zwettl, Stiftsbibliothek, Cod. 261. Ohne Glossen findet sich die Sammlung auch im Cod. 755 der Österreichischen Nationalbibliothek (aus der Kartause Seitz, heute Slowenien). Zu dieser Handschrift vgl. Häring 1970, hier S. 187f.

62 Classen 1959a. Die beiden Handschriften sind Admont, Stiftsbibliothek, Cod. 767 und, daraus kopiert, Rein, Stiftsbibliothek, Cod. 35.

63 Gerhohus de Reichersberg *Epistola ad Petrum*, 359 Z. 8f.; Classen 1960, S. 359.

64 Rüdiger von Klosterneuburg an Mag. Petrus, ed. Weisweiler 1939, hier S. 41 Z. 16f.; Classen 1960, S. 365.

Damit sei dieser knappe und in vielerlei Hinsicht unvollständige Überblick über Möglichkeiten, Probleme und Grenzen der Erforschung von Überlieferung und Rezeption der frühscholastischen Theologie im bayerisch-österreichischen Raum beendet. Daß eine »theologische Mediävistik« wichtig und notwendig ist für ein angemessenes Verständnis der Vergangenheit, ist nicht zu bezweifeln. Die Mediävistik braucht die Theologiegeschichte; umgekehrt braucht die Theologiegeschichte die Mediävistik mit dem Instrumentarium der historischen Hilfswissenschaften wie Paläographie und Kodikologie.

Bibliographie

Quellen

Abaelardus *Collationes*

Peter Abelard: *Collationes*, ed. and transl. by John Marenbon and Giovanni Orlandi (Oxford Medieval Texts), Oxford 2001.

Gerhohus de Reichersberg *De novitatibus*

Gerhohus de Reichersberg: *De novitatibus huius temporis*, ed. Nikolaus M. Häring: *Gerhoch of Reichersberg, Letter to Pope Hadrian about the Novelties of the Day* (Studies and Texts 24), Toronto 1974.

Gerhohus de Reichersberg *Epistola ad Petrum*

Gerhohus de Reichersberg: *Epistola ad Petrum philosophum*, ed. Peter Classen: *Gerhohi praepositi Reichersbergensis Opera inedita*, I (SPAA 8), Roma 1955.

Hermannus de Runa *Sermones festivales*

Hermanni de Runa Sermones festivales, ed. Edmund Mikkers (CChr.CM 64), Turnhout 1986.

Hugo de Sancto Victore *De tribus diebus*

Hugo de Sancto Victore: *De tribus diebus*, ed. Dominique Poirel (CChr.CM 177), Turnhout 2002.

Sententiae Divinitatis

Die Sententiae Divinitatis. Ein Sentenzenbuch der Gilbertschen Schule, hg. von Bernhard Geyer (BGPhMA 7/2–3), Münster [2]1967.

Sententiae Florianenses

Sententiae Florianenses hg. von Heinrich Ostlender (FlorPatr 19), Bonn 1929.

Vita sancti Adalberonis

Vita sancti Adalberonis, hg. und übers. von Irene Schmale-Ott (QFGBW 8), Würzburg 1954.

Vita Altmanni prior

Vita Altmanni prior, ed. Wilhelm Wattenbach (MGH. Scriptores 12), Hannover 1856, 229–243.

Studien

BAHLCKE/EBERHARD/POLÍVKA 1998

Handbuch der historischen Stätten: Böhmen und Mähren, hg. von JOACHIM BAHLCKE, WINFRIED EBERHARD und MIROSLAV POLÍVKA (KTA 329), Stuttgart 1998.

BENSON/CONSTABLE/LANHAM 1982

Renaissance and Renewal in the Twelfth Century. Papers from a conference … commemorating the contribution by Charles Homer Haskins, hg. von ROBERT L. BENSON, GILES CONSTABLE, CAROL D. LANHAM, Cambridge/Mass. 1982.

BOESE 1977

HELMUT BOESE: »Neuerworbene Handschriften österreichischer Provenienz in Stuttgart«, in *Codices manuscripti 3* (1977) 120–125.

BRAUN 1981

JOHANN WILHELM BRAUN: »Gottfried v. Admont«, in *VerLex*[2] 3 (1981) 118–123.

ČERNÍK 1910

BERTHOLD ČERNÍK: »Mittelalterliche Handschriftenverzeichnisse des ehemaligen Zisterzienserklosters Sedlitz in Böhmen«, in *JSK 3* (1910) 345–357.

CLASSEN 1959a

PETER CLASSEN: »Der verkannte Johannes Damascenus«, in *ByZ 52* (1959) 297–303.

CLASSEN 1959b

PETER CLASSEN: »Zur Geschichte der Frühscholastik in Österreich und Bayern«, in *MIÖG 67* (1959) 249–277 [wieder abgedruckt in IDEM: *Ausgewählte Aufsätze*, hg. von JOSEF FLECKENSTEIN (Vorträge und Forschungen 28), Sigmaringen 1983, 279–306].

CLASSEN 1960

PETER CLASSEN: *Gerhoch von Reichersberg. Eine Biographie.* Mit einem Anhang über die Quellen, ihre handschriftliche Überlieferung und ihre Chronologie, Wiesbaden 1960.

CLASSEN 1983

PETER CLASSEN: »Die geistesgeschichtliche Lage im 12. Jahrhundert. Anstöße und Möglichkeiten«, in IDEM: *Ausgewählte Aufsätze*, hg. von JOSEF FLECKENSTEIN (Vorträge und Forschungen 28), Sigmaringen 1983, 327–346.

DE HAMEL 1984

CHRISTOPHER DE HAMEL: *Glossed Books of the Bible and the origins of the Paris booktrade*, Woodbridge/Dover 1984.

DENGLER-SCHREIBER 1979

KARIN DENGLER-SCHREIBER: *Scriptorium und Bibliothek des Klosters Michelsberg in Bamberg* (Studien zur Bibliotheksgeschichte 2), Graz 1979.

DEROLEZ 1979

ALBERT DEROLEZ: *Les catalogues de bibliothèques* (TSMÂO 31), Turnhout 1979.

DEUTINGER 2002

ROMAN DEUTINGER: »Engel oder Wolf? Otto von Freising in den geistigen Auseinandersetzungen seiner Zeit«, in *Ars und Scientia im Mittelalter und in der Frühen Neuzeit.* Ergebnisse interdisziplinärer Forschung, hg. von CORA DIETL und DÖRTE HELSCHINGER, Tübingen/Basel 2002, 31–46.

Egger 2003

Christoph Egger: »The Canon Regular: St Ruf in context«, in *Adrian IV. The English Pope (1154–1159). Studies and Texts,* ed. by Brenda Bolton/ Anne Duggan (Church, Faith and Culture in the Medieval West), Aldershot 2003, 15–28.

Egger 2004

Christoph Egger: »The scholar's suitcase: Books and the transfer of knowledge in twelfth-century Europe«, in *The Church and the Book.* Papers read at the 2000 summer meeting and the 2001 winter meeting of the Ecclesiastical History Society, ed. Robert N. Swanson (Studies in Church History 38), Woodbridge 2004, 87–97.

Ehlers 1996

Joachim Ehlers: »Deutsche Scholaren in Frankreich während des 12. Jahrhunderts«, in *Schulen und Studium im sozialen Wandel des hohen und späten Mittelalters,* hg. von Johannes Fried (Vorträge und Forschungen 30), Sigmaringen 1986, 97–120 [wieder abgedruckt in idem: *Ausgewählte Aufsätze,* hg. von Martin Kintzinger und Bernd Schneidmüller (Berliner historische Studien 21), Berlin 1996, 163–190.

Fichtenau 1938

Heinrich Fichtenau: »Studien zu Gerhoh von Reichersberg«, in *MIÖG 52* (1938) 1–56.

Fichtenau 1944/48

Heinrich Fichtenau: »Ein französischer Frühscholastiker in Wien«, in *Jahrbuch für Landeskunde von Niederösterreich und Wien. NF 29* (1944/48), 118–130.

Fichtenau 1955

Heinrich Fichtenau: *Magister Petrus von Wien,* in *MIÖG 63* (1955) 238–297 [wieder abgedruckt in idem: *Beiträge zur Mediävistik I,* Stuttgart 1975, 218–238].

Fischer 1928

Hans Fischer: *Katalog der Handschriften der Universitätsbibliothek Erlangen.* 1: *Die lateinischen Pergamenthandschriften,* Erlangen 1928.

Foltz 1877

Karl Foltz: *Geschichte der Salzburger Bibliotheken,* Wien 1877.

Frioli 1990

Donatella Frioli: *Lo scriptorium e la biblioteca del monastero cisterciense di Aldersbach* (Testi, studi, strumenti 3), Spoleto 1990.

Frioli 1999

Donatella Frioli: »Per una storia dello scriptorium di Reichersberg: il prevosto Gerhoch e i suoi *segretari*«, in *Scrittura e civiltà 23* (1999) 177–212.

Fuchs 1989

Franz Fuchs: *Bildung und Wissenschaft in Regensburg. Neue Forschungen und Texte aus St. Mang in Stadtamhof* (BQMA 13), Sigmaringen 1989.

Garand 1980

Monique-Cécile Garand: »Manuscrits monastiques et scriptoria aux xie et xiie siècles«, in *Codicologica 3: Essais typologiques,* éd. par A. Gruys, J. P. Gumbert (Litterae textuales), Leiden 1980, 9–33.

Geyer 1951
Bernhard Geyer: »Neues und Altes zu den Sententiae divinitatis«, in *Mélanges Joseph de Ghellinck S.J.*, 2: *Moyen Âge, époque moderne et contemporaine* (ML.H 14), Gembloux 1951, 617–630.

Glassner 1997
Christine Glassner: »Schreiben ist lesen und studieren, der sel speis und des herczen jubiliern. Zu den mittelalterlichen Handschriften des Benediktinerstiftes Melk«, in *SMGB 108* (1997) 283–320.

Gottlieb 1915
Mittelalterliche Bibliothekskataloge Österreichs, 1: *Niederösterreich*, bearb. von Theodor Gottlieb, Wien 1915 [Ndr. Aalen 1974].

Grabmann 1911
Martin Grabmann: *Geschichte der scholastischen Methode*, 1–2, Freiburg i.Br. 1911.

Günster 1955
Josef Günster: »Der ungedruckte christologische Teil einer Denkschrift Gerhohs von Reichersberg«, in *Scholastik 30* (1955) 215–228.

Haidinger 1991
Alois Haidinger: *Katalog der Handschriften des Augustiner Chorherrenstiftes Klosterneuburg*, Teil 2: *Cod. 101–200* (DÖAW 225 = Veröffentl. der Kommission für Schrift- und Buchwesen des Mittelalters II/2/2), Wien 1991.

Häring 1965
Nikolaus M. Häring: »Two Austrian Tractates against the Doctrine of Gilbert of Poitiers«, in *AHDL 40* (1965) 127–167.

Häring 1966
Nikolaus M. Häring: »Eine Zwettler Abkürzung der Vätersammlung Adhemars von Saint-Ruf (Valence)«, in *ThPh 41* (1966) 30–53.

Häring 1970
Nikolaus M. Häring: »Texts Concerning Gilbert of Poitiers,« in *AHDL 45* (1970) 169–203.

Haskins 1927
Charles Homer Haskins: *The Renaissance of the Twelfth Century*, Cambridge, Mass. 1927, [5]1971.

Heilig 1935
Konrad Josef Heilig: »Mittelalterliche Bibliotheksgeschichte als Geistesgeschichte«, in *Zeitschrift für Deutsche Geistesgeschichte 1* (1935) 12–23.

Heilig 1944
Konrad Josef Heilig: »Ostrom und das Deutsche Reich um die Mitte des 12. Jahrhunderts. Die Erhebung Österreichs zum Herzogtum 1156 und das Bündnis zwischen Byzanz und dem Westreich«, in Theodor Mayer/Konrad Heilig/Carl Erdmann: *Kaisertum und Herzogsgewalt im Zeitalter Friedrichs I. Studien zur politischen und Verfassungsgeschichte des hohen Mittelalters* (SRÄDG 9), Berlin 1944, 1–271.

Hermann 1927
Hermann Julius Hermann: *Die romanischen Handschriften des Abendlandes mit Ausnahme der deutschen Handschriften* (Beschreibendes Verzeichnis der illuminierten Handschriften in Österreich VIII/3), Leipzig 1927.

Hödl 1960

Ludwig Hödl: *Die Geschichte der scholastischen Literatur und der Theologie der Schlüsselgewalt* (BGPhMA 38/4), Münster 1960.

Hödl 1985

Ludwig Hödl: »Liebhard von Prüfening«, in *VerLex*[2] 5 (1985) 808–811.

Lhotsky 1961

Alphons Lhotsky: »Studia Neuburgensia. Beiträge zur Grundlegung einer Geschichte der Wissenschaftspflege im spätmittelalterlichen Niederösterreich«, in *JSK. NF 1* (1961) 69–103 [wieder abgedruckt in idem: *Historiographie, Quellenkunde, Wissenschaftsgeschichte. Aufsätze und Vorträge*, 3, Wien 1972, 179–227].

Lhotsky 1964

Alphons Lhotsky: *Grundriß einer Geschichte der Wissenschaftspflege im alten Niederösterreich. Mittelalter* (Forschungen zur Landeskunde von Niederösterreich 17), Wien 1964.

Lobrichon 1984

Guy Lobrichon: »Une nouveauté: les gloses de la Bible«, in *Le Moyen Age et la Bible* (La Bible de tous les temps 4), éd. par Pierre Riché/Guy Lobrichon, Paris 1984, 95–114 [wieder abgedruckt in idem: *La Bible au Moyen Age* (Les Médiévistes français 3), Paris 2003, 158–172].

Losek 2001

Fritz Losek: »De libris scolasticis scolaribusque viris«, in *Tradition und Wandel. Beiträge zur Kirchen-, Gesellschafts- und Kulturgeschichte.* Festschrift für Heinz Dopsch, hrsg. von Gerhard Ammerer, Christian Rohr und Alfred Stefan Weiss, Wien/München 2001, 60–69.

Luscombe 1969

David Luscombe: *The School of Peter Abelard. The Influence of Abelard's Thought in the Early Scholastic Period* (CSMLT 14), Cambridge 1969.

Mazal

Otto Mazal: »Die Salzburger Dombibliothek vom 10.–12. Jahrhundert«, in *Paläographie 1981.* Colloquium des Comité International de Paléographie, München 15.–18. September 1981, Hg. von Gabriel Silagi (MBM 32), München 1982, 71–91.

Mews 1985

Constant Mews: »Peter Abelard's *Theologia Christiana* and *Theologia "Scholarium"* re-visited«, in *RThAM 52* (1985) 109–158.

Mews 1986

Constant Mews: »The Sententie of Peter Abelard«, in *RThAM 53* (1986) 130–184.

Mews 1988

Constant Mews: »In Search for a Name and Its Significance: A Twelfth Century Anecdote about Thierry and Peter Abaelard«, in *Traditio 44* (1988) 171–200.

Möser-Mersky 1961

Mittelalterliche Bibliothekskataloge Österreichs, 3: *Steiermark.* Bearb. von Gerlinde Möser-Mersky, Graz/Wien/Köln 1961.

MÖSER-MERSKY/MIHALIUK 1966
Mittelalterliche Bibliothekskataloge Österreichs, 4: *Salzburg*, bearb. von GERLINDE MÖSER-MERSKY und MELANIE MIHALIUK, Graz/Wien/Köln 1966.

NEBBIAI-DALLA GUARDA 1992
DONATELLA NEBBIAI-DALLA GUARDA: *I documenti per la storia delle biblioteche medievali (secoli IX-XV)* (Collana della Facoltà di Lettere e Filosofia dell'Università di Venezia in San Sebastiano, Sezione di studi storici 8. Materiali e ricerche, ns. 15), Roma 1992.

NIEDERKORN-BRUCK 1989
META NIEDERKORN-BRUCK: »Objektbeschreibung«, in *Katalog der Ausstellung 900 Jahre Benediktiner in Melk.* Jubiläumsausstellung 1989 Stift Melk, Melk 1989, 273–275.

PALMER 1989
NIGEL F. PALMER: »Die *Klosterneuburger Bußpredigten.* Untersuchung und Edition«, in *Überlieferungsgeschichtliche Editionen und Studien zur deutschen Literatur des Mittelalters.* Kurt Ruh zum 75. Geburtstag, hg. von KONRAD KUNZE/JOHANNES G. MAYER/BERNHARD SCHNELL (Texte und Textgeschichte 31), Tübingen 1989, 210–244.

PFAFF 1967
CARL PFAFF: *Scriptorium und Bibliothek des Klosters Mondsee im hohen Mittelalter* (Österreichische Akademie der Wissenschaften, Veröffentlichungen der Kommission für Geschichte Österreichs 2 = Schriften des DDr. Franz Josef Mayer-Gunthof-Fonds 5), Wien 1967.

PFEIFFER/ČERNÍK 1931
HERMANN PFEIFFER/BERTHOLD ČERNÍK: *Catalogus codicum manu scriptorum qui in bibliotheca canonicorum regularium s. Augustini Claustroneoburgi asservantur*, 1–2, Klosterneuburg 1931.

PLANTE 1977
JULIAN G. PLANTE: »The Medieval Library of the Augustinerchorherrenstift Reichersberg, Austria: Towards its Reconstruction from Two Surviving Catalogues (Munich, Staatsbibliothek Cod. Bav. 2)«, in *Studia Codicologica.* In Zusammenarbeit mit JÖRG DUMMER, JOHANNES IRMSCHER und FRANZ PASCHKE hg. von KURT TREU (TU 124), Berlin 1977, 363–373.

ROUSE 1991
RICHARD & MARY ROUSE: »Statim invenire: Schools, Preachers, and New Attitudes to the Page«, in BENSON/CONSTABLE/LANHAM 1982, 201–225 [wieder abgedruckt in IDEM: *Authentic Witnesses.* Approaches to Medieval Texts and Manuscripts (PMS 17), Notre Dame 1991, 191–219].

SCHIMMELPFENNIG 1989
BERNHARD SCHIMMELPFENNIG: »Renaissance/Proto-Renaissance, Renovatio/Renewal, Rezeption. Bericht über eine Begriffs-Diskussion«, in *Kontinuität und Transformation der Antike im Mittelalter.* Veröffentlichung der Kongreßakten zum Freiburger Symposion des Mediävistenverbandes, hg. von WILLI ERZGRÄBER, Sigmaringen 1989, 383–390.

SCHMIDT-KÜNSEMÜLLER 1985
FRIEDRICH ADOLF SCHMIDT-KÜNSEMÜLLER: *Die abendländischen romanischen Blindstempeleinbände* (Denkmäler der Buchkunst 6), Stuttgart 1985.

Schmitz 1975

Hans-Georg Schmitz: *Kloster Prüfening im 12. Jahrhundert* (MBMo 49 = Neue Schriftenreihe des Stadtarchivs München 67), München 1975.

Stammberger 2001

Ralf M. W. Stammberger: »Die Halberstädter Glosse zum Matthäus-Evangelium und zum Buch Josua. Zur Wiederentdeckung der Handschrift Halberstadt, Dom-Gymnasium 47 aus der ersten Hälfte des 12. Jahrhunderts«, in *RPhThAM 68* (2001) 18–33.

Stelzer 1982

Winfried Stelzer: *Gelehrtes Recht in Österreich. Von den Anfängen bis zum frühen 14. Jahrhundert* (MIÖG.E 26), Wien/Köln/Graz 1982.

Weisweiler 1936

Heinrich Weisweiler: *Das Schrifttum der Schule Anselms von Laon und Wilhelms von Champeaux in deutschen Bibliotheken* (BGPhMA 33/1–2), Münster 1936.

Weisweiler 1938a

Heinrich Weisweiler: »Drei unveröffentlichte Briefe aus dem christologischen Streit Gerhohs von Reichersberg. Dogmatische Würdigung und Ausgabe«, in *Scholastik 13* (1938) 22–48.

Weisweiler 1938b

Heinrich Weisweiler: »Das wiedergefundene Gutachten des Magisters Petrus über die Verherrlichung des Gottessohnes gegen Gerhoh von Reichersberg«, in *Scholastik 13* (1938) 225–246.

Weisweiler 1939

Heinrich Weisweiler: »Rudiger von Klosterneuburg an der Seite seiner Brüder Gerhoh und Arno von Reichersberg im christologischen Streit um die Verherrlichung des Gottessohnes. Die dogmatische Stellung und Ausgabe seines ersten neugefundenen Schrifttums«, in *Scholastik 14* (1939) 22–49.

Wielockx 1982/1983

Robert Wielockx: »La sentence *De caritate* et la discussion scolastique sur l'amour«, in *EThL 58* (1982) 50–86. 354–356; *59* (1983) 26–45.

Wind 1996

Peter Wind: »Aus der Schreibschule von St. Peter vom Anfang des 11. Jahrhunderts bis Anfang des 14. Jahrhunderts«, in *Hl. Rupert von Salzburg, 696–1996.* Katalog der Ausstellung im Dommuseum zu Salzburg und in der Erzabtei St. Peter, 16. Mai – 27. Oktober 1996, Hg. von P. Petrus Eder OSB, Johann Kronbichler, Salzburg 1996, 364–404.

Wind 1998/1999

Peter Wind: »Reiner Handschriften des 12. Jahrhunderts in Bibliotheken anderer Klöster und Stifte«, in *ZHVSt 89/90* (1998/99) 31–56.

Wind 2003

Peter Wind: »Die Schreibschule des Stiftes Rein von 1150–1250«, in *Erlesenes und Erbauliches.* Kulturschaffen der Reiner Mönche, Rein 2003, 13–44.

Archa Verbi 1 (2004) 163–177

Tagungsberichte

»Charisma und *vita religiosa* / Carisma e *vita religiosa*« Dresden 10.–12. Juni 2004

von Mirko Breitenstein

Vom 10. bis zum 12. Juni 2004 veranstalteten die beiden mediävistischen Teilprojekte des Dresdner Sonderforschungsbereichs 537 »Institutionalität und Geschichtlichkeit« der Technischen Universität Dresden gemeinsam mit dem Italienisch-Deutschen Zentrum für vergleichende Ordensforschung »Secundum regulam vivere« eine internationale Tagung zum Thema »Charisma und *vita religiosa*«.

Charismatisches Handeln scheint eine der wichtigsten Garantien für die Fortentwicklung der *vita religiosa*, für die Entstehung neuer religiöser Gemeinschaften wie aber auch für deren Reform und Erneuerung gewesen zu sein – so die beiden federführenden Organisatoren der Veranstaltung, Giancarlo Andenna und Gert Melville, in einem den Referenten und Teilnehmern vorab verschickten Thesenpapier. Obgleich sich Charisma und Institution scheinbar ausschließen oder sich zumindest in einem normativen Spannungsfeld begegnen, ist die *vita religiosa* in ihrer Geschichte trotz (oder vielleicht gerade wegen) ihrer Tendenz zur hoch verdichteten Institutionalität immer wieder mit Antrieben durch Einzelpersönlichkeiten von hohem Eigenwillen und starker Führungsqualität konfrontiert worden. Eine genauere und insbesondere vergleichende Analyse solcherart charismatischen Wirkens bot sich somit in besonderem Maße an, um Prinzipien der Institutionengenese zu beschreiben und zu analysieren.

Begonnen wurde die Tagung mit zwei Einführungsreferaten, die aus soziologischer sowie theologischer Sicht generell zum Phänomen Charisma Stellung nahmen. Zunächst sprach Karl Siegbert Rehberg (Dresden) zum Thema »Rationalisierungsschicksal und Charisma-Sehnsucht. Ambivalenzen der Moderne in der frühen Soziologie«. Er wies dabei auf die Schwierigkeiten der begrifflichen Analyse hin, da durch einen inflationären Gebrauch und eine unreflektierte Verwendung von ›Charisma‹ die Gefahr der »begrifflichen Überdehnung« bestehe. Als Typus sei Charisma jedoch vor der Gefahr des Anachronismus gefeit, weil die typologisch-vergleichende historische Soziologie in der Tradition Max Webers »mit jedem Anschein des Authentischen bricht«. Die Dynamik des Weberschen Charisma-Konzeptes liege gerade in seiner gedanklichen Projektion – »über Paulus hinweg« – auf das alttestamentarische Judentum. Als instruktiv und für die Analyse der *vita religiosa* fruchtbar könnte sich der von Rehberg eingefügte Gedanke des Mannheimer Philosophen Helmut F. Spinner erweisen, wonach die Gegenüberstellung normaler Zweck-Mittel-Kalküle und »okkasionaler Rationalitäten«, die vor allem vom personalen Moment bestimmt sind, für eine Analyse der Wirkungsweisen des Charisma hilfreicher zu sein scheint als die traditionelle Distinktion von Rationalität und Irrationalität. Der anti-institutionelle Impuls des Charismas erlaubt es in besonderer Weise die allgegenwärtigen Mechanismen der Verstetigung und Geltungsdurchsetzung zu beobachten; verstanden werden können sie nach Rehberg als »Kampf unterschiedlicher Rationalitätsausprägungen«. Durch den Blick auf die Ausnahmeverhaltensweisen, auf charismatische Provokationen wird so eine genauere Sicht auf die institutionelle Stabilisierung gesellschaftlicher Ordnungen ermöglicht.

Im zweiten, nun theologisch perspektivierten Einführungsvortrag sprach Klaus Tanner (Halle/Dresden) über »Die Macht des Unverfügbaren. Charisma als Gnadengabe in der Thematisierung von Institutionalisierungsprozessen im Christentum«. Auch er brachte die Webersche Projektion des Charismas ins alttestamentliche Judentum zur Sprache. Tanner fragte jedoch vor allem nach dem zwischen jener Dimension des Alten Testamentes und Webers Begriffsbildung Liegenden: nach Paulus. Nicht mehr eine Beobachterperspektive wie in Webers Texten nimmt ein, wer die Paulinischen Aussagen wieder ins Zentrum rückt; statt dessen liest er Dokumente aus der Perspektive eines Betroffenen, der sein eigenes Erleben und Selbstverständnis beschreibt. Charisma verliert bei Weber – so Tanner pointiert – den Paulinischen Charakter der Gabe und wird zum »Besitz«. Während es Weber in erster Linie um die Wirkung des Charismas gehe, werde bei Paulus vor allem die Gebundenheit des Charismas an eine letzte Instanz betont. Der Paulinische Geistbegriff verfüge somit geradezu über eine erkenntnistheoretische Dimension: »Wahrheitserkenntnis ist nur im Geist, durch den Geist möglich«.

Franz Neiske (Münster) eröffnete die Reihe der mediävistischen Referate mit seinem Vortrag »Abt oder Gemeinschaft. Die frühen Äbte Clunys«. Am Beispiel der Frühgeschichte des Klosters Cluny fragte er nach dem, was gewöhnlich als Gründungscharisma einer Gemeinschaft bezeichnet wird und kam zu dem Ergebnis, daß es ein solches in Cluny wohl nicht gab. Wenn jedoch – so Neiske weiter – Heiligkeit als die »ausgeprägteste Form des Unalltäglichen« im Sinne Max Webers verstanden wird, bietet sich seiner Meinung nach der hagiographische Textbestand über die frühen Äbte bis Petrus Venerabilis für die Suche nach dem Terminus 'Charisma' an. Die Vorkommnisse erschöpfen sich jedoch in einer an Paulus angelehnten Beschreibung der Vortrefflichkeiten des jeweiligen Abtes. Das reich überlieferte Urkundenmaterial der Abtei überliefert den Terminus schon in einem weiter verstandenen Sinne: So sind die Schenkungen an das Kloster Charismata des Abtes. Doch könne man, so Neiske, keinesfalls von einem Amtscharisma sprechen, da die Äbte nach Ausweis der Quellen stets in ihr Amt gewählt wurden, weil sie vom Charisma erfüllt waren. Die charismatische Begabung war somit eine wesentliche Voraussetzung der Wahl zum Abt. Die Erfüllung mit Charisma bedeutet im speziellen Falle folglich keinen Bruch mit der Regel, sondern ihre höchstmögliche Erfüllung.

Francesco Panarelli (Potenza) beschäftigte sich in seinem Vortrag »Carisma in discussione: riformatori monastici e communità nel Mezzogiorno italiano tra XI e XII secolo« mit dem Prozeß der Institutionalisierung im Anschluß an die charismatische Phase monastischer Gemeinschaften. Anhand der Beispiele von Giovanni da Matera, Guglielmo da Vercelli sowie Giovanni da Tufara untersuchte er den Verlauf der Gemeinschaftsbildung um einen als charismatisch zu beschreibenden Führer und kommt zu dem Ergebnis, daß das Gründungscharisma zwar für den Prozeß der Entstehung einer Gemeinschaft konstitutiv ist, dieses Charisma jedoch in der weiteren Entwicklung seine Funktion als Gemeinschaftsstiftendes Prinzip verliert und zum bloßen Accessoire wird.

Gert Melville (Dresden) wandte sich in seinem Beitrag »Stephan von Obazine: Begründung und Überwindung charismatischer Führung« ebenfalls dem Problem der Institutionalisierung einer Gemeinschaft im Anschluß an deren charismatische Phase zu. Der Protagonist seines Vortrages, Stephan von Obazine, verkörperte Formen charismatischen Handelns gleichsam als ein »Prototyp«. Die Art und Weise der von ihm initiierten Bewahrung seiner Gemeinschaft ist jedoch ein Phänomen, das im Rahmen der auf der Tagung präsentierten Beispiele als singulär beschrieben werden kann: Stephans lange und ausdauernde Suche nach einem externen Organisationsmodell, und die anschließende konsequent praktizierte Integration seiner charismatischen Gemeinschaft in den Orden der Zisterzienser markieren ein außergewöhnliches Verfahren der Institutionalisierung, das nicht auf die Adaption von Normen sondern deren Oktroyierung zielte. Das Zurücktreten des Charismatikers und die Annahme einer neuen Ordnung durch die Brüder erfolgte dabei aufgrund einer charismatischen Affirmierung der neuen Ordnung durch den Charismatiker; es bedurfte – wie Gert Melville pointiert formulierte – eines Charismas zur »Entcharismatisierung«.

Im Zentrum des Referates von Giuseppe Picasso (Milano) »La spiritualità dell'antico monachesimo alle origini di Monte Oliveto (secolo XIV)« stand mit Bernardo Tolomei ein weiterer Protagonist aus der Reihe der Ordensgründer. Im Rahmen der Varianz der Begriffe von Charisma, entsprach das präsentierte Bild des Gründers der Olivetaner eher der Paulinischen Tradition. Die Olivetaner seien, wie Picasso ausführte, keine Gemeinschaft deren Herrschaftsgefüge als charismatisch beschrieben werden kann, wohl aber ihre auf die Ideen des alten Mönchtums bezogene Spiritualität.

Elke Goez (Passau/Herzogenaurach) widmete sich in ihrem Vortrag »... erit communis et nobis – Verstätigung des Vergänglichen. Zur Perpetuierung des Charismas Bernhards von Clairvaux im Zisterzienserorden« einer unbestritten charismatischen Figur. Das Interesse der Referentin galt insbesondere der Frage, wie Bernhard seine charismatischen Kräfte einsetzte, von denen er selbst ohne Zweifel überzeugt war. Anschaulich wurden die Bemühungen Bernhards um eine gezielte Distribution der eigenen Texte geschildert, ebenso seine Einbindung in die Vorbereitung der eigenen Heiligsprechung. Ein weiterer Schwerpunkt des Vortrages war dem Nachleben Bernhards gewidmet, genauer: den Schritten die Bernhard selbst wie auch die Zisterzienser unternahmen, um sein Charisma zu perpetuieren, sowie – als Ausdruck und Niederschlag des letzteren – den konkurrierenden Bernhard-

Bildern in der einsetzenden Hagiographie, d.h. der Deutungsmacht über den toten Charismatiker. Diese Bemühungen galten sämtlich, wie Elke Goez zeigen konnte, dem Versuch, Bernhard einerseits als Leitfigur der Gemeinschaft festzuschreiben, dabei jedoch gleichzeitig die immense Brisanz seiner Persönlichkeit zu neutralisieren.

Direkten Bezug auf das eingangs erwähnte Thesenpapier der Organisatoren nahm Hubert Houben (Lecce) in seinem Beitrag »Orden ohne Charisma? Bemerkungen zu den geistlichen Ritterorden des Mittelalters (insbesondere zum Deutschen Orden)«. Am Beispiel der vorgestellten Orden gelang es ihm zu zeigen, daß die Entstehung neuer religiöser Gemeinschaften nicht notwendig an die Existenz eines personalen charismatischen Momentes gebunden ist. Die normativen Grundlage der Ritterorden orientierten sich Houben zufolge nicht an Leitvorstellungen charismatischer Persönlichkeiten – seien es zeitgenössische oder auch historische, resp. mythische Figuren –, sondern statt dessen an bestehenden älteren Normen wie den Regeln Benedikts oder Augustinus'. Selbst von einem Charisma des Amtes, bspw. im Falle der Hochmeister des Deutschen Ordens, könne man nicht sprechen. Eine mögliche Erklärung sah Houben im propagierten Postulat der Gleichheit aller Mitglieder, demzufolge herausragende Mitglieder mit besonderem Charisma unerwünscht seien.

In seinem öffentlichen Abendvortrag »Zwischen Berufung und Amt. Norbert von Xanten und Seinesgleichen im ersten Viertel des 12. Jahrhunderts« widmete sich Franz J. Felten (Mainz) dem normativen Spannungsfeld von Charisma und Institution. Norbert markierte dabei sowohl in Feltens Referat als auch im historischen Kontext nur einen, wenn auch herausragenden Punkt in einer Konjunktur charismatischer Bewegungen. Der Gründer des Prämonstratenserordens und spätere Erzbischof von Magdeburg hatte wie kaum ein anderer den Konflikt zwischen Charisma und Amt in seiner Person ausgefochten und ging dabei den Weg »vom Amt zum Charisma und wieder zurück«. Norbert vertraute zu keiner Zeit allein auf die charismatische Wirkung seiner Lehre, sondern betont stets die Notwendigkeit einer Regel. Infolge seines Weggangs nach Magdeburg mußte die auf ihn zentrierte Gemeinschaft in einen Zustand existentieller Gefährdung geraten. Ihr Weiterbestehen, sah Felten durch das präsente Charisma des Abwesenden gesichert, das einerseits durch seine Transformation in institutionelle Formen, andererseits (nach Norbert Tod) durch Hagiographie befestigt wurde.

Achim Wesjohann (Dresden) fragte in seinem Vortrag »Flüchtigkeit und Bewahrung des Charismas: die Dominikaner und Dominikus« vor dem Hintergrund der sich parallel entwickelnden Franziskaner nach der charismatischen Phase in der Geschichte der sich um Dominikus entwickelnden Gemeinschaft. Während Franziskus in allen Quellen als Charismatiker schlechthin erscheint, mute Dominikus eher als dessen Gegentyp, der »Bürokrat«, an. Eine gezielte Lektüre dominikanischer Texte führt jedoch zu einem modifizierten Bild. Als instruktiv im Rahmen der Auseinandersetzung mit dem Weberschen Charisma-Konzept erscheint die Infragestellung des simplen Gegensatzes von Charisma und Institution, die Wesjohann auf seinem Zweifel an der These Webers gründet, wonach Charisma stets mit einem revolutionären Bruch einhergehe: Der Anspruch des Charismatikers ist seiner Meinung nach weniger der Gegensatz als vielmehr die Überbietung der Tradition. Die aus dieser Harmonisierung resultierende Annahme einer Dauerhaftigkeit von Charisma in der religiösen Gemeinschaft stellt die Frage nach einem Ort, an dem das Charisma des Gründers überdauert. Wesjohann erkennt diesen im Mythos; Mythen übernehmen seiner Ansicht nach die Funktion der »narrativen Bewahrung« des Charismas – sie stellen es auf Dauer und werden so zur Begründungsinstanz einer Lebensweise.

Einen lexigraphischen Zugang zum Thema wählte Roberto Rusconi (Rom) in seinem Vortrag »Moneo atque exhortor ... firmiter praecipio: carisma individuale e potere normativo in Francesco d'Assisi«. Er präsentierte seine vergleichende Untersuchung der Schriften des Franziskus hinsichtlich des Gebrauchs der ersten Person (*moneo, consulo, exhortor*, etc.), um so die Stellung des Franziskus als autoritative Instanz zu analysieren. Als Verkörperung der von ihm vertretenen Normen repräsentiert Franziskus – wie Rusconi aufzeigte – in herausragender Weise die Unmittelbarkeit des Charismatikers zum eigentlichen Generator aller Norm.

Zwei verschiedene und durchaus konträre Deutungen einer Charismatikerin verglich Maria Pia Alberzoni (Milano) in ihrem Referat »Chiara d'Assisi. Il carisma controverso«. Anhand der Konfrontation zweier Sinngebungen des gleichen Phänomens, beleuchtete sie so die wichtige Dimension der Wirkung von Charisma in ungewöhnlicher Art – ungewöhnlich weil sie mit der Sicht Gregors IX. auf Klara von Assisi und der Selbstdeutung Klaras sowohl die Sicht von außen als auch die Selbstinterpretation verbinden konnte. Während Gregor IX. bei Klara das Charisma einer Gründerin diagnostiziert und er sie als eine Adlige verehrt, die auf den Ruhm der Welt verzichtete und mit ihrem Leben ein Beispiel gibt, sieht sich Klara vor allem in der Rolle einer Jüngerin des Franziskus. Die emphatische Sicht Gregors auf Klara begründete Maria Alberzoni dabei mit durchaus pragmatischen Motiven des Papstes. So habe dieser ebenso wie seine Nachfolger Klaras Gemeinschaft als weibliches Pendant zu den neu entstandenen männlichen Bewegungen propagieren wollen – unter bewußter Abkehr von der ursprünglichen *forma vitae* Klaras.

Der Beitrag von Michael Cusato (St. Bonaventure, NY), »Esse ergo mitem et humilem corde, hoc est esse vere fratrem minorem: Bonaventure of Bagnoregio and the Reformulation of the Franciscan Charism«, nahm ein Phänomen in den Blick, das man als Charisma der zweiten Generation bezeichnen kann. Für Bonaventura war Franziskus die zentrale Figur der franziskanischen Gemeinschaft. Die Begnadung der franziskanischen Bewegung war für ihn identisch mit der des Franziskus. Jedoch erfährt dieses Charisma in der Sicht Bonaventuras eine vollständige Umdeutung. Cusato diagnostizierte im Werk des Bonaventura eine systematische Transformation franziskanischer Ideale aus dem sozialen in den asketisch-spirituellen Bereich. Minder-Sein – von dem schon Achim Wesjohann angemerkt hatte, daß es eigentlich nur in personaler Hinsicht bestimmbar sei – wird unter ihm zu einer mystischen Qualität, wodurch der Bewegung ein wesentlicher Teil der sozialen Brisanz genommen wurde. Bonaventura sei somit nicht als zweiter Gründer der Franziskaner zu sehen, wohl aber als Generator eines zweiten, nun rein theologischen Charismas der Gemeinschaft.

Giancarlo Andenna (Milano/Brescia/Dresden) wandte sich in seinem Vortrag »Il carisma negato: Gerardo Segarelli« einer geradezu klassisch-charismatischen Gemeinschaft zu. Um Segarelli, der sich zunächst vergeblich um eine Aufnahme in die Gemeinschaft der Franziskaner bemüht hatte, sammelte sich eine stetig wachsende Schar von Frauen und Männern, die mit ihm gemeinsam ein Leben im Geiste wahrer evangelischer Freiheit führen wollten. Zwar genoß die neu entstandene Bewegung zunächst noch das Wohlwollen des Ortsbischofs, doch mehrten sich recht bald Stimmen, die Segarelli als falschen Propheten bezeichneten, der seine Legitimation eben nicht von Gott, sondern nur aus sich selbst bezöge. Einen wesentlichen Teil seiner Ausführungen widmete Andenna der Organisationsstruktur der Gemeinschaft – oder besser: der nicht vorhanden Organisationsstruktur. Offensichtlich bestand weder bei Segarelli noch bei einem erheblichen Teil seiner Anhänger das Bedürfnis nach normativer Definition der Binnenstruktur. So gab es wohl keinerlei fixierte *consuetudines*, und auch eine Phase des ›Einlernens‹ neuer Mitglieder in die Gemeinschaft scheint nicht für nötig erachtet worden zu sein, und dies obwohl – wie Andenna ausführte – die fehlende institutionelle Struktur schon in der Sicht der Zeitgenossen einen wesentlichen Grund für die Zerstreuung der Gemeinschaft markierte.

Wiederum dem Phänomen des theologischen Charismas war der Beitrag von Cosimo Damiano Fonseca (Bari), »Il carisma di un canonico percepito da un monaco: Bartolomeo da Roma e Teofilo Michiel«, gewidmet. Bartolomeo da Roma, Gründer der Kanonikergemeinschaft von Frigionaia wurde mit seinen Maximen zum Vorbild von Teofilo Michiel, Prior des Reformklosters von Polirone, in dem Bartolomeo 1430 starb. Gemäß dem Lebensmodell der Wüstenväter sollte das geistige Leben in Polirone umgestaltet werden. Teofilo versuchte dabei in Anlehnung an sein Vorbild Bartolomeo, den Grad der Institutionalisierung so gering wie möglich zu halten und eher das personale Moment zu betonen.

Einen von den bisherigen Beiträgen gänzlich verschiedenen Zugang zum Thema hatte sich Pavlina Rychterova (Konstanz/Prag) in ihrem Vortrag »Passionsvisionen spätmittelalterlicher Charismatikerinnen: wie Mysterium kommunizierbar gemacht wird« gewählt. Im Zentrum ihrer Ausführungen stand mit Visionärinnen und Mystikerinnen ein ganzer Typus charismatisch begabter Frauen, und deren Visionen der Passion Christi. Unter Zugrundelegung von Victor Turners Begriff der Liminalität konstatiert Rychterova eine Liminalität der Charismatikerinnen »zwischen Himmel und Erde«. Auch der schriftliche Niederschlag ihrer Visionen sei in einem derartigen Grenzbereich »zwischen Literatur und Leben« zu verorten. In dieser Liminalität der Texte liegt nun ihre heilsvermittelnde Funktion begründet. Person und Text verschmelzen auf diese Weise zu einem – wie Rychterova formulierte – »mehrdeutigen Raum zwischen Realität und Darstellung«.

Die Publikation der Beiträge ist für den Beginn des Jahres 2005 geplant.

»What is ›Theology‹ in the Middle Ages?« Religious Cultures in Europe (11th–15th centuries) as reflected in their Selfunderstanding June 23–26, 2004 Warszawa, Poland

von Mareike Böhm
unter Mitarbeit der Moderatoren

Eine Antwort auf die Frage»Was ist ›Theologie‹ im Mittelalter« zu formulieren, war das ehrgeizige Vorhaben des viertägigen Kongresses, der in Warschau stattgefunden hat. Selbst jemandem, der sich nicht speziell mit diesem Thema auseinandersetzt, wird spontan eine Vielzahl von Aspekten einfallen, die auf einer internationalen Tagung unter dieser Fragestellung zu behandeln wären. Die Organisatoren, die Internationale Gesellschaft für Theologische Mediävistik (IGTM) in Frankfurt am Main, und das Institut für Philosophie und Soziologie der Polnischen Akademie der Wissenschaften in Warschau, hatten sich daher entschieden, elf chronologisch oder thematisch konzipierte Sektionen zu bilden. Diese sollten jeweils den Rahmen bilden, in dem die allgemeine Kongreßthematik spezifiziert ausgebreitet und diskutiert werden sollte.

Nach der Begrüßung der Teilnehmer durch den Vorsitzenden der IGTM, Prof. Dr. Rainer Berndt SJ, und dem Grußwort des Stellvertretenden Direktors des Instituts für Philosophie und Soziologie der Polnischen Akademie der Wissenschaften, Prof. Dr. Robert Pilat, eröffnete Bischof Prof. Dr. Stanisław Wielgus, ehemals Rektor der Katholischen Universität von Lublin, die Tagung mit einem Vortrag zur »Bedeutung der mittelalterlichen christlichen Theologie und Philosophie für die Entstehung der neuzeitlichen Naturwissenschaft und für die Entwicklung der modernen Gesellschaften«. Er legte dar, welchen, damals entscheidenden, Beitrag die Theologie erbrachte, nämlich eine Reflexion über die Natur und den Menschen im Verhältnis zu ihrem Schöpfer, damit Wissenschaft und Gesellschaft, so wie wir sie heute kennen, überhaupt wachsen konnten. Angesichts dessen, daß das Mittelalter heute kaum noch Beachtung findet und des immer größer werdenden Verlustes an Kommunikationsfähigkeit unter den zeitgenössischen Religionsgemeinschaften, versuchte die Tagung, in ihren Sektionen sowohl einzelne Zeiträume des Mittelalters als auch bestimmte Autoren im Hinblick auf das übergeordnete Thema zu untersuchen.

Vier Sektionen befaßten sich jeweils mit der Theologie eines Jahrhunderts im Spiegel ausgewählter Autoren. In der Sektion der »Theologie des 11. und 12. Jahrhunderts« stellten sich unter der Moderation von Constant Mews Luigi Catalani (»La teologia nella scuola porretana«), Burcht Pranger (»Theology in a monastic context in the 12th century Latin West«) und Luisa Valente (»Theology in a scholastic context in the Latin West«) die Frage, welche verschiedenen Modelle von Theologie es zu dieser Zeit gab. Dabei zeigte sich, daß das alte Wort Jean Leclercqs von der »théologie monastique« im Unterschied zur »théologie scolastique« nach wie vor soviel Ansehen genießt, daß es gern als Kategorie zur Beschreibung der vielfältigen und nicht leicht zu verstehenden intellektuellen Bewegungen des Frühmittelalters verwendet wird.

Die Sektion »Theologien des 12. Jahrhunderts« setzte sich zum Ziel, einige besondere Problemstellungen dieses Jahrhunderts zu erhellen. Peter Gemeinhardt behandelte eine bisher nicht eingehend untersuchte, spätere Schrift Anselms von Canterbury, die *Epistola de incarnatione Verbi*, um ein revidiertes Bild auf das *Proslogion* zu entwerfen. Elisabeth Reinhardt untersuchte das Theologieverständnis Richards von Sankt Viktor, wobei sie sich auf ausdrückliche Äußerungen des Viktoriners über sein theologisches Vorgehen konzentrierte. Aufgrund ihrer Editionsarbeit an Texten Joachims von Fiore versuchte Julia Eva Wannenmacher, den Standort dieses eigenständigen Denkers im komplexeren Kontext der Theologie der zweiten Hälfte des 12. Jahrhunderts zu bestimmen. Im letzten Vortrag der Sektion leistete Markus Enders eine umfassende Untersuchung zur Bedeutung des Ausdrucks »theologia« bei den Autoren des 12. Jahrhunderts sowie in antiken Quellen. Die Sektionsleitung lag in den Händen von Hideki Nakamura SJ.

Für die inhaltliche Gestaltung, die personelle Besetzung und den unkonventionellen Programmablauf der Sektion »Theologie des 13. Jahrhunderts« haben Ruedi Imbach und Michał Paluch OP (Thomas-Institut Warschau) mit dankenswertem Engagement und Bedacht gesorgt. Da Ruedi Imbach seine Teilnahme an der Tagung kurzfristig absagen mußte, hatte die Moderation Ulrich Horst OP übernommen. Nach dem einleitenden Vortrag mit dem Thema »Zwischen Faszination und Ablehnung: Theologie und Philosophie im 13. Jahrhundert in ihrem Verhältnis zueinander« von Henryk Anzulewicz, der »die spannungsvolle und sich dennoch als enorm produktiv, zukunftsorientiert und zukunftsbestimmend erweisende Wechselbeziehung zwischen Theologie und Philosophie in der Hochscholastik« am Beispiel der Lehrmeinung einiger einflußreicher Pariser Theologen aus dem 13. Jahrhundert umriß, wurde in den nachfolgenden drei Vorträgen die Auffassung der Theologie als praktische bzw./und theoretische Wissenschaft nach Thomas von Aquin von Adriano Oliva OP, Heinrich von Gent von Marialucrezia Leone und Wilhelm von Ware von Mikolaj Olszewski mit eindrucksvoller Klarheit und einer Fülle an neuen Erkenntnissen vorgestellt. Der kurzfristige Wechsel in der Moderation hatte zur Folge, daß der ursprüngliche Plan, die drei in den Vorträgen vorgestellten Auffassungen über die Natur der Theologie als Wissenschaft miteinander ins Gespräch zu bringen, aufgegeben wurde.

Die Sektion »Theologie im 14. Jahrhundert«, deren Moderation Zénon Kaluza (CNRS, Paris) übernommen hatte, ließ mit ihren vergleichsweise sehr unterschiedlichen Themen den derzeitigen Forschungsstand erkennen. Thomas Prügl eröffnete die Sitzung mit dem Vortrag »Medieval Biblical ›principia‹ as reflections on the nature of theology«. Danach stellte Jean-François Genest eines der Hauptmerkmale des 14. Jahrhunderts an einem Beispiel vor, nämlich der »Théologie et expérience spirituelle: Le cas de Thomas Bradwardine«. Chris Schabel mit »Modality, instants of nature, and divine attributes in Parisian reactions to Scotus on divine foreknowledge« sowie Alfonso Maierù mit »Logique et théologie au XIVe siècle« zeigten in ihren Referaten, daß im späteren Mittelalter die Bedeutung der Logik für die Entstehung, aber auch für die Lösung theologischer Fragestellungen unverhältnismäßig stark gewachsen war.

Die übrigen sieben Sektionen waren thematisch ausgerichtet. Zur Konkretisierung gemeinsamer Fragestellungen bot die von Hanns Peter Neuheuser, vertretungsweise für Jochen Schröder, moderierte kunsthistorische Sektion vier Fallstudien. Carsten Fleischhauer äußerte sich skeptisch zur Redeweise vom »bernhardinischen Plan« im frühen Kirchenbau der Zisterzienser. Er konnte die Schwierigkeiten verdeutlichen, durch Werkanalysen zwischen impliziter Theologie und kunsthistorischem Konstrukt zu unterscheiden. Birgit Münch referierte zur Darstellung von Passionsszenen nach der *Vita Christi* Ludolfs von Sachsen, vor allem zur Verzögerungsdauer von Rezeptionsleistungen in der Kunst von Buchillustrationen. Till Busse erörterte den erst im 19. Jahrhundert in die Kunstgeschichte eingeführten Begriff der »Sacra conversazione« als Bezeichnung für alte Topoi aus Epiphanie- und Offertoriumsriten. Bruno Börner setzte sich mit »Christusthemen« der spätmittelalterlichen Skulptur und ihrer Ursprünge in der textlich überlieferten Spiritualität alemannischer Frauenklöster auseinander und veranschaulichte die entsprechende Quellenkritik. Die Diskussion beschäftigte sich mit den metasprachlichen Fachausdrücken, welche in den Disziplinen unterschiedlich hermeneutisch aufgeschlossen werden müssen, aber auch mit der theologischen Mediävistik als übergreifende Perspektive, welche Abgleiche zwischen historischem Sprachgut und dem Forschungsvokabular ermögliche.

Guy Lobrichon eröffnete mit seinem Vortrag »Transfert de connaissances, de l'Université au cabinet de lecture: heurs et malheurs de l'exégèse biblique (France, Italie, XIIIe-XIVe siècles)«, in dem er den Zusammenhang zwischen Textauslegung und Buchform herausstellte, die Sektion »Exegesegeschichte«. Nikolaus von Kues' Idee einer reflexiven Schriftexegese, die der bis dahin gebräuchlichen Unterscheidung zwischen Philosophie und Theologie keine weitere Beachtung schenkt, stellt eine neue Form der Exegese dar. Für den Kusaner ist die Heilige Schrift und ihre Tradition eine Art der Weitergabe von Einsichten in Begründungszusammenhänge des Lebens. Er hält den Menschen für fähig zu diesen Vernunfteinsichten, auch ohne Offenbarung. Diese These vertrat eindrucksvoll Martin Thurner in seinem Vortrag »Tradition und Reflexion. Die Heilige Schrift im Denken des Nikolaus von Kues«. Die Sektion wurde moderiert von Ambrogio Piazzoni.

Aufgabe der von Hanns Peter Neuheuser konzipierten und moderierten liturgiewissenschaftlichen Sektion des Kongresses war es, über die Differenzen zwischen dem objektiven Befund einer mittelalterlichen Liturgie und der stets nachträglichen Redeweise und der Reflexion über mittelalterliche Liturgie zu diskutieren, sowie hieraus das, was unter mittelalterlicher Theologie verstanden werden soll, zu erkunden. Im ersten Beitrag beschäftigte sich Charles Caspers mit dem Autorenkreis aus der Devotio moderna, deren kritischer Blick auf die zeitgenössische Theologie an der Scheide zwischen Mittelalter und früher Neuzeit dazu diente, festzustellen, wie man bereits damals mittelalterliche Liturgie bewertete. Caspers erörterte diese Frage konkret am fortschrittlichen Text des Kommuniontraktates in der *Imitatio Christi* des Thomas von Kempen, wo dieser die Scheu, sakramental zu kommunizieren, ablegt. Im zweiten Beitrag erweiterte Jürgen Bärsch den Blick auf die heutige Forschungssituation, die durch ihre ebenfalls zurückblickende Perspektive und ihre Themenauswahl definiert, was sie unter mittelalterlicher Liturgie resp. Theologie versteht. Bärsch schlug die Ritualität, die Ekklesiologie und das Totengedenken als Gebiete vor, in welche sich die Liturgiewissenschaft in die Mediävistik einbringen könne. Die ergebnisreiche Diskussion vertiefte die Fragen und sprach sich für eine interdisziplinäre Zusammenarbeit unter Einbeziehung der Geschichtswissenschaft und der Kunstgeschichte aus.

In der Sektion »Methoden der mittelalterlichen Theologie und ihr Studium«, moderiert vertretungsweise von Hideki Nakamura SJ, wurden zuerst zwei Autoren aus dem 12. Jahrhundert behandelt, die zur methodischen Entwicklung der mittelalterlichen Theologie einen eigenständigen Beitrag leisteten. Anhand der Untersuchung der zwei Hauptwerke des Peter Abaelard, *Sic et non* und *Scito te ipsum*, versuchte Josep-Ignasi Saranyana, das Hauptanliegen der Theologie Abaelards darzustellen, während Stefan Seit sich auf die Schriften des Johannes von Salisbury konzentrierte, um Johannes' Verständnis der Funktion des Glaubens und dessen Folge in seiner theologischen Methode zu prüfen. In ihrem Vortrag untersuchte Pia Antolić das theologische Denken Roger Bacons, der nach der weitgehenden Aristoteles-Rezeption im 13. Jahrhundert aus theologie-methodischer Sicht einen bemerkenswerten Beitrag im Spannungsfeld seiner verschiedenen Anliegen – Metaphysik, Moralphilosophie und Studium der Heiligen Schrift – leistete. Die Sitzung wurde mit dem Vortrag von Ursula Vones-Liebenstein abgeschlossen, in dem sie sowohl durch systematische Darstellung als auch durch konkrete Beispiele die Leistungen der Prosopographie für die Erforschung der Theologie des Mittelalters hervorhob.

Die Geschichte der Spiritualität im Mittelalter war Thema einer Sektion unter der kundigen Moderation von Walter Senner OP. Francesco D'Elia zog in seinem Vortrag »Omiletica e teologia nei sermones di Gioacchino da Fiore« das geistliche Profil des kalabresischen Abtes nach, insoweit die erhaltenen Predigten dies ermöglichen. Susanne Kaup berichtete mit »Das ›Pratum animarum‹ des Gerhard von Sterngassen OP und seine Quellen« aus ihren Arbeiten über die dominikanische Mystik des Spätmittelalters.

Die Sektion »Entwicklungen im Mittelalter« schließlich, moderiert von Ilona Riedel-Spangenberger, trug mit ihren Vorträgen zur Abrundung der Tagung bei und leitete gleichzeitig zur Öffnung auf neue Fragen und zu weiteren Arbeiten über. Georg Gresser warf erneut die Frage auf, welche Auswirkung die »petrinische Ekklesiologie und eschatologische Grundhaltung Gregors VII. auf die päpstliche Synode« hatten. Thomas Marschler skizzierte »Das Selbstverständnis des theologischen Magisters im Spiegel scholastischer Quodlibetalliteratur« am Beispiel der Persönlichkeit Heinrichs von Gent. Das Referat über die »Theologische Laienkompetenz. Erwägungen zur sozialen Öffnung des theologischen Diskurses im späten Mittelalter« von Volker Leppin ließ erahnen, in welchem Ausmaß das Mittelalter Wegbereiter für die Moderne war, wie Stanisław Wielgus dies bereits in seinem Eröffnungsvortrag erörterte. Markus Graulich stellte abschließend das »Verhältnis zwischen Theologie und Recht im *Decretum Gratiani*« anschaulich dar.

Abgeschlossen wurde die Tagung mit einer Plenumsrunde, die die Frage nach den Herausforderungen in der Zukunft formulierte. Eine zusammenfassende Antwort war kaum zu finden, da nicht zuletzt die Tagung gezeigt hat, daß die Arbeitsfelder der theologischen Mediävistik inhaltlich und methodisch sehr breit sind. Es steht fest, daß die verschiedenen Disziplinen der Theologie die Zusammenarbeit mit allen geschichtswissenschaftlichen Fachrichtungen suchen müssen, um sich inhaltlich und methodisch weiterzuentwickeln.

Die Tagung fand im Gebäude des Instituts für Philosophie und Soziologie der Polnischen Akademie der Wissenschaften, dem Pałac Staszica, statt. Anläßlich einer Exkursion in die Nationalbibliothek wurden den Kongreßteilnehmern einige der ältesten Handschriften Polens, die den 2. Weltkrieg unbeschadet überstanden hatten, gezeigt.

Die IGTM dankt herzlich allen Teilnehmerinnen und Teilnehmern sowie – besonders – den Referentinnen und Referenten, die sich trotz den Schwierigkeiten im Vorfeld von der Reise nicht haben abhalten lassen und die diese erste internationale Tagung der Gesellschaft bereichert haben. Auf dem eingeschlagenen Weg zeigt sich unter den beteiligten Wissenschaftlern die einmütige Erkenntnis, daß der Austausch mit den Vertretern benachbarter Fachdisziplinen notwendig für die eigene Arbeit ist.

Die Publikation der Beiträge ist in den Subsidia des Jahrbuches *Archa Verbi*, Verlag Aschendorff, Münster, vorgesehen.

»Trinitarian Theology in the Medieval West« Workshop im Institut für Europäische Geschichte Mainz (9.–12. September 2004)

von Peter Gemeinhardt

Über die Trinität wurde in den letzten Jahrzehnten viel gesprochen und geschrieben. Das gilt freilich nur bedingt für die mittelalterliche Trinitätstheologie, deren geschichtliche und systematische Entwicklung vergleichsweise selten Aufmerksamkeit erfährt. Gerade für die Anfänge der Scholastik im 12. Jh. und dann für die intensiven Debatten des 13. und 14. Jh. ist trinitarische Reflexion jedoch von eminenter Bedeutung, nicht nur hinsichtlich der Gotteslehre, sondern z.B. auch für die theologische Rezeption der Logik und für die Entfaltung der Anthropologie, speziell des Personbegriffs.

Diese theologische Entwicklung im Besonderen und die geistesgeschichtliche Relevanz trinitarischen Denkens im Allgemeinen vertieft wahrzunehmen war Ziel eines Workshops am Institut für Europäische Geschichte in Mainz, organisiert von Simo Knuuttila und Risto Saarinen (Theologische Fakultät Helsinki). Behandelt wurden vier Themenkomplexe:

– History and Terminology: Augustins Trinitätsdenken (*Roland Kany*); Entwicklung der Trinitätstheologie im 11. und 12. Jh. (*Peter Gemeinhardt*); Trinitarisches Denken in den Schulen des 15. Jh.s (*Maarten Hoenen*).

– Trinity, Logic and Semantics: Dionysius Areopagita (*Stephen Brown*), Trinität und Logik im 12. Jh. (*Simo Knuuttila*), bei Petrus von Pulkau (*Alfonso Maierù*) sowie bei Scotus und Ockham (*Christopher Martin*); Franziskaner und Dominikaner um 1320 (*Lauge Nielsen*).

– Metaphysical Trinity: Der willentliche Hervorgang des Heiligen Geistes (*Russell Friedman*); Utrum essentia generat – Joachim von Fiore (*Bruce Marshall*); trinitarische Hervorgänge nach Thomas von Aquin (*Jeremy Wilkins*).

– Trinitätslehre und religiöse Erfahrung: Die Analogie intelligibler Hervorgänge in Gott (*Frederick Lawrence*); Immanente Trinität bei Boethius (*Paul LaChance*); Die barmherzige Trinität in Luthers Auslegungen von Joh 1,18 (*Risto Saarinen*).

Weit davon entfernt, das Thema erschöpfend behandelt zu haben, zeichnen sich doch gewisse Konvergenzlinien ab, die weitere Bearbeitung verdienten, so etwa die Diskussion über die Behauptung *Deus generat Deum*, der Hervorgang des Heiligen Geistes sowohl als logisches Problem wie auch als Thema religiöser Erfahrung oder die vielfältigen Schuldiskussionen im Spätmittelalter. Eine Veröffentlichung der Beiträge ist angedacht. In jedem Fall bestätigt sich die Annahme, daß die Akten über die mittelalterliche Trinitätstheologie noch keineswegs geschlossen zu werden verdienen.

Mitteilungen

Interdisciplinary Department of the History of Medieval Culture

Katolicki Uniwersytet Lubelski
Al. Racławickie 14Heading 3
20–950 Lublin (Poland)
Tel. 48/81/445 32 37
Fax. 48/81/ 445 41 08
http://www.kul.lublin.pl/m_wydzialowe/sredniowiecze/uk.html

Founded in 1965, the department of the history of Medieval Culture has been headed successively by Rev. Prof. Marian Rechowicz, Rev. Prof. Marian Kurdziałek and, to date, Rt. Rev. Prof. Stanisław Wielgus. Faculty staff have included: Dr. Maria Szafarkiewicz (1965–1992), Rev. Stanisław Wielgus, Dr. Joanna Judycka (1977–1993), Dr. Małgorzata Kawecka (1986–1989) and currently Dr. Wanda Bajor and Rev. Piotr Smoliński. The direction of the research was established by Rev. Kurdziałek and Rev. Prof. Wielgus. Since the study of medieval philosophy was in its early stages at KUL in the 1950s, a project was conceived by Prof. S. Swieżawski and M. Kurdziałek to undertake the edition and publication of a wide range of manuscripts, significant to Polish culture, dating back to the late Middle Ages and early Renaissance generated by or influential at the Academia Cracoviensis. The 15th century was a time of rapid intellectual growth of Polish culture in general and of the Academia Cracoviensis in particular. This was a result of the assumption that demonstrating the originality of Polish scholars' thought would only be possible after the study and publication of sources and research into manuscripts concerning philosophy, philosophy of nature and theology, law and medieval medicine.

The work of the department is focused mainly on medieval manuscripts concerning philosophy, theology, law and science. The main objective of the research is to prepare the edition of the above and conduct analysis reflecting the development of science in medieval Poland. Hence the department provides Polish scholarship with sources of Polish culture, unpublished and hitherto hidden in often decaying medieval manuscripts. The manuscripts under study come from Polish and foreign libraries. The skilled personnel, though few in number, are engaged in a wide range of activities, coordinating the work of medievalists from the university and other circles from Poland and abroad. The activities are: preparing critical editions and publishing them, organizing presentations of papers, international conferences, discussion groups, and conducting specialised courses. The department is also involved in coordinating and supervising the research of young Polish medievalists from the KUL circle. The Interdisciplinary Department of History of Medieval Culture publishes the results of its studies in its own series *Acta Mediaevalia*, circulated internationally.

The Interdisciplinary Department of History of Medieval Culture comprises a team of young scholars, whose work draws the interest of medievalists around the world. The recognition of the 'Lublin editorial school' – as it has already come to be called – was confirmed in 1987 by granting the Tomasso dalla Commissione Leonina and Commissione del Cusano award to the critical edition of *Quaestiones disputatae super octo libros 'Physicorum' Aristotelis cum glossis Ioannis Isneri* prepared by Dr. Lucyna Nowak under the supervision of Prof. Stanisław Wielgus and regarding it as a model edition in medieval studies. The Interdisciplinary Department of History of Medieval Culture, founded in 1965, is meant to be a place of collaboration for medievalists working on various aspects of medieval science and letters. The main objective is preparing critical editions of handwritten medieval commentaries concerning philosophy, theology, law and science. The selection of material corresponds with the research programme of the Institute of Philosophy and Sociology PAN (Polish Academy of Science). Moreover, the department conducts research on medieval commentaries on the Bible from the 15th century. The faculty has embarked upon joint work with Polish and foreign institutes, most of all the Istitute of History, Science, Education and Technology PAN, Institute of Philosophy and Sociology PAN, Fédération Internationale des Instituts d'Études Médiévales, Martin Grabmann Institut der Universität München, and Aristoteles Latinus of the Catholic University in Leuven.

The research projects of the department have included the following eminent Polish medievalists: Prof. M. Rechowicz, Prof. S. Swieżawski, Prof. J. Kłoczowski, Prof. B. Kumor, Prof. M. Kurdziałek, Prof. M. Plezia, Prof. Z. Sułowski, Prof. M. Gogacz, Prof. W. Seńko, Prof. A. Szafrański, Prof. Z. Włodek, Prof. J. Zathey, Prof. M. Markowski, Prof. S. Wielgus. The objects of particular research interest in the department were and are the works of medieval Polish and European authors such as: Jan Elgot, Jan Dąbrówka, Benedykt Hesse, Stanisław of Zawada, Jan Isner, Stanisław of Skarbimierz, Jan Kanty, Maciej of Labiszyn, Henry of Hessen, Nicholas of Dinkesbuhl, Konrad of Soltau, Johannes Dambach, Marsilius of Inghen, Albert of Saxony, Laurentius Londorius and others.

Tagung Weingarten 2005

Kulturkontakte und Rezeptionsvorgänge in der Theologie des 12. und 13. Jahrhunderts

Vom 28. April bis zum 1. Mai 2005 veranstaltet die Katholische Akademie der Diözese Rottenburg-Stuttgart in ihrem Tagungshaus in Weingarten (Oberschwaben) unter diesem Thema eine wissenschaftliche Studientagung in Zusammenarbeit mit dem Institut für Spätmittelalter und Reformation der Universität Tübingen und in Verbindung mit der IGTM. Das Programm sieht folgende Vorträge vor:

1. Ulrich Köpf: Kulturkontakte und Rezeptionsvorgänge in der Theologie des 12. und 13. Jahrhunderts. Zur Einführung.
2. Rainer Berndt: Ps.-Dionysius in der Abtei Sankt Viktor.
3. Hanns-Peter Neuheuser: Zur Problematik der Pseudo-Dionysius-Rezeption in der hochmittelalterlichen Liturgiehermeneutik.
4. Henryk Anzulewicz: Rezeption und Reinterpretation. Ps.-Dionysius, die Peripatetiker und die Umdeutung der Augustinischen Illuminationslehre bei Albertus Magnus.
5. Pia Antolić: Die Kommentierung des pseudo-aristotelischen »Liber de causis« als Buch XII der Metaphysik des Aristoteles im Spiegel der Verurteilung von 1277.
6. Mechthild Dreyer: »sequemur Aristotelem, non omittentes ea quae ex aliis et ex nobis utiliter videbuntur esse addenda«. Zur Aristoteles-Rezeption von Albertus Magnus.
7. Rolf Darge: Die Aristoteles-Rezeption im Ansatz der Ersten Philosophie gemäß Bonaventura und Thomas von Aquin.
8. Rivka Basch: Die Exegese von Hugo von Sankt Viktor und Rabbi Schmuel Meir (»Raschbam«).
9. Ralf M. W. Stammberger: Zur jüdischen Exegese im Werk Hugos von Sankt Viktor.
10. Stefan Schreiner: Abraham ben Me'ir Ibn Esras Rezeption des arabischen Neuplatonismus am Beispiel seiner philosophischen Dichtung ›Chaj ben Meqitz‹ und deren Wirkungsgeschichte.
11. Georg Steer: Meister Eckhart und Moses Maimonides.
12. Mikolaj Olszewski: Reception of Aristotle's gnoseology in the 13th century scholastic metatheology.
13. Lutz Richter-Bernburg: Alpharabius, Algazel, Averroes. Zur lateinischen Rezeption graeco-islamischer Philosophie bis 1300.
14. Matthias M. Tischler: Transfer- und Transformationsprozesse im iberischen Islambild zwischen dem 11. und 13. Jahrhundert.
15. Gotthard Strohmaier: Die islamische Antikenrezeption im Spiegel neuzeitlicher Ideologie.

Rechtzeitig wird die Akademie Detailinformationen und Anmeldeformulare versenden. Anmeldungen nimmt Herr Bauer am Sitz der Stuttgarter Akademie entgegen (Bauer@akademie-rs.de).

Archa Verbi 1 (2004) 179–221

Recensiones

Cecilia Chazelle, Burton V. N. Edwards (eds.): *The Study of the Bible in the Carolingian Era* (Medieval Church Studies 3), Turnhout: Brepols 2003. – xii, 258 pp. – ISBN 2-503-51404-9. – € 60,00.

Mediävistik bleibt ohne eingehende Kenntnis der mittelalterlichen Schriftauslegung ein Ding der Unmöglichkeit. Auch wenn sich die Forschung der Geschichte der Schriftauslegung intensiver zugewandt hat, liegen manche Bereiche noch allzu sehr im Schatten. Dies gilt insbesondere für die lateinischsprachige Exegese des siebten bis zehnten Jahrhunderts. Die von C. Chazelle und B. V. N. Edwards herausgegebene Aufsatzsammlung will die Grundlage für eine Zusammenschau und Neubeurteilung der Bibelstudien und ihrer kulturprägenden Entfaltung in der Karolingerzeit (8.–9. Jahrhundert) bieten (S. 4). Dazu werden elf zumeist englischsprachige Aufsätze zusammengestellt, die entweder Spezialfragen zu biblischen Kommentaren jener Zeit oder die Wechselbeziehungen von Schriftauslegung und Kultur am Beispiel von Kanonistik, Architektur, Hagiographie, Eucharistielehre und Liturgie behandeln. Die Einführung (S. 1–16) umreißt die jüngste Forschung und stellt heraus, daß die lange vorherrschende Sicht, die karolingische Exegese habe sich auf das Zusammenstellen und Weitergeben der Vätertradition beschränkt, viel zu eingeschränkt und ungenau sei und der Subtilität und dem Reichtum der karolingischen Schriftwerke nicht gerecht werde. Dies erhärten auch einige der Einzelbeiträge, so daß man diesen Sammelband als kräftigen Impuls, auch diesem Stiefkind der bisherigen Editions- und Forschungstätigkeit mehr Aufmerksamkeit zu schenken, nur begrüßen kann. Der Sammelband selbst stellt allerdings anders, als sein Titel vermuten läßt, nicht die erhoffte Gesamt- oder Überblicksdarstellung dar. Dazu bleiben die einzelnen Artikel zu speziell und thematisch unverbunden. Der Sammelband enthält *glossae* oder *quaestiones*, aber keinen *tractatus* oder *commentarius* zur karolingischen Exegese. Bei der Fülle von Einzelinformationen in allen hier veröffentlichten Aufsätzen sei nur einer besonders hervorgehoben, da er deutlich macht, wie erst der Blick fürs Detail die Eigenart der karolingischen Exegese erkennbar werden läßt. Alle anderen Artikel seien nur kurz beschrieben. John C. Cavadini untersucht, welche Mechanismen und Ziele hinter dem massiven Tradierungsprozeß von Kirchenväterliteratur in den frühscholastischen Werken stecken. Statt des Begriffes Sammlung oder Überlieferung schlägt er – einem Bild Alkuins folgend – den des ›Konfekts‹ vor, d. h. den der ›Zubereitung‹, denn die Tradition werde beim Überlieferungsvorgang ›synthetisiert und entwickelt‹ (S. 140). Dies zeigt Cavadini am Beispiel von Hilarius von Poitiers auf. Die Theologen des achten und neunten Jahrhunderts greifen auf Hilarius' antiarianische Theologie zurück, um mit ihm in einem neuen Kontext adoptianistisch-nestorianische Fragen zu klären. Dazu werden gezielt und durchdacht Zitate aus Hilarius' Werken ausgewählt, gekürzt und zurechtgeschnitten und dann zusammengestellt. Noch stärker baut Hinkmar von Reims im Prädestinationsstreit Hilarius als eine weitere Väterautorität auf, die die hauptsächlich augustinisch geprägte Tradition ergänzen soll, und zwar um ein komplementäres, auf Origenes zurückführendes Verständnis der Erlösung. Diese Eigenständigkeit des Denkens wird nur dann erkennbar, wenn man die Eigenarbeit im Prozeß der Überlieferung durch Feinanalysen herausarbeitet, was Cavadini in besonders überzeugender Weise gelungen ist. Die weiteren Artikel seien der Orientierung halber kurz mit Autor und Inhalt genannt. John J. Contreni stellt die *Glossae divinae historiae* von Johannes Eriugena in einem Vergleich mit den Glossen von Canterbury anhand zahlreicher Beispiele vor (vgl. den Appendix S. 29–38). Michael Fox widmet sich Alkuins *Quaestiones in Genesim*, die weit mehr Originalität aufweisen, als bisher angenommen. Einer kritischen Edition arbeitet er mit einem Verzeichnis der Handschriften und einem groben Stemma vor. Carol Scheppard bereitet eine Edition der *Eclogae Tractatorum in Psalterium* vor und gibt einen Einblick in die darin hervortretende und zur Zeit verstärkt diskutierte irische Exegese und ihre Eigenheiten. Johannes Heil entwickelt ähnlich wie in seiner einschlägigen Monographie das Judenbild der Paulus-Kommentare, um daran die Unterschiedlichkeit, aber auch Originalität der Exegese des 9. Jahrhunderts aufzuzeigen. Der Herausgeber B. V. N. Edwards stellt die Incipits der Kommentare zum Deuteronomium samt Handschriftenverzeichnissen von Haimo von Auxerre (unveröffentlicht), Walahfrid Strabo (unveröffentlicht) und Hrabanus Maurus (PL 108) zusammen und klärt ihre Abhängigkeit (S. 108–113). Mary Alberi analysiert Alkuins Deutung der zwei Schwerter (Lk 22,36–38) in dessen Epistola 136. William J. Diebold ergänzt die Studie von Günther Binding zum *sapiens architectus* mit einem Blick auf die relevanten Schriftstellen und ihre Deutung. E. Ann Matter beleuchtet die Verwendung der Heiligen Schrift in einigen hagiographischen Werken, insbesondere von Paschasius Radbertus. Die Herausgeberin C. Chazelle umreißt den ersten Abendmahlsstreit, den sie zu Recht auch als exegetischen Streit verstanden wissen will. Abigail Firey untersucht den Gebrauch der Schrift in den pseudo-isidorischen Dekretalen und weitet damit den Blick auf die Kanonistik aus. Dominique Iogna-Prat wendet sich in dem einzigen französischen Aufsatz des Bandes der Deutung der Kirche in mehreren Liturgiekommentaren zu. Das Buch ist sehr schön gedruckt, die Bibliographie (S. 245–258) mit einschlägigen Veröffentlichungen ab 1989 besonders nützlich. Das umfassende Sammelwerk von MAGNE SÆBØ (ed.): *Hebrew Bible, Old Testament. The history of its interpretation*, Göttingen 1996ff. hätte noch auf alle Fälle aufgenommen gehört. Allerdings fallen auch einige handwerkliche Mängel auf. Das Buch hat keine Register, dabei wäre ein Personenregister der Mühe wert gewesen, denn viele nützliche Einzelbeobachtungen bleiben so in den Artikeln vergraben. Daß ein Hauptwerk der Herausgeberin von 2001 einem der Mitautoren nicht zugänglich gewesen sei (S. 134, Anm. 3), verwundert den Rezensenten, ebenso welchen Sinn es trotz aller Verwandschaft machen soll, für das neunte Jahrhundert die Vulgata in der Ausgabe der Clementina vom Ende des 16. Jahrhunderts anzugeben (S. 186–188). Kopfschütteln rufen auch einige Tippfehler hervor, wobei es für den deutschsprachigen Leser ein besonderer Wermutstropfen ist, daß gehäuft deutsche Wörter falsch geschrieben werden. Doch ermutigt der Sammelband, sich verstärkt der Frühphase der mittelalterlichen Exegese zuzuwenden, wofür ihm weite Beachtung gewünscht und den Vf.n Dank ausgesprochen sei.

Ulli Roth, Pforzheim

HENRY CHADWICK: *East and West. The Making of a Rift in the Church. From Apostolic Times Until the Council of Florence* (Oxford History of the Christian Church), Oxford: Oxford University Press 2003. – x, 306 pp. – ISBN 0-19-926457-0. – £ 60,00.

Die ökumenischen Dialoge einschließlich der jüngsten Diskussionen über die Mitarbeit der orthodoxen Kirchen im ÖRK haben deutlich vor Augen geführt, daß das ökumenische Problem von ›Ost‹ und ›West‹ noch lange nicht Gegenstand distanzierter historischer Betrachtung sein kann. Wohl aber ist es unverzichtbar, sich die Geschichte dieses komplexen Problems zu vergegenwärtigen, um zu verstehen, welche theologischen und ekklesiologischen Diskrepanzen heutigen Debatten – mindestens implizit – zu Grunde liegen. Einen wichtigen Beitrag zur ökumenischen Selbstaufklärung liefert der Grandseigneur der angelsächsischen Patristik, Sir Henry Chadwick (= Ch.). Auf rund 300 Seiten werden fast 1500 Jahre Kirchengeschichte komprimiert und problemorientiert dargestellt – basierend auf souveränem Umgang mit den Quellen, dabei immer mit scharfem historischem Urteil und nicht selten auch mit feiner Ironie gegenüber den Akteuren der Geschichte der Spaltung zwischen Ost und West. Aus einer Fülle von kirchen- und dogmengeschichtlichen Einzelheiten werden luzide die großen Linien entwickelt, die z.T. bis heute die Selbst- und Fremdwahrnehmung im ökumenischen Gespräch prägen. ›Making‹ deutet an, daß neben dem ›kirchenspaltenden‹ Agieren einzelner Persönlichkeiten die Konstruktion von Geschichtsbildern Beachtung verdient. Das prominenteste Beispiel dafür ist das ›Schisma von 1054‹, das zum Integral der sukzessiven Spaltung zwischen Ost und West avancierte, obwohl das historische Aufeinandertreffen von Michael Kerullarios und Humbert von Silva Candida zwar eruptiv verlief (›a declaration of cold civil war in the Church‹, S. 216), zunächst aber folgenlos blieb: ›Churches are out of communion with one another if they come to think and feel that they are. The events of 1053–54 were more symptomatic of a state of mind than a primary cause‹ (S. 218). In Aufnahme der neueren Forschung benennt Ch. das Jahr 1204 als ›the time when the divorce of Latin west and Greek east came to be made permanent‹ (S. 275). Konsequenterweise stehen nicht Humbert und Kerullarios im Mittelpunkt, sondern die Auseinandersetzung des konstantinopolitanischen Patriarchen Photius mit den römischen Päpsten Nikolaus I., Hadrian II. und Johannes VIII. im 9. Jh., die fast ein Drittel des Buches einnimmt (S. 95–192). In Nikolaus' und Photius' Briefen treten die schon seit längerem latenten Differenzen in Theologie (*Filioque*), Ritus (Samstagsfasten) und Ekklesiologie (Primat) gebündelt zu Tage, die fortan das Motivinventar ost-westlicher Dialoge bilden sollten (im elften Jahrhundert kam die Azymenfrage hinzu; vgl. dazu G. Avvakumov, *Die Entstehung des Unionsgedankens* [VGI 47], Berlin 2002). Nikolaus' Versuch, den internen Streit zwischen Photius und Ignatius um das Patriarchenamt von Rom aus autoritativ zu entscheiden, führte auf den Synoden von Konstantinopel 869/70 und 879/80 zur Grundsatzfrage, ob die Autorität in der Kirche ›primatial‹ oder ›pentarchisch‹ ausgeübt werden solle, ob also dem römischen Papst ein letztinstanzliches Recht zukomme, disziplinäre und theologische Entscheidungen zu fällen, oder ob dies den ökumenischen Synoden unter Beteiligung der fünf höchstrangigen Patriarchen vorbehalten sei, unter denen der Bischof von Rom nur den Ehrenvorsitz inne habe. Daher entpuppt sich die Autoritätsfrage für die wachsende Entfremdung zwischen Ost und West quasi als ›Meta-Kontroverse‹: ›Nicholas' pattern of dominance appears as a Christianized version of centralized imperial power, and without that, he felt, the unity and universality of the one universal and apostolic Church could never be realized in the mess of human history‹ (S. 109). Entsprechend beanspruchte er im Rückgriff auf die Synode von Serdika 342, daß in Rechtsfällen die unterlegene Partei an den römischen Papst appellieren könne – was gegenwärtig die Ignatianer taten (S. 135f.) und was seinerzeit Athanasius den Rückhalt von Papst Julius I. verschaffte (S. 15). Daß Nikolaus zur Begründung seiner Autorität die pseudo-isidorischen Dekretalen heranzog, d.h. die Setzung kanonischen Rechts durch (gefälschte) Entscheidungen früherer Päpste, die deren Nachfolger sowohl über Konzilsentscheidungen als auch über weltliche Instanzen erhoben (S. 97f.), war mit der byzantinischen ›Symphonia‹ von Kaiser und Patriarch ebenso wenig vereinbar wie mit Kanon 28 der Synode von Chalkedon 451, der dem ›Neuen Rom‹ den gleichen Rang zubilligte wie dem ›alten‹ (S. 45f.), und zwar aufgrund der jeweiligen politischen Bedeutung, während die Päpste seit Damasus ihre Autorität – und die der ›petrinischen‹ Stühle von Antiochien und Alexandrien – von Petrus herleiteten (S. 22). Die Konsequenzen werden an der Azymenfrage im Hochmittelalter deutlich: Nur im Rahmen der Anerkennung seines Primats war Rom bereit, Unterschiede in kirchlichen Riten zu tolerieren, während für die Ostkirchen die Legitimität disziplinärer Unterschiede durch den Konsens im Glauben begründet war, den allein die ökumenischen Synoden zum Ausdruck brachten

(S. 176). Als theologisches Symbol der Entfremdung wird das *Filioque* identifiziert, also die Frage, ob der Heilige Geist nach dem Nizäno-Konstantinopolitanum von 381 nur aus dem Vater oder – so die lateinische Theologie seit Augustin (S. 28f.) – auch aus dem Sohn hervorgehe. Der Beginn dieser Kontroverse ist später anzusetzen, als es Ch. im Gefolge der Forschungstradition tut – das angeblich schon 769 in Rom vorgelegte ›profilioquistische‹ Florilegium aus Cod. Paris. Graec. 1115 (vgl. S. 73) gehört ins 13. Jahrhundert (so K.H. Uthemann, in: *ByZ 92* (1999) 502–511, gegen A. Alexakis), und Maximus Confessors Verteidigung der lateinischen Seite wurde zwar auf dem Florentinum zum Schlüsselbeleg (S. 268f.), blieb aber bis ins neunte Jahrhundert (Anastasius Bibliothecarius) und weit darüber hinaus unbeachtet. Verfechter des *Filioque* war zunächst Karl der Große, nicht die Päpste seiner Zeit (Hadrian I., Leo III.). Zutreffend folgert Ch. daher als Pointe der photianischen Streitigkeiten: ›The *Filioque*, so far from being vindicated by the supreme authority of St Peter's successor, was the principal factor discrediting the absoluteness of that authority‹ (S. 192). Erst Petrus Damiani und Anselm von Canterbury versuchten im elften Jahrhundert in päpstlichem Auftrag, das *Filioque* zu systematisch zu begründen (vgl. S. 219, 224f.), ohne dabei bereits ein Schisma vorauszusetzen. Im Hochmittelalter verlagerte sich die Diskussion auf die hermeneutische Frage nach der Vereinbarkeit beider Theologien (mit bemerkenswerten Versuchen, die Fronten aufzuweichen, so Johannes Bekkos und Barlaam; S. 250–254) und nach der ›Deutungshoheit‹ über das Verbot des Konzils von Ephesus 431, den ›nizänischen‹ Glauben zu verändern: Bezog sich dies auf den Text oder auf den theologischen Gehalt des Bekenntnisses? Das Konzil von Ferrara-Florenz bezeugt die beiderseitige Akzeptanz für das Axiom, daß nur auf der Grundlage der Vätertradition eine Lösung gefunden werden könne (S. 271f.). Das Unionsdekret vom Juli 1439 erscheint jedoch gerade im Blick auf das *Filioque* als intransigente Fortschreibung ›einer‹ (der lateinischen) Position statt als Versuch, eine als schmerzlich empfundene Differenz im ›gemeinsamen‹ Glauben und Bekennen zu überbrücken. Ch.s Buch lenkt den Blick treffsicher auf die vielen Facetten der Auseinanderentwicklung von Ost und West, die nur in ihrem Zusammenwirken das Entstehen einer derart nachhaltigen ›Kirchenspaltung‹ verständlich machen. Die sparsamen Literaturangaben in den Fußnoten (knappe Bibliographie S. 277–280) erschließen zusammen mit dem Register (S. 281–306) die Quellen, ohne einzelne Forschungskontroversen zu entfalten; Fachleute werden erkennen, wo weiterhin Erörterungsbedarf besteht. Einer ökumenisch sensiblen Mediävistik eröffnet sich ein reiches Feld zur Betätigung, gerade im Blick auf die lateinische und griechische Trinitätstheologie und ihre Interdependenzen. Insgesamt ist Ch.s Buch als meisterhafte Darstellung zu würdigen. Angesichts des hohen Alters des Vf.s kann man nur wünschen, daß auch kommende Generationen von Historikern, Patristikern und Mediävisten (und vielleicht nicht nur Angelsachsen!) solchen Mut zur Synthese beweisen – zum Nutzen des eigenen Faches und zum Nutzen der Ökumene. Statt Kontroversen zu prolongieren, eröffnet sich die Chance, geschichtliche Deutungsmuster zu dechiffrieren und dadurch Selbst- und Fremdwahrnehmungen in Fluß zu bringen. Das wird im 21. Jahrhundert nicht leichter sein als auf dem Konzil von Ferrara-Florenz. Ch.s Buch lädt aber nachdrücklich dazu ein, die Geschichte von ›Ost und West‹ gemeinsam neu zu lesen.

Peter Gemeinhardt, Jena

Peter Gemeinhardt: *Die Filioque-Kontroverse zwischen Ost- und Westkirche im Frühmittelalter* (Arbeiten zur Kirchengeschichte 82), Berlin, New York: De Gruyter 2002. – xv, 644 S. – ISBN 3-11-017491-X. – € 138,00.

Die Kontroverse um den *Filioque*-Zusatz in der lateinischen Version des nizäno-konstantinopolitanischen Glaubensbekenntnisses (= NC) bietet trotz zahlreicher Studien in der Vergangenheit der Forschung weiterhin Anlaß zu Nachfragen und Klarstellungen. Die unter Betreuung von Wolfgang Bienert (Marburg) entstandene Promotionsschrift des evangelischen Kirchenhistorikers Peter Gemeinhardt wirft neues Licht auf das Problem in der entscheidenden Phase seiner Entfaltung und Zuspitzung während des Frühmittelalters. Obwohl der Vf. in einer kundigen Einleitung (S. 1–40) beweist, daß er mit der aktuellen Relevanz seines Gegenstands im ökumenischen Diskurs wohl vertraut ist, versteht er den Beitrag seines Projekts für die heutige Situation weniger im Sinne einer eigenen Stellungnahme als vielmehr der ihr vorangehenden historischen Grundlagenforschung. Daß der Vf. dabei durchaus mit einem systematischen Interesse Geschichte schreibt, beweist die Formulierung des Fernziels seiner Analyse – ›die Diskussion über das *Filioque* von dem Ballast traditional gewachsener Begrifflichkeiten, Vorurteile und Assoziationen zu befreien bzw. die Disputanten mindestens darüber aufzuklären‹ (S. 33) – ebenso wie die Abgrenzung seiner hermeneutischen Methode von klassisch orthodoxen wie auch römisch-katholischen Zugangsweisen zum Thema (S. 38). Nur holzschnittartig können hier einige der Ergebnisse referiert werden, die Vf. mit Blick auf seinen rund vier Jahrhunderte umspannenden Untersuchungszeitraum herausarbeitet. Die pneumatologischen Grundentscheidungen fallen in der patristischen Trinitätstheologie des Westens schon vor Bekanntwerden des NC, namentlich im epochalen Entwurf des hl. Augustinus, der den Hervorgang des Geistes aus Vater und Sohn klar vertritt (S. 41–75). Diese ›Spielart des Neunizänismus‹ wird für die Symbolgeschichte des lateinischen Frühmittelalters in durchgängiger Weise konstitutiv (S. 66f.). Nicht was das theologische Konzept, wohl aber was das Eindringen des *Filioque* in die Bekenntnistexte betrifft, bleibt Rom an der Schwelle zum Mittelalter hinter Gallien oder Spanien zurück. ›Kontroverstheologisch‹ wird das *Filioque* erstmals in der karolingischen Epoche bedeutsam (S. 76–164), in der das neu aufgelebte Kaisertum des Westens nicht nur die politische, sondern auch die religiöse Autorität des Kaisers in Byzanz infragestellt. Mit Blick auf das *Filioque* als Element karolingischer ›Normaltheologie‹ deutet sich schon die Tendenz an, ›eine einzige Formel als orthodoxes Bekenntnis zu proklamieren‹ (S. 123). Der erste kirchenpolitische Konflikt um das *Filioque* entbrannte ab 808 nicht zwischen Lateinern und Griechen, sondern ›zwischen dem theologischen wie politischen Selbstbewußtsein Karls des Großen einerseits und der von ihm grundsätzlich anerkannten, faktisch aber eingeschränkten päpstlichen Autorität andererseits‹ (S. 141). Anlaß waren griechische Häresievorwürfe gegen fränkische Mönche in Jerusalem wegen des *Filioque*-Zusatzes im NC. Papst Leo III. scheint sich damals klar gegen die Hinzufügung ausgesprochen zu haben, worauf die Aachener Synode von 809 mit einer theologischen Denkschrift antwortete, die ›das erste literarische Erzeugnis der *Filioque*-Kontroverse‹ (S. 148) darstellt. Wie sich die Position der römischen Bischöfe und damit auch die Fronten der Kontroverse in den folgenden Jahrzehnten änderten, beschreibt der Vf. ausführlich bei seiner Darstellung der wechselhaften Epoche des Patriarchen Photius von Konstantinopel (S. 165–298). Er möchte dabei den Patriarchen nicht mehr zum Alleinverantwortlichen für das ›photianische Schisma‹ erklären, sondern ist bemüht, den ersten offenen Konflikt zwischen Ost und West um das *Filioque* als ›eskalierende[n] Interaktionsprozeß‹ zu beschreiben (S. 165), der auf dem Hintergrund eines durch politische Faktoren wesentlich mitbedingten neuen Verhältnisses zwischen römischem Papsttum und byzantinischer Kirchenführung (etwa im Konflikt um die Bulgarenmission) zur Ausfaltung kam. Auch in der unruhigen Phase der 860er Jahre, die Photius' Absetzung und spätere Wiedereinsetzung im Patriarchenamt erlebten, behielten die Päpste ihre ›ambivalente, zwischen Text und Theologie des Bekenntnisses unterscheidende Haltung‹ (S. 289) hinsichtlich des *Filioque* bei. Daß Photius dies nicht begriffen hat, zeigt die einseitige Verschärfung seiner Kritik an den Lateinern im theologischen Spätwerk, mit dessen Rezeption das *Filioque* ›in das antihäretische Potential der griechischen Homiletik‹ einging (S. 301). Wie dieses in der ›Dynamik der unaufhaltsamen kulturellen und politischen Entfremdung‹ (S. 313) zwischen Ost und West 150 Jahre später zur Entfaltung kommen konnte, zeigt der Vf. in der Schilderung der Ereignisse von 1054 (S. 299–398). Zu Beginn des 11. Jahrhunderts hatte das *Filioque* endlich auch in das NC der römischen Liturgie Einzug gehalten. Doch waren es zunächst wiederum politische Fakten, vor allem die Verbündung des Papsttums mit den Normannen, die das Verhältnis zu Byzanz derart destabilisierten, daß am Ende der offene theologische Bruch stand. In der römischen Bannbulle des 16. Juli 1054 wird das *Filioque* erstmals ›nicht nur als adäquate pneumatologische Lehre, sondern auch als unverzichtbarer Bestandteil des normativen Glaubensbekenntnisses behauptet‹ (S. 355). Daß Humbert von Silva Candida den Griechen nun sogar den Vorwurf machen konnte, sie hätten die allein rechtgläubige Formel aus dem NC gestrichen, darf nach dem Vf. nicht als historischer Irrtum des Kardinals gewertet werden, sondern ist in der Weise ›gezielt überzogene[r] Polemik‹ (S. 367) bewußter Ausdruck der Überzeugung, daß allein das *Filioque* die im ursprünglichen NC enthaltene Pneumatologie in rechter Weise expliziert. Die griechische Theologie, namentlich in der Person des Niketas Stethatos, hat daraufhin die eigene Lehre im photianischen Sinne verfestigt. Der ursprünglich eher an rituellen Differenzen (wie den Fasten- und Azymenfragen) entzündete Streit zwischen Lateinern und Griechen ist somit seit 1054 endgültig und radikal theologisiert worden. In der rationalen Trinitätsspekulation des Anselm von Canterbury, die der Vf. in einem eigenen Kapitel in ihren breiten historisch-systematischen Kontext einordnet (S. 399–510), wird das *Filioque* zur theologischen Wahrheit erklärt, die ›mit unwiderleglichen Gründen‹ erweisbar ist. Zwar sollte das Ziel dieser ›rationalen Rekonstruktion des Glaubens‹ ausdrücklich ›nicht Konfrontation, sondern Konsens‹ (S. 486) sein; doch war die Erwartung, die Griechen könnten den so fortentwickelten Grundprinzipien der augustinischen Trinitätslehre zustimmen, kaum realistisch. Das Konzil von Bari 1098 als Versuch der Verständigung auf höchster Ebene unter Beteiligung Anselms blieb am Ende erfolglos. Im 12. Jahrhundert, dem der Autor den Ausblick seines Schlußkapitels widmet (S. 511–534) haben u.a. die Erfahrungen der Kreuzzüge sowie eine verhärtete Kontroversliteratur das nun auch offiziell als solches anerkannte Schisma befestigt. Vermittlungsbemühungen wie den Gesandtschaftsreisen des Bischofs Anselm von Havelberg war kirchenpolitisch kein Erfolg beschieden, wofür der Vf. letztlich das ›Streben der Päpste nach Sicherung und Ausbau ihrer Macht‹ (S. 531) verantwortlich erklärt. Das *Filioque*-Problem, so resümiert die Studie (S. 535–556), ist in seiner frühmittelalterlichen Gestalt erstaunlich vieldimensional. Zwei unterschiedliche theologische Grundtendenzen in der Auslegung des NC sind erst im Verlauf langwelliger politischer Verschiebungen im Kräftedreieck des römischen und byzantinischen Kaisertums sowie des (zwischen Ost und West erstaunlich flexiblen) Papsttums zu unversöhnlichen Fronten geworden, die am Ende ein Schisma markieren. Freilich übersieht der Vf. nicht, daß sich hinter den politischen Vorgängen in theologischer Hinsicht ›Prinzipien der Schrift- und Traditionsdeutung verfestigten, die die inhaltliche Diskussion präfigurierten‹ (S. 541): Dem ›materialen‹ Kriterium der Treue zu den sieben Ökumenischen Konzilien im Osten steht das ›formale‹ Kriterium des lebendigen päpstlichen Jurisdiktions- und Lehrprimats im Westen gegenüber. Der auf eine sehr prinzipielle ekklesiologische Alternative zielende Ausgang der ›doppelten Rezeptionsgeschichte des NC‹ (S. 548) dürfte auch in Zukunft eine hohe Hürde auf dem Weg der ökumenischen Verständigung zwischen West und Ost bleiben, die mit den Mitteln der Trinitätstheologie allein nicht zu überwinden ist. Diesen Konflikt *in statu nascendi* vor Augen geführt zu bekommen, macht allein die Lektüre der aufwendigen Dissertation Peter Gemeinhardts lohnend. In der Fülle des Quellenmaterials, mit der sie eine häufig vernachlässigte Epoche der Theologiegeschichte erschließt, in der gelungenen Kombination von ideen- und ereignisgeschichtlicher Darstellung, in der souveränen Auswertung, die den minutiös erhobenen Fakten durchweg zuteil wird, und schließlich in der tadellosen formalen Gestalt (allein fast 50 Registerseiten!) stellt die Studie eine hervorragende Forschungsleistung dar, von der historisch wie systematisch orientierte Theologen gleichermaßen profitieren werden.

Thomas Marschler, Bochum

Georgij Avvakumov: *Die Entstehung des Unionsgedankens. Die lateinische Theologie des Hochmittelalters in der Auseinandersetzung mit dem Ritus der Ostkirche* (Veröffentlichungen des Grabmann-Institutes 47), Berlin: Akademie 2002. – 433 S. – ISBN 3-05-003715-6. – € 64,80.

Das Ereignis des Jahres 1054 – in der (kirchen-)geschichtlichen Forschung ist der Terminus »Schisma« umstrittener denn je – und die darauf folgende Jahrhunderte andauernde Diskussion um das Verhältnis zwischen dem lateinischen und dem byzantinischen Christentum mit dem Ziel der Überwindung des Trennenden und der Suche nach dem Verbindendem stehen im Zentrum dieser umsichtigen, scharfsinnigen und zugleich flüssig lesbaren Darstellung. Bereits im Vorwort gibt der Vf. sein besonderes Interesse, seine Intention und seine besondere Qualifikation zur Behandlung dieses Themas selbst an: »Es gibt kaum einen Bereich der Theologiegeschichte, der in Rußland so wenig bekannt, so ungern erforscht und mit so vielen Vorurteilen behaftet ist, wie die scholastische Theologie des lateinischen Mittelalters. Eben diese Ausgangslage wirkte für den Autor der vorliegenden Studie, einen gebürtigen Russen, der seine Ausbildung in russisch-orthodoxer Theologie ... erwarb, seit langem als Herausforderung und Ansporn«. Und gleichzeitig ist damit auch schon die Ausrichtung der Arbeit umrissen: Es geht um eine Geschichte des Unionsgedankens, also um die »Gesamtheit jener theologischen Prinzipien und Ideen« die »den Unionsversuchen des Westens mit der Ostkirche im Mittelalter und der frühen Neuzeit zugrunde lagen. Der Vf. versucht im ersten Teil seiner Untersuchung die verschiedenen Diskussionen sowohl im Osten als auch im Westen hinsichtlich ihres Aussagewertes in Fragen der Liturgie und des Ritus nachzuzeichnen und beschränkt sich daher zu Recht auf die drei großen Themen Azymenstreit (S. 29–160), Problem der Wasserbeimischung (S. 161–198) und Tauf formelstreit (S. 199–220; der *Filioque*-Streit wird dagegen weitestgehend ausgeklammert). Hierbei bietet der Vf. ein eindrucksvolles Bild von der Vielfalt der theologischen Argumentationen und stellt umsichtig und unter Berücksichtigung eines breiten Quellenmaterials die östlichen und westlichen Positionen in ihrer Wechselwirkung dar. Besonders differenziert wird dem Leser die Dimension des Azymenstreits verdeutlicht. Das »Judaisierungsargument« in der byzantinischen Polemik wirft den Lateinern vor, sie wollten zurück zum Judentum und gipfelt in der Frage: »Wenn ihr schon Azymen essen wollt, warum laßt ihr euch nicht gleich auch beschneiden?«. Das »Einsetzungsargument« geht der Frage nach, ob das letzte Abendmahl ein jüdisches Passamahl war oder nicht. Das physische (etymologische) Argument geht der Frage nach, ob man einen ungesäuerten Teig überhaupt als Brot bezeichnen kann. Und das »typologisch-symbolische« Argument geht davon aus, »daß es zwischen der physischen Beschaffenheit des Brotes, das in der Eucharistie dargebracht wird, und dem Leib Christi eine gewisse Entsprechung und symbolische Ähnlichkeit geben muß.« Der zweite Teil der Arbeit (S. 221–372: »Die lateinischen Zugänge zur Eigenart der Ostkirche«) versucht nun, die Ergebnisse des ersten Teils in einen politischen Kontext zu stellen. Hierzu werden die historischen Hintergründe und politischen Motivationen der jeweiligen Handlungsträger dargestellt und problematisiert. Hier sieht der Vf. verschiedene Stadien der Entwicklung gegeben. Wichtig ist die feine Trennung der Auffassungen über die Tragweite der Ereignisse von 1054. Im Jahr 1089 wurde eine wichtige Synode gehalten: die päpstliche Synode unter Urban II. in Melfi, die sich vordergründig zunächst mit der Frage der weiteren Entwicklung in Unteritalien, dann aber auch weitergehend mit Fragen des Ritus und des Dialogs beschäftigte. Der Vf. kommt hier zu einem interessanten Urteil: »Der Konflikt von 1053/54 hat sich nicht weiterentwickelt, sondern scheint in den darauffolgenden Jahrzehnten zum Erliegen gekommen sein. Dreiundfünfzig Jahre nach den Exkommunikationen von 1054 konnten die griechischen Bischöfe in der Hagia Sophia und im Patriarchalarchiv keine Schriften ausfindig machen, die erkennen ließen, ob die Kirche von Rom von uns getrennt sei und ob deshalb der Name des Papstes in den heiligen Diptychen nicht angeführt werde« (S. 233). In seiner Analyse der Ereignisse rund um die Kreuzzüge und die Errichtung der lateinischen Patriarchate im Heiligen Land kann der Vf. glaubhaft machen, daß gerade die Vertreibung der griechischen Patriarchen aus Antiochia und Jerusalem »der beste Beweis dafür« seien, »daß das »Schisma von 1054« zumindest im Bewußtsein der Lateiner an der Wende zum 12. Jahrhundert nicht als normatives Ereignis wahrgenommen wurde«. Nach einer Analyse der Problemfelder in der theologischen Reflexion der Lateiner über die rituelle Eigenart der Byzantiner (ekklesiologisch, sakramententheologisch, kirchengeschichtlich und kirchenrechtlich) kommt der Vf. in einem letzten Schritt zu der entscheidenden Frage: »Wie soll die rituelle Eigenart der Byzantiner gehandhabt werden?« Hier entwirft der Vf. drei Modelle, die mit den Schlagworten »Mißbilligung«, »Duldung« und »Anerkennung« umschrieben werden. Als »Zauberformel« des lateinischen Westens im 12. Jahrhundert wird dann die Lösung bezeichnet, die von diesem Zeitpunkt an immer wieder die Spaltung zu heilen versuchte: *diversa, non adversa*... verschieden, aber nicht entgegengesetzt. »Diese Anerkennung der Multiformität im religiösen Leben und Denken erstreckte sich auch auf die Haltung gegenüber der rituellen Eigenart der Ostkirche in dieser Zeit« (S. 357). Im Nachwort faßt der Vf. noch einmal die wesentlichen Ergebnisse zusammen. Hier soll eines besonders hervorgehoben werden: »In der Ostkirche gab es fast keine Versuche, im Rahmen einer orthodoxen Jurisdiktion unierte Kirchen des westlichen Ritus zu etablieren, während von Seiten des Papsttums bis in das 18. Jahrhundert hinein eine aktive Unionspolitik betrieben wurde. ... Im Westen standen die rituellen Unterschiede zwischen Lateinern und Griechen selten einer vollständigen *communio* zwischen den beiden Kirchen im Wege. Im Osten wurde dagegen diese Verschiedenheit als wichtiges, nicht selten gravierendes Hindernis zur vollen Gemeinschaft empfunden« (S. 379). Man darf diesem engagiert und kompetent geschriebenen Buch ein möglichst großes Publikum wünschen. Hier wird zum ersten Mal das Thema auch aus der Sicht des selbst Betroffenen behandelt. Der Vf. greift mit seiner Studie in die aktuelle Diskussion zur interkulturellen Kommunikation ein und liefert als Praktiker (Pfarrer der russischsprachigen katholischen Seelsorge in München) Einsichten, die man in anderen Darstellungen nicht finden kann.

Georg Gresser, Bamberg

BERNARD MCGINN, PATRICIA FERRIS MCGINN: *Early Christian Mystics. The Divine Visions of the Spiritual Masters*, New York: Crossroad 2003. – 256 pp. – ISBN 0-824-5210-6. – $ 18.95.

Spätestens seit dem Erscheinen der (bisherigen) drei Bände der *Geschichte der Mystik im Abendland* (engl. Originaltitel: *The Presence of God. A History of Western Mysticism*) erübrigt es sich, Bernard McGinn vorzustellen. Er ist bei einem breiten Publikum als einer der profiliertesten und kompetentesten Interpreten der christlichen Mystik bekannt. Seine neue Monographie *Early Christian Mystics*, die er zusammen mit seiner Frau verfaßt hat, weckt daher zweifellos große Erwartungen. Wer sich aufgrund des Titels nun eine Behandlung der frühchristlichen Mystik erhofft hat, wird freilich schon beim Blick ins Inhaltsverzeichnis seine Erwartungen zum Teil revidieren müssen: Unter ›Early Christian Mysticism‹ verstehen die beiden Autoren die gesamte christliche Mystik bis zum Jahr 1200, das heißt alle wichtigen Autoren der Patristik und des frühen Mittelalters, bei denen eine unmittelbare Präsenzerfahrung Gottes zur Sprache kommt: Origenes, Evagrius, Cassian, Gregor der Große, Hildegard, Richard von St. Victor, Gregor von Nyssa, Augustinus, Pseudo-Dionysius Areopagita, Johannes Scotus, Bernhard von Clairvaux und Wilhelm von St. Thierry. Mit der Nennung dieser zwölf Namen ist auch schon Wesentliches zur formalen und materialen Struktur des Werks ausgesagt: Die McGinns bieten einen prosopographischen Rundgang durch die Geschichte der Mystik anhand von zwölf Portraits der wichtigsten Autoren der abendländischen Mystik. In den einzelnen Portraits wird der jeweilige Vertreter mit einer Kurzbiographie vergegenwärtigt, seine Schriften knapp besprochen und die spezifischen Theologumena und Konzepte gedeutet. Die Darstellungen münden in prägnante Zusammenfassungen, die den Ertrag durch Motti sichern, und enden schließlich mit (auf den angelsächsischen Sprachraum zugeschnittenen) Literaturempfehlungen. In einer den Portraits vorangestellten Einführung benennen die Autoren selbst die Intention, mit der sie sich an den Leser wenden: Das Hauptwerk Bernard McGinns, die *Geschichte der Mystik im Abendland,* hat den theologiegeschichtlich vorgebildeten Leser im Auge. Um einem breiteren Publikum einige Ergebnisse dieser breit angelegten Studie zu vermitteln, haben sich die McGinns entschieden, die Geschichte der Mystik gleichsam auf den Punkt zu bringen und für ein nichtakademisches Publikum auszulegen. Patricia Ferris McGinn zeichnet dabei vor allem für die Vorarbeiten, Bernard McGinn für die Endredaktion des Textes verantwortlich. In der Einleitung resümiert McGinn ein Modell von Mystik, das er in seiner Geschichte der Mystik ausführlich begründet hat: Mystik ist der Aspekt des christlichen Glaubens, der sich mit der Erfahrung der unmittelbaren Gottesgegenwart, einschließlich deren Vorbedingungen und Wirkungen, beschäftigt. Diese Formel wird in einem ersten Rundgang anhand von sechs Portraits illustriert, wobei der Akzent auf der Gottessuche liegt. Bei Origenes kann man lernen, daß sich der mystische Aufstieg aus einer geistlichen Schriftauslegung nährt. Evagrius zeigt, wie das asketische Leben über die *apatheia* zur Kontemplation führt. In Cassians Schriften wird die fruchtbare Übertragung der östlichen eremitischen Theologie in den lateinischen Westen und die Bedeutung der *puritas cordis* für den Gebetsaufstieg sichtbar. Gregor der Große ist der große Lehrer der *compunctio,* der *contemplatio* und der gegenseitigen Durchdringung von Liebe und Wissen. An Hildegard von Bingen wird das visionäre Element als ein möglicher Bestandteil der Mystik offenkundig. Richard von St. Viktor ist der große Systematiker, der den Aufstieg richtungsweisend psychologisch hierarchisiert hat. In einem zweiten prosopographischen Komplex liegt der Akzent auf dem transformativen Element der mystischen Begegnung. Danach hat Gregor von Nyssa die nicht auszuschöpfende unendliche Erkennbarkeit Gottes herausgearbeitet. Bei Augustinus wird der Zusammenhang zwischen Mystik einerseits und Bildtheologie, Trinitätstheologie, Ekklesiologie sowie Christologie andererseits mustergültig aufgewiesen. Dionysius zeigt, daß die Präsenz Gottes immer auch als die Präsenz der Absenz Gottes gedacht werden müsse und mystische Einung ein wissendes Nichtwissen sei. Johannes Scotus erhellt die kosmologische Dimension der mystischen Einung. Der Zisterzienser Bernhard zeigt, daß der Aufstieg zur Einung als *ordinatio amoris* verstanden werden muß und bietet eine Phänomenologie der kontemplativen Liebe. Wilhelm von St. Thierry schließlich arbeitet das trinitarische Moment der Mystik heraus und verdeutlicht die Bedeutung des Hl. Geistes als ›Medium‹ der Gotteserfahrung. Den McGinns ist mit *Early Christian Mystics* eine in sich geschlossene, ausgewogene und die ganze Bandbreite der Mystik bis 1200 umfassende Monographie gelungen. Die Einsatzmöglichkeiten des Büchleins liegen auf der Hand: Diese grundlegende Einführung in die Mystik eignet sich vorzüglich zum Einsatz in der Lehre, sowohl in den höheren Klassen des Religionsunterrichts wie in Einführungsseminaren an der Universität. Auch im Bereich der Seelsorge und der Exerzitien ist das Buch vielseitig verwendbar. Der theologische Mediävist freilich wird für seine wissenschaftliche Arbeit eher auf das Hauptwerk McGinns zurückgreifen.

Karl-Heinz Steinmetz, München

Ralf M.W. Stammberger: *Scriptor und Scriptorium. Das Buch im Spiegel mittelalterlicher Handschriften* (Lebensbilder des Mittelalters), Graz: Adeva 2003. – 136 S. – ISBN 3–201–01797–3. – € 49,00.

Wenn in der Epoche des weltweiten Internets mittelalterliche Bücher eine größere Breitenwirkung haben können, dann vor allem in ihrer künstlerischen Dimension der Buchmalerei. Nachdem der Grazer Adeva-Verlag dazu schon seine *Glanzlichter der Buchkunst* (bisher 11 Bde.) und seine *Codices illuminati* (bisher 3 Bde.) vorgelegt hat, ediert er mit seinen *Lebensbildern des Mittelalters* (bisher 4 Bde.) kunsthistorisch-thematische Meisterwerke zur Buchmalerei. Speziell für die Buchreligion des Christentums ist die Geschichte und Technik der Buchherstellung vor der Gutenberg-Epoche des mechanischen Buchdruckes von zentraler Bedeutung. Von daher deckt dieser (3.) Band der Reihe, zusammengestellt vom Geschäftsführer der IGTM und dem Gründer und Leiter des Hugo-von-St.-Viktor-Instituts, P. Prof. Dr. Rainer Berndt SJ (Frankfurt) gewidmet, über Schreiber und Schreibwerkstatt für mittelalterlich-europäische Bücher ein zentrales Thema gut, fundiert und allgemein verständlich ab. In seiner prägnanten, inhaltlich gut (wenn auch formal nicht weiter) gegliederten Einleitung (S. 9–29) skizziert Stammberger mit vier weiteren Abbildungen und Bezug zu den 50 anschließenden Tafeln, schwerpunktmäßig, ausgehend von den alttestamentlichen Schriftrollen, die Buchform des mittelalterlichen Pergamentcodex. Dazu paßt gut die ausgewählte Aufgabenbeschreibung des *armarius* (Bibliothekars) aus dem *liber ordinarius* der Pariser St. Viktor Abtei aus der ersten Hälfte des 12. Jahrhunderts (S. 17f.). Für die aufkommenden Notwendigkeiten der mittelalterlichen Universitäten stellt der Autor abschließend das sogenannte Pecia-System als erste Form der Buchvervielfältigung vor. Die alttestamentliche Sicht des Buches u.a. als Medium der Rückerinnerung an das Wissen der Väter, die Gottes Willen kannten und nach ihm lebten, wird im Neuen Testament, im frühen Christentum und in der christlichen Liturgie bis zur Identifizierung des Evangelienbuches mit Jesus Christus selbst (Joh 1,1: Gott war das Wort) gesteigert. Durch die Inspirationslehre bekamen die biblischen Bücher ihre zentrale Bedeutung für die Glaubenspraxis und den mittelalterlichen Studienbetrieb, der sich fast ausschließlich als Autoritäten- und Text-Studium verstand. Zwar bietet der Autor dazu ein gutes, aktuelles und zumindest auch englische Titel enthaltendes Quellen- und Literaturverzeichnis (S. 133f.), aber keine näheren Kriterien zur Auswahl seiner 50 Tafeln, welche von den Schreibstoffen über die Evangelien bis zum Zweiten Konzil von Konstantinopel (381) reichen und die jeweils auf einer Doppelseite links die Fundstelle und einen guten Kommentar bieten sowie rechts die farbigen Abbildungen. Die Auswahl der gut kommentierten und farblich brillianten Abbildungen – aus europäischen Handschriftenbeständen und nordamerikanischen Sammlungen – des 5. bis 15. Jahrhunderts überzeugt nicht nur, sondern kann in ihrer vorliegenden Zusammenstellung als vorbildlich gelungen und hilfreich (z.B. für mediävistische Lehrveranstaltungen) angesehen werden; denn sie bietet ein gutes Gleichgewicht von allgemein bekannter Buchmalerei (z.B. Tafel 5: Codexherstellung, Bamberg, 12. Jh.) und weniger bekannten Stücken (z.B. Tafel 10: schreibender Mönch Eadwin, England, 1150) bis hin zu den Franziskaner (Tafel 26) und schreibenden Frauen (Tafel 20: Christine de Pizan, London, 15. Jh.). Zwar wäre ein Stichwortregister für eine gezielte Benutzung des Bandes hilfreich gewesen, aber so muß sich auch der eilige Benutzer des IT-Zeitalters die Zeit nehmen und die höchst ansprechenden Farbabbildungen aus 1000 Jahren mittelalterlicher Kultur- und Kirchengeschichte hoffentlich genüßlich und bereichernd durchblättern. Dem Autor und Verlag ist damit eine vorbildliche Einführung in die mittelalterliche Buchmalerei gelungen.

Reimund Haas, Essen/Köln

NIKOLAS JASPERT: *Die Kreuzzüge* (Geschichte kompakt), Darmstadt: Wissenschaftliche Buchgesellschaft 2003. – ix, 180 S. – ISBN 3-534-15129-1. – € 14,90.

In Reaktion auf das ständig wachsende Wissen und die veränderten Fragestellungen auch in den Geisteswissenschaften hat die Wissenschaftliche Buchgesellschaft Darmstadt im Jahr 2002 eine neue geschichtswissenschaftliche Reihe eröffnet, die Schülern der gymnasialen Oberstufe, Studierenden, Lehrern sowie allen geschichtlich Interessierten in einer knappen, konzis konzipierten Form geschichtliches Überblickswissen zu zentralen Themen und Fragestellungen der gegenwärtigen Geschichtswissenschaften vermitteln möchte. Die bislang ausschließlich von jüngeren Wissenschaftlerinnen und Wissenschaftlern verfaßten Publikationen tragen den Veränderungen in diesen Disziplinen weg von einer reinen Fakten-, Polit- oder Nationalhistoriographie hin zu einer Struktur-, Sozial- und Wirtschafts-, sowie vergleichenden Geschichtsschreibung Rechnung und öffnen sich auch einem generell kulturwissenschaftlichen Zugriff. Die Lesetexte der auf dem neuesten Forschungsstand geschriebenen Handbücher sind mit Zeittafeln (am Anfang der chronologischen Kapitel), Erläuterungen zu den wichtigsten Personen, Ereignissen und Begriffen (typographisch durch das Schlagwort als Überschrift, durch kleinere, eingerückte Schrift und einen grauen Randbalken sowie einem marginalen E hervorgehoben) und mit Graphiken ausgestattet. Zahlreiche Zwischenüberschriften und Marginaltitel portionieren das Wissen und sind eine geeignete Suchhilfe. Zur schnelleren Einarbeitung in das Thema sind die Bände mit kommentierten, nach den Sachkapiteln angeordneten Quellen- und Literaturverzeichnissen versehen und werden über ein Personen- und Sachregister gut erschlossen. Gelungen erscheint dem Rezensenten das Konzept der den Sachkapiteln zugrundegelegten Quellenauszüge (auf grauen Flächen und am Rande mit einem Q gekennzeichnet) zu sein, anhand derer nicht nur der jeweilige Charakter des Themenabschnitts deutlich werden kann; die kurz zitierten Quellen regen auch zum Weiterlesen an. Zu den im Jahr 2002 erschienenen drei mediävistischen Themenbänden *Ottonen und Salier* (LUDGER KÖRNTGEN), *Klöster und Orden im Mittelalter* (GUDRUN GLEBA) und *Interregnum* (MARTIN KAUFHOLD), die im Folgejahr um das sozial- und medizingeschichtliche Überblickswerk *Krankheit und Heilkunde im Mittelalter* (KAY PETER JANKRIFT) erweitert wurde, tritt als vierter Band mit dem Überblick von Nikolas Jaspert eine kompakte Darstellung des umfassenden mittelalterlichen Phänomens der Kreuzzüge. Dabei setzt der Autor mit einem erweiterten Kreuzzugsbegriff, der gerade in jüngster Zeit in Europa, Israel und den USA – auch vor dem Hintergrund seines fälschlich-gefährlichen Gebrauchs im aktuellen politischen Tagesgeschäft (S. 163) – besondere Aufmerksamkeit erlangt hat, durchaus neue Akzente in der deutschen Forschungslandschaft. Ausgehend von dem traditionellen Verständnis, daß ein Kreuzzug ein vom Papst ausgerufener, mit der Zusage eines Ablasses versehener Kriegszug gegen Glaubens- und Kirchenfeinde ist, wird hierunter nicht mehr nur der traditionelle Kreuzzug ins Heilige Land oder in den Vorderen Orient verstanden und aus christlicher Perspektive beschrieben. Denn auch wenn dieser Geschichtskomplex ereignis- und strukturgeschichtliches Schwerpunktthema des Bandes bleibt (Kreuzzugsgeschichte S. 33–57; Kreuzfahrerherrschaften S. 78–108) und durch ausführliche Abschnitte zu den religiösen, soziopolitischen und ideengeschichtlichen Voraussetzungen der Kreuzzüge (S. 1–32) sowie zur Praxis, Theorie und Kritik des Kreuzzuggedankens abgerundet wird (S. 58–67), so ist er doch sinnvollerweise um die muslimische Perspektive auf das Geschehen ergänzt (S. 67–77). Ebenso werden die zeitgleichen Kriege gegen jegliche Form von Andersgläubigkeit in Europa (Muslime und Juden auf der Iberischen Halbinsel S. 110–119; Heiden im Ostseeraum S. 119–128) sowie die Auseinandersetzung mit Abweichlern innerhalb der *Christianitas* seit dem 13. Jahrhundert (Ketzerkreuzzüge) thematisiert (S. 129–137). Hinzu tritt eine umfassende Beurteilung der europaweiten Rolle der geistlichen Ritterorden, zu welcher der Autor aufgrund seiner einschlägigen Forschungen v. a. zur Iberischen Halbinsel besonders berufen ist (S. 138–157). Seine Abrundung findet der Band in einem kurzen Kapitel zu den Auswirkungen und dem Nachleben der Kreuzzüge und ihrer Idee (S. 158–163), drei Karten zu Vorderem Orient, Iberischer Halbinsel und Ostseeraum (S. 164f.), einer nach den Kapiteln zusammengestellten Auswahlbibliographie (S. 167–172) und einem Personen- und Sachregister (S. 173–180). Das Phänomen ›Kreuzzug‹ wird in einer umfassenden geistesgeschichtlichen Perspektive als das der älteren religiösen Begegnungsphase in kleinräumigen Lebenswelten nachgeordnete erstmalige systematische Aufeinanderprallen der religiösen Großgruppen ›Christen‹ und ›Muslime/Heiden/Andersgläubige‹ verstanden (S. 1). Als Geschehens- und Erfahrungszeitraum von geistlicher, militärischer und kultureller Mobilität des gesamten Abendlandes habe das Kreuzzugszeitalter wesentliche Voraussetzungen für die mit der Neuzeit einsetzende weltumspannende Expansions- und Kolonialisierungsbewegung Europas geschaffen (S. 12 und 163). Das vornehmlich in den Blick genommene, historisch interessierte Zielpublikum dürfte erklären, warum die theologie- und philosophiegeschichtliche Perspektive des Buches eher weniger stark ausgebildet ist. Freilich wird man vom Genre eines einführenden Studienbuches kaum eine stringente Verwebung der allgemeinen gesellschafts-, politik- und kulturgeschichtlichen Entwicklungen des Kreuzzugszeitalters mit der komplexen Theologie- und Philosophiehistorie des Hoch- und Spätmittelalters sowie eine Beurteilung der wechselseitigen Bedingtheit in den verschiedenen Raum- und Zeitkontexten erwarten dürfen, zumal es hierzu noch an modernen monographischen Vorarbeiten fehlt. Es sei hier nur an das große Desiderat einer Gesamtdarstellung der Reconquista der Iberischen Halbinsel im Spiegel der zeitgenössischen lateinischen und volkssprachlichen Literaturen erinnert. An kleineren inhaltlichen Korrekturen seien genannt S. 18f.: Die hier skizzierte *miles Christi*-Vorstellung sähe man gerne noch etwas schärfer profiliert. S. 21: Statt Bischof ›Günther‹ von Bamberg sagte man besser ›Bischof Gunther von Bamberg‹. S. 26: Man kann kaum von ›Tochterhäusern Clunys‹ oder dem ›Mutterhaus‹ Cluny sprechen; auch hatte Cluny nicht von Anfang an einen ›Klosterverband‹ ausgebildet. Das würde Cluny doch einen zu sehr zisterziensischen Charakter verleihen. S. 59 und 65: In einer neuen Auflage sollte nicht mehr für die traditionelle monastische Ortsbeständigkeit der vorgeblich allgemein im Gebrauch stehende Begriff der *stabilitas loci* verwendet werden, der wohl eine karolingische Neudeutung der in der Benediktregel (4, 78) formulierten Verbandsbeständigkeit (*stabilitas in congregatione*) ist. Auf S. 65 Z. 4f. muß es heißen: ›der Propst Gerhoh von Reichersberg‹ statt ›der Rottenbucher Chorherr‹. Auch könnte man in einer Neuauflage die Einführung in inhaltlich-konzeptioneller Hinsicht bereichern. S. 31f. etwa werden die dynamischen Verschiebungen in der Entwicklung der Kreuzzugstheorie zu wenig problematisiert. Bemerkenswerter aber ist die Nichtnennung des für die theologische Fortentwicklung der kirchlichen Kriegsvorstellung und des Kreuzzugsgedankens maßgeblichen Denkers Thomas von Aquin, zumal Augustins Gedankengebäude zum gerechten Krieg thematisiert ist (S. 13 und 129). Im Kontext der Türkengefahr des 15. Jahrhunderts sollten der große Kreuzzugsprediger Johannes von Capestrano (1386–1456) und sein Zeitgenosse Papst Pius II. (1458–1464) nicht unerwähnt bleiben (S. 57). In einer neuen Auflage wünschte man sich zudem eine Auseinandersetzung mit Jan Assmanns aufregender These vom Intoleranz- und Gewaltpotential der Monotheismen hinsichtlich der möglichen Implikationen für die Kreuzzugsthematik, ferner eine etwas deutlichere Hervorhebung der intellektuellen Bedeutung Clunys für die spanische Reconquista. So wird etwa die durch Petrus Venerabilis veranlaßte Koranübersetzung und ihr historischer Kontext mit keinem Wort gewürdigt (vgl. dazu D. Iogna-Prat, *Ordonner et exclure. Cluny et la société chrétienne face à l'hérésie, au judaïsme et à l'islam, 1000–1150*, Paris 1998 [²2002], S. 324–

359). Das gleichfalls nicht erwähnte, bislang freilich kaum beleuchtete, aber wesentliche Thema des christlich-muslimischen Kriegsgefangenen- und Lösegeldwesens in den lateinischen Kreuzfahrerherrschaften und seiner gesamteuropäischen Auswirkungen ist inzwischen bearbeitet: Y. FRIEDMAN, *Encounter between enemies. Captivity and ransoms in the Latin Kingdom of Jerusalem* (Cultures, Beliefs and Traditions 10), Leiden 2002. Auch könnte das Buch mehr als nur vier, zudem sehr kurze übersetzte Quellenstücke (vgl. S. 11 und 97: Fulcher von Chartres, *Historia Hierosolymitana* I, 3, 2; S. 18: *Gesta Francorum et aliorum Hierosolimitanorum* I, 1; S. 76: Usāma ibn Munqiḏ) vertragen. In einer Neuauflage sollte in der Auswahlbibliographie (S. 169f.) Sekundärliteratur zur reichen, im Darstellungsteil nur punktuell erwähnten (S. 17, 59, 64, 66, 114f., 130 und 161) lateinischen und nationalsprachlichen Kreuzzugsliteratur bzw. -dichtung berücksichtigt werden, die sich in Kreuzzugschronistik, -gedicht (auch Lyrik), -epen (bzw. *Chansons de geste*) und -romane auffächert (vgl. etwa die diversen Artikel im *Dictionnaire des lettres françaises. Le Moyen Âge*, Paris 1994: J. SALVAT, »Chanson de la Croisade contre les Albigeois«, S. 243–247; I. WEILL, »Croisade (Cycle de la)«, S. 356–358; G. TYL-LABORY, »Croisade et Mort de Richard Cœur de Lion«, S. 358; CL. CAHEN/I. WEILL/G. TYL-LABORY, »Croisades (Littérature des)«, S. 358–363; oder der Artikel »Kreuzzugsdichtung« von L. S. CRIST/M.-R. JUNG/U. SCHULZE/G. H. M. CLAASSENS/K. BITTERLING/H.-P. NAUMANN, in *LexMA 5* [1991] 1519–1525). In der Sektion ›Heiliger Krieg, Rittertum und Pilgerfahrt‹ der Bibliographie (S. 169) dürfen die beiden jüngst erschienenen Bücher von JEAN FLORI, *La guerre sainte. La formation de l'idée de croisade dans l'Occident chrétien* (Paris 2001) und *Guerre sainte, jihad, croisade. Violence et religion dans le christianisme et l'islam* (Paris 2002) ergänzt werden. Inzwischen ist das auf S. 172 genannte Buch von ALAIN DEMURGER zu den geistlichen Ritterorden des Mittelalters auch auf deutsch erschienen: *Die Ritter des Herrn. Geschichte der geistlichen Ritterorden*, München 2003.

Matthias M. Tischler, Frankfurt am Main

ANTON LEICHTFRIED: *Trinitätstheologie als Geschichtstheologie. ›De sancta Trinitate et operibus eius‹ Ruperts von Deutz (ca. 1075–1129)* (Studien zur systematischen und spirituellen Theologie, 37), Würzburg: Echter 2003. – xi, 362 S. – ISBN 3-429-02375-0. – € 24,50.

Das exegetische Werk Ruperts von Deutz und besonders sein monumentaler Kommentar *De sancta Trinitate et operibus eius* ist eines der bedeutendsten Schriftzeugnisse des 12. Jahrhunderts. In ihm gewann seine Konzeption der geschichtsmächtigen Wirksamkeit des dreieinigen Gottes, eines der wichtigsten Themen Ruperts und seines Jahrhunderts, ihren vollendetsten Ausdruck. Dabei befand sich ihr Autor in ebenso engem Dialog mit der exegetischen Tradition der Väter, wie er auch die Probleme seiner eigenen Zeit und ihrer Kirche, ihrer Gegenwart und Zukunft, im Blick hatte. Mit dieser Schrift beschäftigt sich Anton Leichtfried in seiner Untersuchung, ursprünglich eine Freiburger Dissertation. Nachdem der Gegenstand der Arbeit, die geplante Vorgehensweise und der Forschungsstand erörtert werden, gibt der Autor in einem ersten Teil einen Überblick über Leben und Werk sowie über die theologische Methode Ruperts von Deutz. Im zweiten Teil widmet er sich Ruperts Trinitätstheologie, wobei Eigenart, wechselseitiges Verhältnis der drei göttlichen Personen und ihr jeweiliger Anteil am Heilswerk in der Geschichte anhand des Textes von *De sancta Trinitate* betrachtet wird, während in einem dritten Teil als Ergebnis Ruperts Trinitäts- als Geschichtstheologie vorgestellt und eine theologiegeschichtliche Einordnung versucht wird. Eine Liste der Werke Ruperts, Quellen- und Literaturverzeichnis (leider kein Index) schließen die Untersuchung ab. Der Autor hat sich vorgenommen, Ruperts Kommentar dem Verständnis des Lesers besser zu erschließen und dabei auch weiterführende Erkenntnisse über Ruperts theologisches Denken und besonders sein Trinitätsverständnis zu gewinnen. Außerdem beabsichtigt er, den theologiegeschichtlichen Standorts Ruperts zu bestimmen, in Bezug auf seine Vorgänger wie Augustin und Hieronymus, aber auch im

Verhältnis zu zeitgenössischen theologischen Richtungen der scholastischen Theologie, Geschichtstheologie oder Mystik des 12. Jahrhunderts. Die Übersicht über Forschungsstand und Literatur zu Rupert von Deutz und seinem Werk ist reichhaltig (Verweise auf Lexikonartikel sowie bibliographische Nachschlagewerke wie *Medioevo Latino* wären in einer wissenschaftlichen Arbeit verzichtbar); ausführlichere Informationen über Inhalt und Thesen der durchaus gegensätzlichen wichtigsten Untersuchungen zum Thema hätten dieses Kapitel noch bereichert. Über Ruperts Leben und Werk informiert der Autor in Anlehnung vor allem an John H. van Engen zuverlässig, wenn auch ohne neue Ergebnisse. Besonders die Berichte über das Visionserlebnis Ruperts und sein Weg aus einer geistlichen Krise, aber auch das Erlebnis der Anfeindungen und des Nichternstgenommenwerdens, schließlich des Häresievorwurfs und der darauffolgenden Isolierung und Selbstzweifel des jungen Mönchs sind sehr anschaulich. Für die Chronologie der Werke Ruperts, die sich zumeist aus ihnen selbst erschließt, ergeben sich keine neuen Erkenntnisse. Leider wird nicht immer klar, welche der vorgebrachten Daten und Anschauungen bereits aus der Literatur bekannt sind und inwiefern sich die Meinung des Autors davon unterscheidet, so daß ein möglicher Forschungsfortschritt nicht immer erkennbar ist. Manche Kenntnisse sollten beim Leser vorausgesetzt werden, weshalb beispielsweise die zweimalige Beschreibung des Umstands, daß Rupert als Oblate ins Kloster kam, und die Erläuterung über die Natur des Oblatenwesens (S. 11 und S. 15) verzichtbar wäre. Die Bezeichnung des Archidiakons Heinrich, vor dem Rupert sich rechtfertigen mußte, als Diözesanoffizial (S. 25 bzw. S. 27), ist zumindest fragwürdig, da von diesem Amt eigentlich erst ein Jahrhundert später die Rede sein kann. Mehrfach klingt die Schilderung der Ereignisse durch van Engen in den Formulierungen des Vf.s noch nach, möglicherweise ohne daß ihm dies selbst bewußt war, wie bei der Beschreibung der Achtung Ruperts vor seinem Kontrahenten im Lütticher Prozeß, Alger (S. 28 bzw. van Engen, S. 163). Die Darstellung des Lebens Ruperts ist dennoch durchaus lesenswert. Problematischer wirkt sich aus, daß die Vertrautheit des Vf.s mit der exegetischen Literatur vor Rupert größer sein könnte. So ist entgegen seiner Annahme auch in der ersten Hälfte des 12. Jahrhunderts die Kommentierung der Evangelien und weiterer Teile der Heiligen Schrift keine exotische oder gar gewagte Beschäftigung, der seit der Antike nur Rupert oblag. Das umfangreiche Kommentarwerk verschiedener Autoren seit dem frühen Mittelalter, wie Beda Venerabilis, Rabanus Maurus, Paschasius Radbertus, Haimo und Remigius von Auxerre, Bruno von Segni und anderen mehr wird von ihm nicht einmal im Quellenverzeichnis zur Kenntnis genommen. Ruperts Kommentar zu den zwölf Kleinen Propheten etwa bezeichnet er als erste Neuinterpretation seit Hieronymus (S. 41) und ignoriert den (früheren) Kommentar Haimos. Das Kapitel über das Wesen der monastischen Theologie wie auch der Exkurs über den Begriff des Deutschen Symbolismus enttäuschen. In beiden Fällen wird die Chance einer spannenden Begriffsdiskussion zugunsten extensiver Zitate aus der Sekundärliteratur aufgegeben. Die Kritik, die etwa an den Auffassungen Horst Dieter Rauhs (*Das Bild des Antichrist im Mittelalter: Von Tyconius bis zum Deutschen Symbolismus*, Münster^{2}1998) immer wieder geübt wird, bleibt mangels gebotener Alternativen letztlich unverständlich; die vielfältigen Möglichkeiten, die sich aus der Aufnahme der Denkanstöße und Hinweise der Werke Wilhelm Kamlahs, Henri de Lubacs oder eben (gern in kritischer Auseinandersetzung) Horst Dieter Rauhs ergeben hätten, bleiben ungenutzt. Von den Titeln des umfangreichen Verzeichnisses der Sekundärliteratur (von denen manche nicht verwendet zu sein scheinen) hätte der Autor dabei viel profitieren können. Den Hauptteil der Untersuchung bildet die paraphrasierende Erläuterung des Heilswirkens der drei göttlichen Personen in *De sancta Trinitate*, verbunden mit Querverweisen innerhalb der Werke Ruperts und Hinweisen aus der Sekundärliteratur. Der Vf. bemüht sich, die Gedankengänge Ruperts nachzuvollziehen und ihre wesentlichen Grundzüge herauszuarbeiten. Obwohl er zuvor (S. 67) verspricht, das neuartige Verhältnis der Exegese Ruperts zu den Vätern zu untersuchen, findet dies an keiner Stelle über allgemeine Thesen hinausgehend statt. Nirgends wird der Versuch unternommen, Ruperts Auffassungen mit denen seiner Vorgänger oder Zeitgenossen zu vergleichen, um im Kontrast zu deren Werken und Meinungen Charakteristisches und Neues im Denken Ruperts herauszuarbeiten. Dies ist umso unverständlicher, als auf überlieferte Bibliothekskataloge und vorhandene Untersuchungen über die Bibliothek in Lüttich verwiesen wird, hier also die gewiß nicht alltägliche Chance bestünde, gewissermaßen Schreibpult und Handapparat eines mittelalterlichen Autors in Augenschein zu nehmen. An keiner Stelle wird die Frage nach den Quellen und Vorbildern der Aussagen Ruperts anders als in allgemeiner Form beantwortet. Dabei sind die Werke Ruperts bei aller Vielfalt und Originalität in höherem Maß als die jedes anderen Autors seines Jahrhunderts der exegetischen Tradition verpflichtet und mit ihr verwoben. Beinahe jedes Element der traditionellen Exegese findet sich bei ihm wieder und könnte unschwer nachgewiesen werden, wobei die von Rupert verwendete Quelle und seine Interpretation dieser Quelle interessante Perspektiven erschließen könnten. So sind die sieben Gaben des heiligen Geistes, die Rupert und mit ihm der Vf. mehrfach thematisiert (S. 83, 270–283 und 308f.), zum Zeitpunkt der Beschäftigung Ruperts mit ihnen ein seit Jahrhunderten bekanntes Motiv der exegetischen Literatur mit einer vielfältigen Geschichte, die Rupert selbstverständlich vertraut war. Doch davon kein Wort. Obwohl der Autor versucht, die herausragende Bedeutung der Werke des Geistes in der Schöpfung wie der Erlösung bei Rupert deutlich zu machen, verzichtet er hier auf die Chance, Rupert bei der Herausarbeitung seiner These von der Rezeption der Überlieferung bis zur Neugestaltung in *De sancta Trinitate* beobachtend nachzuspüren. In den verdienstvollen Editionen früherer Jahrzehnte wäre dies aus arbeitstechnischen Gründen, aber auch aufgrund der damals in weit geringerem Maß vorhandenen Hilfsmittel kaum möglich gewesen. Daß in einer Zeit, in der nicht nur gute Editionen Ruperts und vieler anderer Autoren vorliegen, sondern auch elektronische Datenbanken den Zugang zu einem Großteil dieser Texte und somit vergleichende Untersuchungen erheblich erleichtern, dieser Blick über die Texte Ruperts hinaus gänzlich unterlassen wird, ist ebenso unverständlich wie bedauerlich. Es ist aller Ehren wert, das Werk und das Denken Ruperts einer rechten Würdigung zuführen zu wollen und es als einzigartig zu erklären, aber darum steht es dennoch im Kontext seiner Zeit, der Tradition der Kirche und ihrer Autoritäten. Ruperts Originalität und Größe werden dadurch nicht geringer, vielmehr sollte beides vor diesem Hintergrund erst recht hervortreten und in seiner Eigenart deutlich werden. Eine begründete Einordnung in den theologiegeschichtlichen Kontext, die über bereits bekannte Ergebnisse hinausgeht, wie sie für den dritten Teil des Buches versprochen wurde, könnte jedenfalls nur im Hinblick und im Dialog mit diesem Kontext vorgenommen werden. Die Darstellung des Verhältnisses Ruperts zur scholastischen Theologie, zu anderen Vertretern geschichtstheologischer Konzeptionen und zur zeitgenössischen Mystik bestätigt auf der Basis der Sekundärliteratur die dort vertretenen Auffassungen. Allenfalls hätte man sich eine eigene und detailliertere Beschäftigung mit einzelnen, in den Kapitelüberschriften genannten Autoren gewünscht, mit denen der Vf. Rupert vergleicht oder von denen er sie abgrenzt. Insgesamt ist zu sagen, daß die Untersuchung eine gründliche Beschäftigung mit dem Werk Ruperts ebenso zur Voraussetzung hatte wie sie zu ihr auffordert und damit sicher ihr Ziel erreicht: Rupert als lohnende Lektüre ins Bewußtsein zu rücken ist ein zweifelsfreies Verdienst dieses Buches, ebenso wie die Gegenüberstellung einzelner Thesen und Sichtweisen der beiden großen, fast gleichzeitig erschienenen Rupert-Monographien Arduinis und van Engens. Die Hoffnung auf neue Perspektiven oder ein tieferes Verständnis für das Denken Ruperts, das über die vorhandene Literatur hinausgeht, wird jedoch ebenso enttäuscht wie die Erwartung einer angemessenen Neueinordnung Ruperts in der intellektuellen Landschaft des 12. Jahrhunderts, zu der gerade anläßlich einer Untersuchung von *De sancta Trinitate et operibus eius* viel Neues zu erforschen und zu sagen gewesen wäre.

Julia Eva Wannenmacher, Berlin

JEFFREY P. HERGAN: *St. Albert the Great's Theory of the Beatific Vision.* New York u.a.: Lang 2002. – x, 160 pp. – ISBN 0–82045–790–6. – $ 52.95 (€ 56,70).

In 1241 the Bishop of Paris and the Chancellor of the University of Paris issued a proclamation condemning the proposition that the essence of God was not seen in the beatific vision. This condemnation was the cause of a number of theologians to attempt to develop an account of the beatific vision that incorporated the divine essence and excluded intermediaries. Jeffrey Hergan's book is a study of the repeated efforts of Albertus Magnus to formulate a theory of the beatific vision that was consistent with the condemnation. Hergan orders the book historically, beginning with Albert's *Quaestio de visione Dei in patria* (1245/46), and then presenting the section of his *De resurrectione* (1246) that pertains to this vision, then the relevant section of Albert's commentary on the *Sentences* of Peter Lombard, followed by Albert's discussion of the matter in his *Summa theologiae* (1268). Hergan devotes a chapter to each of these works by Albert. He carefully develops the context for the discussion in each work, presents the key texts, analyzes them and draws conclusions. His method of analysis is both critical-historical and analytic. What Hergan is anxious to show, what indeed appears to be the thesis of the book, is that Albert struggled with the problem of developing a theory of the direct vision of the divine essence because of his commitment to Neoplatonic metaphysics that resulted in his holding what Hergan calls a "monism of light". By this he means that for Albert, light was the essential constituent of all creatures (p. 71). Consequently, the distinction in the beatific vision between knower and known, that is between man and God, would be redundant. The distinction between creature and creator is destroyed. Albert tries to repair this damage. But he does so, according to Hergan, on the epistemological level instead of the metaphysical level where the root of the problem lies. Furthermore, Hergan observes that Albert employs the language of Aristotle but does not commit himself to his metaphysics. As a result Albert finds himself forced to try to make sense of the role of species in his account of the vision of God. Without the support of Aristotle's metaphysics the concept of species cannot be accounted for and as a result Albert keeps trying to reformulate his theory. Hergan shows that if Aristotle's metaphysics is assumed, as it is in the case of Thomas Aquinas, then the problem of species disappears. And so he sets up an interesting contrast in chapter five in which he shows the reader the movement of thought in Albert's *Summa* in contrast to that of Aquinas in the fifty-third chapter of part one of his *Summa contra gentiles.* In order to show an alternative metaphysics of light within the Neoplatonic tradition Hergan appends a discussion of beatific vision as found in Bonaventure's *Itinerarium mentis in Deum.* Here the language of Aristotle is not present in any crucial way. The result is that Albert can be seen as a hybrid thinker who is trapped by an epistemology that his metaphysics cannot accommodate. Hergan's analysis is very interesting and his thesis about Albert being a victim of a monism of light is intriguing. The main criticisms of the book, however, is that Hergan does not give a convincing argument for holding that Albert's metaphysics was a monism of light. There needs to be a textually based account of the fundamental components of Albert's metaphysics. To be sure this is difficult to do. Texts in the *opera* of Albert often are commentaries or epitomes. Because of his intellectual honesty it is not always easy to disentangle Albert's views on a matter from Aristotle's or the Pseudo-Dionysius. In fact using Albert's commentaries on the Pseudo-Dionysius to sort out the Neoplatonic elements of his own metaphysics will not work because Albert keeps himself in the background as he tries to present as clear an interpretation as he can. There are also some minor criticisms that must be addressed. One has to do with the format of the book. Hergan summarizes each chapter as he brings it to a close. Chapter six promises to be a summary of his results. To a certain extent it is. But it is also a resume of the first five chapters that is needless and redundant. Major points that should have been highlighted in earlier chapters appear more as afterthoughts than as genuine summary. The tendency of the book to needless reiteration is also found elsewhere. For example Hergan repeats verbatim on p. 73 an explanation of the requirements of the journeyman theologian that he had already given on p. 60. This also happens on pp. 59 and 60 (although this might be a printer's error). In the second chapter of the book where the problem of light and vision first appears Hergan could have helped his reader by giving more background on Albert's scientific account of vision. Such an account may have helped to put the thesis of a monism of light into another context that would provide more evidence of its possible status. In the same way Albert's theory of creation needs to be expanded in order to correctly assess his analogy of divine creation and beatification (pp. 23–24). In chapter three Hergan needs to explain where Albert derives the principle that *intellectus convertitur supra se sine medio* since it is crucial to Albert's argument. For here is one of those Neoplatonic principles that, when properly explained, may change the thesis of a monism of light. In chapter four Hergan wonders whether Albert holds a theory of participation, but he does not explain how knowing this would help Albert's analysis. The comparison of Albert with Thomas Aquinas and Bonaventure is indeed important. Hergan's account is interesting and helpful. But in a way the comparison is not altogether fair to Albert. To be sure Aquinas was his student. He also provides an alternative account of beatitude from the perspective of a metaphysics concordant with the epistemology needed to give the account. But Aquinas was not exactly an "Albertist" the way Ulrich of Strassburg or Dietrich of Freiberg were. These men were closer to Albert intellectually. They reacted similarly to the same ideas that he did. Would it not have been profitable to compare Albert's account with say Dietrich, who wrote a treatise specifically on the beatific vision? In this way it would have been possible to provide a context of comparison that was intellectually closer to Albert than Aquinas or even Bonaventure for that matter.

Markus Führer, Augsburg College

TIMOTHY L. SMITH: *Thomas Aquinas' Trinitarian Theology. A Study in Theological Method*, Washington: The Catholic University of America Press 2003. – xiii, 258 pp. – ISBN 0–8132–1097–6. – $ 59.95.

Die Renaissance einer heilsgeschichtlich orientierten Trinitätslehre, wie sie konfessionsübergreifend seit einigen Jahrzehnten zu verzeichnen ist, blickt mit spürbarer Distanz auf die scholastischen Entwürfe und ihre vorwiegend philosophische Reflexion der dogmatischen Grundbegriffe zurück. Daß die systematische Kritik der Gegenwart aber auch zu einer Relecture der mittelalterlichen Texte motivieren kann, bezeugt die vorliegende Arbeit des in Kalifornien lehrenden Theologen Timothy L. Smith. Die seit de Regnon übliche schematische Zweiteilung der klassischen trinitarischen Entwürfe in einen lateinischen und einen griechischen Traditionsstrang kennt Smith ebenso wie die Kritik gegen das westliche Modell, die seit Rahner oft wiederholt wurde. Wenn er dennoch gerade das Beispiel der Trinitätslehre für geeignet hält, die theologische Methode des Thomas von Aquin in der Rede über Gott zu würdigen, so auch deswegen, weil er einige dieser gängigen Vorbehalte für unberechtigt hält. Die Studie gliedert sich in fünf Kapitel. Im ersten Kapitel über den Kontext der Trinitätslehre im Aufbau der *Prima Pars* der thomanischen *Summa Theologiae* [= ST] (S. 12–47) ist Smith bemüht, mit Bezug auf die seit Chenu intensiv geführten Diskussionen zur Gliederung des Werkes Thomas gegen die neuscholastische Lesart in Schutz zu nehmen, in welcher ein Traktat *De Deo uno* vom nachfolgenden *De Deo trino* unterschieden und zu seiner Grundlage erklärt wird. Dagegen setzt Smith mit C. Straeter, daß mit ST I, 27–43 nicht ›neue Realitäten‹ in Gott behauptet, sondern nur Unterscheidungen in der einen, bereits eingeführten Realität des göttlichen Wesens vorgenommen werden. Gegen die These einer Funktionslosigkeit der thomanischen Trinitätsspekulation wird deren unverzichtbare Bedeutung für das rechte Verständnis der Freiheit göttlicher Schöpfung und Ursächlichkeit hervorgehoben. Wiederholt weist Smith in seiner Studie darauf hin, daß die Komposition der thomanischen Summa nicht auf eine Ableitung der Personen aus dem Wesen abzielt. Als *articulus fidei* im strengen Sinn ist die Wahrheit über sie keines rationalen Beweises fähig. Am Ursprung der neuscholastischen Traktatunterscheidung sieht Smith den Kommentar Cajetans und seine Thomas mißverstehende These von der absoluten Subsistenz der göttlichen Wesenheit. Erst durch sie hat sich der Eindruck verfestigt, daß die bei Thomas noch fraglos als ›*una divina essentia trium personarum*‹ betrachtete Wesenheit auch ohne die Relationen quasi monopersonal existieren und folglich theologisch erörtert werden kann. Der zweite Abschnitt über Aufbau und Methode der Trinitätserörterung (S. 48–108) versucht zunächst den Sinn herauszuarbeiten, den der Übergang ›from unity to distinction‹ verfolgt, der bei Thomas zwischen ST I, 26 und 27 geschieht. Smith wendet sich gegen die von Jorissen und Schmidbaur vertretene These, wonach die Rede von ›Gott‹ bei Thomas stets eine der Personen als Handelnden implizieren müsse. Denn damit wird fälschlich vorausgesetzt, daß es unmittelbare Kenntnis einer trinitarischen Person aus dem Handeln Gottes (ohne Bezug auf die übrigen Relationen) geben könnte. Bei Thomas erfolgt nach Smith ab q. 27 nicht ein Übergang ›vom Wesen zu den Personen‹, sondern von der (im Handeln Gottes nach außen ununterscheidbaren) Einheit der Personen zu ihrer Differenzierung. Eine Analyse des Aufbauschemas der thomanischen Trinitätslehre zeigt, daß Thomas keineswegs Augustins *De Trinitate* imitiert, sondern sich von ihm in der umgekehrten Anordnung des Stoffes, einer stärkeren Gewichtung der Relationen gegenüber den Hervorgängen und einer spürbaren Zurückhaltung beim Einsatz des imago-Begriffs unterscheidet. Die Rede von einer einheitlichen lateinischen Tradition der Trinitätslehre ist darum nach Smith nur unter Vorbehalten möglich (S. 70). Es folgt eine Darstellung der trinitätstheologischen Zentralbegriffe ›Hervorgänge‹, ›Relationen‹ und ›Personen‹ im thomanischen Entwurf. Mit M. E. Williams wird das Verständnis der innergöttlichen Relation bei Thomas in die Nähe der Vorgaben des Gilbert von Poitiers gestellt (S. 93). Wenn Kapitel 3 das Verhältnis der essentiellen und personalen Attribute Gottes thematisiert (S. 109–159), ist dabei zunächst das Problem der Appropriationen zu behandeln, auf das Thomas weit kürzer als Augustinus eingeht. Doch auch aus inhaltlicher Perspektive ist Smith wiederum bemüht, die Vorstellung einer Einheitlichkeit ›von Augustinus zu Thomas‹ aufzubrechen. Anders als Abaelard, Anselm und in gewisser Weise auch noch Albert gibt es für Thomas im Blick auf die personalen Eigentümlichkeiten in der Trinität keine gültigen rationalen Zugänge. Für Thomas sind die mit der Appropriationslehre verbundenen Vernunftargumente nur Manifestationen und Illustrationen der heilsgeschichtlich, durch Gottes Freiheitstat erfolgten Trinitätsoffenbarung. ›Thus, in the end, theological investigation remains exegetical‹ (S. 150). Aufgabe des Theologen ist es, eine offenbarungsgerechte Sprache zu formulieren, die sich bewußt ist, durch ihre Verhaftetheit an geschöpfliche Aussagemodi hinter dem Bezeichneten zurückzubleiben. Der folgende vierte Abschnitt über ›Kontext and Charakter‹ der theologischen Sprache des Aquinaten (S. 160–203) fragt vor allem nach möglichen Beziehungen zur spekulativen Grammatik der Modisten des 13. Jahrhunderts. Die bei ihnen verfolgte Tendenz, *modus significandi* und *modus essendi* streng zu parallelisieren, eine Realität der grammatikalischen Regeln *extra animam* zu behaupten und damit die Logik als wahre Metaphysik anzusehen, findet sich in dieser Weise bei Thomas nicht. Er gehört vielmehr zu denjenigen mittelalterlichen Denkern, welche die Grundbedeutung eines Wortes von übertragenen Verwendungen, Signifikation und Supposition unterscheiden. Menschliche Rede von Gott bleibt stets kreatürlich vermittelt und wahrt den Raum für ›apophatische Kritik‹. Doch verliert eine so verstandene theologische Sprache nach Smith keineswegs generell die Fähigkeit, etwas zu bezeichnen (S. 192ff.). Unsere Begriffe vermögen nämlich korrekt Dinge der Wirklichkeit zu benennen, auch wenn unsere Explikation der Begriffe ihnen nicht gerecht wird. ›We name as we know‹, lautet die Grundregel der analogen Sprache des Aquinaten, die sich damit sprachtheoretisch sowohl von einem Ultrarealismus wie von einem bloßen Konventionalismus distanziert. Diese entscheidende Charakterisierung der theologischen Rede über Gott exemplifiziert Smith im Schlußkapitel (S. 204–230) am Verhältnis zur ps.-dionysischen Lehre über die Gottesnamen bei Thomas im Vergleich zu seinem Lehrer Albert. Während für Albert die Unfähigkeit zu vollkommenem Wissen über Gott stets auch die Unmöglichkeit mit sich bringt, Gott richtig zu benennen, so daß sie den ›theoretischen‹ Charakter der Theologie grundlegend in Frage stellt, löst sich Thomas stärker von der negativen Theologie des Areopagiten, ohne sie völlig aufzugeben. Eine Unmöglichkeit, über Gott zu sprechen, besteht nicht schlechthin, sondern nur, soweit uns vollkommene Erkenntnis und Benennung versagt bleiben. – Die vorliegende Studie stellt einen intelligenten und originellen Beitrag zur systematischen Reflexion der thomanischen Gotteslehre dar. Smith zeigt sich in seinen Ausführungen sowohl mit den Themen der aktuellen Trinitätsdiskussion wie auch mit den entscheidenden Ergebnissen der historischen Scholastikforschung zu seinem Gegenstand gut vertraut. In Einzelfragen, zu denen etwa der trinitätstheologische ›Rationalismus‹ Anselms und Abaelards (S. 125–129) oder die Rolle des Aquinaten in der Herausbildung der Traktattrennung *De Deo uno/trino* zählen, wird man die Position des Vf.s nicht immer teilen müssen. Ebenso hätten einige der angeschnittenen Themen eine noch differenziertere Erörterung verdient, wie etwa die in der Barocktheologie aller Schulen zu findende These einer absoluten Subsistenz der göttlichen Wesenheit. Die wesentliche Intention des Vf.s allerdings, die theologische Sprachtheorie des Aquinaten auf der Grundlage der Trinitätslehre herauszuarbeiten, um so zum theologischen Kernproblem seiner Gotteslehre vorzustoßen, wird in den Ausführungen der Studie überzeugend eingelöst. Der Satz ›we refer to God better than we know‹ (S. 235) umreißt präzise Möglichkeit und Grenzen einer Theologie im Dienst des nach Einsicht strebenden Glaubens, die sich bewußt ist, den Zugang zu ihrem Gegenstand nicht rationaler Konstruktion, sondern göttlicher Selbstoffenbarung zu verdanken.

Thomas Marschler, Bochum

François Daguet: *Finis omnium ecclesia. Théologie du dessein divin chez Thomas d'Aquin.* (Bibliothèque Thomiste 54), Paris: Vrin 2003. – 544 p. – ISBN 2-7116-1621-5. – EUR 42.00.

La recherche de F. Daguet expose les éléments constitutifs de l'idée fondamentale d'Église (*ratio ecclesiae*) et met en lumière l'unité du dessein de Dieu dans la théologie de Thomas d'Aquin. La première partie de l'ouvrage étudie l'économie prélapsaire, la «première Église» avant le péché, c'est-à-dire le dessein primordial de Dieu pour ses créatures spirituelles, anges et hommes (p. 39–187). Dans une deuxième partie, F. Daguet présente une synthèse de l'économie de la rédemption chez Thomas d'Aquin (p. 189–345). L'étude traite en particulier la rupture apportée par le péché et le motif de l'incarnation du Verbe, en comparant les explications de Thomas d'Aquin sur l'économie originelle et sur l'économie du salut. La troisième partie discute enfin les éléments constitutifs de «l'Église de la rédemption» : les âges du monde, l'universalité du salut dans le Christ, la «personnalité» de l'Église, le rôle de l'Esprit, le rapport de l'Église au Christ et la structure de la société ecclésiale

(p. 347–509). La conclusion de ce livre (p. 511–519) résume les composantes que F. Daguet a réunies dans la «*ratio ecclesiae*» suivant Thomas d'Aquin: le dessein, formé par Dieu, de s'unir toutes les créatures spirituelles, chacune et toutes ensemble, ce dessein ne portant sur rien d'autre que l'Église comprise dans toute sa profondeur et son étendue : *finis omnium ecclesia*. Cette dissertation doctorale constitue une véritable *thèse* théologique. D'une part, elle établit de façon positive et systématique l'omniprésence du thème de l'Église chez Thomas d'Aquin. D'autre part, elle montre de façon convaincante que, pour Thomas d'Aquin, l'idée fondamentale de l'Église ne se réduit pas à l'économie de la rédemption: le dessein de Dieu est ecclésial à sa racine même. Pour l'établir, l'auteur précise tout au long de sa recherche la distinction qu'il faut faire entre le *dessein de Dieu* et ses *modes de réalisation*. Le dessein de Dieu est unique. Il s'agit de la même filiation adoptive des anges et des hommes, à savoir la conformation au Fils de Dieu par le don du Saint-Esprit, donnant de participer à la béatitude trinitaire au terme d'une vie de mérite, c'est-à-dire de charité (p. 94–114, 126–171, etc.). En leur essence filiale et pneumatique, la grâce et le mérite qui font partie des éléments constitutifs de l'Église demeurent identiques dans toutes les économies successives. Tout comme le dessein de Dieu, l'Église est donc *unique*. Mais le mode de réalisation du dessein de Dieu diffère: tandis qu'il s'accomplit exclusivement par les missions invisibles du Verbe et de l'Esprit dans l'économie originelle, après la faute ce dessein trouve sa réalisation dans la participation au Christ, le Verbe incarné. L'Église ne devient celle du Verbe incarné qu'en raison de la chute et des dispositions prises par Dieu pour le salut (p. 171). Il y a donc, pour Thomas d'Aquin, *deux économies distinctes* à l'intérieur d'un *unique dessein* divin. La principale différence entre les deux économies réside dans le mode selon lequel le Verbe donne la grâce de la filiation adoptive (p. 235–237, 279, etc.), ce mode impliquant notamment, en régime d'incarnation, l'édifice des sacrements de la foi et l'aspect hiérarchique. Dans les économies successives de l'unique dessein de Dieu, F. Daguet montre la place centrale que Thomas d'Aquin attribue au mérite et à sa communication par le lien de la charité (p. 241–270), ainsi qu'aux rapports internes de la *societas* ecclésiale, c'est-à-dire au régime de vie sociale qui appartient à la notion fondamentale d'Église (p. 114–124, 172–187, 477–509), suivant l'enseignement thomasien concernant le «*duplex ordo rerum*»: la relation à la fin ultime transcendante, et les relations immanentes des parties entre elles. L'auteur établit que ce second aspect, souvent négligé par la tradition thomiste, possède une valeur structurante qui caractérise l'idée fondamentale de l'Église. Les relations d'aide des membres de l'Église appartiennent tant à l'économie primordiale qu'à celle de la rédemption. Cela montre que l'ordre interne ou immanent de l'Église n'est pas un ordre figé mais profondément dynamique : la communication de la charité réalise la communion des saints. Pour établir cette *ratio ecclesiae*, la recherche de F. Daguet opère une magistrale relecture de toute la théologie de Thomas d'Aquin sous le signe de l'Église. Elle touche tous les domaines de ce que nous appelons aujourd'hui la théologie dogmatique : le traité de Dieu Trinité, la création, l'angélologie, l'anthropologie, le gouvernement divin, le béatitude et la grâce, l'agir humain, la christologie, les sacrements et l'eschatologie. Cette relecture comporte d'importantes discussions et des choix d'interprétation. Parmi les thèmes les plus significatifs, signalons la vive critique du «christocentrisme absolu» que certains auteurs thomistes projettent parfois dans les textes de Thomas d'Aquin (p. 210–239). L'auteur dénonce une certaine tradition thomiste qui place le Christ en son incarnation au cœur du dessein initial de Dieu. Il écarte également, à juste titre, l'interprétation posant la supériorité d'ensemble du régime de la rédemption (la grâce christique) par rapport à l'économie originelle (p. 252–259). L'auteur critique aussi sévèrement les disciples de Thomas d'Aquin qui ont tenté de justifier la permission divine du mal au nom de la primauté ou de la gloire du Christ. François Daguet montre plutôt que, pour Thomas d'Aquin, le mal du péché est l'*occasion* pour Dieu de procurer un bien, mais que ce mal n'est pas de soi permis par Dieu *pour* qu'un plus grand bien survienne (le Christ). Des ombres demeurent cependant (p. 324–342), car certains textes de Thomas d'Aquin semblent bien résister à une interprétation uniforme. Concernant le mal moral, François Daguet répond à la difficulté en expliquant, un peu facilement peut-être, que Thomas «maintient l'aporie du péché sans chercher à la résorber en l'intégrant à un schéma cohérent» (p. 259). Il s'applique à montrer que, pour Thomas d'Aquin, la volonté divine est réellement «contrariée par le péché» (323–345, 515). La doctrine restrictive de la prédestination que l'on trouve chez Thomas d'Aquin, en raison de l'influence de saint Augustin, mettrait Thomas en contradiction avec lui-même (p. 514). Notons encore que, concernant la connaissance et la permission du mal moral par Dieu, l'interprétation de l'auteur est proche de celle de Maritain (p. 304–310). François Daguet a adopté une lecture systématique et synchronique, de type «inductif», plutôt qu'une approche historique des textes de Thomas d'Aquin. Cette méthode contribue à l'intérêt de l'ouvrage mais elle risque peut-être d'entraîner, sur certains points, une sorte de «reconstruction» de la théologie de Thomas d'Aquin. Les thèses centrales de cet essai sont pourtant bien fondées et les choix d'interprétation sont discutés avec beaucoup d'intelligence. Ce livre offre une lumière originale et de grande valeur pour mieux saisir la théologie thomasienne de l'Église, c'est-à-dire le dessein de Dieu et son accomplissement dans la pensée de Thomas d'Aquin.

Gilles Emery op, Fribourg

ANDREW TRAVER: *The Opuscula of William of Saint-Amour. The Minor Works of 1255–1256* (Beiträge zur Geschichte der Philosophie und Theologie des Mittelalters. NF 63), Münster: Aschendorff 2003. – 220 S. – ISBN 3-402-04014-X. – € 35,00.

Die erste Phase des Pariser Mendikantenstreits, dessen Protagonist auf Seiten des Weltklerus Wilhelm von Saint-Amour war, beschäftigt seit langem Historiker der Universität und der Bettelorden. Besondere Aufmerksamkeit haben die ekklesiologischen Implikationen jener Kontroverse gefunden. Für Bonaventura und Thomas von Aquin waren die Auseinandersetzungen ein Wendepunkt in ihren Reflexionen über Stellung und Funktion ihrer Orden in der Kirche mit großen Konsequenzen für die Nachgeschichte. Dank vorbildlicher Editionen der Quästionen und Opuscula der beiden Theologen können wir einen Teil der Diskussionen in allen Einzelheiten verfolgen. Anders verhält es sich mit den Werken ihrer Kontrahenten. Die kritische Edition der zentralen Schrift Wilhelms von Saint-Amour *De periculis novissimorum temporum* hat der Tod M.-M. Dufeils, des besten Kenners der Materie, verhindert. Die allgemein benutzte Edition von M. Bierbaum ist ein unvollständiger Ersatz, da die komplexe Entstehungsgeschichte von *De periculis* nicht berücksichtigt ist. Eine Lücke schließt die hier zu besprechende Publikation. Den zu edierenden Texten (der *Quaestio de mendicitate* sowie drei nachher zu nennenden Predigten) schickt der Vf. einen instruktiven Überblick über alle Werke Wilhelms voraus, in der deren Anlaß, Inhalt, Charakter, Datierung und Überlieferung mit leichten Korrekturen an Dufeils großer Studie präzise vorgestellt werden (S. 7–81). Dem schließt sich eine Beschreibung der Handschriften an (S. 83–122). Angemerkt zu werden verdient, daß sowohl *De periculis* wie der Sermo *Qui amat periculum* im 15. Jahrhundert in Mittel- und Osteuropa (Prag) verbreitet waren, wobei auffällt, daß die Predigt zusammen mit Texten aus dem Umkreis der Konzilien von Konstanz und Basel, sowie im Zusammenhang mit hussitischem Material überliefert wird (S. 105–107). Neu ediert wird Wilhelms *Quaestio de mendicitate* (S. 122–154), die Antwort auf Bonaventuras Disputation von 1255/56, in deren Text die Bemerkungen Wilhelms eingefügt sind. Aufschlußreich für die Redaktion durch Bonaventura sind die Beobachtungen des Vf.s zu einigen Passagen, die typisch franziskanische Argumentationen reflektieren (S. 22–28). Im Mittelpunkt der Einwände steht die minoritische Armutskonzeption, die als nicht evangeliumsgemäß erwiesen wird. Ekklesiologische Gedanken stehen nur am Rand, bedeutsam ist allein die Zurückweisung der von den Mendikanten beanspruchten *subauctoritas* (vgl. nrr. 79, 139, 145, 153). Die in der Forschung nicht sonderlich beachteten und hier edierten Predigten sind bemerkenswerte Zeugnisse für den Eindruck, den die Mendikantenpredigt in allen sozialen Schichten hinterlassen hat, und für die bittere, teilweise maßlose und unsachliche Polemik, mit der sie konfrontiert wurde. Wilhelm und die hinter ihm stehenden Kreise haben offenbar gesehen, daß sie ihre Position angesichts der Popularität und der Unterstützung, die die neuen Orden fanden, nicht würden auf Dauer halten können. Das impliziert andererseits, daß Thomas und Bonaventura, die strikt theologisch argumentierten und sich populistischer Schlagworte enthielten, von der Stärke ihres Standpunkts überzeugt gewesen sein müssen. Der Sermo *Qui amat periculum* (S. 155–178) nennt Franziskaner und Dominikaner Heuchler und Pseudopropheten, die ihren Erfolg beim Adel, beim Bürgertum und beim einfachen Volk einem scheinheiligen Auftreten und schönen Worten verdanken. In vielen Variationen dient die Hypokrisie der Mendikanten als Erklärung für den Anklang, den ihr Wirken gefunden hatte. Daß ihre seelsorgliche Arbeit der Legitimität entbehrt, wird durch die alte Auffassung begründet, daß es in der Kirche nur zwei hierarchische Stufen gibt, Bischöfe und Presbyter, während die neuen Orden keinen rechten ekklesiologischen Ort haben, so daß ihre Predigt- und Beichtvollmacht angemaßt und daher für sie selbst und ihr Publikum Ursachen ewigen Verderbens sind. Da sich die Bettelbrüder geschickt zu tarnen wissen, bedarf es sicherer Kriterien, um sie als Eindringlinge zu entlarven (S. 173–177). Die Tatsache, daß das *Evangelium sempiternum* Gerhards von Borgo San Donnino auch in Paris zirkuliert, spricht für die Größe der Gefahren. Die Predigt *Si quis diligit me* dominiert wiederum der Vorwurf der Heuchelei, der aber diesmal eine pikante Note erhält. War diese Sünde früher auf einen kleinen Kreis beschränkt, so ist sie heute in allen sozialen Schichten zu finden, sogar bei Königen. Unter den Herrschern gibt es nämlich solche, die zum nächtlichen Stundengebet aufstehen und danach sechs Messen beiwohnen, aber die Anliegen der Armen, die um Audienz nachsuchen, vernachlässigen. Sie tragen zwar keine kostbare Robe, führen aber Kriege, in denen viele Christen getötet werden. Das waren außerordentlich gewagte Sätze, denn es besteht kein Zweifel daran, daß sie auf König Ludwig gemünzt waren, der daraus auch seine Konsequenzen gezogen hat. Der zuletzt edierte Sermo *De pharisaeo et publicano* befaßt sich ebenfalls, wie die ihm zugrundeliegende Perikope nahelegt, mit Hypokrisie und Scheinheiligkeit. Wilhelms Predigten vermitteln ein lebhaftes Bild von den heftigen Kontroversen in Paris, in die auch die Gläubigen einbezogen wurden. Die maßlose Polemik verrät zugleich, daß Wilhelm von Saint-Amour und die hinter ihm stehenden Kollegen bereits die schwächere Partei waren. Die besseren Argumente lagen anderswo. Einleitung und Edition der ›Minor Works‹ Wilhelms von St. Amour, wie sie A. Traver vorgelegt hat, verdienen hohe Anerkennung. Mein Wunsch: Er möge auf dieselbe vorbildliche Weise auch *De periculis novissimorum temporum* edieren.

Ulrich Horst op, Blieskastel

KEVIN MADIGAN: *Olivi and the Interpretation of Matthew in the High Middle Ages* (University of Notre Dame Press 2003). – xv, 224 pp. – ISBN 0-268-03715-9 (hardcover), $ 47.50. – ISBN 0-268-03715-9 (paperback), $ 27.50.

Die Auseinandersetzungen um die Franziskanerspiritualen und ihren geistigen Führer

Petrus Johannis Olivi (1247/48–1269) wurden in den letzten Jahren und Jahrzehnten vor allem durch die Studien von David Burr and David Flood grundlegend erforscht. Zusammen mit der kritischen Edition der Werke Olivis, die vor einigen Jahren von den Patres Editores von Grottaferrata in Angriff genommen wurde (*Collectio Oliviana*), tritt das Werk und die Person Olivis heute zunehmend klarer hervor und bildet einen wichtigen aktuellen Forschungsbereich theologischer Mediävistik. Lange Zeit als schillernde Figur vernachlässigt und vergessen, wird Olivi heute als origineller Theologe und als eine zentrale, wenn auch umstrittene Figur im Ringen um die Identität des Minoritenorden am Ende des 13. Jahrhunderts rehabilitiert. Als verheißungsvoller junger Gelehrter zum Studium nach Paris gesandt, verweigerte er sich (aus noch unbekannten Gründen) der universitären Karriere und wandte sich statt dessen einem intensiven Schriftstudium zu. Den Großteil seines exegetisches Werkes verfaßte er als Konventsmagister an verschiedenen Orten in Südfrankreich, wo er schließlich zum intellektuellen Führer der frühen Spiritualenbewegung avancierte. Freilich, sein Schicksal wurde erst Jahre nach seinem Tod durch die Verurteilung seiner unverhüllt joachitisch inspirierten Schriftkommentare, vor allem seines Apokalypsekommentars, durch Papst Johannes XXII. besiegelt. Das vorliegende Buch, das auf einer von Bernard McGinn betreuten Dissertation an der University of Chicago aus dem Jahre 1992 basiert, nimmt sich mit dem Matthäuskommentar eines weiteren wichtigen Schriftkommentars Olivis an. Der Autor hat sich zwar zum Ziel gesetzt, Olivis Kommentar im Zusammenhang der gesamten mittelalterlichen Auslegung des Matthäusevangeliums zu untersuchen, jedoch darf bereits hier festgehalten werden, daß das Buch vorrangig an Olivi interessiert ist und andere Kommentare nur stichpunktartig zum Vergleich heranzieht. Es ist erklärte Absicht des Autors, vor allem den joachitischen Ideen Olivis nachzuspüren, die in erstaunlich dichter Weise auch in dem Matthäuskommentar verarbeitet wurden. Sich auf Beryl Smalley stützend, beklagt Madigan zunächst die im großen und ganzen unspektakuläre, um nicht zu sagen langweilige Universitätsexegese des 13. Jahrhunderts, die sich darin gefiel, alte patristische Lehren zu kompilieren und dabei von jeglichem aktuellen Tagesbezug abzusehen. Erst der aufflammende Bettelordenstreit um die Mitte des 13. Jahrhunderts habe vor allem im Franziskanerorden dazu geführt, die Streitpunkte um die rechte Auslegung der *vita apostolica* und der Nachfolge Jesu sowie die Vorwürfe gegen die mendikantische und näherhin franziskanische Lebensweise in der schulmäßigen Auslegung der Evangelien aufzugreifen und zu debattieren. »From 1250 to roughly 1315, Franciscan gospel commentaries became increasingly ›Franciscan‹, polemical, and, finally, with Olivi, apocalyptic« (S. 11). Danach sei das Interesse an solch ›Franciscanizing exegesis‹ radikal abgeflaut. »Indeed, reading gospel commentaries written in the early fourteenth century is very much like reading ones written in the early thirteenth« (ebd.). Madigan unterscheidet in den Jahrzehnten vor Olivi bereits drei Traditionen von Matthäusauslegungen: eine ›scholastische‹, wozu er die Kommentare der Kathedralmagister des 12. Jahrhunderts, Hugo v. St. Chers Postille und auch Alexander von Hales rechnet, eine ›franziskanische‹, repräsentiert von Johannes Pecham und Johannes de la Rochelle, sowie die ›joachitische‹ vorgetragen und repräsentiert durch den Abt von Fiore allein. Damit ist auch der Aufbau des Buches abgesteckt. Das erste Kapitel (›The Scholastic Gospel‹, S. 13–28) untersucht in recht knapper Weise Matthäusauslegungen in der *Glossa ordinaria*, den anonymen *Enarrationes in Matthaeum* (entstanden wohl nach 1150), sowie in Hugo von St. Chers *Postilla*. Während die stilistischen Merkmale dieser Werke den Charakterisierungen von Beryl Smalleys folgend kurz abgehandelt werden, unterzieht Madigan zwei Perikopen, den Bethlehemitischen Kindermord (Mt 2,13–23) und die Versuchung Jesu (4,1–11), einer genaueren Untersuchung nach inhaltlichen Gesichtspunkten. Da beide Perikopen bei Olivi eine wichtige Rolle spielen werden, wird an dieser Stelle gleichsam die ›traditionelle‹, um nicht zu sagen konventionelle Auslegung vorgestellt. Kapitel 2 (›The Joachite Gospel‹, S. 29–44) widmet sich dem *Tractatus super quatuor evangelia* des Joachim von Fiore und dessen heilsgeschichtlich-prophetischer Auslegung. Madigan arbeitet hier sehr schön und knapp die typisch joachitische Gedankenwelt heraus, die später die Spiritualen in den Mendikantenorden so nachhaltig begeisterte. Obwohl Madigan den *Tractatus* Joachims nicht als unmittelbare Vorlage für Olivi stichhaltig nachweisen kann, vermutet er dennoch über das ganze Buch hinweg eine indirekte, aber spürbare Beeinflussung Olivis durch diese Schrift des Abts von Fiore – eine Vermutung, die den Rezensenten nicht zu überzeugen vermochte. Während das dritte Kapitel (»Franciscan Apocalyptic«, S. 45–55), beginnend mit Hugo von Digne, über Bonaventura bis hin zu Olivi, die begeisterte Aufnahme joachitischen Gedankenguts im Franziskanerorden erzählt, folgt das vierte Kapitel den Ereignissen und Motiven des Mendikantenstreites zwischen 1250 und 1325 (»Franciscan Order under Attack«, S. 57–66). Im fünften Kapitel (S. 67–78) informiert Madigan über das bewegte Leben und Werk Olivis, vor allem über dessen Schriftkommentare, wobei er weithin auf die Vorarbeiten von David Burr zurückgreifen kann. Die meisten Bibelkommentare Olivis entstanden demzufolge zwischen 1279 und 1283, als Olivi Konventslektor in Narbonne und Montpellier war. Der Matthäuskommentar wird auf 1279–1281 datiert. Im Gefolge des *Opus imperfectum in Matthaeum* (Ps.-Chrysostomus) unterteilte Olivi das Buch in sieben Teile. Daneben erfährt man über Methode und Stil Olivis, etwa daß er seine historischen Kenntnisse aus der *Historia Scholastica* des Petrus Comestor bezog und häufigen Gebrauch der *Catena aurea* des Thomas von Aquin machte. (Hier hätte sich ein Verweis auf den entsprechenden Artikel von J. Bataillon in dem Sammelband *Pierre de Jean Olivi*, ed. A. Boureau u. S. Piron, Paris 1999, nahegelegt). Die folgenden beiden Kapitel wenden sich schließlich ausgewählten Perikopen des Matthäusevangeliums zu, in denen der Joachimismus Olivis klar zutage tritt. Das sechste Kapitel (»The new evangelical order«, S. 79–91) untersucht bestimmt Perikopen, wie etwa die Anbetung der Weisen (Mt 2,1–11), die Heilung der Tochter des Jairus (Mt 9,23–26) oder die Gleichnisse vom Himmelreich (Mt 13), in denen die historisch-eschatologische Auslegungsmethode Olivis deutlich wird. Wie schon Joachim von Fiore so erblickte Olivi in den Ereignissen der Evangelien auch Prophezeiungen für die Endzeit der Kirche, die auf die Verwirklichung der Geistkirche im hl. Franz und seinen Ordensgefährten hinzielt. Obwohl Olivi im Matthäuskommentar nicht das Kommen des dritten Zeitalters des hl. Geistes in Aussicht stellte (wie er es später im Apokalypsekommentar tat), versäumte er doch selten, das Entstehen und die Ausbreitung der Franziskaner als Typus und Erfüllung neutestamentlicher Geschehnisse herauszustellen. Das siebente Kapitel (»Franciscan Persecution«, S. 93–128) bringt die franziskanisch-spiritualistische Evangelienauslegung noch mehr zum Vorschein. Madigan präsentiert eindrucksvolle Texte, in denen Olivi die Anfeindungen des franziskanischen Armutsideals und Verfolgungen des Ordens (und der Spiritualen?) im Evangelium prophezeit sieht. Der Bethlehemitische Kindermord (Mt 2,13–18) etwa, oder die Versuchung Jesu durch den Teufel (Mt 4,1–11) sind solche Textstellen, in denen Olivi die Verfolgung der wahren Kontemplativen und der Jünger des hl. Franz vorausgesagt sah. Ferner finden sich zahlreiche Texte, in denen Olivi das Ideal der vollkommenen Armut und den *usus pauper* verteidigt. In diesem Zusammenhang reitet der Franziskaner auch eine Attacke gegen Thomas von Aquin wegen dessen abweichender Interpretation des Geldverbotes in dem mendikantischen Schlüsseltext Mt 10,9f (S. 106–113). Madigans Auswahl und Anordnung der Texte Olivis geben einen exzellenten Eindruck von dem franziskanischen Selbstverständnis, den ordensinternen und -externen Spannungen und den joachitischen Überzeugungen Olivis. Daß Olivi seine Schriftkommentare als kritische und polemische Werkzeuge seiner Überzeugungen benutzte, läßt auch Rückschlüsse auf die enorme Bedeutung der Heiligen Schrift für die Spiritualen zu. Im letzten ging es bei den Kämpfen um die franziskanische Identität um das rechte Verständnis von Schrift und Schriftauslegung. In dieser Schärfe wurde daher die »Franciscanizing exegesis« von keinem der von Madigan zum Vergleich herangezogenen früheren und späteren Kommentare geteilt. Das achte und letzte Kapitel (»Papal condemnation and possible consequences«, S. 129–140) schließt daher ganz folgerichtig mit einem Blick auf die Postille des Nikolaus von Lyra, die eben zu jener Zeit entstand, als Olivis Apokalypsekommentar vom Papst verurteilt wurde. Auf diesem Hintergrund erstaunt es nicht, daß die joachitisch-spiritualistische Evangelienauslegung in der Postille des Lyraners nicht die geringste Spur hinterlassen hat. Madigan schrieb ein spannendes, flüssig zu lesendes Buch über Petrus Johannis Olivi und dessen ideologische Schriftauslegung, das sich gut in die Forschungen David Burrs über Olivi einfügt. Was man vermißt, ist eine Würdigung der breiteren Matthäusauslegung im Mittelalter, die der Titel des Buches verspricht. Die Querverweise auf einige zeitgenössische oder frühere Matthäuskommentare dienen nur als Negativfolie für die abweichende joachitische Auslegung bestimmter Perikopen bei Olivi, eine tiefere Auseinandersetzung wird nicht geleistet. Madigan bemüht sich auch nicht um eine Untersuchung der exegetischen Methoden an sich, weder bei Olivi noch bei den zum Vergleich herangezogenen Kommentaren, sondern übernimmt unbesehen die Charakterisierungen und Schlußfolgerungen von Beryl Smalley *The Gospels in the Schools, c. 1100–1280* (London 1985). Dabei hätte es sich unter anderem nahegelegt, auch Olivis theoretische und hermeneutische Überlegungen zur Schriftauslegung heranzuziehen, vor allem die von E. Stadter edierte Quaestio 1 der *Summa quaestionum super Sententias* (in: *Franziskanische Studien* 44 [1962]), oder die 1997 von D. Flood und G. Gál edierten *Principia in sacram scripturam*. Schließlich hätte man es begrüßt, wenn Madigan neben den Klassikern von Beryl Smalley auch die neueren Ergebnisse mittelalterlicher Exegeseforschung zu Rate gezogen hätte, wie etwa das Buch von G. Dahan, *L'exégèse chrétienne de la Bible en Occident médiéval, XIIe-XIVe siècle* (Paris 1999), das im übrigen häufig auf Olivi eingeht. Was m.E. allerdings noch schwerer wiegt, ist die nachlässige, ja oberflächliche Behandlung der Matthäusvorlesung des Thomas von Aquin. Von einer unangebrachten Voreingenommenheit Madigans gegen Thomas abgesehen (›that ever-vigilant Dominican hammer of heretics, Thomas Aquinas‹, S. 26), stimmt vor allem die Einschätzung nicht, daß der Mendikantenstreit den Matthäuskommentar des Aquinaten in keinster Weise beeinflußt habe. Thomas nimmt darin sehr wohl Stellung zu den Vorwürfen im erneut aufgeflammten Mendikantenstreit, allerdings auch deutlich gegen bestimmte franziskanische Positionen (vgl. dazu U. Horst, *Evangelische Armut und Kirche*, Berlin 1992, S. 77–81, oder E. Panella, »La ›Lex nova‹ tra Storia ed Ermeneutica«, in: *Memorie domenicane* n.s. 6 (1973) 11–106, v.a. 40–59). Wenn Madigan mutmaßt, daß Thomas über Matthäus während seines ersten Pariser Aufenthaltes gelesen habe (S. 184, Anm. 15), so gibt er ferner zu erkennen, daß er nicht auf dem neuesten Stand der Forschung ist, die den Matthäuskommentar des Aquinaten mit sehr guten Argumenten in die Jahre 1268–1270 datiert. Zu dieser Zeit war Olivi selbst Student in Paris und könnte vom Kommentar des Aquinaten ohne weiteres Kenntnisse aus erster Hand erhalten haben. Madigan schrieb ein instruktives Buch über Olivi und dessen joachitische Bibelexegese, aufgezeigt am Beispiel des Matthäuskommentars. Das Matthäusevangelium mit all seinen theologischen Präferenzen steht dabei nicht im Vordergrund. Für eine umfassendere Geschichte der Matthäusauslegung im Mittelalter stellt das Buch jedoch eine gute Vorarbeit dar.

Thomas Prügl, Notre Dame

Bernhard McGinn: *The Mystical Thought of Meister Eckhart. The Man from Whom God Hid Nothing*, New York: Crossroad, Herder & Herder 2001. – xiii, 305 pp. – ISBN 0-8245-1914-0 (hardcover), $ 45.00. – ISBN 0-8245-1996-5 (paperback), $ 24.95.

In dieser 2001 erschienenen Monographie stellt einer der weltweit führenden Kenner der christlichen Mystik das mystische Denken Meister Eckharts in sechs Kapiteln, einem Anhang über die Quellen Eckharts und einem umfangreichen Anmerkungsteil dar. Der Autor zog aufgrund der gesammelten Materialfülle die Veröffentlichung dieses Bandes dem Eckhart-Teil des angekündigten vierten Bandes seiner voluminösen Geschichte der Mystik im Abendland (*The Presence of God. The Harvest of Mysticism: 1300–1500*) vor, welche nur eine gekürzte Form der vorliegenden Untersuchung beinhalten wird. Nach einer Einführung zum Leben und Werk Meister Eckharts, worin der Autor die Werke nach dem neuesten Forschungsstand chronologisch ordnet, inhaltlich kurz skizziert und zu aktuellen Forschungsfragen Stellung nimmt (Kap. 1: ›Meister Eckhart: Lesemeister and Lebemeister‹, S. 1–19), beschäftigt er sich in einem zweiten Kapitel (›Approaching Eckhart: Controversies and Perspectives‹, S. 20–34) mit den Kontroversen und Problemen der Eckhart-Interpretation, die trotz des in den letzten Jahrzehnten zunehmend feststellbaren Bestrebens, Meister Eckhart in seinem Selbstverständnis zu erfassen, bisher keineswegs zu einer allgemeinen Übereinstimmung gekommen ist. Die Forschermeinungen bleiben insbesondere in der Frage der Charakterisierung Eckharts als Mystiker oder als Philosoph/Theologe gespalten. Zu dieser Problematik nimmt der Autor Stellung, indem er die Entweder-Oder-Mentalität und das unangemessene Mystikverständnis jener, die eine antimystische Position vertreten, als dem einheitlichen Verständnis der Wahrheit Eckharts entgegenstehend, kritisch hinterfragt. Nach einer Darlegung der Beziehung zwischen Philosophie und Theologie bei Eckhart entwickelt er, ausgehend von programmatischen Aussagen Eckharts, eine ›Theorie‹ der hermeneutischen Praxis des Predigers und schließt, ohne genauer auf den bereits breit erforschten mystischen Sprachgebrauch Eckharts einzugehen, exemplarisch einige Überlegungen zu dessen Rhetorik an. Bezüglich der Streitfrage über das Verhältnis zwischen dem Lateinischen und dem Deutschen Werk des Dominikaners wäre es seiner Meinung nach wichtig, sowohl eine einfache Opposition als auch ein Ignorieren der Unterschiede zu vermeiden; vielmehr solle die Beziehung zwischen beiden erfaßt und so die Fülle Eckhartschen Denkens rekonstruiert werden. Das dritte Kapitel (›Eckhart and the Mysticism of the Ground‹, S. 35–52) charakterisiert nach einer Kritik herkömmlicher Beschreibungen nach geographischen, religiösen oder ideellen Gesichtspunkten Eckharts Mystik mit dem in seinem Werk zentralen und zugleich proteischen Begriff des Grundes als ›Mystik des Grundes‹ und bezeichnet den deutschen Terminus als ›Meister- bzw. Sprengmetapher‹, die es ermögliche, die ganze Spannweite sprachlicher Strategien zur Beschreibung der Gott Mensch Beziehung zusammenzufassen und alle früheren Kategorien mystischer Rede zu durchbrechen. Nach einer ausführlichen Erforschung der Semantik und der Quellen dieses Begriffs im Vergleich mit den traditionellen lateinischen Begriffen für die Tiefe der Seele und die innerste Natur Gottes, die jeweils nur einen Teilaspekt des mittelhochdeutschen Ausdrucks ›grunt‹ wiedergeben, erkennt der Autor in dieser Metapher eine Wortschöpfung, deren Hauptbedeutung (die sich aus einer Untersuchung der Zusammenhänge und Bedeutungen innerhalb der mittelhochdeutschen Predigten und Traktate ergibt) darin liegt, die ganz neue und für das traditionelle christliche Verständnis herausfordernde Konzeption einer unterschiedslosen Einung von Gott und Mensch (›fused identity‹) auszudrücken. Der Begriff des Grundes liefert einen Angel- oder Brennpunkt, der es erlaubt, die wichtigen Aspekte Eckhartscher Mystik lebendig zu verbinden. Im vierten Kapitel (›The Preacher in Action: Eckhart on the Eternal Birth‹, S. 53–70) präsentiert McGinn eine detaillierte Analyse des im Werk Eckharts einmaligen systematischen Predigtzyklus' von vier Predigten über die ›ewige geburt‹, die er als volkssprachliche *Summa* der Eckhartschen Mystik qualifiziert. Das fünfte und sechste Kapitel (Kap. 5: ›The Metaphysics of Flow‹, S. 71–113; Kap. 6: ›Going without a Way: The Return to the Ground‹, S. 114–161) geben dem Eckhart-Leser einen Schlüssel zum Verständnis des ›theologischen Skeletts‹, d. h. der in seinen Werken mitenthaltenen Systematik an die Hand, indem der Autor die Hauptthemen der mystischen Lehre am großen ›Diptychon‹ des grundlegenden metaphysischen Gesetzes der Wirklichkeit des Ausfließens aller Dinge aus dem verborgenen Grund Gottes (*exitus-emanatio/ûzganc-uzfliessen*) und des Zurückfließens des Universums zu seiner wesentlichen Identität mit dieser göttlichen Quelle (*reditus-restoratio/inganc-durchbrechen*) in fünf respektive vier Punkten darlegt. Zunächst in der Untersuchung des von Eckhart herausgearbeiteten Zusammenhangs zwischen der innertrinitarischen Emanation und der Schöpfung (›*Bullitio-Ebullitio*‹), wobei der Begriff des Ausfließens beides umfaßt und das ›innere Brodeln‹ Gottes Quelle und Vorbild des ›Übersprudelns‹ aller geschaffenen Dinge nach außen und Prinzip der gnadenhaften Rückkehr der vernünftigen Kreaturen zu Gott ist. In einem zweiten Unterkapitel (›*Principium/Trinitatis*‹) wird dann zwischen dem Begriff ›grunt‹ als Möglichkeit für die formale innertrinitarische Emanation und deren aktiven Quelle oder dem Ursprung, dem ›principium‹ unterschieden und Eckharts Dreifaltigkeitslehre im Zusammenhang mit seinem Gebrauch der transzendentalen Prädikate *esse/unum/verum/bonum* zum Verständnis des innertrinitarischen Dynamismus analysiert und die Originalität seines apophatischen und dialektischen Ansatzes, der zugleich trinitarisch und an manchen Stellen supratrinitarisch zu sein scheint, herausgestellt. Der oft vergessenen Pneumatologie wird neben der Christologie volle Rechnung getragen, der mütterliche Aspekt Gottes bei Eckhart ergänzend hervorgehoben. Anschließend beantwortet der Autor im Unterkapitel ›Speaking about God: *De Nominibus Dei*‹ erstens die Frage nach dem allgemeinen Sprachgebrauch in Bezug auf Gott und zweitens, welches Licht dieser auf die Anwendung der transzendentalen Begriffe auf die göttliche Natur als solche, nicht nur auf die Dreifaltigkeit der Personen, wirft. Drei Arten des Sprachgebrauchs Eckharts werden unterschieden und analysiert: Aussage, Analogie und Dialektik, wobei besonders der dialektische Gebrauch von *unum* und seine Beziehung zu *esse* und *intelligere* Berücksichtigung findet. Henologie und Ontologie werden einander nicht gegenübergestellt, vielmehr wird an den apophatischen Horizont von Eckharts Denken erinnert, der jede Form des Wissens und Sprechens über Gott begrenzt und sich mittels oft unerhörter Predigtaussagen Ausdruck verschafft, um zur stillen Einung im Unwissen zu führen. *Exitus/ûzganc* ist nicht auf Gottes innere *bullitio* beschränkt, sondern sprudelt in der Schöpfung über, die in einem vierten Punkt als *ebullitio* zunächst in sich selbst als *creatio continua* und dann in der inneren Seinsstruktur der Geschöpfe betrachtet wird, um im folgenden Unterkapitel in der Beschreibung der Schöpfung der Menschheit als *imago/intellectus* zu gipfeln, die bei Eckhart eine Sonderstellung im Aus- und Rückfluß aller Dinge zu Gott einnimmt. Die Betrachtung der Rückkehrbewegung zu Gott wird durch die Beschreibung der Christologie Eckharts eingeleitet, mit der Darlegung seiner Gnadentheologie weiterentwikkelt, mit der Analyse der drei zentralen Aktivitäten des Abscheidens, Gebärens und Durchbrechens fortgeführt, durch welche die Seele ihr Ziel erreicht, und mit Überlegungen zur Einheit mit Gott abgeschlossen, die zu einem Leben ohne Warum führt, in welchem die Kontemplation in der fruchtbaren Aktion ihre Erfüllung findet. Der Autor gibt in dieser mit Recht bereits als ›die beste Einführung in Eckharts Denken‹ bezeichneten Studie einen einmaligen historischen und inhaltlichen Überblick über das Gesamtwerk Eckharts und beweist in seiner Stellungnahme zu den schwierigsten Themen des Meisters sowie zu den aktuellen Forschungsfragen höchste Kompetenz, die er für jeden, der sich wissenschaftlich mit Meister Eckhart beschäftigen möchte und für jeden in Eckharts Gedankenwelt nach Orientierung Suchenden fruchtbar macht.

Sigrun Jäger, Freiburg

BRUCE MILEM: *The Unspoken Word: Negative Theology in Meister Eckhart's German Sermons*, Washington: The Catholic University of America Press 2002. – ix, 192 pp. – ISBN 0-8132-1019-4. – $ 44.95.

In dem vorliegenden Buch untersucht der für seinen Essay ›Meister Eckhart and the Image: Sermon 16b‹ im Jahr 1998 mit dem Eckhart Society Essay Prize ausgezeichnete Autor vier bekannte deutsche Predigten mit besonderem Augenmerk auf den Sprachgebrauch Eckharts. Das Buch ist in sechs Kapitel gegliedert: ›1. Reading Eckhart's German Sermons‹ (S. 1–21), ›2. Suffering God: Sermon 52‹ (S. 22–49), ›3. Time, Eternity, and Images in Sermon 2‹ (S. 50–85), ›4. Eckhart's Understanding of the Image: Sermon 16B‹ (S. 86–111), ›5. ›God and I we are one in this work‹: Sermon 6‹ (S. 112–142), ›6. Eckhart's Preaching‹ (S. 143–180). Die vier zentralen Kapitel sind der Analyse je einer Predigt gewidmet, die in Anlehnung an den von Eckhart selbst vorgegebenen Predigtaufbau in je vier bis fünf Abschnitten vorgenommen wird. Die wichtigsten Ergebnisse werden dann im Schlußkapitel thematisch in weiteren vier Abschnitten zusammengefaßt. Im ersten Kapitel erfährt der Leser zunächst in aller Kürze das Wichtigste über Leben und Werk Meister Eckharts, die Textgeschichte der Deutschen Predigten sowie die Methode, den Inhalt und den Aufbau der Studie. Der Autor betrachtet Meister Eckharts Predigten als bewußt produzierte Sprachprodukte, deren rhetorische Strategie er, ausgehend von Predigt 53, mit Hilfe von A. Sell »apophatic discourse« nennt. Diese besondere Form von Rede respektiert die Unaussprechlichkeit des Transzendenten, indem sie jede Aussage über Gott *ad infinitum* selbst korrigiert. Ihr Einsatz soll, vergleichbar mit Bertolt Brechts Theaterstrategie, den Zuhörerkreis zu einer kritischen Annäherung an die Predigten führen. Die Berücksichtigung des von Eckhart selbst betonten linguistischen Status der Predigten ist für den Autor interpretationsentscheidend; die Beachtung des im Moment der Predigt stattfindenden Ereignisses, das ›Wie‹ der Sprache, ist ebenso wichtig wie der Predigtinhalt. Methodisch werden jedem Eckhartinterpreten drei Leitlinien zum Lesen der Predigten nahegelegt und in vorliegender Studie angewandt: Erstens soll die Predigt als Ganzes unter Berücksichtigung der internen Organisationsprinzipien gelesen werden, zweitens sollen individuelle Behauptungen in Bezug auf andere Behauptungen in der Predigt interpretiert werden, und drittens soll der Akt des Sprechens selbst ausgelegt werden. Mit dem Vorschlag einer solchen Interpretationsstrategie umgeht der Autor bewußt zwei kritische Bereiche moderner Eckhartforschung, zu denen er aber dennoch kurz Stellung nimmt: Erstens die Beziehung zwischen den deutschen Predigten und dem lateinischen Werk Eckharts. Milem spricht sich für eine zunächst getrennte Untersuchung von deutschem und lateinischem Werk aus, um ihre wahre Beziehung zueinander eventuell in einem zweiten Schritt entdecken zu können. Zweitens die Frage nach der Mystik. Im zweiten Kapitel zeigt der Autor auf, daß Eckhart in der 52. Predigt zunächst eine scharfe Unterscheidung zwischen zwei Existenzordnungen zeichnet: der göttlichen, transzendenten und ewigen einerseits, und der geschaffenen, endlichen und zeitlichen andererseits, um sie dann aber in der menschlichen Seele zusammenfallen zu lassen, die paradoxerweise beides ist – göttlich und geschaffen, ewig und zeitlich. Indem die Predigt ewige Wahrheit innerhalb der zeitlichen Sprache hervorbringt, kombiniert die Predigt, wie die Seele, paradoxerweise Ewigkeit und Zeit und funktioniert so als ein indirektes Bild der Seele und ihrer Begegnung mit Gott. Nach Milem benützt Eckhart in dieser Predigt das Konzept der geistigen Armut nicht in erster Linie, um ein praktisches geistiges Ideal, das es in der Zeit zu erreichen gälte, vorzustellen, sondern um die ewige ontische Einheit der Seele mit Gott zu beschreiben, in der die Seele sich immer schon in einer gewissen Hinsicht, nämlich in ihrem ewigen Aspekt, im Zustand dieser Armut befindet. Der genannte paradoxe Status der Seele wird besonders anhand einer ausführlichen Analyse des berühmten ›Ich‹ der Predigt, ihrer Rhetorik und der Bitte Eckharts an Gott, ihn von Gott frei zu machen, herausgearbeitet. Predigt 2, die im dritten Kapitel behandelt wird, wirft laut Milem die Frage nach der Rolle der Bilder (Worte und Konzepte miteingeschlossen) im Denken und Sprechen über einen unaussprechlichen Gott explizit auf. Der Autor argumentiert, daß Eckhart das offensichtliche Defizit der Bilder zu einem Vorteil verwandelt, indem er Bilder von Gott zeichnet, die offen ihre Unfähigkeit zugeben, Gott fassen zu können. Die Bilder der Jungfrau und des Weibes, die für Eckhart die Gottempfänglichkeit und Gottesgeburt des menschlichen Geistes symbolisieren und die Einheit des menschlichen Geistes mit Gott beschreiben, werden mit dem Bild des Bürgleins in eine dialektische Beziehung gesetzt, das die in den ersten beiden Bildern in einer trinitarischen Sprache gegebene Beschreibung der Einheit Gottes mit der Seele kritisiert und somit die Unaussprechlichkeit und Unfaßbarkeit dieser Einheit klar macht. Der ewige und zeitliche Aspekt des menschlichen Geistes bleiben deutlich unterschieden; insofern der Intellekt zeitlich ist, bleibt er für jeglichen Erkenntnisgewinn auf Bilder angewiesen. Die Ununterschiedenheit von Gott und den Geschöpfen eliminiert nicht deren Unterscheidung und Verschiedenheit. Der Großteil der Predigt 16b (Kapitel 4) ist dem Verständnis des Bildes gewidmet, das Eckhart in erster Linie durch sein ontologisches Abhängigkeitsverhältnis zu seiner Quelle charakterisiert. Dies führt zur Schlußfolgerung, daß die Geschöpfe als Bild Gottes wirken, indem sie durch ihre Kontingenz, ihre Unvollkommenheit und Begrenztheit, ihre Abhängigkeit von Gott, dem Geber des Seins, offenbaren. Die gleichzeitige Unterscheidung und Einheit von Mensch und Gott werden auch anhand von Predigt 6 im fünften Kapitel aufgezeigt, in der Eckhart von einer ersten Definition der Gerechtigkeit, die eine scharfe Unterscheidung zwischen Gott und Mensch impliziert, zu einer zweiten, diese Unterscheidung korrigierenden und ergänzenden Definition der Gerechtigkeit des abgeschiedenen Menschen übergeht, welche die Einheit zwischen Gott und Mensch betont. Im dritten Abschnitt wird die Beziehung zwischen Gott und dem Gerechten als Gleichheit beschrieben, die wiederum als ontologische Abhängigkeitsbeziehung zwischen dem Gerechten und der Gerechtigkeit begriffen wird, als Einheit der beiden, und nicht als Ähnlichkeit. Im vierten Abschnitt ist die Einheit und Unterschiedenheit von Gott und den Geschöpfen im Wirken herausgearbeitet, das menschliche Wirken ›ohne Warum‹ als einem Aspekt jeder Handlung und Teilhabe an Gottes schöpferischem Wirken und am inneren Leben der Dreifaltigkeit beschrieben. In der hinsichtlich der Form, der Ausgewogenheit zwischen wissenschaftlicher Genauigkeit und Kürze und der klaren Gedankenführung vorbildlich durchgeführten Studie ist es dem Autor gelungen, Eckharts Denken und rhetorisches Vorgehen in den deutschen Predigten um eine konsequent durchgehaltene Grundachse, nämlich der Unterscheidung eines zeitlichen und eines ewigen Aspektes der menschlichen Seele, die sich in den Predigten linguistisch widerspiegelt, anzuordnen. Die unaussprechliche Beziehung zwischen Gott und der Seele auf rationaler Ebene erschöpfend zu beschreiben, ist laut Aussage des Autors unmöglich. Eine neue, überzeugende Annäherung an diese letztlich unsagbare und undenkbare Wirklichkeit ist ihm besonders in der Analyse des Bürgleins in der Seele geglückt. Alle diejenigen Formulierungen, die trotz aller Differenzierungsversuche in irgendeiner Weise die Identität von Gott und der Seele nahelegen, sind kritisch zu hinterfragen. Eine genaue Untersuchung der Eckhartschen Christologie und der Grundmetapher könnte die Ausführungen des Autors noch weiter erhellen. Die vorgeschlagene Methode scheint mir ein sehr angemessenes Instrument zur Analyse der Predigten zu sein.

Sigrun Jäger, Freiburg

Amador Vega: *Ramon Llull and the Secret of Life*; transl. by James W. Heisig, New York: Crossroad, Herder & Herder Book 2003. – ix, 277 pp. – ISBN 0–8245–2117–X. – $ 29.95. [Span. Originaltitel: Amador Vega Esquerra: *Ramon Llull y el secreto de la vida* (El árbol del paraíso 26), Madrid: Ediciones Siruela 2002. – 311 pp. – ISBN 84–7844–600–1. – € 21,00.]

Amador Vega Esquerra versucht mit seinem Buch einen neuartigen Blick auf das Gesamtphänomen Ramon Llull zu werfen. Hierzu behandelt er drei Themenkreise und gliedert entsprechend seine Darstellung in drei Abschnitte, die zunächst Llulls Leben, dann sein Denken bzw. die darin erkennbare Weisheit und schließlich die beiden angemessene Sprache behandeln. Dieser erste Teil nimmt zusammen mit den Anmerkungen die erste Hälfte des Bandes ein. Danach folgt eine Anthologie aus zahlreichen Werken Llulls in englischer Übersetzung, die es dem Leser ermöglichen soll, die Darstellung Vegas an den Texten selbst nachzuvollziehen. Vega geht von der hermeneutischen Grunderfahrung aus, daß sich das Welt- und vor allem auch das Selbstverständnis des Menschen in einem Dialog zwischen Sichtbarem und Unsichtbarem entfalte, genauer zwischen individuellen Erfahrungen und der Suche nach ihrer Bedeutung, sprich dem Sinn des eigenen Lebens (S. 1). Dieses Wechselverhältnis, in dem sich das Leben als erfahrenes zunächst als Geheimnis darbietet, das im Laufe des Lebens selbst enthüllt werden soll, gewinne aber nur dann den adäquaten Sinnhorizont bzw. werde nur dann transparent, wenn das Geheimnis des Lebens im Licht einer übergeschichtlichen Größe gesehen werde, die Vega ›Weisheit‹ nennt, für das Christentum etwa in Gestalt der Heiligkeit. Aus diesen einführenden Überlegungen wird schon ersichtlich, daß Vegas Buch keine philologisch-historische Abhandlung über Llull als eine Art Ausnahmedenker des 13. Jahrhunderts sein will. Im Laufe der Untersuchung wird aber auch deutlich, daß Vega keine esoterische Lebensphilosophie oder eine unmittelbar verwertbare Lebenskunst à la Llull vorlegen möchte. Der Autor verquickt jedoch Erfahrungsdenken mit Anklängen an existenziale, existenzialistische oder auch religionspsychologische Terminologie mit der Idee, das Leben Ramon Llulls mit allen seinen Ausfaltungen als eine einheitliche Gestalt unter der mittelalterlichen Bestimmung des Menschen, der ›Heiligkeit‹, erkennbar werden zu lassen. Der Leser weiß manchmal nicht, ob Llull als mittelalterlicher Mystiker vorgestellt oder eine neue Art Universalmystik aus Llull herausentwickelt wird, zumal Vega immer wieder Brückenschläge v. a. zum Buddhismus versucht. Dabei ist die Grundidee, Llulls Leben als ein Spiegelbild seines Denkens und das Werk als Entfaltung seiner Visionserlebnisse darzustellen – letztlich das Programm von Llulls Autobiographie *Vita coetanea* (1311) –, durchaus plausibel. Auch erscheint es bedenkenswert, wenn Vega Llulls Leben und Werk mit klassischen mittelalterlichen Schemata beleuchtet wie dem der vierfältigen Liebe nach Richard von St. Viktor (S. 66f.) oder dem der drei Stufen des mystischen Aufstieges. Diese werden um eine *via predicativa* (S. 83) ergänzt, d.h. um den Schritt, das Betrachtete weiterzugeben und von der *unio* wieder in die Welt herabzusteigen, bei Llull etwa in Form seines schriftstellerischen Wirkens durch seine *Ars*. Dennoch kann der Rezensent die Rolle, die das Phänomen des ›Geheimnisses‹ in Llulls Denken einnehmen soll, nicht nachvollziehen, zumal der Autor selbst darauf hinweist, daß eigentlich Llulls ›kontemplatives System ein klar apologetisches Ziel hat, das eher Vernunft als Dogmen braucht‹ (S. 51). Llulls System betont ja die Vernunft und die rationale Durchsichtigkeit auch der Theologie, wie der Streit um die notwendigen Vernunftgründe zeigt. Symptomatisch für Vegas anders gelagerte Gewichtung ist der Versuch, den bei Cusanus zu beheimatenden Begriff *coincidentia oppositorum* auf Llull anzuwenden. Damit überspringt er die große Unterschiedlichkeit ihrer Denkweisen (S. 80, 89, 125–127, Anm. 168). Auch der Abschnitt über Llulls Sprache erhellt die Frage nach dem Stellenwert des ›Geheimnisses‹ in Llulls Werk nicht. So klar es ist, daß Llull ein eigenes symbolisches System und neuartige

Begriffe schafft, um sich allgemein, und das heißt vor allem auch interreligiös, verständlich zu machen, so mißverständlich wird Vegas Unternehmen, wenn er diesen Aspekt unter die Überschrift ›The Alchemy of Language‹ stellt. Während Vega das *Buch vom Freund und vom Geliebten* zurecht als mystische Schrift liest, rückt er die berühmten Figuren der *Ars* in eine zu große Nähe zur Kabbalah (bes. S. 82). Llulls Kombinatorik und Buchstabenkunst hat nur eine rein heuristische, erkenntnistheoretische und mnemotechnische Funktion, besitzt aber in sich keinen Erkenntniswert (vgl. A. Kilcher: *Die Sprachtheorie der Kabbalah als ästhetisches Paradigma*, Stuttgart/Weimar 1998, S. 154). Vegas Buch führt knapp und anregend in das Leben Llulls ein (S. 2–30) und präsentiert dem Leser hierzu zahlreiche Quellen in englischer Übersetzung. Die Darstellung des Denkens und der Sprache unter dem Gesichtspunkt ›Geheimnis des Lebens‹ überzeugt dagegen nicht, so daß das Werk nicht geeignet ist, wenn man sich ein Grundverständnis des Llullschen Denkens verschaffen möchte. Dabei ist das Buch sehr schön gemacht mit einem umfangreichen Literaturverzeichnis, einem Lebenslauf Llulls (S. 259–261) und einem umfassenden Personen- und Sachindex. Sehr gut sind auch die Schwarzweißillustrationen geworden, insbesondere die Miniaturen zu Llulls Leben aus dem *Breviculum*. Nützlich für eine Behandlung von Llulls Leben sind die englischen Übersetzungen, auch wenn sie meist nur Auszüge bieten können. Von Vega stammen die Übersetzungen aus *Llibre de contemplació en Déu* (Prolog u. Kap. 169, 170, 174), *Arbre de ciència* (Prolog und Auszüge), *Cant de Ramon*, vor allem von Anthony und Eve Bonner, *Llibre del gentil i dels tres savis* (Prolog und Epilog), *Blanquerna* (Buch V, Kap. 96f.), *Llibre de amic i amat* (Auszüge), *Fèlix o Llibre de meravelles* (Buch IV Anfang), *Lo desconort*, *Ars brevis* (Prolog und pars 1–3), *Vita coetanea*. In der Bibliographie hätte man in den Zeiten des Internets auch einige wertvolle Links nennen können, so zu den farbigen Bildern aus dem *Breviculum* (http://www.ub.uni–freiburg.de/referate/04/breviculum–miniaturen.htm) oder zur umfassenden Online-Datenbank (http://orbita.bib.ub.es/ramon/index.asp), besonders zu den online-edierten Werken (http://orbita.bib.ub.es/llull/ velec.asp).

Ulli Roth, Pforzheim

Hubert Schröcker: *Das Verhältnis der Allmacht Gottes zum Kontradiktionsprinzip nach Wilhelm von Ockham* (Veröffentlichungen des Grabmann-Institutes zur Erforschung der mittelalterlichen Theologie und Philosophie, 49), Berlin: Akademie 2003. – 536 S. – ISBN 3–05–003747–4. – € 69,80.

Wilhelm von Ockham, dessen Werk und Gestalt sich gerade in jüngster Zeit wieder besonderer Beachtung von Historikern, Theologen und Philosophen erfreut, suchte einen geistigen Prozeß zu erfassen, der zunächst ein Prozeß seiner Zeit war. Hans Blumenberg charakterisiert ihn durch die Verurteilung von 1277 durch den Bischof von Paris: »Dieses Dokument bezeichnet genau den Zeitpunkt, in dem der Vorrang des Interesses an der Rationalität der Schöpfung und ihrer humanen Intelligibilität umschlägt in die spekulative Faszination durch das theologische Prädikat der absoluten Macht und Freiheit« (*Säkularisierung und Selbstbehauptung*, Frankfurt/M. 1983, S. 186). Die Wende im Bewußtsein der Freiheit bei Ockham ist durch das Verhältnis von Freiheit und Ordnung virulent geworden. Ockham entwickelt den Begriff der Freiheit Gottes durch die in der Tradition vorhandene Unterscheidung von absoluter und geordneter Macht (*potentia absoluta et ordinata*). Während nach Blumenbergs philosophiegeschichtlicher Deutung der Gedanke der Allmacht Gottes den neuzeitlichen Menschen zur Selbstkonstitution als autonomes Subjekt genötigt hat, macht er nach neuscholastisch geprägter Darstellung Ockham zum Urheber des Verlustes der hochscholastischen Synthese von Philosophie und Theologie. Schröcker will in seinem Buch beide Interpretationen hinterfragen und dementsprechend klären, »in welchem Ausmaß Ockhams Denken von seinem Glauben an den allmächtigen Gott geprägt ist« (S. 20). Anders als Autoren vor ihm kehrt Schröcker allerdings die Fragestellung um: »Statt zu fragen, was Gott alles tun kann, frage ich, was er *nicht* tun kann und weshalb er es nicht tun kann. Ich frage also nach der Grenze der göttlichen Macht« (ebd.). Gottes Macht ist nach Ockham (wie auch nach den meisten mittelalterlichen Theologen) nicht schlechthin grenzenlos: »Sie besagt nur, daß Gott all das tun kann, was keinen logischen Widerspruch enthält. Die Grenze der Allmacht – und nach Ockham ist es ihre einzige Grenze! – bildet also das Kontradiktionsprinzip« (ebd.). Richtig erkennt der Vf., daß diese Grenze die Allmacht nicht aufhebt, sondern im Gegenteil erst die Voraussetzung schafft, um die Allmacht Gottes überhaupt sinnvoll denken zu können. Der Satz vom (ausgeschlossenen) Widerspruch gehört zu den obersten Grundsätzen der Logik und Metaphysik. Wer überhaupt über etwas argumentieren will, muß anerkennen, daß es unmöglich ist, daß dasselbe Prädikat demselben Subjekt in derselben Hinsicht zugleich zukommt und nicht zukommt. Entsprechend seiner Problemstellung, was Gott *nicht* tun kann, orientiert der Vf. den ersten Hauptteil seines Buches an drei negativen Behauptungen Ockhams: ›*Deus nihil potest facere inordinate*‹, ›*Deus non potest peccare*‹ und ›*(Deus) non potest efficere Deum*‹, und führt sie auf das Kontradiktionsprinzip zurück. Ziel der Textanalysen ist dabei, unter schrittweisen Verbesserungen eine kohärente Definition des Begriffs ›Allmacht‹ aufzustellen. Das Ergebnis lautet: »Eine göttliche Person P ist allmächtig genau dann, wenn für jede Entität X, die sich mit ausschließlich absoluten Begriffen beschreiben läßt, gilt: Wenn die Aussage ›X wird gemacht‹ widerspruchsfrei ist, ist die göttliche Person P fähig, X zu erschaffen oder zu erhalten« (S. 205). Der Vf. lehnt sich bei der Erarbeitung dieser Definition (oder Beschreibung), die sich so bei Ockham nicht findet, methodisch an Verfahren der zeitgenössischen Analytischen Philosophie an. Auf diese Weise trägt er viele einzelne Überlegungen und zahlreiche Sonderfälle systematisch zusammen, wertet sie aus und gewinnt am Ende eine höchst willkommene terminologische Klarheit. Im Zuge dieses schrittweisen Aufbaus der Definition von ›Allmacht‹ zeigt sich Schröcker als umfassender Kenner aller einschlägigen Werke Ockhams. Er kann überzeugend darlegen, daß Ockham seinen Allmachtsbegriff über Entitäten, Handlungen und mögliche Sachverhalte bestimmt. Durch alle begrifflichen Verfeinerungen hindurch erkennt der Leser, daß es für Ockham nur eine einzige Grenze der göttlichen Macht gibt, eben das Kontradiktionsprinzip. Gott vermag alles, nur eines kann er nicht: einen Widerspruch verwirklichen. Damit rückt der Begriff des Möglichen in das Zentrum der weiteren Überlegungen (S. 209–508). »Die Allmacht Gottes und das Kontradiktionsprinzip bestimmen einen jeweils eigenen Begriff der Möglichkeit. Denn einerseits ist möglich, was irgendjemand vermag. Alles aber, was irgendjemand vermag, vermag auch Gott. Daher ist in diesem Sinn alles möglich, was Gott vermag. Andererseits gilt auch als möglich, was in sich widerspruchsfrei ist … Diese beiden Möglichkeitsbegriffe sind nach Ockham wenigstens dem begrifflichen Umfang nach gleich« (S. 210). Die genannten Zusammenhänge werfen die Frage nach dem Verhältnis der Allmacht Gottes zum Kontradiktionsprinzip und zum Grund der Möglichkeit des Möglichen (bzw. der Unmöglichkeit des Unmöglichen) auf. Historisch richtig setzt der Vf. für diese Probleme mit einer Erörterung des Sinns der traditionellen Ideenlehre an, und zwar bei Heinrich von Gent und Johannes Duns Scotus, den beiden wichtigsten indirekten und direkten Quellen Ockhams. »Gott selbst weiß und erkennt alles, was möglich ist. Seine Erkenntnis erfolgt durch die ewigen Ideen, die sich im göttlichen Geist befinden. Die Ideenlehre läßt uns einen Blick in die ersten Prinzipien der wirklichen und bloß möglichen Geschöpfe tun und erlaubt daher Einblicke in erste Gründe der Möglichkeit.« (S. 211). Als Resümee ergibt sich für Heinrich von Gent der Grundgedanke, daß die Möglichkeit des Möglichen auf der absoluten Vollkommenheit Gottes beruht, die unfähig ist, Widersprüche zu erzeugen. Scotus legt für seine Lösung das göttliche Wesen samt seinen Attributen Intellekt und Macht zugrunde. Der

Intellekt bringt ein *esse intelligibile* hervor, dessen Darstellung sich als widerspruchsfrei mit dem Sein vereinbar erweist. Es ist nicht aus sich notwendig, wohl aber möglich und besitzt daher ein *esse possibile.* Ockhams Lösung für das Problem des Grundes des Möglichen bzw. Unmöglichen liegt in der Annahme einer ›natürlichen Simultanität‹ der Allmacht Gottes und des Möglichen. Allerdings verändert Ockham die Fragestellung in einer für ihn charakteristischen Weise. Er fragt in seiner *Ordinatio* (dist. 43, q. 2) nicht, woher das Mögliche und das Unmögliche kausal stammen, sondern »ob es Gott ›früher‹ (*prius*) zukomme, das Unmögliche nicht machen zu können, als es dem Unmöglichen zukommt, von Gott nicht gemacht werden zu können« (S. 493). Damit verlegt Ockham das Problem von der ontologischen Ebene auf die sprachkritische. Er verneint die Frage und gibt damit indirekt zu verstehen, daß es dem Möglichen nicht früher zukommt, gemacht werden zu können, als es Gott zukommt, das Mögliche machen zu können. Die Macht Gottes und die Möglichkeit des Möglichen sind also nach Ockham der Natur nach zugleich. Daß Gott etwas kann und daß etwas möglich ist, sind die beiden Seiten desselben Sachverhalts. Diese Lösung muß man nicht, wie Schröcker es tut (S. 462, 501), als ›merkwürdig‹ und ›unbefriedigend‹ ansehen. Es entspricht Ockhams grundsätzlicher Auffassung von Wissenschaft und daher auch von Theologie, daß diese sprachlich verfaßt ist. In der Theologie geht es wesentlich um Aussagen und um die Supposition der in diesen vorkommenden Termini an Subjekts- und Prädikatsstelle. Begriffe des Möglichen supponieren personal für Mögliches, Begriffe des Unmöglichen supponieren weder für Mögliches noch für Unmögliches, daher für nichts. Das Mögliche hat aber nach Ockham kein eigenes *esse possibile* und ist keine mögliche Entität. Mögliches und Unmögliches sind, wie es der Vf. selbst richtig sagt (S. 462), beide nichts, aber nicht auf dieselbe Weise. Hier wäre es gut gewesen, auf die Unterscheidung der Modalitäten *de dicto* und *de re* einzugehen. Und wenn ich schon bei kritischen Anmerkungen bin: Der Vf. gebraucht die Wörter »Widerspruch«, »widerspruchsfrei« u.ä. unterschiedslos für Aussagen, Handlungen (z.B. S. 147), Begriffe (z.B. S. 200) und Entitäten (z.B. S. 84, 200, 201, 205). Das ist nur dann akzeptabel, wenn einem klar ist, daß diese Wörter im eigentlichen Sinn nur auf der Ebene der Sprache ihren Platz haben. (Dann noch einige Flüchtigkeitsfehler: S. 37 statt ›Totenbett‹ lies ›Sterbebett‹; S. 79 statt ›brilliant‹ lies ›brillant‹, S. 505 statt ›lassen‹ lies ›läßt‹). Die hier aufgeführten kleineren Mängel des Buches schmälern aber nicht Schröckers Verdienste. Wir haben es bei dem vorliegenden Buch mit einem Werk zu tun, das außergewöhnlich viel zu bieten hat. Es folgt dem Denken Ockhams (und nicht nur diesem, weshalb der Titel etwas zu einschränkend ist) in sehr viele Verästelungen und läßt doch die Problemzusammenhänge immer wieder deutlich werden. Eine herausragende Dissertation!

Gerhard Leibold, Innsbruck

VOLKER LEPPIN: *Wilhelm von Ockham. Gelehrter, Streiter, Bettelmönch* (Gestalten des Mittelalters und der Renaissance), Darmstadt: Primus, 2003. – x, 309 S. – ISBN 3-89678-476-5 (Primus); 3-534-14752-9 (wbg). – € 29,20.

Der Kirchenhistoriker aus Jena Volker Leppin hat das nicht leichte Unterfangen auf sich genommen, eine Biographie Wilhelms von Ockham zu schreiben. In diesem Fall war es nicht die Fülle, sondern der Mangel an Information über das Leben dieser bedeutenden Gestalt des 14. Jahrhunderts, welcher die Sache erschwerte. Die wenigen sicheren Lebensdaten Ockhams sind allseits bekannt: die Subdiakonenweihe 1306, welche die Geburt auf zwischen 1280 und 1285 zurückdatieren läßt, Studium der Theologie in Oxford ab ca. 1308 ohne Abschluß der Promotion, der Streit mit dem Oxforder Universitätskanzler Lutterell, der 1324 die Abreise nach Avignon zur Verteidigung gegen den Vorwurf der Häresie mit sich brachte, die Flucht von dort mit dem Ordensoberen Michael von Cesena nach Italien im Jahr 1328 und der Aufenthalt bis zum Lebensende in München unter dem Schutz

Ludwigs des Bayern, der Tod ziemlich sicher 1347, vermutlich nicht an der Pest, sondern »der natürliche Tod eines entkräfteten Mannes« (S. 270). Da in der Forschung seit den grundlegenden Arbeiten für die kritische Edition und den Studien von Jürgen Miethke, William Courtenay, Fritz Hoffmann und Gedeon Gál keine neuen Details zur Person des Franziskaners William aufgetaucht sind, blieb es bei einem unvollständigen Knochengerüst an Daten, die für eine Biographie mit Fleisch bestückt werden mußten. Der Autor freilich hat aus der Not eine Tugend gemacht. Wo die Details fehlten, führt er den Leser in die Lebenszeit und das historische Umfeld Ockhams ein – sei es im Hinblick auf Oxford mit seinen Streitigkeiten zwischen den Bettelorden und der Universität, dem geistigen Flair nach den Verurteilungen von 1277 und den Thesen des Duns Scotus; sei es im Hinblick auf die veränderte Situation Ockhams am Ordensstudium in London, wo er der gängigen Forschungsmeinung nach Philosophie lehrte; oder im Hinblick auf das geschäftige Avignon oder das im Umbruch befindliche München mit ihren jeweiligen opponierenden Kräften, Papst und Kaiser. Diese historischen Situierungen der Person Wilhelms von Ockham lesen sich streckenweise wie Einführungen in die mittelalterliche theologische Literatur, in religiöse Bewegungen oder in die Grundzüge mittelalterlicher Politik. Der Mangel an bekannten Details zum konkreten Leben läßt das Zeitgeschehen zu Wort kommen und den Hintergrund plastisch werden, vor dem sich der in historischen Daten kaum greifbare Franziskaner bewegte. Und dennoch, obwohl nur als Schatten einer Gestalt sichtbar – die Zeugnisse lassen nicht viel über sein Innenleben erahnen – machte Ockham dennoch Geschichte – und zwar mit der Feder. Dies ist das Charakteristikum Ockhams, welches der Autor der Biographie stark macht: Ockham als Mann, der unabhängig von Anklagen, Häresieverdächtigungen und später Exkommunikation weiter mit akademischen Argumenten kämpft, der in der Regel weniger auf die Polemik als auf die Vollständigkeit der Argumente baut und bereits fern von der Universität noch Einführungen in die Logik verfaßt, ein hoffnungsloser Intellektueller, der in dem Glauben schreibt, mit Argumenten überzeugen zu können und der erst spät, in der existentiellen Abhängigkeit vom Schutz des Kaisers, sich von politischen Umständen beeinflußt Schweigen auferlegt oder sich für die Zwecke des Kaisers benutzen läßt. Diese intellektuelle Tätigkeit, die Ockham auch fern von ihrem eigentlichen Bestimmungsort, der Universität, weiterpflegt, charakterisierte V. Leppin durch den anachronistischen Begriff der ›virtuellen Universität‹, mit dem er sowohl die schriftstellerische Tätigkeit Ockhams während des Untersuchungsverfahrens in Avignon als auch während seiner de facto Gefangenschaft in München bezeichnet. Im Zusammenhang mit der ›virtuellen Universität‹ kommt der Autor zu einer bemerkenswerten Neudatierung der *Quodlibeta* Ockhams, jener den umfangreichen neunten Band der *Opera Theologica* füllenden Erörterungen in magistralem Stil, die bislang in die Zeit des Londoner Aufenthaltes datiert worden waren. Leppin argumentiert zu Recht, daß die schriftstellerische Produktion in London damit ungeheuerlich gewesen sein müßte: Ockham verfaßte dort neben seinen Philosophievorlesungen noch seine zwei Eucharistietraktate und die Summe der Logik, in der er zu seiner veränderten Auffassung in der Universalienlehre fand und die deontologisierte Logik zur Grundlage aller Wissenschaften machte, und hätte dann pro Vorlesungsmonat noch zwei Quaestionen der *Quodlibeta* disputieren müssen. Daher argumentiert der Autor, Ockham habe in Avignon die literarische Form der *Quodlibeta* aufgegriffen, um seine Position zu klären, ohne diese *Quodlibeta* tatsächlich zu halten (S. 140–143). Für Ockhams theologische Lehre interessant ist diese These durch den engen Zusammenhang der Inhalte der Quodlibeta mit den Anklagepunkten gegen Ockham in Avignon, was die schärferen Formulierungen in den *Quodlibeta* gegenüber denen seines Oxforder Sentenzenkommentars erklären könnte: Gottes absolute Macht nicht wie bei Duns Scotus als zweiter Handlungsraum, mit dem der reguläre Weltablauf durchbrochen werden konnte, sondern als denkerische Rahmenbedingung der nur vom Widerspruchsprinzip begrenzten theoretischen Möglichkeiten Gottes – um den Preis, daß auch Wunder als von Gott im Rahmen der Ordnung vorgesehen gelten mußten und so zur Anfrage an die Gültigkeit von Kausalzusammenhängen wurden (S. 147–148); oder die Position, daß es keine Verdienstlichkeit einer Handlung ohne Gnade gebe, gegen den Pelagianismus-Vorwurf (S. 152–155). Erstaunlich bleibt die noch ungebrochene Anerkennung der Macht des Papstes zu dieser Zeit, nach dessen Vorbild Ockham Gottes Allmacht erklärte und die er erst später einer Revision unterzog (S. 148–149; 181). Interessant für den Historiker die Verbindung, die sich in den Augen Johannes XXII. zwischen Ockham und den u.a. von Petrus Johannis Olivi inspirierten Beginen herstellen ließ: beide schienen eine direkte Gottesschau und damit eine Heilsunmittelbarkeit zu vertreten, welche zu einer Relativierung kirchlicher Autorität und Macht führen mußte (S. 156–165) und eine Angst vor unkontrollierter Laienfrömmigkeit hervorrief, die noch hundert Jahre später, z.B. bei Johannes Gerson, als Schreckbild fungiert. Auch im Hinblick auf das Verbot der Ockhamlektüre in Paris 1339 läßt sich auf dem Hintergrund des Buches erkennen, in wie großem Maße Kirchen- und Realpolitik auf die Wahrnehmung der theologischen und philosophischen Positionen Ockhams Einfluß genommen haben, auch wenn sie die Verbreitung seiner zentralen Werke – der *Summa Logicae* und des Fragment gebliebenen *Dialogus* – nicht unterbinden konnten. Es mag jedes Buch seine Mängel haben – die Philosophen hätten sich vielleicht mehr Aufmerksamkeit für die Physik gewünscht, und der Leser, der rasch einen Kurztitel auflösen will und nicht weiß, ob dieser nun unmittelbar Ockham oder dessen Umfeld betrifft, eine weniger gegliederte Literaturliste –, es hat sicherlich die Kernpunkte der Ockhamschen Lehre ebenso wie die relevanten historischen Fakten berücksichtigt und für den theologisch und historisch interessierten Leser aufbereitet. Dabei hat der Autor nicht nur teilweise zuvor vertretene Ansichten revidiert (z.B. die Datierung der *Ordinatio,* d.h. der Überarbeitung des ersten Sentenzenbuchs, vgl. S. 39), sondern auch eine Form und einen Stil gewählt, der sich wohltuend von der fachspezifischen Arbeit der eigenen Dissertation und ebenso von Ockham selbst abhebt, dessen Argumentation ›oft von geradezu eisiger Kälte geprägt‹ ist (S. 80). Sowohl die Form der Darstellung als auch die sich anschließenden Resümees und Wertungen des Autors samt den knappen Skizzen zur Wirkungsgeschichte Ockhams machen das Lesen, sei es im Ausschnitt oder am Stück, nicht nur für den Laien wie Fachmann anregend, sondern sogar zum Vergnügen. Ein Prädikat, das in der theologischen Fachliteratur nicht sehr häufig vergeben werden kann!

Sigrid Müller, Nijmegen

Eva Luise Wittneben: *Bonagratia von Bergamo. Franziskanerjurist und Wortführer seines Ordens im Streit mit Papst Johannes XXII.* (Studies in Medieval and Reformation Thought 90), Leiden/Boston: Brill 2003. – viii, 424 pp. – ISBN 90–04–12817–4. – € 96,00 ($ 130.00).

Mit dem Juristen Bonagratia von Bergamo († 1340), der 1319 Generalprokurator des Franziskanerordens wurde, hat sich Eva Luise Wittneben in ihrer Heidelberger historischen Dissertation eine, ja zeitweise die entscheidende Figur im theoretischen Armutsstreit, den die Franziskaner mit Johannes XXII. durchfochten, zum Thema gewählt. Sein Wirken in den Jahren 1311–1328 wird gründlich und umfassend aufgearbeitet und in seinen zeitgenössischen Kontext gesetzt. Das erste Kapitel zeichnet zunächst durchaus kritisch sein Wirken gegen die Spiritualen im eigenen Orden nach: Seine Polemik gegen die Begrifflichkeit des *usus pauper* sei der Versuch gewesen, »der gegnerischen Seite den Mund zu verbieten« (S. 32), er selbst war in Auseinandersetzung mit den Spiritualen ein »Scharfmacher« (S. 39). Solche deutlichen Wertungen erfolgen stets auf einer verläßlichen philologischen Grundlage: Neben ausführlichen Paraphrasen und Transkriptionen in den Anmerkungen, die die eigene Urteilsbildung des Lesers insbesondere bei dem vielfach herangezogenen unedierten Material erleichtern, zeichnet Wittneben auch die Glossierungstätigkeit Bonagratias nach, so daß seine Verfasserschaft – oder mindestens Redaktionstätigkeit – an Ordensschriften erhärtet werden kann (S. 73–81). Der Darstellung von Bonagratias spezifischem Beitrag zum theoretischen Armutsstreit dient das zweite Kapitel. Sorgfältig wird Bonagratias *Tractatus de paupertate* in die zeitgenössische Armutsdiskussion eingeordnet. Besonders wird das Verhältnis zum Manifest der Franziskaner von Perugia dargestellt, das die franziskanische Position zur Armutsfrage bekräftigte, wie sie durch *Exiit qui seminat* (1279) päpstlicherseits abgesichert, nun aber von Johannes XXII. zur Disposition gestellt worden war. W. zeigt, daß Bonagratia in seinem *Tractatus* auf die ausführlichere Variante dieses Manifests zurückgriff. Seine Ausführungen dienten der theoretischen Vertiefung und juristischen Absicherung der Position von Perugia; auffällig ist, daß er hierzu auch auf Überlegungen des Spiritualen Petrus Johannis Olivi zurückgreift, ohne dessen Namen zu nennen – daß dies, wie W. erwägt (S. 156), unbewußt geschehen sein könnte, scheint jedoch angesichts des zuvor geschilderten Kampfes gegen die Spiritualen und der wenig später von W. deutlich herausgearbeiteten Olivi-Kenntnisse Bonagratias (S. 172f) eine wenig wahrscheinliche Variante: Vielmehr scheint Bonagratia, indem er Olivis Konzept die eschatologische Spitze nahm und die eigentumsrechtliche Restitution des Urzustandes als Spezialrecht der Franziskaner proklamierte (S. 148), die Aussagen so entschärft zu haben, daß sie in sein Konzept passen konnten. Eben diese Proklamierung eines Ausnahmerechts ist nach W. »der eigentlich originäre Beitrag« Bonagratias zum Armutsstreit (S. 157). Damit war auf theoretischer Seite der dramatische Höhepunkt, Bonagratias Appellation gegen die Bulle *Ad conditorem* (1322) und seine sofortige Verhaftung, weitgehend vorbereitet (S. 164–185). Von hier an verschränkt sich Bonagratias Leben und Wirken vollends mit den Auseinandersetzungen seines Ordens mit Johannes XXII. In Anlehnung an die Rede von einer ›Politik des dissimulierenden Ausgleichs‹ bei ihrem Doktorvater Jürgen Miethke beschreibt W. zunächst Bonagratias Beteiligung an den Ausgleichsbemühungen von Seiten der Franziskaner und setzt damit gegenüber der kritischen Sicht der Franziskaner in der gelehrten Abhandlung Ulrich Horsts über *Evangelische Armut und päpstliches Lehramt* (Stuttgart 1996) erkennbar eigene Akzente; hier wäre auch eine deutlichere und explizitere Auseinandersetzung möglich gewesen. In diesem Zusammenhang kann W. die Autorschaft Bonagratias an den *Responsiones ad oppositiones* (1323/4) bestätigen, die weitgehend auf dem *Tractatus* und der Appellation gegen *Ad conditorem* beruhen. Für den Minoritenexkurs der Sachsenhäuser Appellation hingegen kann W. mit guten Gründen die Verfasserschaft Bonagratias bestreiten (S. 251) – und so Bonagratia weiterhin im Sinne einer Ausgleichspolitik deuten. Zum ›Bruch mit dem Papst‹ kommt es dementsprechend nach W. erst im Zusammenhang der im folgenden Kapitel geschilderten Geschehnisse: 1328 flohen Bonagratia, Michael von Cesena und andere Franziskaner aus Avignon – und stellten sich nun eindeutig in Opposition zum Papst und an die Seite Ludwigs des Bayern. Dies hatte nun auch theologisch interessante Folgen. Wie bei anderen Autoren, etwa Wilhelm von Ockham, so kann man auch bei Bonagratia beobachten, daß die Konfrontation mit einem in seinen Augen zweifelsfrei häretischen Papst die Frage nach eindeutigen Kriterien für Häresie verschärfte. Und W. kann zeigen, wie Bonagratia in der Appellation von Pisa (1328) gegenüber Bonaventura, aber auch gegenüber eigenen früheren Aussagen die Bindung des Papstes an einmal kirchlich definierte Glaubenswahrheiten durch den Gedanken, daß die römische Kirche niemals irren könne, hervorhebt (S. 317). Daß diese ekklesiologische Umorientierung auch rechtsformale Auswirkungen hatte, zeigt W. im Anschluß an H.-J. Becker im letzten, fünften Kapitel über Bonagratia als Autor franziskanischer Appellationen: Die Instanz, an die er sich mit seinen Appellationen wendet, verschiebt sich vom Papst über den Apostolischen Stuhl und die *Romana ecclesia catholica et apostolica* zum Konzil (S. 378), ohne daß hier je von einem prinzipiellen Konziliarismus die Rede sein könnte. Die gründliche Untersuchung W.s hat durch alle Detailfreude und gelegentlich allzu ausführliche Paraphrasierung der einschlägigen Schriften hindurch einen klar erkennbaren roten Faden. Bonagratia wird als versierter Jurist und Politiker erkennbar, und auch die theologischen Implikationen seiner Argumentationen werden angedeutet. Sie machen die Nähe innerhalb der gegen Johannes XXII. verbundenen franziskanischen Argumentationsgemeinschaft deutlich. Die Arbeit bedeutet einen wichtigen Fortschritt in der Erschließung des nicht nur rein äußerlich, sondern auch analytisch schwer zugänglichen Œuvres Bonagratias.

Volker Leppin, Jena

Rik van Nieuwenhove: *Jan van Ruusbroec, Mystical Theologian of the Trinity* (Studies in Spirituality and Theology), Notre Dame: The University of Notre Dame Press 2003. – 264 pp. – ISBN 0–268–03261–0 (hardcover), $ 45.00. – ISBN 0–268–03262–9 (paperback), $ 22.00.

Die kompakte Studie von Rik van Nieuwenhove, Dozent für Theologie am Trinity College in Dublin, nimmt die mystische Trinitätstheologie von Jan van Ruusbroec (1293–1381) (= R.) in den Blick und ist schon aufgrund dieses dezidiert theologischen Interesses ein beachtenswerter Neuansatz innerhalb der R.-Forschung. Wie der Autor in seiner Einleitung schreibt, ist in den letzten 50 Jahren keine größere Arbeit über R.s Theologie erschienen. So ist sein Ziel: »I hope to demonstrate that Ruusbroec has an exciting theology worth investigating« (2). Dementsprechend orientiert sich die Arbeit in ihrem Aufbau an theologischen Gesichtspunkten. Nachdem in einem ersten Kapitel R.s Leben und Werk souverän und knapp dargestellt werden (S. 7–27), beschäftigt sich das zweite Kapitel (S. 29–76) mit der grundlegenden theologischen Einordnung des flämischen Mystikers. Ist er ein apophatischer Theologe, der die gnadenhafte Einheit Gottes mit den Menschen theologisch reflektiert, oder doch eher – wie es viele Studien bisher suggerierten – ein Mystiker im engeren Sinn, der die Erfahrung Gottes rein phänomenologisch beschreibt? Der Autor läßt keinen Zweifel daran, daß er zur ersten Sichtweise tendiert, nach der R. die geistliche Idee eines gemeinsamen Lebens (*vita communis*) zwischen Gott und der Seele hat, in dem Aktivität und bleibender ›Genuß‹ harmonisch zueinander stehen. »Ruusbroec does not describe a psychological *experience* in which memory, intellect, and will have an immediate contact with God but a *state* of the deified person who relates in an entirely new manner to God and world« (S. 75). Es geht ihm um die Teilhabe am göttlichen trinitarischen Leben, nicht um eine aller Objektivität entzogene mystische ›Erfahrung Gottes‹. Nachdem der Autor so seine Grundthese formuliert hat, entwickelt er sie in den folgenden Kapiteln. Kapitel 3 (S. 77–99) beschreibt die Trinitätstheologie R.s, wobei vor allem der Begriff der *regiratio*, des Zurückfließens der göttlichen Personen in die communiale Einheit, eine zentrale Rolle spielt. Dem Autor gelingt es dabei, sowohl R.s Abhängigkeiten vom Neuplatonismus und scholastischen Theologen wie Albert dem Großen, Thomas von Aquin, Bonaventura einerseits sowie dem deutschen Mystiker Meister Eckhart andererseits deutlich zu machen, als auch seine Originalität in dieser Lehre herauszustellen. So zeigt er beispielsweise, daß bei Eckhart der *regressus* (oder die *regiratio*) vor allem durch den Sohn bzw. das Wort vermittelt ist, während R. den Akt des Zurückfließens besonders mit der Person des Geistes verbindet. Als mystischer Theologe beschreibt er einen dynamischen Gott, der wie Ebbe und Flut in Bewegung ist und den Menschen in diesen Fluß hinein nehmen will. Im vierten Kapitel (S. 101–120) geht es um R.s Anthropologie. Hier zeigt der Autor, daß die menschliche Seele zwar als ein »trinitarian blueprint« (S. 113 u.ö.) angesehen werden kann, daß aber diese natürliche Gottebenbildlichkeit durch die göttliche Gnade vollendet werden muß. R. kann daher nicht für eine Meinung ins Feld geführt werden, nach welcher der Mensch von Natur aus göttlich sei (auch wenn er als Idee in Gott schon vor aller Zeit existierte, wie R. mit Eckhart betont). Vielmehr spielt die Sünde, die uns Gott unähnlich gemacht hat, eine wichtige Rolle. Der Mensch muß wieder in die Beziehung zu Gott eintreten, um erlöst zu werden. Das Wesen des geschaffenen Seins ist also keine substanzhafte Größe, sondern besteht in seiner Beziehung zu Gott. Diese Beziehung macht den Menschen eigentlich erst zum Menschen. An dieser Stelle kommt nun im fünften Kapitel (S. 121–156) die Christologie ins Spiel, insofern Jesu Leben und Tod für uns die entscheidenden Vermittlungsinstanzen bei der Rückkehr zu Gott sind. Mit und in Christus und seinem Erlösungswerk sind uns Objektivierungen der göttlichen Gnade gegeben, vor allem das Kreuz und die Sakramente der Kirche (und hier noch mal besonders die Eucharistie). »The trinitarian love requires reciprocity and it is in the cross (and the eucharist) that we are given the possibility of reciprocating God's love« (S. 145). In diesem Zusammenhang wendet sich R. vehement gegen die sogenannten Brüder vom freien Geist, die meinten, ohne die Kirche und deren Sakramente zu einer Einheit mit Gott gelangen zu können. Deutlich macht der Autor klar: »When Ruusbroec talks of union with God, what he has in mind is knowledge and love of God that we acquire through the ordinary means of Christian faith and worship« (S. 70). Damit geht ein weiterer wichtiger Punkt einher: Die Einheit des Menschen mit Gott verlangt von diesem Aktivität, d.h. ein Leben nach den Tugenden in Glaube, Hoffnung und Liebe und ist kein Akt reiner Passivität, wie es ›freigeistliche Brüder‹ damals wie heute zu behaupten versuchen und damit R. in die Nähe von buddhistischen Erlösungslehren bringen. Diese seine Position unterstreicht der Autor noch einmal im sechsten Kapitel (S. 157–191). Die Vergöttlichung besteht nach R. in der Teilhabe am communialen Leben Gottes und vollzieht sich in drei Schritten: 1. Empfangen der Gnade Gottes; 2. Bekehrung des eigenen, selbstsüchtigen Willens; 3. Reinigung des Gewissens. Noch einmal wird damit die aktive Rolle des Menschen bei der Vergöttlichung hervorgehoben. Ziel ist für den Theologen R. nicht die *vita contemplativa*, in welcher der Mensch Gott einfach nur genießt, sondern die *vita communis* mit Gott, in der Genuß und Aktivität, Freude am ewigen Bleiben in Gott und ständiges Sich-Verschenken, harmonisch integriert sind. Dabei ist die theozentrische Intention sehr wichtig: »The common life is a life of enjoyment and activity, just as the Trinity itself is both activity in the Persons and enjoyment in their mutual interpenetration or *perichoresis*« (S. 177). Christus ist dabei Vorbild und Mittler für die Teilhabe des Menschen am innertrinitarischen Leben. Inwieweit diese Sicht einen Einfluß auf die spanische Mystik des 16. Jahrhunderts hatte, insbesondere auf Johannes vom Kreuz, wie der Autor mehrere Male (S. 46, 62, 190) erwähnt, ist eine spannende Frage und ein Feld für weitere Forschungen. Zusammenfassend können wir sagen, daß Nieuwenhoves Arbeit eine wichtige Korrektur des bisherigen R.-Bildes einleitet. Die theologisch-mediävistische Relevanz des Buches besteht vor allem darin, deutlich gemacht zu haben, daß R. kein Außenseiter ist, der in gewagter, womöglich theologisch bedenklicher Weise über das Wesen der Erfahrung Gottes spekuliert, sondern ein mystischer Theologe im besten Sinne des Wortes, der in einer Reihe mit Gregor von Nyssa, Augustinus, Pseudo-Dionysius Areopagita, Bonaventura und Meister Eckhart genannt werden muß. Er gehört in die Mitte mittelalterlicher mystischer Theologie und sollte viel stärker als bisher als solcher beachtet werden. Die Kirche hat dem übrigens dadurch schon Rechnung getragen, daß sie ihn 1909 selig gesprochen hat (was den wenigsten wohl bekannt ist). Der Vorteil der Studie liegt zudem darin, daß die These kompakt und klar auf 200 Seiten dargestellt wird. Der Autor verliert sich nicht in wilden Spekulationen, sondern bleibt immer streng an den Texten (vor allem an R.s wichtigstem Werk *Die Geestelike Brulocht*). Schließlich wird auch deutlich, daß es unzulässig ist, R. esoterisch im Sinne einer unpersönlichen Einheitserfahrung Gottes zu vereinnahmen. Die einzige kleine Anfrage, die weniger an den

Autor als an R. selbst zu stellen wäre, ist, warum er für diese faszinierende Sicht der Teilhabe des Menschen am göttlichen Leben relativ selten biblische Bilder benutzt (eine Kritik, die schon Gerson an R. übte). Die metaphorische Sprache R.s, auf die auch Nieuwenhove aufmerksam macht (S. 164), versucht das Unaussprechliche manchmal in einer Sprache auszudrücken, die mißverständlich ist und den Mißinterpretationen vergangener Zeiten Vorschub geleistet hat. Vielleicht hätte der Autor darauf aufmerksam machen können. Letztlich bleibt aber die Studie eine überzeugende Darlegung der Theologie R.s, an der die weitere Forschung nicht vorbeikommen wird.

Cornelius Roth, Fulda

Martin Thurner (Hg.): *Nicolaus Cusanus zwischen Deutschland und Italien: Beiträge eines deutsch-italienischen Symposiums in der Villa Vigoni* (Veröffentlichungen des Grabmann-Institutes zur Erforschung der mittelalterlichen Theologie und Philosophie 48), Berlin: Akademie 2002. – 691 S. – ISBN 3–05–003583–8. – € 69,80.

Das Jahr 2001 gab aufgrund des 600. Geburtstages des Kardinals Nikolaus von Kues Anlaß zu zahlreichen Veröffentlichungen und Veranstaltungen, denen ihrerseits Veröffentlichungen folgten. Der sich über neueste Entwicklungen in der Erforschung von Lebens- und Denkwelt des Cusaners zu informieren Gewillte sieht sich vor eine Masse an Literatur gestellt, die sich aus vielerlei Kontexten mit verschiedenen Interessen und daraus resultierenden differierenden Fragestellungen des Phänomens Cusanus annimmt. Auch im zu besprechenden Buch handelt es sich um einen Tagungsband, und zwar zum Symposion im Centro italo-tedesco Villa Vigoni vom 28.3.–1.4.2001, und die Pluralität der Fragestellungen und Blickrichtungen ist hier sogar zum Programm erhoben: Vereint sind Beiträge aus italienischer und deutscher Sicht, aus philologisch-historischen und philosophisch-theologischen Blickrichtungen. Herausgekommen ist ein Sammelband, der geknüpft an die übergeordnete Frage nach dem Stand des Cusaners zwischen Deutschland und Italien lebendig Vielfalt und Reichtum der Interessen, Themen und Beziehungen sowohl der Person Cusanus als auch des kulturellen Lebens des Quattrocento in 24 Beiträgen in deutscher, italienischer und englischer Sprache auf 691 Seiten gleichsam vor Augen führt. Immer wieder klingt aus naheliegenden Gründen die Frage an, ob und inwieweit Cusanus ›Humanist‹ gewesen sei, wobei eigenartigerweise die grundsätzliche Frage nach der Verhältnisbestimmung von Humanismus und Theologie im 15. Jahrhundert unterbelichtet bleibt. Die cusanischen Predigten als Quellen für seine Philosophie bleiben weitgehend ungenutzt. Eine weitere die Beiträge durchziehende Frage ist die nach Kenntnis und Bedeutung des Cusaners für Ficino; es werden Mittlerfiguren, gemeinsame Quellen und strukturelle Ähnlichkeiten aufgezeigt. Zusätzlich zu der Qualität der einzelnen Beiträge liegt das Besondere dieses Buches darin, daß gerade durch die Darstellung der verschiedensten Lebens- und Denkbewegungen des Cusaners dieser in seiner Vielschichtigkeit erscheint, wohingegen er sonst meist das Schicksal erleiden muß, auf wenige Facetten reduziert zu werden. Insofern regt das Buch dazu an, in dem eigenen Blick auf den Cusaner die vielfältigen Fragestellungen im Kopf zu behalten, mit denen man ihm begegnen kann. Einführend gibt der Organisator M. Thurner einen instruktiven Forschungsüberblick, der an der von E. Cassirer ins moderne Bewußtsein gebrachten Frage nach dem Verhältnis des Cusaners zum italienischen Renaissancehumanismus orientiert ist und die verschiedenen methodischen Lösungsansätze vorführt (S. 11–24). Der folgende grundlegende Beitrag von C. Vasoli »Niccolò Cusano e la cultura umanistica fiorentina« (S. 75–90) zeigt anhand des mit Cusanus befreundeten Toscanelli die mannigfaltigen Diskurse quer durch die verschiedenen Kreise im Florenz der Frührenaissance auf und ist insofern programmatisch, als in den folgenden Beiträgen der Florentiner Platonismus und somit Pico della Mirandola und Marsilio Ficino immer wieder zur Sprache kommen. Die weiteren Beiträge sind unter fünf Obertitel gestellt, zunächst die ›Einflüsse der deutschen und italienischen Kultur auf Cusanus‹, hier Cusanus Studium in Padua (G. Federici Vescovini, S. 93–113), Fulgosio, Valla und Cusanus in bezug auf die konstantinische Schenkung (G. Piaia, S. 115–128), Albertus Magnus und Cusanus in bezug auf den hermetischen Asclepius als einer entscheidenden Quelle für cusanische Zentralthemen (P. Arfé, S. 129–151) und Meister Eckhart und Cusanus in bezug auf die Gabe, ausgehend von christlicher Glaubenserfahrung und des Gott als Geber aussprechenden Schriftwortes Jak. 1,17 (M. Thurner, S. 153–184). Der zweite Block versammelt unter der Überschrift ›Cusanus und die Handschriften- und Bibliothekskultur des 15. Jahrhunderts‹ Beziehungen des Cusanus zu Humanisten in seiner Padovaner Studienzeit (H. Schnarr, S. 187–213), sein Erlernen der griechischen Sprache incl. einer Edition der (meist von Cusanus stammenden) Marginalien zu der Übersetzung des Georg von Trapezunt von Platons Parmenides in Ms Guarnacci 6201 (J. Monfasani, S. 215–252), die Cusanus-Handschriften der Bibliothek des Pierleone da Spoleto, einer möglichen Mittlerfigur eines Einflusses auf Ficino (M. Rotzoll, S. 253–287) und die Präsentation des Cusaners in zeitgenössischen Stellungnahmen und den ersten Editionen seiner Schriften (L. Perini, S. 289–301). Der nächste Block kündigt die ›Wirkungen des Cusanus auf seine deutschen und italienischen Zeitgenossen‹ an (die Überschriften von Block eins ›Einflüsse‹ und Block drei ›Wirkungen‹ entsprechen somit formal Cassirers These von Cusanus Aufnahme italienischer Kultur und anschließender Rückwirkung). Politisch kommt Cusanus als Kirchenreformer in den Blick (A. Landi, S. 305–313), und das Verhältnis von Cusanus zu Enea Silvio Piccolomini wird entgegen einer gängigen Stilisierung als Freundschaft mit einigen Seitenhieben Richtung Kirchengeschichtsschreibung als rein diplomatisch entlarvt (W. Baum, S. 315–337). Es schließt sich eine Untersuchung über mathematische Unendlichkeitsbetrachtungen der Renaissance an, ausgehend von der Bestimmung von π (L. de Bernart, S. 339–381). Den Block beendet eine Darstellung des philosophisch-theologischen Unendlichkeitsbegriffs des Cusaners, vorgeführt an *De docta ignorantia* und *De visione Dei* (M. Enders, S. 383–441). Der vierte Block beschränkt sich als einziger nur auf ›Cusanus und Italien‹ mit dem Thema ›Cusanus und die italienische Philosophie des 15. Jahrhunderts‹, und unwillkürlich drängt sich die Frage auf, ob man deutsche Philosophie im fünfzehnten Jahrhundert hier auch hätte beifügen können. Porphyrius und Jamblich als Vertreter zweier neuplatonischer Richtungen werden in bezug auf ihre Verbindung von Mathematik und Theologie befragt, da deren Ideen auf Cusanus und den Renaissanceplatonismus wirkten (G. Girgenti, S. 445–461); der Umschwung im Musikverständnis der Renaissance wird anhand bedeutender Autoren vorgeführt und als Zugang zu Cusanus genutzt (F. Santi, S. 463–479), das Verhältnis von Ficino zu Cusanus wird sowohl anhand der Frage nach einem gemeinsamen, in der Metapher der Jagd nach Weisheit zum Ausdruck kommenden Denkhorizont angegangen, indem das Verständnis von *spiritus* bei beiden Denkern entfaltet wird (A. Tarabochia Canavero, S. 481–509), als auch in der Untersuchung ihres jeweiligen Religionsverständnisses (W. A. Euler, S. 511–526), wobei ›beachtenswerte strukturelle Übereinstimmungen‹ erkannt werden. Das Religionsverständnis ist auch Untersuchungsgegenstand des Beitrages von P. R. Blum (S. 527–554); er stellt die ›Modelle‹ von Cusanus, Ficino, Pico della Mirandola, Machiavelli, Suárez und Campanella vor dem Hintergrund der Konfessionalisierungsdebatte vor und betont im Unterschied zu Euler die Differenz in der Blickrichtung von Cusanus und Ficino, die daraus erwachsen ist, daß letzterer sein Konzept mit einer anthropologischen Anlage zur Religiosität begründet habe. Verschiedene Blickrichtungen bestimmen auch den Beitrag über Anthropologie bei Cusanus und Pico della Mirandola (H. Schwaetzer, S. 555–574), da nach Schwaetzer die Denkbewegung der *imago Dei*-Vorstellung bei Cusanus anthropologisch ansetzt und er von den Fähigkeiten des Menschen ausgehend dessen kosmologische Stellung begründet, Pico hingegen die Fähigkeiten des Menschen aus seiner kosmologischen Stellung ableitet. Die Stärke einer fähigkeitsbezogenen Konzeption der Anthropologie liege darin, daß sie die kosmologische systematisch integrieren könne. Abschließend finden sich unter der Überschrift ›Cusanus in der Gesamtperspektive der deutsch-italienischen Philosophie vom Spätmittelalter zur Frühneuzeit‹ verschiedene Beiträge geeint. Ausgehend von der *imago Dei*-Vorstellung und deren Auswirkungen auf die Frage nach menschlicher Kreativität und Erkenntnis ergibt sich für W. Haug (S. 577–600) eine Differenz zwischen Cusanus und Eckhart, da bei Cusanus angeblich anders als bei Eckhart jegliche Erkenntnis über die sinnenfällige Welt bildhaft vermittelt wird, während es bei jenem zu zwei Erkenntnisformen käme. Die Parallele von Erkennen zu Schöpfung vermöge dann zu zeigen, daß Cusanus gerade die Grenzen der menschlichen Kreativität aufzeigen will und insofern weit von dem selbstverständlich ausgesprochenen Dictum eines Landino vom schöpferischen Dichter entfernt ist, aber den Geist als kreativen Spielraum aufgezeigt habe, dessen Grenzen nur noch fallen müssen, um zur Idee eines freien kreativen Menschen zu gelangen. Der Frage nach der ›Epochenschwelle‹ stellt sich M. Falcioni (S. 601–615), indem er ausgehend von der These Blumenbergs, daß bei Bruno das unendliche Weltall die Stelle der zweiten Person der Trinität einnimmt, die *anima mundi* bei Cusanus und Bruno analysiert und neben den Differenzen die Transzendenz in der Immanenz als das Gemeinsame bestimmt. Der Rezeption des Cusaners im deutschen Renaissancehumanismus geht S. Meier-Oeser nach (S. 617–632), und H. G. Senger (S. 634–653) stellt Wissenskonzeptionen und Ignoranzkompensationen von Petrarca, Cusanus, Agrippa von Nettesheim und Erasmus vor.

Stefanie Frost, Göttingen

Quellen zur Kirchenreform im Zeitalter der großen Konzilien des 15. Jahrhunderts: Zweiter Teil: Die Konzilien von Pavia/Siena (1423/24), Basel (1431–1449) und Ferrara/Florenz (1438–1445); ausgewählt und übersetzt von Jürgen Miethke und Lorenz Weinrich (Ausgewählte Quellen zur Deutschen Geschichte des Mittelalters: Freiherr vom Stein-Gedächtnisausgabe, 38b), Darmstadt: Wissenschaftliche Buchgesellschaft 2002. – 510 S. – ISBN 3-534-02436-2. – € 132,00.

Sieben Jahre nach Erscheinen des ersten Bandes, in dem die beiden Autoren 16 verschiedenste Texte zur Kirchenreform im Umfeld der Konzilien von Pisa (1409) und Konstanz (1414–1418) in Übersetzung vorgelegt haben, erfährt das Werk mit dem zweiten Band, der sich den Konzilien von Pavia/Siena, Basel und Ferrara/Florenz zuwendet, seinen Abschluß. Nichts braucht mehr über Idee und Qualität der Freiherr vom Stein-Gedächtnisausgabe gesagt zu werden, für welche auch diese beiden Bände wiederum Standards setzen. Sie lösen das mehrfache Desiderat ein, wichtige Texte, die bislang in alten, teils schwer zugänglichen Drucksammlungen verstreut waren, in einer handlichen Neuausgabe zur Verfügung zu stellen und diese mit einer zeitgemäßen Übersetzung zu versehen, die jedoch zu keinem Zeitpunkt den Primat des Primärtextes aus dem Blick verliert. Gerade bei der mit Fachterminologie reich befrachteten und spezialisierten Diskussion um die Reform kirchlichen Lebens im Spätmittelalter stößt jede Übersetzung an ihre Grenzen, weshalb der auf der gegenüberliegenden Seite abgedruckte lateinische Originaltext umso willkommener, ja unverzichtbar ist. Sämtliche Texte wurden anhand ausgewählter Handschriften überprüft und in aller Regel ›verbessert‹. Emendationen gegenüber den früheren Drucken oder Abweichungen in den Handschriften sind hinreichend in mit Kleinbuchstaben versehenen Fußnoten dokumentiert. Ein zweiter Apparat (mit numerischen Fußnoten) bietet knappe Erläuterungen zu Personen, Ereignissen, zitierten Quellen oder Fachtermini. Direkte Textverweise, sei es aus der Schrift oder dem Kirchenrecht, sind hinreichend nachgewiesen. Auch wenn die Autoren bewußt keine ›kritische Edition‹ vorlegen wollten, darf diese zweisprachige Ausgabe mit ihrem knappen, aber für den Studienzweck ausreichenden und handlichen Apparat als neue Standardedition der darin enthaltenen Stücke angesehen werden. Jürgen Miethke besorgte für beide Bände die Auswahl der Texte und verfaßte die Einleitungen, während Lorenz Weinrich vor allem für die Textgestaltung und Übersetzung verantwortlich zeichnet. Gleichwohl betonen beide Autoren ihre wechselseitige Kooperation und gemeinsame Verantwortung für das Werk. Die formalen Vorgaben und methodischen Richtlinien sind für beide Bände dieselben. Was den Inhalt betrifft, will ich mich im folgenden jedoch auf eine Darstellung und Würdigung nur des zweiten Bandes beschränken, in welchem die Reformdiskussion auf dem Basler Konzil klar im Vordergrund steht. Von den insgesamt 31 Texten stammen nur vier aus Pavia/Siena: neben zwei offiziellen Texten eine Reformeingabe der französischen Nation sowie eine Predigt des Dominikaners Girolamo da Firenze (S. 98–149). Ferrara/Florenz kann gar nur mit drei Stücken aufwarten: einer deutschen Reformvorlage von 1438 (S. 452–457) sowie kurzen Auszügen aus der Unionsbulle *Laetentur coeli* und der Verlegung des Konzils nach Rom (1443). Diesem schmalen Bestand stehen die weitaus zahlreicheren Texte gegenüber, die im Kontext des Konzils von Basel verfaßt wurden. Sie sind in vier Gruppen unterteilt, zunächst solche, die »Im Vorfeld des Konzils« anzusiedeln sind (S. 152–177), näherhin eine päpstliche Reformkonstitution von 1425 sowie die Reformvorschläge der Salzburger Kirchenprovinz von 1431, die hier erstmals im Druck veröffentlicht werden. Eine zweite Abteilung widmet sich der ›Selbstbehauptung des Konzils‹ in den ersten Monaten seines Bestehens (S. 178–187) sowie einiger privater oder halboffizieller Stellungnahmen bekannter oder anonymer Konzilsteilnehmer (S. 188–317). Die dritte Sektion vereinigt die eigentlichen Reformdekrete des Konzil, und in einem vierten Abschnitt wird deren ›Rezeption‹ hervorgehoben. Innerhalb dieser vierten Sektion finden sich solch häufig zitierte, aber selten studierte Texte wie die Pragmatische Sanktion von Bourges (1438) und das deutsche Gegenstück dazu, die Mainzer Akzeptation von 1439. In derselben Reihe darf auch das spätere Fürstenkonkordat von 1447 gesehen werden, worin der Papst nach der erfolgreichen Abwehr konziliarer Reformbestrebungen dem deutschen König und den Kurfürsten die Konstanzer Reformbestimmungen, aber auch die Mainzer Akzeptation bestätigte. Unter der Sparte ›Rezeption‹ der Basler Reformen werden ferner jene Reformstatuten eingereiht, die der Konzilspräsident Kardinal Cesarini für das Basler Domkapitel anläßlich der Visitationen in der Stadt Basel im Jahre 1434 zusammenstellte. Das Herzstück der Sammlung freilich bilden die Reformdekrete des Basiliense selbst (S. 318–401). Hier nahm das Konzil auf insgesamt zehn seiner Sitzungen zwischen 1433 und 1439 offiziell u.a. zu Wahlen, Provinzialkonzilien, Judenbekehrungen, Konkubinariern, Annaten und Liturgie, zu Papstwahl und Kardinälen, zum Kommunionempfang, Prozessen und Pfründen Stellung. Nicht weniger wichtig, wenn nicht sogar noch interessanter sind die privaten oder repräsentativen Stellungnahmen einzelner Konzilsteilnehmer, die die Reformdiskussionen engagiert, differenziert und bisweilen auch polemisch begleiteten und formten. Insbesondere gilt es dabei auf den bereits 1432 verfaßten *Dialogus inter Iohannem et Iacobum* des Juan de Palomar hinzuweisen, der typisch für zahlreiche Basler Reformschriften recht unbestimmt und allgemein zunächst an die moralisch-religiöse Selbstreform der Konzilsteilnehmer appellierte und dabei zelotische Absichten kritisierte, die dem Papsttum und der Kurie jegliche Kompetenz hinsichtlich der Pfründenvergabe entziehen wollten. Wesentlich konkreter waren dagegen die Reformvorstellungen des Lübecker Bischofs Johannes Schele, der vor allem typisch deutsche Anliegen und Sorgen zur Sprache brachte und dessen *Avisamenta reformacionis in curia et extra* wohl aus einer breiteren Konsensbildung innerhalb der deutschen Nation hervorgingen. Die deutsche Nation trat ein weiteres

Mal in den Vordergrund mit den Reformanträgen, die der Freisinger Generalvikar Johannes Grünwalder im Februar 1433 präsentierte (S. 286–301). Weiterhin von Interesse ist schließlich die Vorlage des Konzilspräsidenten Cesarini, die dieser Ende März 1434 einreichte (S. 307–317). Die bemerkenswerten Äußerungen zur Ekklesiologie und Kirchenreform des Bischofs von Cádiz, Juan González, stellte vor Jahren bereits Erich Meuthen heraus. Hier werden nun zwei seiner Texte abgedruckt, wobei sich der erste mit der in Basel lauthals geforderten Suspension des Papstes auseinandersetzte, während das zweite Gutachten, das hier erstmals in ganzer Länge veröffentlicht wird, zum geplanten *Decretum irritans* Stellung bezog. Ein buntes Bild spätmittelalterlichen Lebens bietet der Reformaufruf des ansonsten weniger bekannten Guillaume Maurel von 1434 (S. 266–277). Das letzte Stück der Sammlung, gleichsam der krönende Abschluß, stellt die umfangreiche *Reformacio generalis* des Nikolaus von Kues dar (S. 468–499). Dieses längste Dokument des gesamten Bandes wurde unter Heranziehung aller vier bekannten Handschriften neu abgedruckt. Die Einleitung (S. 15–82) stellt die ausgewählten Stücke kurz vor und ordnet sie in die Gesamtdiskussion ein. Mit reichen Literaturangaben versehen vermittelt dieser Überblick ein gut dokumentiertes, ja vorzügliches Bild von den Stoßrichtungen und Schwerpunkten, der Komplexität und den verschiedenen Erwartungshorizonten, aber auch von den Erfolgen und den Grenzen der konziliaren Reformbemühungen. Ein Register erschließt den Band auch jenen, die nur kurzen Rat suchen oder nach gezielten Themen suchen. Man darf hoffen und wünschen, daß diese exzellente Quellenauswahl intensive Verwendung in der Lehre findet und damit auch die weitere Erforschung der spätmittelalterlichen Kirchenreform, die im Grunde immer noch in den Kinderschuhen steckt, inspiriert und beflügelt.

Thomas Prügl, Notre Dame

DIRECTIONES AUCTORUM

Dr. Christoph Egger, Institut für Österreichische Geschichtsforschung, Universität Wien, Dr.-Karl-Lueger-Ring, 1, A–1010 Wien

Prof. Dr. Barbara Faes de Mottoni, Istituto per la storia del pensiero filosofico, Via de Togni, 7, I–20123 Milano

Prof. Dr. Volker Leppin, Theologische Fakultät, Universität Jena, Fürstengraben 6, D–07743 Jena

Prof. Dr. Constant J. Mews, Centre for Studies in Religion and Theology, School of Historical Studies, Box 11A, Monash University, Victoria, Australia 3800

Dr. Matthias Perkams, Philosophische Fakultät, Universität Jena, Fürstengraben 1, D–07743 Jena

Prof. Dr. Thomas Prügl, University of Notre Dame, 130, Malloy Hall, Notre-Dame IN, 45665

Dr. Matthias M. Tischler, Hugo von Sankt Viktor-Institut, Phil.-Theol. Hochschule Sankt Georgen, Offenbacher Landstraße 224, D–60599 Frankfurt am Main

Ralph Walterspacher M. A., Schoferstraße 1, D–79098 Freiburg im Breisgau

Die Internationale Gesellschaft für Theologische Mediävistik e.V.

Die Gesellschaft ist hervorgegangen aus dem Arbeitskreis Theologische Mediävistik und wurde am 20. April 2002 in Frankfurt am Main gegründet.

»Die Gesellschaft zielt auf den wissenschaftlichen Austausch zum Zweck der Förderung von Forschung und Lehre im Bereich der theologischen Mediävistik. Sie vertritt die Anliegen der Disziplin gegenüber staatlichen, kirchlichen und anderen Stellen, die mit wissenschaftsorganisatorischen Fragen befaßt sind. Sie kooperiert mit anderen mediävistischen Forschungseinrichtungen, Gesellschaften und Vereinen. Sie bemüht sich um die Förderung der Kooperation zwischen den Forschenden der eigenen Disziplin und ihrer Teildisziplinen, insbesondere der Kirchen- und Theologiegeschichte und ihrer Teildisziplinen (insbesondere der Exegesegeschichte, der Spiritualitäts- und Frömmigkeitsgeschichte, der Liturgiegeschichte, der Historischen Kanonistik und der Sermonesforschung) und fördert den interdisziplinären Austausch mit den Forschenden der anderen mediävistischen Disziplinen, insbesondere der Geschichtswissenschaft, der Historischen Hilfswissenschaften, der Philosophiegeschichte, der Kunstgeschichte, der Musikgeschichte und der historischen Sprach- und Literaturwissenschaften.« (Satzung § 1 Abs. 2).

Die Arbeit der Gesellschaft ist als gemeinnützig anerkannt.

Die Gesellschaft veranstaltet eine jährliche Tagung und kooperiert mit ihren Mitgliedern bei der Ausrichtung weiterer Tagungen und Publikationsprojekte. Zur Förderung des wissenschaftlichen Austausches hat sie das Jahrbuch *Archa Verbi* begründet, das im Hause Aschendorff erscheint. In einer Subsidia-Reihe werden Tagungsakten und herausragende Forschungsarbeiten veröffentlicht.

Mitglied der Gesellschaft kann jeder im Bereich der theologischen Mediävistik qualifizierte Wissenschaftler werden, der von zwei Mitgliedern vorgeschlagen und dessen Antrag auf Mitgliedschaft vom Vorstand der Gesellschaft angenommen wurde. Der Mitgliedsbeitrag beträgt pro Jahr 50,– € für Einzelpersonen und 100,– € für Institutionen und schließt den Bezug des Jahrbuches mit ein. Der reduzierte Beitrag für Studierende beträgt 10,– €. Gegenwärtiger Vorsitzender der Gesellschaft ist P. Prof. Dr. Rainer Berndt SJ (Frankfurt am Main). Dem Vorstand gehören an Dr. Henryk Anzulewicz (Bonn) als Schatzmeister, Prof. Dr. Marianne Schlosser (Wien) als Schriftführerin und Ralf M. W. Stammberger (Frankfurt am Main) als Geschäftsführer.

Weitere Informationen über:
Internationale Gesellschaft für Theologische Mediävistik
c/o Hugo von Sankt Viktor-Institut für Quellenkunde des Mittelalters
Offenbacher Landstraße 224
D–60599 Frankfurt am Main (Germany)
Fon: +49/69/6061–222; Fax: +49/69/6061–307
email: igtm-geschaeftsstelle@gmx.de
homepage: http://www.st-georgen.uni-frankfurt.de/igtm/

Archa Verbi. Yearbook for the Study of Medieval Theology

Das Jahrbuch wird von der Internationalen Gesellschaft für Theologische Mediävistik e.V. herausgegeben. Publikationssprachen sind Deutsch, Englisch, Französisch, Italienisch und Spanisch.

Das Jahrbuch nimmt in seiner Abteilung Recensiones Stellung zu Büchern und anderen Medieneinheiten, die für die theologische Mediävistik in all ihren Fachgebieten bedeutsam sind.

In *Archa Verbi* werden als Artikel wissenschaftliche Beiträge und Textausgaben aufgenommen, die dem thematischen Profil der IGTM entsprechen, wobei prinzipiell alle mediävistischen Disziplinen relevant sind, sofern sie sich die Christentumsgeschichte zum Gegenstand (als Kirchengeschichte, Exegese- und Theologiegeschichte, Kirchliche Rechtsgeschichte, Kunstgeschichte, Historische Hilfswissenschaften, etc.) wählen.

Die bei der Schriftleitung eingehenden Artikel werden im double-blind-Verfahren begutachtet, d.h. zwei von den scriptores bestimmte unabhängige Gutachter prüfen die Qualität der Artikel. Dabei ist weder der Autor des Artikels den Gutachtern bekannt noch kennen umgekehrt die Autoren die Gutachter. Bei den eingereichten Artikeln sind auf einem Deckblatt Name des Autors und Titel des eingereichten Artikels vermerkt. Dieses Deckblatt verbleibt bei den scriptores. Der Text des Artikels darf keine Hinweise auf die Person des Autors enthalten.

Aufgrund der Gutachten entscheiden die scriptores und der coetus editionis, ob der jeweilige Artikel zur Publikation angenommen wird. Die Entscheidung erfolgt durch Mehrheitsentscheid. Die scriptores haben ein Veto-Recht, das sie nur gemeinsam ausüben können.

Die von den Gutachtern, den scriptores und dem coetus editionis formulierten Anmerkungen und Änderungswünsche werden dem Autor im Falle der bedingten Annahme zur Einarbeitung zugeleitet. Den überarbeiteten Text besprechen die scriptores gemeinsam mit den sachlich und sprachlich kompetenten Mitgliedern des coetus editionis. Die scriptores entscheiden über die endgültige Annahme.

Die Redaktionsrichtlinien finden Sie im Internet unter:
http://www.st-georgen.uni-frankfurt.de/igtm/Dateien/Richtlinien.wpd

Manuskripte bitten wir an die Schriftleitung zu richten:

Prof. Dr. Volker Leppin
Theologische Fakultät
Friedrich-Schiller-Universität Jena
Fürstengraben 6
D–07743 Jena.

Absprachen über Rezensionen sind zu treffen mit

Prof. Dr. Thomas Prügl,
University of Notre Dame,
130, Malloy Hall, Notre-Dame IN, 45665.